P9-ARM-777

"Man was born free,
and is everywhere
in chains!"

— J.J. Rousseau

GEORGE WOODCOCK was born in Winnipeg in 1912 and came to England as a child, remaining until 1949. He taught English at the University of Washington, and English and Asian Studies at the University of British Columbia, but resigned from teaching in 1963 to devote himself to writing. He has edited various journals and papers including *Now*, *War Commentary* and *Freedom* and was one of the founder editors of the American journal *Dissent*. He has won many literary awards and in 1973 received the Molson Prize, the highest Canadian award for achievements in the arts and humanities. He has published over thirty books including *The Crystal Spirit* (1966), a study of George Orwell, *Anarchism* (1970) and biographies of Kropotkin, Proudhon, Wilde, Gandhi and Huxley.

The Anarchist Reader

Edited by George Woodcock

WITHDRAWN

Harvester Press/Humanities Press
In association with Fontana

Burg
HX
833
.A57
1977

First published in England in 1977 by
THE HARVESTER PRESS LIMITED
Publisher: John Spiers
2 Stanford Terrace,
Hassocks, Sussex, England
and in the USA by
Humanities Press Inc.,
Atlantic Highlands, NY 07716

This edition first published in 1977 in
association with Fontana Books

The Anarchist Reader copyright in the introduction
and in this selection
© George Woodcock 1977

Harvester Press
British Library Cataloguing in Publication Data

The anarchist reader.
 1. Anarchism and anarchists—Addresses,
essays, lectures
 I. Woodcock, George, b. 1912
335'.83'08   HX833

ISBN 0–85527–889–7

Humanities Press
Library of Congress Cataloging in Publication Data
Main entry under title:

The Anarchist reader.

 Bibliography: p.
 1. Anarchism and anarchists—Addresses, essays,
lectures.   I. Woodcock, George, 1912–
HX833,A57 1977   335'.83   77–2990
ISBN 0–391–00709–2

Printed in Great Britain by
Redwood Burn Limited
Trowbridge, Wiltshire

Contents

6 Contents

Whoever puts his hand on me to govern me is an usurper and a tyrant; I declare him my enemy.

Pierre-Joseph Proudhon

Let us put our trust in the eternal spirit which destroys and annihilates only because it is the unsearchable and eternally creative source of all life. The urge to destroy is also a creative urge.

Michael Bakunin

With what delight must every well informed friend of mankind look forward, to the auspicious period, the dissolution of political government, of that brute engine, which has been the only perennial cause of the vices of mankind, and which . . . has mischiefs of various sorts incorporated with its substance, and no otherwise removable than by its utter annihilation.

William Godwin

The loathsome mask has fallen, the man remains
Sceptreless, free, uncircumscribed, but man
Equal, unclassed, tribeless, and nationless,
Exempt from awe, worship, degree, the king
Over himself; just, gentle, wise, but man
Passionless? – no, yet free from guilt or pain,
Which were, for his will made or suffered them,
Nor yet exempt, though ruling them like slaves,
From chance, and death, and mutability,
The clogs of that which else might oversoar
The loftiest star of unascended heaven
Pinnacled deep in the intense inane.

Percy Bysshe Shelley

Proletarians of the world, look into the depths of your own beings, seek out the truth and realize it yourselves: you will find it nowhere else.

Peter Arshinov

Give flowers to the rebels who failed . . .
Italian anarchist song

Acknowledgements

The author and publisher gratefully acknowledge permission to reproduce the following extracts:

'Topless Federations' from *Anarchy in Action* by Colin Ward reprinted by permission of the author, George Allen and Unwin Ltd, and Harper & Row, Publishers;

'A Commune in Aragon' reprinted by permission of Faber and Faber Ltd from *The Spanish Cockpit* by Franz Borkenau;

'A Song for the Spanish Anarchists' reprinted by permission of Faber and Faber Ltd and Horizon Press, New York from *Collected Poems* by Herbert Read;

'An Aesthetic Approach to Education' reprinted by permission of David Higham Associates Ltd from *The Grassroots of Art* by Herbert Read published by Faber and Faber Ltd;

'Anarchism and the Religious Impulse' reprinted by permission of David Higham Associates Ltd from *Anarchy and Order* by Herbert Read published by Faber and Faber Ltd;

'Barcelona, 1936' reprinted by permission of Mrs Sonia Brownwell Orwell, Secker and Warburg Ltd and Harcourt Brace Jovanovich, Inc. from *Homage to Catalonia* by George Orwell;

'Revolution and Social Reality' reprinted by permission of David Higham Associates Ltd and the author from *Authority and Delinquency in the Modern State* by Alex Comfort, published by Routledge and Kegan Paul Ltd;

'Affinity Groups', 'Paris, 1968', and 'Anarchism and Ecology' reprinted by permission of the author, Wildwood House Ltd and Ramparts Press, Palo Alto, California from *Post-Scarcity Anarchism* by Murray Bookchin;

'The Violence of Laws', 'Resistance to Military Service' and 'Arranging Our Lives' from *Leo Tolstoy's Works*, translated by Louise and Aylmer Maude and published by the Oxford University Press. Reprinted by permission of the publisher;

'Makhno's Anarchism in Practice' reprinted by permission of Black and Red and Solidarity, Detroit from *History of the Makhnovist Movement* by Peter Arshinov;

'The Failure of the Russian Revolution' reprinted by permission of Doubleday and Co. Inc. from *My Further Disillusionment with Russia* by Emma Goldman;

'Normal Politics and the Psychology of Power' reprinted by permission of Random House Inc. from *People and Personnel* by Paul Goodman;

'Alternatives to Miseducation' reprinted from *Compulsory Miseducation* by Paul Goodman, copyright 1964 by permission of the publishers Horizon Press, New York.

While every effort has been made to trace copyright holders, this has not always been possible. The publishers would be pleased to hear from any copyright holder not here acknowledged.

Anarchism:
A Historical Introduction

GEORGE WOODCOCK

1 TRADITION AND TERRAIN

Anarchism is a word about which there have been many confusions. Anarchy is very often mistakenly regarded as the equivalent of chaos, and an anarchist is often thought of as at best a nihilist – a man who has abandoned all principles – and at worst a mindless terrorist. The anarchists whose works I shall be quoting in this collection were men of elaborate principles, a tiny minority of whom indeed did perform acts of violence, though they never aspired to compete, in terms of destructiveness, with the military leaders of the past or the nuclear scientists of our own day. In other words, I shall be presenting the anarchists as they were and are rather than as they have appeared in the fantasies of cartoonists, journalists and politicians, whose favourite way of abusing an opponent is to accuse him of promoting anarchy.

What we are concerned with, in terms of definition, is a cluster of words which in turn represents a cluster of doctrines and attitudes whose principal uniting feature is the belief that government is both harmful and unnecessary. A double Greek root is involved: the word *archon,* meaning a ruler, and the prefix *an,* indicating without; hence *anarchy* means the state of being without a ruler. By derivation, *anarchism* is the doctrine which contends that government is the source of most of our social troubles and that there are viable alternative forms of voluntary organization. And by further definition the *anarchist* is the man who sets out to create a society without government.

That concept of society without government is essential for an understanding of the anarchist attitude. In rejecting government, the true anarchist does not reject the idea or the fact of society; on the contrary, his view of the need for society as a living entity becomes intensified when he con-templates the abolition of government. As he sees it, the pyra-midical structure imposed by a government, with power pro-ceeding from above downwards, can only be replaced if society becomes a closely-knit fabric of voluntary relationships. The difference between a governmental society and an anarchic society is in his view the difference between a structure and an organism; one is built and the other grows according to natural laws. Metaphorically, one can compare the pyramid of government with the sphere of society, which is held to-gether by an equilibrium of stresses. Anarchists are much concerned with equilibriums, and two kinds of equilibrium play a very important role in their philosophy. One is the equilibrium between destruction and construction that domin-ates their tactics. The other is the equilibrium between liberty and order which dominates their view of the ideal society. But order for the anarchist is not something imposed from above. It is a natural order, and is given expression by self-discipline and voluntary co-operation.

The roots of anarchist thought are ancient; I shall trace some of them thoroughly in the next section of this intro-duction. Libertarian doctrines, which argued that as a moral being man can live best without being ruled, existed among the philosophers of ancient Greece and China, and among the heretical Christian sects of the Middle Ages. Elaborately argued philosophies that were anarchist in all but name began to appear during the Renaissance and Reformation periods, between the fifteenth and seventeenth centuries and, even more copiously, in the eighteenth century, as events built up towards the French and American Revolutions which ushered in the modern age.

But as an activist movement, seeking to change society by collective methods, anarchism belongs only to the nineteenth and twentieth centuries. There were times when millions of European and Latin American working men and peasants followed the black or black-and-red flags of the anarchists, re-volted under their leadership and set up transitory models of a free world, as in Spain and in the Ukraine during the periods of revolutionary upheaval. There were also great writers, like Shelley and Tolstoy, who expressed in their poems and novels and in their other writings the essential viewpoints of anarchism. The fortunes of the movement have fluctuated greatly and, being a movement rather than a party, it has shown extraordinary powers of revival. As late as the early 1960s it seemed a moribund, forgotten movement, yet today it seems once again, as it did in the 1870s, and the 1890s and again in the 1930s, a phenomenon of urgent relevance.

Perhaps the best point to begin a survey of anarchist attitudes is with the first man to accept the title of anarchist, Pierre-Joseph Proudhon, a prophet of intellectual fury who once declared: 'To be governed is to be watched over, inspected, spied on, directed, legislated over, regulated, docketed, indoctrined, preached at, controlled, assessed, weighed, censored, ordered about, by men who have neither right, nor knowledge, nor virtue. That is government, that is its justice, that is its morality.'

Proudhon was a largely self-educated printer from the mountainous French province of Franche-Comté, who in 1840 published a book, *Qu'est-ce que la Propriété?* (*What is Property?*), which became extremely influential in nineteenth-century radical circles; even Marx, later Proudhon's bitter enemy, approved of it. Proudhon's answer to the question his title posed was 'Property is Theft', and the phrase, which identified capitalism with government as the two main enemies of freedom, became one of the key slogans of the century.

Proudhon took part in the 1848 French Revolution, and it was largely under his influence that the famous, ill-fated alliance of European socialists, the International Workingmen's Association (better known as the First International), was founded in 1864, the year before his death. Proudhon's books provided the intellectual infrastructure for the European anarchist movement, and Michael Bakunin, who became the greatest of the anarchist activists, always referred to Proudhon as 'the master of us all'.

Perhaps the most significant thing about Proudhon is that, despite his influence and his following, he refused to establish a dogmatic doctrine such as Marx bequeathed to his followers. When an admirer congratulated him on his system, Proudhon replied indignantly: 'My system? I have no system!' He distrusted theoretical structures as much as governmental structures. Doctrines, for him, were never complete; their meanings emerged and their forms changed according to the situation; he believed that, within broad channels of principle, political theory – like thought of any kind – was in a process of constant evolution.

Proudhon also denied that he had founded a political party – he condemned all parties as 'varieties of absolutism'. In the formal sense this was true, though he did in fact gather a group of disciples out of whom the first anarchist movement emerged. Related to Proudhon's rejection of the idea of a political party was his action when he was elected to the Constituent Assembly of France during the Revolution of 1848. He was one of a tiny minority of representatives who voted against a Constitution approved by the Assembly and, when he was asked his reasons, he emphasized that he did not vote against the specific form of the Constitution: 'I have voted against the Constitution because it was a Constitution.' By this he implied that he rejected fixed forms of political organization.

The attitudes which Proudhon exhibited during the 1840s on questions of system, party and political organization not only reflected the views of earlier libertarian thinkers, like William Godwin, who had raised precisely the same objections. They also anticipated, before an actual anarchist movement came into being, the attitude it would adopt towards political action and the form it would take. Thus, it has never been possible to talk of anarchism as a philosophic or political system of the same kind as Marxism, which assumes that the writings of a man who died in 1883 provide oracular answers to all problems ever afterwards. And anarchism has never been represented by a political party, because its followers have wished to retain their freedom to react spontaneously to concrete situations and have regarded political parties as sharing the same faults as governments. As for constitutions, the anarchists have continued to regard them as fixed and guaranteed political systems which rigidify the state and institutionalize the exercise of power; neither of these effects is acceptable to libertarians, who believe that the organization of community life on a political level should be replaced by its social and economic organization on the basis of free contractual agreement between individuals.

Freedom, as all these objections imply, is not something to be decreed and protected by laws and states. It is something you shape for yourself and share with your fellow men. States and laws are its enemies, and from every corner of the varied spectrum of anarchist beliefs opinion on this point is quite unanimous. The state is evil and brings not order but conflict. Authority thwarts the natural impulses and makes men strangers to each other. As early as 1793, in his great *Political Justice*, William Godwin put the point in his resounding periods:

> Government lays its hands upon the spring that is in society and puts a stop to its motion. It gives substance and permanence to our errors. It reverses the genuine propensities of mind, and instead of suffering us to look forward, teaches us to look backward for perfection. It prompts us to seek the public welfare, not in innovation and improvement, but in a timid reverence for the decisions of our ancestors, as if it were the nature of mind always to degenerate and never to advance.

The objection which anarchists have always sustained to fixed and authoritarian forms of organization does not mean that they deny organization as such. The anarchist is not an individualist in the extreme sense of the word. He believes passionately in individual freedom, but he also recognizes that such freedom can only be safeguarded by a willingness to co-operate, by the reality of community, and for this reason, as we shall later see, the discussion of various kinds of non-coercive organization plays a great part in anarchist literature. Yet if the anarchist refuses to be ruled by the dead hand of the past, he accepts the corollary of that refusal; he does not expect the future to be determined by the present, and for this reason it is wrong to identify the anarchist with the utopian. The essential characteristic of utopian thought is the creation of an ideal society, beyond which there will be no progress, no change, because the ideal is by definition perfect and therefore static. But the anarchists have always argued that we cannot use our experience in the present to plan for a future where conditions may be quite different. If we demand freedom of choice, we must expect a similar demand from our successors. We can only seek to remove the injustices we know.

The anarchist is really a natural disciple of the Greek philosopher Heraclitus, who taught that the unity of existence lies in its constant change. 'Over those who step into the same river,' said Heraclitus, 'the waters that flow are constantly different.' The image is a good one for anarchism, as it has been and as it remains, since it conveys the idea of a doctrine with many variations, which nevertheless moves between the banks of certain unifying principles. And thus, even though there are many different anarchist points of view, there is a definable anarchist philosophy, just as there is a recognizable anarchist temperament. It involves three elements – a criticism of society as it is, a vision of a desirable alternative society, and a plan for proceeding from one to the other. Everything is involved in the question: Having decided that government is undesirable, can we – and how can we? – make the further step and show that it is unnecessary as well, and that there are alternative means of human organization that will enable us to live without it?

This question involves us in a consideration of the anarchist view of man's place in the scheme of things. Generally speaking, anarchists believe in a modified version of the view of the natural world that was celebrated in the Renaissance, and especially in the eighteenth century, as the Great Chain of Being. In its most familiar form the Great Chain of Being was seen as a continuity proceeding from the humblest form of life to the Godhead, usually deistically conceived. Alexander Pope expressed the concept admirably in the *Essay on Man*:

> Vast chain of being! which from God began,
> Natures ethereal, human, angel, man,
> Beasts, birds, fish, insect, what no eye can see,
> No glass can reach; from Infinite to thee,
> From thee to nothing . . .

Everything, in other words, had its place in the order of being, and if it followed its own nature, all would be well.

But let any species break the chain by departing from its nature, and disaster would ensue. It was a doctrine that would appeal to a modern ecologist. The concept derived ultimately from the Greek idea, most clearly developed by the Stoic philosophers, that man belonged to nature, responded to its primal laws, and that in nature he might find the model for his own societies. It had its analogues in the philosophies of ancient China, and thirty years ago, as I remember, anarchists were fond of quoting some remarks the Taoist sage Lao Tse is said to have made in reproaching Confucius for devising means to make people behave morally.

> When the actions of the people are controlled by prohibitive laws, the country becomes more and more impoverished. Therefore the wise man says: 'I will design nothing, and the people will shape themselves. I will keep quiet and the people will find their rest. I will not assert myself, and the people will come forth. I will discountenance ambition, and the people will return to their natural simplicity.'

But Chinese wisdom was a late discovery so far as European anarchists were concerned. For them the concept of the unity of the natural law came by a devious route from the world of classical antiquity, through the neo-Platonists of Hellenistic Alexandria, and thence by way of the rediscovery of ancient wisdom during the Renaissance and the consequent erosion of the hierarchical cosmogony of the Middle Ages. By the time the essential idea of the Great Chain of Being had reached the anarchists, God had been displaced from its head or had been rationalized into a principle of harmony, and probably the most influential individual in carrying out the transmission was the Swiss writer, author of the famous *Confessions*, Jean-Jacques Rousseau.

Rousseau had been widely acclaimed and widely blamed, as a proto-liberal, a proto-communist, a proto-anarchist. Many of his critics, thinking only of his authoritarian aspect, regard him as mainly responsible for the deification of the State which emerged in the French Revolution and in all subsequent revolutions. His theory of a tacit social contract by which authority was established in ancient times and made binding on subsequent generations was especially repugnant to the anarchists with their concept of an unfettered future, and all the principal anarchist theoreticians from Godwin to Kropotkin criticized him unreservedly on this point.

Yet despite their objections to his idea of a primeval social contract, there is a great deal the anarchists derived from Rousseau, including his romantic stress on spontaneity, his idea of education as a drawing out of what is latent in the child so that the natural instincts for good are developed, and his sense of the primitive virtues. Though Rousseau was not the first writer to adumbrate the concept of the Noble Savage, there is no doubt that the anarchists received principally from him their predilection for pre-civilized man, so that their writings have been full of descriptions of primitive societies able to arrange their social affairs and even to create fairly elaborate cultures without resorting, at least openly, to a system of authority. And the whole of the anarchist viewpoint is neatly summed up in one phrase of Rousseau: 'Man was born free and is everywhere in chains!'

Essentially, the anarchists believe that if man obeys the natural laws of his kind, he will be able to live at peace with his fellows; in other words, man may not be naturally good, but he is – according to the anarchists – naturally social. It is authoritarian institutions that warp and atrophy his co-operative inclinations. During the nineteenth century, a great deal of support was given to this belief by the various types of evolutionary doctrine that gradually became accepted by scientific opinion as the century built up to the publication of Darwin's epoch-making *Origin of Species* in 1859. Darwin and his predecessors established firmly that man belonged in the chain of evolution, and that the same basic laws governed his physical make-up and instinctual behaviour as governed those of the animal world. Indeed, as it was finally admitted with reluctance and heart-searching, he belonged to the animal world. Thus it became possible to compare human societies and those of other species, and when Peter Kropotkin, the Russian anarchist who was also a trained scientist, examined the evidence for evolution and reinforced it with his own field studies in Siberia, he came to the conclusion that one of the key factors in the evolution of successful species was not so much their power to compete as their inclination to co-operate. He developed this theory in *Mutual Aid* which, as soon as it was published in 1902, became one of the seminal works of anarchist theory.

Kropotkin argued that even the intellectual faculty is 'eminently social', since it is nurtured by communication – mainly in the form of language, by imitation, and by the accumulated experience of the race. He admitted that the struggle for existence, of which such evolutionists as Thomas Henry Huxley made a great deal, was indeed important, but he saw it as a struggle against adverse circumstances rather than between individuals of the same species, and he sug-gested that where it did exist within a species it was always injurious. Kropotkin argued that far from thriving on com-petition, natural selection sought out the means by which competition could be avoided, and those means he called *mutual aid*; that, henceforward, would be one of the key concepts of anarchism.

Since evolutionary doctrine had strengthened the links in the chain that united man to the animal world, Kropotkin argued that the same laws applied to human societies as to animal societies. Man, he contended, was not naturally solitary, as Rousseau had suggested. He was naturally social. And his natural form of social organization was that based on voluntary co-operation. Since it precluded the need for government, such organization would result in the fulfilment of the apparent paradox of order in anarchy, and order in anarchy is natural order. Organization that depends on co-ercion for its existence, on the other hand, is a perversion of natural order, and far from producing social peace, it ends always in strife and violence.

Some of the anarchists went beyond Kropotkin's biological and sociological arguments to the margins of psychology, and Proudhon in a way anticipated Jung's doctrine of the collective unconscious when, in that great work of his matur-ity, *De la Justice dans La Révolution et dans l'Eglise*, he suggested that deep in the human psyche, in the minds of all of us, lies a sense of justice that we have only to recognize for it to become active.

An integral part of a collective existence, man feels his dignity at the same time in himself and in others, and thus carries in his heart the principle of a morality superior to himself. This principle does not come to him from outside; it is secreted within him, it is immanent. It constitutes his essence, the essence of society itself. It is the true form of the human spirit, a form which takes shape and grows towards perfection only by the relationship that every day gives birth to social life. Justice, in other words, exists in us like love, like notions of beauty, of utility, of truth, like all our powers and faculties.

The final corollary of this belief that man should live by natural law, and that natural law establishes co-operation – voluntary co-operation – as the fundamental basis of society, is the argument that differentiates most anarchists from the pure individualists like Max Stirner; the argument that freedom is a social virtue. What the anarchists are really trying to find is a way out of the alienation that in the contemporary world, in spite of – or perhaps rather because of – its vast organizational ramifications, leads to man being isolated among the masses of his fellows. What has happened is a kind of polarization, in which the State has taken over from the individual the communal responsibilities that once gave his personal life the extended dimension of fellowship, both in the local setting and in the world in general; in most modern societies responsibility is in urgent danger of being strangled by paternalistic authority. Both the gigantism and the impersonality of the modern state are repugnant to anarchists. They wish not only to re-create a living fellowship between man and man, but also to eliminate the distance which authority places between individual men and the initiation of socially necessary activities. This involves two concepts which one finds in all the varieties of anarchism. The first is one of social organization; it is the principle of *decentralization*. The second is one of social action; it is the principle which I think can best be described by the phrase *individual capability*.

The basis of the principle of decentralization is the anarchist view that what characterizes the State, apart from its foundation on authority and coercion, is the way in which it cumulatively centralizes all social and political functions, and in doing so puts them out of the reach of the citizens whose lives they shape. Hence men are deprived of freedom to decide on their own futures, and this means that they lose the sense of purpose in their lives. Some people are cushioned by wealth and privilege from feeling the direct impact of this process, though they too are affected in insidious ways, but the poor and the underprivileged experience the impositions of the paternalistic state in a very direct way.

For these reasons the anarchist proposes, as the necessary basis for any transformation of society, the breaking down of the gigantic impersonal structures of the State and of the great corporations that dominate industry and communications. Instead of attempting to concentrate social functions on the largest possible scales, which progressively increases the distance between the individual and the source of responsibility even in modern democracies, we should begin again from the smallest practicable unit of organization, so that face-to-face contacts can take the place of remote commands, and everyone involved in an operation can not only know how and why it is going on, but can also share directly in decisions regarding anything that affects him directly, either as a worker or as a citizen. Such an attitude, of course, implies that the activity of the functional groups into which society divides itself will be voluntary. In areas into which the State has not penetrated, this happens already in our society, as it did to a far greater extent in the past, and a great deal of socially useful work – as Kropotkin and Tolstoy so abundantly pointed out – is carried on entirely by voluntary organizations. Many anarchists have drawn from this fact the conclusion that if the structure of the State were dismantled, there might be an initial period of disorganization, but that given man's social inclinations there would be little difficulty in establishing a network of voluntary arrangements; in fact, they would probably spring up in response to the need for them.

All this, of course, is echoed in the theory of participatory democracy put forward in the 1960s by North American radicals who had been influenced, directly or indirectly, by the teachings of the anarchists. The great argument that has always been brought against anarchist decentralization and participatory democracy is that both will lead to the fragmentation of society. To this I can imagine an anarchist theoretician answering that decentralization indeed means the fragmentation of the State, but that the fragmentation of the State would lead to the strengthening of society and of the social bonds among its members. He would urge that the social alienation which occurs in modern society through the rule of gigantic corporations is itself the worst of all sources of social fragmentation, and that by inducing people to co-operate regularly in decisions relating to their own lives, decentralization will in fact eliminate the alarming atomization of modern communities into lonely individuals dependent on authority personified by the policeman and the social worker.

Thus, far from advocating the breakdown of society at the same time as they seek the destruction of authority, the anarchists are in fact hoping to strengthen social bonds and social virtues by reinforcing community relationships at the most basic grassroots level. What they envisage is a reversal of the pyramid of power which the State exemplifies. Instead of authority descending from some political heaven by a ladder of bureaucracy, they see responsibility beginning among individuals and small groups given dignity by freedom. The most important unit of society, in their view, is that in which people co-operate directly to fulfil their immediate needs. Nobody can assess these needs better than those who experience them. This basic nuclear unit appears in various forms among the anarchist writers. Godwin called it the parish; Proudhon called it the commune; the syndicalists called it the workshop. The name matters very little; the fact of direct collaboration and consultation between the people most intimately involved in a phase of living is the important thing.

Most social problems in fact crop up at this level of the house, the street, the village, the workshop, and many of the libertarian writers have, like Proudhon and Godwin, been extremely cautious in discussing organization beyond this stage. Living on the edge of a pre-industrial age, Godwin thought that no more was needed than the occasional national assembly of local delegates called to discuss exceptional matters of common interest, plus a system of juries of arbitration. And even these he envisaged as only a temporary measure, a transitional device to tide us over until the day when men would be mature and would need no political machinery whatever.

The industrial revolution forced the modification of such splendid speculations; as soon as railways and factories appeared, it was obvious that even without government a more elaborate system of co-ordination than scattered and loosely linked parishes and communes was needed.

At this point it may be appropriate to step into parenthesis and draw the most vital distinction between the anarchists and the Marxists – at least so far as the Marxists have performed in history. Because of Marx's view of the dominance of the economic factor in the exploitation of one man by another, his followers were inclined to ignore the lethal characteristics of other forms of power. As a result, they not only elaborated a theory of dictatorship of the proletariat, but also proved its lack of validity by allowing the dictatorship to become in all Communist countries a hidebound party rule. By ignoring the processes of power, the revolutionists who claimed to follow Marx destroyed freedom as effectively as any confraternity of South American generals.

The anarchists have the ironic advantage over the Marxists that they have never established a free society shaped according to their ideals, except for short periods in small areas, and therefore they cannot be accused of failure in its development. At the same time, from the early 1870s, Bakunin and his followers prophesied quite accurately that the Marxist failure to understand that power is psychologically as well as economically based would lead to a recreation of the State in a new form. For their part, they recognized that economic and political inequality were interdependent, and from the beginning they attacked what Godwin called 'accumulated property' as strongly as they criticized centralized government. In this way they were the true descendants of those heretical sects of the Reformation who combined the condemnation of earthly government with a kind of communitarianism. Godwin substituted the idea of justice – as Proudhon would do after him – for that of the deity, but essentially his reasoning belonged in the dissenting tradition.

> Our animal needs, it is well known, consist in food, clothing and shelter. If justice means anything, nothing can be more unjust than that any man lack them. But justice does not stop here. So far as the general stock of commodities holds out, every man has a claim not only to the means of life, but to the means of a good life. It is unjust that a man works to the point of destroying his health, or his life, while another riots in superfluity. It is unjust that a man has not leisure to cultivate his mind while another does not move a finger for the general welfare. Justice demands in fact that each man, unless perhaps he be employed more beneficially to the public, should contribute to the cultivation of the common harvest, of which each man consumes a share. This reciprocity . . . is of the very essence of justice.

None of the late anarchists ever went beyond Godwin's statement that reciprocity is the essence of justice. But they modified its application. Once the industrial revolution had changed patterns of manufacture and transport, it was impossible for even an advocate of the small peasant and the individual craftsman like Proudhon to ignore the fact that complexity of organization was a social if not a political necessity. The anarchists tried to accommodate this fact in industrial terms by falling back on the concept the utopian socialist Saint-Simon compressed into the aphorism: 'We must replace the government of men by the administration of things.' A late nineteenth-century generation deeply involved in trade union activity evolved a theory of anarcho-syndicalism, which envisaged union-controlled workshops as the setting in which men might learn to organize the production of necessary goods and services. They also recognized that within limits it might be possible to delegate certain functions to technological experts, and even an anarchist so distrustful

[handwritten margin note: – Immstenil / labor of the / social / factory]

of domination by the syndicates as Errico Malatesta could say: 'Government signifies delegation of power, that is, abdication of the initiative and sovereignty of all men into the hands of a few. Administration signifies delegation of *work*, that is, the free exchange of services founded on free agreement.'

Today we look with a justified cynicism upon the trust which earlier anarchists like Malatesta were inclined to place in administrators; on any level, even outside government, we have learnt how easily administrative work, unlike most other forms of work, can convert itself into power, and today, among anarchists as among others, there is a lively vigilance wherever administration shows signs of becoming converted into bureaucracy. Administration is like a medicinal drug, excellent in homeopathic portions but fatal – to freedom at least – in large doses. But the need for it in some degree cannot be denied even by the man who rejects government.

If administration as opposed to government has been one way the anarchists thought of mitigating the centrifugal tendencies of a decentralized society, the other was the semi-political device of federalism. Even politicians who are far from being anarchists have recognized the perils of attempting to run a large or even a small country by a monolithically centralized State machine, and the result has been a variety of semi-federal constitutions like those of the United States, Canada and Switzerland. In no case have these countries entirely abandoned the principle of authority, and power in all of them is still inclined to flow from above downwards, often with great force, as recent American history has demonstrated. The anarchist envisages a different kind of federal society, one in which responsibility begins in the vital nuclei of social life, the workplace and the neighbourhoods where people live. In such a vision all matters of purely local concern – matters by which no outside interests are affected – should be decided locally by the people most directly involved. Where neighbourhoods have interests in common, they should federate loosely to discuss co-operation and arbitrate differences, and so upwards, through provinces to larger geographical entities, until, with all frontiers abolished, the whole world becomes a federation of federations of federations,

bringing together every small community in a kind of symbiotic unity like a great structure of coral.

Such a radical and radiant concept of federalism is linked with the principle I have called *individual capability*. Anarchists have always argued that, given the right conditions of free development, every man is capable of deciding directly on social and political issues. The question became urgent in the mid-nineteenth century when working men first began to think that their interests might be better served by seceding from political parties which were dominated by middle-class leaders. The First International was founded in 1864 on this basis; one of its leading principles was summed up in the slogan: 'The liberation of the workers is the task of the workers themselves.' Some interpreted this to mean that they should set up political parties of their own, and the various labour parties and Marxist socialist parties arose from their efforts. But as the anarchists translated it, the idea involved the rejection of ordinary political action; they opposed not only the more authoritarian forms of government, but also parliamentary democracy in its customary form, by which the people elect a representative for a period and abandon their affairs to his discretion until the next election. Proudhon summed up the anarchist attitude to this kind of system, in which demagogues can gain and keep power by manipulating the will of the people, when he declared that 'Universal Suffrage is Counter-Revolution.' This was not meant as an anti-democratic statement; it was meant to condemn a system in which voters choose a spokesman every few years and for the rest of the time abdicate their rights and duties as citizens.

The anarchist preference is for an arrangement by which people decide directly on what affects them immediately, and, where issues affect large areas, appoint assemblies of delegates rather than representatives, chosen for short periods and subject to recall. They favour devices that can give rapid expression to public opinion, like the referendum, but they also seek to ensure that every minority is as far as possible self-governing, and above all that the will of the majority does not become a tyranny over dissidents. The anarchist view of social organization is, indeed, summed up in the phrase *direct action*, but so is their view of the means of changing society.

What direct action means in practical terms has varied from generation to generation and from one type of anarchism to another, and I shall allow its form to emerge in the later sections of this introduction as I pass on from the theory with which up to the present I have been involved to the historical development of anarchism as theory modified by action.

2 THE ANARCHIST FAMILY TREE

Anarchism, as I have just suggested, is not merely an abstract theory about society. It has developed out of social conditions; it has been shaped by cultural influences; it has expressed itself in varying forms of action, by which in turn it has been modified.

As a doctrine that criticizes actual contemporary society and proposes both an alternative arrangement and a means to attain it, anarchism really began to take shape about four centuries ago during the period of the Reformation. Significantly, this was also the period when the modern nation-state, to which anarchism is the extreme antithesis, began to take shape. But before dealing with that vital historical conjunction, it is well to look at some of the more devious historic threads that over the centuries have helped to shape the anarchist viewpoint.

At the same time as they proclaim their urgent desire to liberate themselves from the dead hand of tradition, anarchists like to believe that their roots run deep into the past, and the paradox is only apparent. As we have seen, the whole world-view within which anarchism is embraced depends on an acceptance of natural laws manifested through evolution, and this means that the anarchist sees himself as the representative of the true evolution of human society, and regards authoritarian political organizations as a perversion of that evolution. It follows naturally that anarchists should be concerned to validate their claims to speak on behalf of natural and historic man, and Kropotkin carried this process to a logical end when he maintained that the roots of anarchism were to be found in a long war between liberty and authority that had already begun in the Stone Age. In *Mutual Aid* he made much of the anarchic character of tribal societies that live by elaborate patterns of customary co-operation with no visible system of authority. He failed to take into account that authority does not have to be embodied in a person, such as a king or a high chief; it also thrives in the elaborate systems of taboo and obligation that govern most primitive groups. Primitive man is rarely free in our sense of the word. What Kropotkin did prove – and this had its importance to the anarchist viewpoint – was that primitive man seems quite naturally to seek out patterns of co-operation.

Freedom in a form we might recognize seems to be a product of those communities on a harsh and rocky seacoast which became the city states of ancient Greece. Yet the freedom Athenians enjoyed was not of a kind the anarchists would have approved, since it was based on the institution of slavery, and even utopian political philosophers like Plato and Aristotle conceived societies where the freedom of some would depend on the servitude of others. Only a few mystics, like the devotees of the Eleusinian mysteries, and a few philosophers like the much-maligned Epicurus and Zeno the Stoic, conceived a society accepting all moral men as equals, and only Zeno and his followers seem to have combined that vision with a clear rejection of government.

The same applies to the Roman Republic, which at the time of the French and American Revolutions was regarded as the ancestral home of liberty. Brutus was held to be a great republican hero, and even today radicals regard the slave leader Spartacus as a spiritual ancestor. In fact it is doubtful if either Brutus or Spartacus would understand freedom as anarchists do, since they had not yet made the vital conjunction between freedom and equality. Brutus represented a patrician oligarchy; when he stabbed Caesar it was to defend the rights and authority of the social class from which he sprang. Even the slave rebellion Spartacus led was unconcerned with general liberation; Spartacus and the gladiators associated with him in leading the rebellion merely wanted to return to their own countries and take up their lives again among their own peoples.

But though a modern anarchist would find few congenial voices in the ancient world, by the fourteenth century the way discontented men began to speak had changed, as the words Froissart puts into the mouth of John Ball make quite clear.

Things cannot go well in England, nor ever will, until all goods are held in common, and until there will be neither serfs, nor gentlemen, and we shall be equal. For what reason have they, whom we call lords, got the best of us? How did they deserve it? Why do they keep us in bondage? If we all descended from one father and one mother, Adam and Eve, how can they assert or prove that they are more masters than ourselves? Except perhaps that they make us work and produce for them to spend!

Those words were spoken when the feudal system of the Middle Ages was breaking apart in England and the peasants were in a state of revolt against the imposition of serfdom. John Ball was one of their leaders, and the significant thing about him is that he was what men in those days called a hedge priest – a wandering preacher with no church who propounded a heretical and millenarian form of Christianity.

With millenarian Christianity we are approaching one of the two most vital historical strands in the anarchist tradition – the line of dissent which first took on a religious form, and then in the eighteenth century became secularized and welded to more rationalist currents of thought connected with the changes in political organization that the Renaissance precipitated. Already, long before the Reformation, millenarian sects were keeping the medieval rulers of Church and State in a constant ferment of anxiety. Bishops and kings united in the great war that had to be fought in the south of France to exterminate the so-called Albigensian or Catharist heresy which was regarded as a major threat to the stability of the medieval social order, and long before Luther appeared, radical ideas were being preached among conventicles of lowly people who believed that in the very near future the powerful were due to be laid low and the meek to inherit the earth.

The rigorous persecution of medieval heretics was directed largely towards expunging their doctrines from the popular mind, and our information regarding them has come down to us mainly in the distorted form to which their opponents chose to give publicity. Nevertheless, it seems certain that many such sectarians went beyond mere doctrinal arguments to changes in behaviour directed towards social and political adjustments of a radical type, including the abolition of poverty and the dissolution of political government. All this was bound up with the very idea of the millenium, the thousand-year reign of Christ in which men would return to a simple and holy life, sharing all and accepting the direct rule of God and his saints. Internally the millenarian sects, like such modern radical sects as the Doukhobors and Mennonites, were less libertarian than they may seem over the spaces of history, yet their conflict with earthly authority did have eventual political consequences as secular dissent emerged out of the need for freedom of worship demanded by religious dissent. In the Netherlands, in France, in Britain, the religious dissenters rose to the leadership of movements opposed to the despotic monarchies established in most of Europe after the breakup of feudalism.

In long-term consequences the most important of these movements uniting political and religious dissent was the seventeenth-century English Revolution, which reached its peak in the Civil War of the 1640s and in the Commonwealth, England's only interlude of republican rule. It was under the Commonwealth that, among a whole cluster of radical groups such as the Fifth Monarchy Men and the Levellers, there emerged the first real proto-anarchists, the Diggers who, like later anarchists, identified economic with political power and who believed that a social rather than a political revolution was necessary for the establishment of justice.

Gerrard Winstanley, the Diggers' leader, had gone all the way along the road of dissent to the point where he made the final identification of God with the principle of Reason. Winstanley's doctrine of God as reason was identical with what Leo Tolstoy, the other great Christian anarchist, meant when he declared that 'The Kingdom of God is within you.'

In fact, Winstanley used the same phrase.

> Where does that Reason dwell? He dwells in every creature according to the nature and being of the creature, but supremely in man. Therefore man is called a rational creature. This is the Kingdom of God within man. Let reason rule the man and he dares not trespass against his fellow creatures, but will do as he would be done unto. For reason tells him – is thy neighbour hungry and naked today? Do thou feed him and clothe him; it may be thy case tomorrow and then he will be ready to help thee.

Winstanley decided that it was his mission to speak up for the disinherited, for the common people who had been very little helped by Cromwell's victory, and in 1649 he published a pamphlet called *The New Law of Righteousness* which began with a denunciation of authority as thorough and as basic as anything in later anarchist literature. 'Everyone that gets an authority into his hands tyrannizes over the others,' Winstanley declared, and went on to show that not only masters and magistrates, but also fathers and husbands 'do carry themselves like oppressing lords over such as are under them . . . not knowing that these have an equal privilege with them to share the blessing of liberty.' He went on to link the absence of liberty with what he calls 'this particular property of mine and thine', to whose presence he also attributes the existence of crime. Finally, after many variations on this theme, he sketches out his vision of the free society, based on the teachings of Christ whom he gives the name of Universal Liberty. The passage in which he does so is worth quoting, since it does get surprisingly near – considering the gap of two centuries – to the kind of social arrangement nineteenth-century anarchists projected in their imaginations.

> When this universal equity rises up in every man and woman, then none shall lay claim to any creature and say, This is mine and that is yours. This is my work, that is yours. But everyone shall put their hands to till the earth and bring up cattle, and the blessing of earth shall be common to

all; when a man hath need of any corn or cattle, he shall take from the next store-house he meets with. There shall be no buying and selling, no fairs and markets . . . And all shall cheerfully put to their hands to make those things that are needful, one helping another. There shall be none lords over others, but everyone shall be a lord of himself, subject to the law of righteousness, reason and equity, which shall dwell and rule in him, which is the Lord.

Living in an agrarian age, Winstanley saw the main problem as ownership of the land, and, like a true anarchist, he believed the problem could be solved only by the direct action of the common people. So in the spring of 1649 he led a company of his followers to squat on unused land in southern England and cultivate it for their own sustenance. The local land-owners and the State went into alliance against this threatening little company. The landlords sent men to drive away their cattle and destroy their crops. Cromwell sent soldiers, but withdrew them when he found they were being converted by the Diggers. The Diggers practised passive resistance as long as they could endure, and then departed.

Winstanley, who has a fair claim to being the first of the anarchists, withdrew into an oblivion so deep that even the date of his death is not remembered (though it is known he influenced the earlier and more militant Quakers), and once the English Revolution had spent its course it was not until the era of the French Revolution, more than a century later, that a recognizable strain of anarchistic thought again emerged.

When it did, it combined with elements derived from English dissent a great deal that was developed from – or often in reaction to – the Renaissance idea of the proper ordering of society. The political order of the Middle Ages had been organic in form, a balance of Church and king, of baronies and free cities, whose haphazard nature was illustrated most vividly by the fact that the kings had no permanent capitals, but travelled from royal castle to royal castle fol-lowed by vast trains of wagons bearing the royal property. At the same time there was – in theory at least – a tightly graded social order in which every man knew his place, which compensated for the lack of an elaborate political system; there were also cracks in the medieval order in which men might enjoy freedom and good community life, as happened in some of the cities of Italy and Germany.

The medieval social order, never so stable as its later defenders have argued, disintegrated between the twelfth and fourteenth centuries, a development that coincided with the revival of humanist learning, which is one way of defining the Renaissance. Man now became important for his qualities as an individual rather than for the position he held in a graded society, but whether this was a net gain for freedom must be judged in the light of the fact that at the same time the organic order of the medieval world was replaced by a faith in rationally devised political patterns.

Renaissance individualism was culturally invigorating, but not necessarily anarchist in quality. It stressed self-development at the expense of others; it was freedom without equality, liberty without community. It produced splendid artists but also remorseless villains. One can illustrate the difference between Renaissance individualism and historic anarchism by comparing the two men who made the name of Malatesta famous in Italian history. Sigismondo Malatesta was a ruthless fifteenth-century soldier of fortune who ruled his own domain with such brutality that he became known as the Tyrant of Rimini. He was at the same time a freethinker and a perceptive patron of the arts, but at no stretching of the phrase could he be called a socially motivated man. The other Malatesta, Errico, was a nineteenth-century wouldbe doctor who turned anarchist and abandoned his career to spend his life wandering the earth as a poor man and helping people in a dozen countries to rebel against tyranny. This Malatesta combined a genuinely individualist temperament with a sense of the indivisibility of liberty.

The other aspect of the Renaissance lay in its emphasis on order. This was reflected in the many rationally planned cities built at that time, and in the search for political order which led to the concepts of ruthless political action developed by men like Machiavelli, and to the plans of ideal social orders devised by Thomas Moore in *Utopia* and Tomasso Campanella in *The City of the Sun*. Most such utopian writers, even when they advocated common property, portrayed essentially authoritarian societies, as rigidly controlled as the new cities. Such an attitude was in keeping with the rise of the modern national state, which began in Cromwell's England, was developed in the France of Louis XIV, and, ironically, was completed during the French Revolution when conscription was introduced and gave Napoleon the means to extend nationalism into imperialism.

Yet at the same time the Renaissance inclination to liberate thought from dogma tended to produce thinkers who offered libertarian alternatives to the total rule of authority. Diderot and Etienne de la Boëtie were examples in France; in Britain perhaps the most important representatives of this trend were the philosopher John Locke and the radical Tom Paine, who took part in both the American and French Revolutions and was condemned to death *in absentia* by the English for writing *The Rights of Man.* Paine was in many ways near the anarchists, particularly when he emphasized the vital distinction between society and government. 'Society is produced by our wants,' said Paine, 'and government by our wickedness; the former promotes our happiness positively by uniting our affections, the latter negatively by restraining our vices . . . Government, like dress, is the badge of lost innocence; the palaces of kings are built on the ruins of the bowers of paradise.'

Paine's influence permeated the native libertarian movement of nineteenth-century America and helped to shape the thought of anarchists as varied as Henry David Thoreau, Josiah Warren and Benjamin Tucker. One of his personal friends was William Godwin, whose *Enquiry concerning Political Justice* (1793) deeply influenced Coleridge, Wordsworth and Shelley, provided the foundation for Robert Owen's utopian efforts, and was probably the most complete study of the faults of government as government ever written. Godwin derived from both ancestral strains of modern anarchism, religious dissent and Renaissance rationalism. As a young man he belonged to a tiny sect called the Sandemanians who denied Church government, believed in sharing goods among the faithful, and argued that religious men had no place in the affairs of State. For a while Godwin served as a dissenting pastor; then he was converted to rationalism and substituted reason for faith without abandoning the social ideas that stemmed from his religious dissent. He was also influenced by the ideas of the French Enlightenment, and wrote *Political Justice* largely to clarify his own views of recent developments in the French Revolution.

There were in fact proto-anarchists at work in France at that time, *enragés* like Jacques Roux and Jean Varlet, but such men were too involved in action to develop a written ideology, and it was Godwin, from the distance of London, who criticized the authoritarian direction which the Jacobins had given the Revolution.

In *Political Justice* he attacked the theory and practice of government with what was to become the classic anarchist argument: that authority is against nature and that social ills exist because men are not at liberty to act according to reason. As an alternative he sketched out a decentralized libertarian society in which small autonomous communities will be the essential units and in which even democratic political practices will be minimized because majority rule is a form of tyranny and voting for representatives is an abdication of personal responsibility.

Godwin developed theoretical anarchism as thoroughly as it has ever been done. What later libertarians added to his arguments was the dimension of action as they moved from the thinker's study to the social jungle.

3 THE CLASSIC ANARCHIST MOVEMENT

The seeds of great movements often lie in what seem at the time mediocre lives or small and insignificant encounters. Certainly, a time traveller who returned to the cafés of Paris and the wretched hotel rooms of the Latin Quarter, where revolutionaries gathered in the early years of the 1840s, would be hard put to it to recognize the men who would become the great rallying names of the century. France was then a monarchy once again, but it was ruled by the most liberal of the Bourbons, Louis Philippe, the so-called Citizen King, and in those years, when the ferment of French discontent was building up to the revolutionary peak of 1848,

Paris gave rather grudging asylum to those who had fled from harsher regimes. One could meet there Spanish federalists, Italian carbonarists and Poles intriguing to re-establish their country, then divided up between Russia, Prussia and Austria-Hungary. There were many Russians who had fled from the oppressive tyranny of the Tsar Nicholas I, and a fair number of Germans who had found it discreet to absent themselves from Prussia and from the petty states of the Rhineland.

Among the more obscure expatriates who lived in this atmosphere of intrigue and expectancy were a Russian and a German who were to be seen often together and sometimes in the company of a French radical journalist who was more inclined than most of his countrymen to mingle with the foreign revolutionaries. They were all young and all poor, and as they talked into the small hours of many a Parisian morning nobody detected the long shadows they were already casting into the future.

For the stocky Frenchman in the seedy green *redingot*, with a broad peasant face fringed with monkey whiskers, was Pierre-Joseph Proudhon, who had just given the nineteenth century one of its greatest battle cries – Property is Theft! He had already declared himself an anarchist, and was the first man ever to accept that label with pride and defiance. The Russian, a penniless nobleman of gigantic stature and inexhaustible charm, was Michael Bakunin; he was busily inciting insurrection among the lesser Slav peoples in the Austrian Empire, and had just attracted attention by an essay entitled *Reaction in Germany* which in a series of pungent phrases had summed up the paradoxes that lie at the heart of anarchist doctrines. 'Let us put our trust in the eternal spirit which destroys and annihilates only because it is the unsearchable and eternally creative source of all life. The urge to destroy is also a creative urge.'

The German in the trio was Karl Marx, himself a notable creator of historic phrases and in those days an almost irrepressible fountain of German metaphysics; his contribution to the gatherings apparently consisted largely of long expositions of the philosophy of Hegel for the edification of his companions. Marx, of course, was to be the ancestor of modern authoritarian communism, though he and Engels would not issue their *Communist Manifesto* for several years to come; Proudhon and Bakunin were to become the founders of anarchism as a social revolutionary movement. In time bitter enmities would divide the three, and even in the 1840s their relationship was guarded. There is extant a correspondence between Marx and Proudhon leading to a breach of relations in 1846. In it they discuss the possibility of establishing a liaison between social revolutionaries, and the difference in approaches is already evident as one contrasts Marx's rigid dogmatism with Proudhon's exploratory flexibility. Bakunin left an actual record of his encounters with Marx in the 1840s.

Marx and I were friendly enough in those days. We saw one another often, for I respected him a great deal for his science and for his passionate and serious devotion – mingled though it was with a certain personal vanity – to the cause of the proletariat, and I sought avidly his ever instructive and intelligent conversation. Yet there was really no intimacy between us. Our temperaments did not suit each other. He called me a sentimental idealist – and he was right. I called him vain, perfidious and sly – and I was right too!

Yet for a little time Marx and the two anarchists were united in their realization that the great pre-nineteenth-century revolutions, the English Revolution of the seventeenth century and the American and French Revolutions of the eighteenth, had proceeded only part of the way towards a just society, because they had been political rather than social revolutions. They had rearranged the patterns of authority, giving power to new classes, but they had in no fundamental way changed the social and economic structure of the countries in which they had taken place. The great slogan of the French Revolution – liberty, equality, fraternity – had become a mockery, since political equality was impossible without economic equality, liberty was dependent on people not being enslaved by property, and fraternity was impossible across the chasm that at the end of the eighteenth century still divided the rich from the poor.

Neither Marx, Proudhon nor Bakunin considered the possibility that such results might be inherent in the revolutionary process, which twentieth-century experience seems to suggest may always entail the substitution of one élite for another. But one thing Proudhon and Bakunin both understood more clearly than Marx: that a revolution which does not get rid of authority will always create a power more pervasive and more durable than that which it has replaced. They believed that a revolution without authority, that destroyed power-wielding institutions and replaced them by voluntary co-operative institutions, was indeed possible and could happen in their time. Marx was at once more realistic and more deluded. He recognized the vital role power plays in revolutions, but he believed it possible to create a new kind of power, the power of the proletariat working through the party, which in the end would dissolve itself and produce the ideal anarchist society which he too believed the final, desirable goal of human endeavour; Bakunin was right in accusing Marx of excessive optimism and in prophesying that a Marxist political order would turn out to be a rigid oligarchy of officials and technocrats.

But when Marx, Proudhon and Bakunin met in the Latin Quarter all this was in the future. Looking to the past, between these men and the French Revolution lay the generation of the so-called utopian socialists, like Cabet and Fourier and Robert Owen who recognized that the French Revolution had failed to attack the radical questions of social injustice, and who proposed as a remedy various forms of the socialization of wealth and productivity. They were called utopian because they wished to create here and now experimental communities that would demonstrate how a just society might work. From Proudhon on, the anarchists were influenced in many ways by the utopian socialists, and particularly in their notion of the small community as the basis of society. But they differed from them in rejecting the rigidity of utopian socialist planning, which they believed would lead to new kinds of authority, and they also believed that there was a reprehensible élitism in the idea of a socialist elect demonstrating to the people how an ideal society should work. The anarchist mystique was based on the idea that people could create for themselves, spontaneously, the social and economic relations they needed. What one really required, they argued, was not to fabricate new and artificial social forms but to find ways of activating the people so that out of their natural groupings and popular traditions the institutions appropriate to a free society might evolve.

Not until the 1860s did these aspirations begin to coalesce into an actual anarchist movement. During the wave of revolutions that swept Europe in 1848 both Bakunin and Proudhon were actively engaged. Bakunin took part in risings in Paris and Prague and fought beside Wagner on the barricades in Dresden. Captured in Saxony, he ended as a prisoner of the Tsar in the notorious Peter-and-Paul Fortress, and only in 1861 did he escape via Siberia, Japan and the United States to western Europe where he resumed his revolutionary activity. Proudhon took part in the 1848 revolution in Paris and became an early disillusioned member of the National Assembly. He learnt quickly how parliamentary activity puts a man out of touch with the people, and spent much more of his time during the revolutionary year on fierily independent journalism in a series of newspapers – *The People, The Representative of the People* and *The People's Friend* – which were successively suppressed because the revolutionary authorities could not endure his impartial attacks on all sides in the new republic, which he accused of being devoid of ideas. Proudhon also tried to organize the workers economically in the People's Bank, which was really a kind of Credit Union where goods and services could be exchanged on the basis of labour costs. He hoped this would be the start of a network of free relationships between producers – such as peasants, artisans and co-operative workshops – which would displace ordinary market relationships and liberate the worker from dependence. The People's Bank was perhaps the first anarchist mass organization; it had gained a membership of 27,000 when Proudhon was imprisoned in 1849 for his criticisms of the newly elected President, Napoleon Bonaparte, who later became Emperor as Napoleon III.

Almost all of Proudhon's remaining life was spent in prison or exile. He remained a minority of one, glorying in the fact that he led no party. Yet precisely because he was

independent his influence grew immensely during the Second
Empire. Towards the end of his life, which came in 1865, he
wrote *De la Capacité Politique des Classes ouvrières*, in
which he argued that political parties were operated by members of the social élite and that working men would only
control their own destinies when they created and operated
their own organizations for social change. Many French
workers were influenced by such ideas, and they formed a
movement aimed at the regeneration of society by economic
means. They called themselves Mutualists, but essentially
they were anarchists who hoped to gain their ends peacefully
by means of producers' co-operation.

Out of meetings between 1862 and 1864 between these
French disciples of Proudhon and English trade union representatives emerged the International Workingmen's Association – the First International. Marx's followers foster the
legend that he founded the International, but he took no part
in the early negotiations and at the final meeting in London
on 28 September 1864 at which the Association was set up,
he was only – as he put it – 'a mute figure on the platform'.

Thus the First International was never a Marxist body. It
included socialists, anarchists of many kinds, and people who
were neither. Nobody knows how large its membership
became. Both its supporters and its enemies for their own
varying reasons tend to exaggerate its membership and its
influence. Yet there is no doubt that, especially in the Latin-
speaking lands of southern Europe, the Association gave
workers and peasants a stimulus to struggle on their own
behalf as they had never done before. But behind all the devotion and the grand and elevating aspirations, the International
became a battleground of ideologies and personalities. Proudhon was dead by the time the Association became an active
organization in 1865, yet the differences that had already
begun to emerge between the trio of revolutionaries in those
early days in Paris survived to become magnified in the setting
of the International, and the conflict between Marx and the
Mutualists, and later between Marx and Bakunin personally,
not only reflected the temperamental differences of the
protagonists, but also the fundamental differences in means –
which automatically means a difference in ends – between the

authoritarian socialists and the libertarian anarchists.

Marx and his followers, being more astute tacticians, managed to entrench themselves in positions of organizational power. It was Marx who drafted the rules of the Association and gained virtual control of the General Council, established in London. His influence in the branches, mainly in Latin countries, was less certain, and the annual Congresses turned into battles between Marx and Bakunin, who headed the Italian, Spanish and French Swiss contingents. Having already created a secret brotherhood of revolutionaries in Italy, Bakunin had joined the International in 1868. His methods as an organizer were eccentric but curiously effective, and he created the world's greatest anarchist movement – in Spain – by sending to Barcelona an Italian engineer who knew no Spanish yet possessed the kind of charisma that made a common language unnecessary. Anselmo Lorenzo, who later became a leader of the Spanish anarchists, left a fascinating description of the incident which Gerald Brenan quoted in *The Spanish Labyrinth.*

Fanelli was a tall man with a kind and grave expression, a thick, black beard, and large black expressive eyes which flashed like lightning or took on the appearance of kindly compassion according to the sentiments that dominated him. His voice had a metallic tone and was susceptible of all the inflections appropriate to what he was saying, passing rapidly from accents of anger and menace against tyrants and exploiters to take on those of suffering, regret and consolation, when he spoke of the pains of the exploited, either as one who, without suffering them himself, understood them, or as one who through his altruistic feelings delights in presenting an ultra-revolutionary ideal of peace and fraternity. He spoke in French and Italian, but we could understand his expressive mimicry and follow his meaning.

The battle within the International assumed many aspects. It was a duel between Marx and Bakunin. It was also a battle between Germanic and Latin groups. But the fundamental differences were other than those of personality or culture. They became defined in the endless debates that consumed the

years between 1868 and the split which destroyed the International in 1872. The Marxists argued for political organization aimed at transforming the proletariat into a ruling class.
The anarchists argued for the economic organization of the
workers according to their occupations. Authoritarian versus
libertarian, political action versus industrial action, transitional
proletarian dictatorship versus immediate abolition of all State
power: the debate went on and the two points of view were
irreconcilable. Debate turned into conflict. At the Basel
Congress of 1872 the Marxists expelled Bakunin and trans-
ferred the General Council to New York where it would be
out of reach of the anarchists; it was dead by 1874. The
anarchists meanwhile set up their rival International; it survived the Marxist rump by three years and was dead by
1877.

Yet the anarchist movement lived on, as a pattern rather
than an organization, in scattered groups and individuals,
always in contact, holding melodramatic conferences which
scared the respectable, and rarely united. A few dedicated
and talented men like Peter Kropotkin and Errico Malatesta
shaped the ideology of anarchism, and between 1880 and
1900 it flowered amazingly. At one extreme were the followers
of Leo Tolstoy, who advocated non-violent resistance and
strongly influenced Gandhi in his strategy of *satyagraha* or
civil disobedience, which finally won Indian independence.
Others devoted their energies to free schools or to communities where people tried to live communally without the
restrictions implied in utopian theory. Yet others sought an
alliance between anarchism and the revolution in the arts
which at the turn of the century initiated the Modernist
movement in Europe and especially in France. Painters like
Pissaro and Signac and Vlaminck and the young Picasso
called themselves anarchists; so did poets like Mallarmé and
men of letters like Oscar Wilde.

All anarchists saw themselves as propagandists for freedom but while some confined their propaganda to writing and
speaking, others elaborated the theory and practice of propaganda by deed. This was an early form of an idea favoured
in our own day, that a political theory becomes valid only
when it is activated. It originated, not among the anarchists,

but with an extreme Italian republican, Carlo Pisacane (who had discarded his title of Duke of San Giovanni), and who probably expressed the idea more succinctly than anyone has since done: 'The propaganda of the idea is a chimera. Ideas result from deeds, not the latter from the former, and the people will not be free when they are educated, but educated when they are free.'

Borrowing Pisacane's insight, Italian anarchists exemplified the propaganda of the deed by starting small Quixotic insurrections which had no hope of success but which it was mistakenly thought would arouse the people to undertake their own liberation. Then, during a brief interlude which has plagued the record of anarchism ever since, a few mainly isolated individuals took to the practice of assassinating symbolic figures to draw attention to injustice. During the 1890s a king of Italy, a president of France, a president of the United States, an empress of Austria and a prime minister of Spain fell victim to these strange and terrible enthusiasts. Most anarchists had nothing to do with such acts, and regarded them with very mixed feelings, until in the end most of them reacted in horror, as the French anarchist novelist, Octave Mirbeau, did when Emile Henry threw a bomb into a crowded café and killed innocent people. 'A mortal enemy of anarchism,' said Mirbeau, 'could have acted no more effectively than this Henry when he threw his inexplicable bomb into the midst of peaceful and anonymous persons. Henry says and affirms and claims that he is an anarchist. It is possible. Every party has its criminals and fools, because every party has its men.'

Terrorism quickly died away as an anarchist method, except in Spain and Russia, where all kinds of politics had traditionally been violent. Only a few individual anarchists ever practised it, and to think of the anarchist as a man with a bomb is like considering every Roman Catholic a dynamiter because of Guy Fawkes. Movements are indeed manifested through the actions of individuals, but one must distinguish between the person and the idea, and the idea of anarchism has never been invalidated by the extremities of its fanatics.

Nineteenth-century anarchism in fact recovered very quickly from the damage done by the terrorists, and in the last years of the century moved into its phase of broadest influence through the development of a movement to create libertarian unions of syndicates. The movement called itself anarcho-syndicalism; essentially its viewpoint was that unions should be regarded not merely as instruments for getting better wages, but also as agents for the transformation of society. The unions would be involved in a constant struggle to change society by the classic method of the general strike and, taking over and running the places of production during a revolution, to form the infrastructure of the new society.

Anarcho-syndicalism had much early success in France, where the CGT was run by anarchists until 1914. There were large syndicalist movements in Italy and Latin America, while the International Workers of the World (IWW) in the United States was syndicalist in its approach. But it was in Spain that anarcho-syndicalism, like anarchism itself, reached its apogee. There it appealed for its moral and idealistic qualities; it became not merely a political movement but also a quasi-religious movement of puritanical tinge which gave Spaniards a surrogate Reformation. Anarchism won over the factory workers of Barcelona; it spread like evangelical wildfire among the landless peasants of Andalucia and Valencia. In the 1930s, at its height, the great anarchist union, the National Con-federation of Labour (CNT), had more than two million members. Spain represented the true peak of the nineteenth-century anarchist movement, extending far into the twentieth century, for Spanish anarchism reached its apogee and its end during the Spanish Civil War of the later 1930s.

In Spain the anarchists showed that in local and spontaneous efforts their methods were effective; where they failed was in co-ordination on a larger scale. For example, in Barcelona it was the anarchist grasp of street fighting tactics that defeated the attempt by Franco's generals to seize power. Similarly, in the rural areas the villagers established free communes, and even critical commentators were impressed by the natural efficiency and Spartan fortitude with which the people set about rearranging their lives on the lines indicated by the nineteenth-century anarchist prophets.

Yet all this comradeship and self-sacrifice, which showed so admirably that small, dedicated groups could indeed put anarchist teachings into practice, was doomed to vanish, largely because the anarchist virtues of spontaneity and voluntary action are alien to the spirit of war – even of civil war – which is totalitarian in nature. They failed to resist effectively the fascists who advanced on the village communes from the south and destroyed them, or the communists who undermined the anarchist position behind the republican lines. Two years of war and political intrigue broke the spirit of the Spanish anarchists. The historic movement created by Bakunin and Proudhon died when Franco's armies marched unopposed into anarchist Barcelona. But the anarchist idea, as distinct from the movement, did not, and in the last decade it has risen like a phoenix from the fire of its own transformation.

4 PHOENIX IN THE AWAKENING DESERT

In these pages I have been stressing the differences between anarchism and more dogmatic political orthodoxies, and especially between anarchist groups and the tightly hierarchical structures of political parties whose aim is power. When anarchism existed as an identifiable movement, it had intellectual leaders but no organizational leadership. It always included within itself a variety of viewpoints on tactics and on the nature of the desirable society that co-existed with a remarkable degree of mutual tolerance, rather like the religious sects of India. In the last resort, it was always the idea expressed directly in action that was dynamic rather than the movement.

In fact, even when anarchism was most popular and its organizations numbered their followers in the millions, as the CNT did in Spain, the structure was always a fragile and flexible frame within which the power of spontaneous thought remained the important motive force. It is because anarchism is in essence an anti-dogmatic and unstructured cluster of related attitudes that it can flourish when conditions are favourable, and then, like a plant in the desert, lie dormant for seasons and even for years, waiting for the rains to make it blossom again. In an ordinary political faith, the party is needed as a kind of church, a vehicle of the dogma, but anarchism has been nearer to the mystical faiths that rely on personal illumination, and for this reason it has never needed a movement to keep it alive. Many of its important teachers, as we have seen, were solitary, dedicated individualists like Godwin and Thoreau and Stirner. Those who granted the need for organization wanted it to be minimal, so that even Pierre-Joseph Proudhon, intellectual mentor of the historic anarchist movement, warned his followers against any rigidity of thought or action. With few exceptions, the anarchist originators avoided the trap of becoming infallible gurus, and it is significant that there has never been a single anarchist book that has been put forward and accepted as a political gospel in the same way as Marx's *Das Kapital*. In fact, widely-read anarchist books like Kropotkin's *Memoirs of a Revolutionist* or Herbert Read's *Poetry and Anarchism*, or the essays of Paul Goodman, to give a few varied examples, retain their freshness and appeal precisely because their intent is to awaken thought, not to direct it.

It is this peculiarly unpartisan element in anarchist thought that makes it resilient and durable, and explains why the downfall of the movement in Spain with Franco's victory, though it certainly meant the end of the movement founded by Proudhon and Bakunin, did not mean more than a temporary eclipse of the anarchist idea. Between 1939 and the beginning of the 1960s, anarchism did not play a great part in the affairs of any country or in the thoughts of anyone but a few libertarian intellectuals and a few ageing veterans of past battles. Yet from the early 1960s there has been a rebirth, the ideas of anarchism have emerged rejuvenated, have clothed themselves in action, have stimulated the young in age and spirit, and have disturbed established hierarchies on both the Right and the Left. In the process, anarchist doctrines and methods have been carried far beyond the remnants of the old anarchist movement. New kinds of organization have appeared, new modes of action have evolved, but they reproduce surprisingly faithfully – even among people who hardly know what the word *anarchism* means or who perhaps have never heard it – the ideas on the defects of present society and the desiderata of a better society that have been taught by seminal thinkers in the libertarian tradition from seventeenth-century Winstanley down to Herbert Read and his successors in our own generation.

Turn now to the sequence of events. World War II, following Franco's victory, completed the breakdown of the international anarchist movement. The process began as early as 1918. In Russia, after the 1917 October Revolution, the Bolsheviks recognized the anarchists as their main rivals and eliminated them, but only after a struggle in which large areas of the Ukraine became a kind of anarchist peasant community under a guerilla leader Nestor Makhno, who fought brilliantly against Whites and Reds but finally fled to western Europe in 1921 to escape destruction by Trotsky's legions. The advent of fascism in Italy and nazism in Germany meant the end of the anarchist movement in both countries, and by the time the Reichswehr had completed its conquests of the Second World War, the only anarchists at large and active were in Britain, the United States, Switzerland and the more liberal Latin American states, of which Mexico was the most important. Every country where a mass anarchist movement had once existed – Russia, France, Italy and Spain – was by 1942 existing under a totalitarian regime.

There ensued a situation quite new in anarchist history, for during the Second World War it was in the English-speaking countries that anarchism demonstrated the greatest vitality and the tradition was interpreted in completely new ways. The stimulus did not come only from Spanish, Italian and Russian refugees who represented the movement created by Proudhon, Bakunin and Kropotkin. It came also from writers reared in the modernist movement who had learnt their anarchism as much from Oscar Wilde and William Morris and William Godwin.

In Britain this interim movement, as I call it because it represents a transition between nineteenth-century and late-twentieth-century anarchism, drew together not only British writers and painters who had emerged between the 1920s and the 1940s, but also many refugee artists from eastern Europe, from France and Belgium. There were English painters like Augustus John and John Minton, Russian constructivists like Naum Gago and Polish expressionists like Jankel Adler. Herbert Read and John Cowper Powys represented the older writers, but Dylan Thomas was a declared anarchist, and so were Alex Comfort, George Woodcock and Denise Levertov.

In the United States also, anarchism escaped from its traditions to be transformed by younger interpreters. In New York it centred around Dwight Macdonald, then running *Politics*, and Paul Goodman, already relating accepted libertarian doctrine to contemporary American problems of rural decay and urban chaos. In San Francisco, even during the early 1940s, a literary anarchist movement which had floating links with the more traditional movement among Italian emigrés arose under the leadership of the poet Kenneth Rexroth; other poets like Robert Duncan and Philip Lamantia and, later on, Kenneth Patchen and Allen Ginsberg became closely involved, so that anarchism was one of the motivating philosophies of the beat movement in California.

This tendency for anarchism during the 1940s to become lodged like a seed germ in the minds of a few English-speaking intellectuals led to interesting theoretical developments, particularly in the fields of science and education. Ever since Kropotkin modified evolutionary theory by publishing *Mutual Aid*, libertarian thinkers have attempted to relate their doctrines to whatever sciences of man seem to be currently important. During the present century the place biology had held in the speculations of Kropotkin and of his associates like Elisée and Elie Reclus was assumed by psychology. Long before he became the improbable guru of geriatric sexology, Alex Comfort wrote a valuable anarchist treatise in the psychology of power, *Authority and Delinquency*. The teachings of Erich Fromm – particularly in *The Fear of Freedom* – made their appeal to anarchists in the 1940s, and so did the heretical Freudian teachings of Wilhelm Reich, which related psychological to political repression and sought in neurosis the origins of coercive power. The most important anarchist writer to be influenced by modern psychological theory was Herbert Read, who drew copiously on the theories of Freud, Adler and especially Jung to support the other characteristic departure of anarchist theory during the 1940s – an intensified recognition of the need for a new type of education that would enable men to accept and also to endure freedom. (I say *endure* quite deliberately because – as the very title of Fromm's *The Fear of Freedom* suggested – it had dawned on libertarians in the mid-twentieth century [as it had dawned earlier on

Proudhon] that freedom is an austere discipline whose advantages may not be immediately evident to the masses accustomed to State tutelage and the welfare society.) Herbert Read believed that the educational system as it existed, with its emphasis on merely academic learning, prepared men for obedience, not for freedom; in his books, such as *Education through Art* and *The Education of Free Men*, he argued that the schools should be transformed to educate the senses before they touched the mind, and that the harmonious personality which resulted from education through art would not only live a more balanced individual life, but would also achieve, with a minimum of disturbance, the peaceful transformation of society of which the anarchists had long dreamed, a transformation in which people who were inwardly at peace and therefore at peace with each other could make equality and fraternity compatible with freedom.

When the war ended in 1945, and countries like Italy and France were liberated, there was a kind of rattling of the bones in the movement Bakunin had created. Old anarchists met again; an uneasy liaison appeared between them and the English-speaking intellectuals who had extended anarchist theory during the 1940s. There were even international congresses; but the one I attended at Berne in 1946 was a strangely spectral affair, with a few old men and a few young men gathering beside the grave of Bakunin, to orate, to play Mozart in his memory and to dream of repeating his achievement.

The old movement was not resurrected in any meaningful way, yet the anarchist idea, as distinct from the organization, has certainly been born again, and the rebirth has taken place largely outside the gallant but scanty groups of veterans. The crucial decade was the 1960s. The 1950s – the decade of cautious careerist youth – had been a period of hibernation for anarchist ideas, though they were kept alive by a few poets and essayists. But as that decade ended, the idea seemed suddenly active again. It developed in two different ways.

First, there was the scholarly interest. Nowadays, in view of the wealth of available material, it is hard to remember how little had been written on anarchism up to 1950 in a spirit of scholarly enquiry. There were the apologias of the anarchists and the diatribes of their opponents, but few objective records of what anarchism meant and what anarchists had done. The first complete history of anarchism ever written, in English or any other language, was my own *Anarchism: A History of Libertarian Ideas and Movements*, which appeared in 1962. Other general histories followed, and also biographies of the more important anarchist thinkers and activists, as well as reprints of their works, so that anarchism during the 1960s became at last academically respectable.

But that was the anarchism of the past, of the classic thinkers, the historic movement that had been moribund since 1939. What began to emerge in the 1960s was the actual revival of the anarchist current of thought accompanied by active movements among young people in many European and American countries. Often the name did not re-emerge; often the dogma was diluted by other strains of radical thought; rarely was there an attempt to re-establish continuity with a movement in the past. But the idea re-emerged, clear and recognizable, and in countries as varied as Britain and Holland, France and the United States, it attracted adherents on a scale unparalleled since the days before the First World War.

Like the New Left, to which it was loosely related, the movement which one might call neo-anarchism had double roots. It sprang partly from the experience of those who became involved in the civil rights movement in the United States as early as the mid-1950s, and partly from the great mass protests against nuclear disarmament that were held in Britain during the early 1960s. In Britain the protest movement was developed by the Campaign for Nuclear Disarmament, and within the CND there appeared a more militant group called the Committee of One Hundred, in which Bertrand Russell was active but which also included a number of anarchist intellectuals from earlier decades. Quite apart from these links with classic anarchism, there was within the Committee of One Hundred, as always happens when militant pacifism encounters a government irremediably bent on warlike preparations, a spontaneous surge of anti-State feeling, that is to say, anarchist feeling still unnamed. Arguments surfaced in the Committee of One Hundred in favour of methods advocated by the anarchists. Groups dedicated to direct action and to exploring the implications of a society without war and violence and hence without coercion sprang up all over Britain. At the same time the remnants of the anarchist movement was revivified, and the anarchists – in the new sense as well as the old – became a vocal and active element in British political life, few in comparison with the larger political parties, but more numerous and more influential than they ever were in the England of the past.

A striking characteristic of the neo-anarchism that emerged in Britain and the United States at this time was that, like so many modern protest movements, it represented mainly a trend among the young, and the middle-class young especially. In 1962, at the beginning of the upsurge, the British anarchist periodical *Freedom* conducted a survey of the occupations and class backgrounds of its readers. Past anarchist movements had consisted mainly of artisans and peasants, with a few intellectual leaders recruited from the upper- and middle-class intelligentsia. The *Freedom* survey revealed that in the Britain of the 1960s only 15 per cent of the anarchists willing to answer questions about themselves belonged to traditional groupings of peasants and workers; of the remaining 85 per cent, the largest group consisted of teachers and students, and there were also many architects, doctors, journalists and people working independently as artists and craftsmen. Even more significant was the class shift among the young; 45 per cent of the readers over 60 were manual workers, as against 23 per cent of those in their thirties and 10 per cent of those in their twenties. Very similar proportions exist in anarchist and near-anarchist movements in most Western countries. The new libertarianism has been essentially a revolt, not of the under-privileged, and certainly not of the skilled workers, who are busy defending their recent gains in living standards, but of the privileged who have seen the futility of affluence as a goal.

Undoubtedly one of the factors that has made anarchism popular among the young has been its opposition to the increasingly centralized and technocratic industrial cultures of western Europe, North America, Japan and Russia. In this context an important mediating figure – though the orthodox anarchists have never accepted him – was Aldous Huxley. Huxley's pacifism and his early recognition of the perils of population explosion, of ecological destruction and psychological manipulation, all combined in a social vision that in many ways anticipated the preoccupations of neo-anarchism during the 1960s and 1970s. Already in the 1930s, with *Brave New World*, Huxley had presented the first warning vision of the kind of mindless, materialistic existence a society dominated by technological centralization might produce. In his Foreword to the 1946 edition of that book, Huxley declared that the perils implicit in modern social trends could only be averted by switching over to rapid decentralization and simplification in economic terms, and to political forms that – as he put it – would be 'Kropotkinesque and co-operative'. In later books, and especially in his novel, *After Many a Summer*, Huxley enlarged on his acceptance of the anarchist critique of the existing order, and it was largely through these late works of his, often taught in college English courses, that the libertarian attitude was transmitted to the generation of the 1960s and welded on to their concern for environmental regeneration.

Even in mood, in its insistence on spontaneity, on theoretical flexibility, on simplicity of living, on love and anger as complementary and necessary components of social as well as individual action, anarchism had a special appeal to a generation that rejected the impersonality of massive institutions and the pragmatic calculations of political parties. In terms of social organization, the anarchist rejection of the State, and the insistence of decentralism and grassroots responsibilities, have found a strong echo in a contemporary movement which demands that its democracy be not representative but participatory and that its action be direct. The recurrence of the theme of workers' control of industry also shows the enduring influence of the ideas Proudhon created and passed on to the anarcho-syndicalists.

The movement in which anarchist ideas perhaps came most dramatically to the surface in recent years was the Paris insurrection of 1968. It was a largely spontaneous affair, in which left-wing party leaders and trade union leaders had little control, and in which something resembling the old anarchist scenario for a libertarian revolution was actually enacted. The students occupied their colleges, they raised the black flag of the anarchists on the Bourse, and they inspired the workers to strike and sit in their factories. For a few days De Gaulle's power, and the vainglorious nationalism he represented, hung in the balance; only by making a deal with his enemies in the army could his rule survive long enough for the basic conservative forces in French society to reassert themselves. The events in Paris demonstrated, as similar events in Athens and Bangkok and elsewhere have later done, that despite their sophisticated techniques of holding power, modern governments are almost as vulnerable as their predecessors, and in some ways more vulnerable, since contemporary society has become such an elaborately interlocking structure of bureaucratic machinery that even a slight failure of function quickly becomes magnified in its effects. In such circumstances the rebel becomes rather like a small State in a world seemingly dominated by nuclear superpowers; his ability to disturb the intricate balance gives him certain advantages, and there is no doubt that because of the dynamics of the situation contemporary radicals have managed to change social attitudes and induce retreats on the part of authority that would not have been likely even a decade ago. But we have to bear in mind that these retreats are largely tactical. Nowhere has a spontaneous rebellion in recent years resulted in a radical change in the actual structure of power. Governments may have changed; the pattern of authority has not been fundamentally disrupted.

A recognition of this fact has led some contemporary anarchists to abandon the direct attack on the citadel of power, on the assumption that it may collapse through undermining if they can change the attitudes of people at the grassroots level. Two interesting examples of this approach – interesting largely because of their mutual contrasts – came respectively from Holland and India.

In Holland – where Domela Nieuwenhuis and Bart de Ligt had created a considerable pacifist-anarchist movement before the Second World War – there have been two neo-anarchist movements, the Provos in the 1960s and the Kabouters in the 1970s. The differences between the two groups illustrate fairly well the scope of variation in terms of tactics that has existed among anarchists in recent years. *Provo* is a contraction of *provocation*, and it was precisely by provocation, in the form of noisy demonstrations, eccentric happenings, original forms of mutual aid, that the Provos set out to stir the Dutch people from a too complacent acceptance of the welfare state into which Holland had transformed itself. The actions of the Provos were reminiscent of one of the anonymous posters that appeared in Paris during the insurrection of 1968: 'The society of alienation must disappear from history. We are inventing a new and original world. Imagination is seizing power.' By using their imagination, the Provos sought to give the tactics of rebellion a new twist so that the despair of ever attaining a free society – which gnaws secretly at every anarchist – became in its own way a weapon to be used in forcing governments to show their true faces. The weak provoke; the strong unwillingly expend themselves. Having stirred the imagination of the Dutch, the Provos showed their difference from ordinary political parties by voluntarily disbanding themselves. Three years later some of them came together in a new group, the Kabouters or Goblins, dedicated to working through local administrations at the municipal level, ignoring the higher levels of government.

In India anarchism has been a respected if not much implemented concept ever since Gandhi described himself as 'a kind of anarchist', and planned a decentralized society based on autonomous village communes. When India became independent, mainly through a civil disobedience movement which Gandhi had developed to a great extent under the influence of Tolstoy and Thoreau, Gandhi's associates abandoned his plan since they wished to make India a State with a great army and a vast bureaucracy modelled on that of the British Raj; the result has been the virtual dictatorship which Mrs Indira Gandhi has recently established by abrogating all the essential freedoms. Nevertheless, some of Gandhi's followers decided to develop his more anarchistic thoughts, and one of the most important libertarian movements in the contemporary world has been Sarvodaya, the movement led by Vinova Bhave and Jayaprakash Narayan, which has sought to make Gandhi's dream a reality by means of *gramdan* – the ownership of the land by autonomous communities. By 1969 a fifth of the villages of India had declared themselves in favour of *gramdan*, and while there is much more of intent than achievement in such a situation, it represents an extensive basic commitment to fundamentally anarchistic ideas. Sarvodaya has also been one of the more significant nuclei of resistance to Mrs Gandhi and her rule by force.

Anarchism, in summary, is a phoenix in an awakening desert, an idea that has revived for the only reason that makes ideas revive: that they respond to some need felt deeply by people – and, since activists are always the tip of any social iceberg, by more people than overtly appear concerned. Anarchism's recent popularity has been in part due to a general reaction against the monolithic welfare state, and already some of the libertarian proposals, like the greater involvement of workers in industrial control and the greater decisive say by people in matters that affect them locally and personally, were beginning to take shape in the 1960s as part of a general shift towards participatory democracy.

Up to now, indeed, there has been little progress towards using anarchist concepts in the wider organization of society, and it is here that the critics feel they are on stronger ground as they talk of the difficulty of handling mass industry – and mass populations – by anarchist methods. Yet it is not impossible that technology might offer some of the means to that end. For technology itself is neutral; there is – as Lewis Mumford pointed out long ago in *Technics and Civilization* – nothing to suggest that a technologically developed society need be either centralized or authoritarian or ecologically wasteful. And one can – to give an example – conceive a time arriving when people in control of their technology might use electronic communications to inform themselves of all sides of a public issue and use the same means to make their wishes known and effective without intermediaries. In this way, the institution of the referendum, which is now so clumsy that it is rarely used, could be applied to all important decisions, and referenda could be adjusted to the particular constituencies actually affected by a decision. Democracy might then be direct and active again, as it once was, for the citizens at least, in ancient Athens. And if a live democracy, participatory and direct, may not yet be the naturally ordered society of anarchy, it would still represent a historic step in that direction.

A Note on the Text

In preparing the anthology of anarchist writings which follows. I have inevitably had to formulate voluntary limitations and then, since they are voluntary, to follow them. A good book might have been compiled merely of the writings and oral traditions of those libertarians who preceded the post-French-Revolutionary men we now recognize as the Anarchists. To include them in the present volume would have made a collection far larger in volume than the present handbook. So I have contented myself with mentioning and modestly quoting in my Introduction some at least of the more interesting precursors of anarchism; my actual examples of anarchist writings begin chronologically with William Godwin who offered, when he published *Enquiry Concerning Political Justice* in 1793, the first thorough libertarian criticism of government in its various aspects, including the forms of economic domination that are associated inevitably with the exercise of power. It has been with genuine reluctance that I have left out some of Godwin's predecessors; I would like especially to have included long extracts from Gerrard Winstanley, who wrote in the 1640s, but I must trust that the slight quotations from his writings included in the Introduction will lead my readers to explore his work more deeply.

Having decided to exclude all Godwin's forbears, I still find myself with between thirty and forty anarchist writers who, it seems to me, *must* be heard; the number of those who *should* be heard is many times larger, and one day I hope to compile the immense and many-volumed anthology that would give representative voice to them all. Yet even the three dozen writers who do appear in this selection display a variety of pre-occupations and styles that one could not expect to encounter in any revolutionary tradition but the anarchist. The literature of Marxist-Leninism, for example, consists of the writings of Marx, Engels and Lenin, usually presented out of context, and little else that does not – in Orwell's phrase – seem to be spoken by gramophones. The whole ideological stance of anarchism is entirely different from that of any authoritarian socialist movement. It tolerates variety, and rejects the idea of political as much as religious gurus. There is no founding prophet whom all his successors must echo. The anarchists have their respected – though not reverenced – teachers, but merely as the first among equals, and what distinguishes any representative collection of anarchist writings, if it is a good one, will be the undogmatic freedom with which the writers develop their own ideas in original and uninhibited ways. The present collection, I think, will exhibit very clearly this characteristic of anarchist writing; it will also exhibit the broadness and flexibility which such an undogmatic attitude allows in the exploration of man's many facets as a social being. For anarchism presents only one aspect of freedom: that of man among other men. It is concerned with the gaining of freedom; what freedom itself creates must lie in the realms of the contemplative and creative lives, and therefore outside the bounds of this collection.

Certain classic anarchist thinkers – Godwin and Proudhon, Bakunin and Kropotkin and Tolstoy – have tended to shape the general outline of libertarian thinking owing to their pre- cedence in time and also to the mental versatility that en- abled them to grasp the anarchist vision in all its scope and also its details. They have been given a larger share of space than most of the later writers, mainly because they so often made the first statement – and sometimes the best statement – on particular issues. I have tried to correct any disproportion that may arise from such a situation by quoting relatively little from those anarchist classics – Kropotkin's *Mutual Aid, Conquest of Bread* and *Fields, Factories and Workshops* are notable examples – that have been reprinted and are now readily available.

For the most part I have confined myself to two kinds of items – the exposition of ideas and arguments, and the descrip- tion of episodes that give a physical projection to such argu- ments, hence the pieces I have included on the Paris Com- mune, the Russian Revolution, the Spanish Civil War, Paris

in 1968. Tempted though I was by reminiscent memoirs like
those of Kropotkin, Emma Goldman and Rudolf Rocker, I
have for the most part avoided the use of mere autobiography;
I have also avoided reproducing manifestos, proclamations,
and other topical documents, since, whatever their historical
significance, they suffer from the distortions of propaganda as
distinct from polemics. Certain kinds of apologetic texts I have
included sparingly where they have put a point of view in an
especially illuminating way; examples are the statement made
by the terrorist Emile Henry to the court that tried and condemned him, and the fine speeches of Pierre Monatte and
Errico Malatesta on opposing sides in the historic debate on
syndicalism that was the high point of the 1907 Anarchist
Congress in Amsterdam.

Since few of the items I include reproduce *in toto* the writings from which they are derived, I have more often than
not created my own title which as near as possible projects
the spirit of the actual extract; the original title of the work
from which it is drawn is also noted at the beginning of the
piece. Some pieces by Proudhon, Bakunin, Henry, Monatte,
Malatesta and others I have translated specially for this collection, either because no translation existed, or because I found
the existing translation inadequate.

I confess to a defeat in planning. I began this collection
with schematic outline in mind: I would divide it into three
main sections, 1, the anarchist criticism of existing society, 2,
anarchist views on the way to bring that society to its end,
and 3, anarchist speculations on the society that might appear
on the morrow of the revolution. Within each main section I
proposed to make a series of sub-sections, echoing on from
one section to the other, on such special subjects as distribution, criminality, education, etc. I quickly found that anarchist writers are much too idiosyncratic and too antipathetic
to structured arrangement for a rigidly defined pattern of this
kind to work. I had to abandon myself to the claims of the
writings that seemed most intrinsically interesting, and then they
seemed to fall quite naturally into loose groups that showed
the main areas of anarchist interest. What surprised even me,
with all my past knowledge of anarchist writings, was how

richly and in what variety the positive and constructive aspects of anarchism were exemplified. In rejecting the temptations of utopia, the anarchists did not abandon themselves to negation.

G.W.

Part 1
The Anarchist Stance

Here are presented the essential definitions of anarchist thought and the anarchist temperament. What is anarchism? What is the stance from which anarchists approach society and the world?

Sébastien Faure, nineteenth-century creator of the first anarchist encyclopedia, suggests the open, undogmatic nature of the anarchist approach. His Italian contemporary, Errico Malatesta, justifies the acceptance of the title of *anarchist*, and in the extract from Proudhon we encounter the first man who did accept the title, and learn of his views on freedom as the social destination of society and on authority – expressed most flagrantly in the institution of property – as the barrier to progress towards that destination. Oscar Wilde talks, as all anarchists have done, on disobedience as a necessary and creative virtue; he represents the current artistic revolt that has always been a strong component of anarchism. A later writer and aesthete, Herbert Read, recognizes a philosophic element that distinguishes anarchism from the merely political creeds and speculates that anarchism may eventually provide a substitute for the spiritual quality that vanished from most men's lives as the traditional religions lost impetus and credibility.

ANARCHY–ANARCHIST

SEBASTIEN FAURE
(From *Encyclopédie anarchiste*, n.d.)

There is not, and there cannot be, a libertarian *Creed* or *Catechism*.

That which exists and constitutes what one might call the anarchist doctrine is a cluster of general principles, fundamental conceptions and practical applications regarding which a consensus has been established among individuals whose thought is inimical to Authority and who struggle, collectively or in isolation, against all disciplines and constraints, whether political, economic, intellectual or moral.

At the same time, there may be – and indeed there are – many varieties of anarchist, yet all have a common characteristic that separates them from the rest of humankind. This uniting point is *the negation of the principle of Authority in social organizations and the hatred of all constraints that originate in institutions founded on this principle.*

Thus, whoever denies Authority and fights against it is an Anarchist.

ANARCHY DEFINED

ERRICO MALATESTA
(From *Anarchy*, 1907)

Anarchy is a word that comes from the Greek, and signifies, strictly speaking, 'without government': the state of a people without any constituted authority.

Before such an organization had begun to be considered possible and desirable by a whole class of thinkers, so as to be taken as the aim of a movement (which has now become one of the most important factors in modern social warfare), the word 'anarchy' was used universally in the sense of disorder and confusion, and it is still adopted in that sense by the ignorant and by adversaries interested in distorting the truth.

We shall not enter into philological discussions, for the question is not philological but historical. The common interpretation of the word does not misconceive its true etymological significance, but is derived from it, owing to the prejudice that government must be a necessity of the organization of social life, and that consequently a society without government must be given up to disorder, and oscillate between the unbridled dominion of some and the blind vengeance of others.

The existence of this prejudice and its influence on the meaning the public has given to the word is easily explained.

Man, like all living beings, adapts himself to the conditions in which he lives, and transmits by inheritance his acquired habits. Thus, being born and having lived in bondage, being the descendant of a long line of slaves, man, when he began to think, believed that slavery was an essential condition of life, and liberty seemed to him impossible. In like manner, the workman, forced for centuries to depend on the good-will of his employer for work, that is, for bread, and accustomed to see his own life at the disposal of those who possess the land and capital, has ended in believing that it is his master who gives him food, and asks ingenuously how it would be possible to live, if there were no master over him?

In the same way, a man whose limbs had been bound from birth, but who had nevertheless found out how to hobble about, might attribute to the very bands that bound him his ability to move, while, on the contrary, they would diminish and paralyze the muscular energy of his limbs.

If then we add to the natural effect of habit the education given him by his master, the parson, the teacher, etc., who are all interested in teaching that the employer and the government are necessary, if we add the judge and the policeman to force those who think differently – and might try to propagate their opinions – to keep silence, we shall understand how the prejudice as to the utility and necessity of masters and governments has become established. Suppose a doctor brought for-

ward a complete theory, with a thousand ably invented illustrations, to persuade the man with bound limbs that, if his limbs
were freed, he could not walk, or even live. The man would
defend his bands furiously and consider anyone his enemy
who tried to tear them off.

Thus, if it is believed that government is necessary and that
without government there must be disorder and confusion, it
is natural and logical to suppose that anarchy, which signifies
absence of government, must also mean absence of order.

Nor is this fact without parallel in the history of words.
In those epochs and countries where people have considered
government by one man (monarchy) necessary, the word
'republic' (that is, government of many) has been used precisely like 'anarchy', to imply disorder and confusion. Traces
of this meaning of the word are still to be found in the
popular languages of almost all countries.

When this opinion is changed, and the public are convinced
that government is not necessary, but extremely harmful, the
word 'anarchy', precisely because it signifies 'without government', will become equal to saying 'natural order, harmony of
the needs and interests of all, complete liberty with complete
solidarity'.

Therefore, those are wrong who say that anarchists have
chosen their name badly, because it is erroneously understood
by the masses and leads to a false interpretation. The error
does not come from the word, but from the thing. The difficulty which anarchists meet in spreading their views does not
depend upon the name they have given themselves, but upon
the fact that their conceptions strike at all the inveterate prejudices which people have about the function of government,
or 'the State', as it is called.

THE BIRTH OF ANARCHY: THE DEATH OF PROPERTY

PIERRE-JOSEPH PROUDHON
(from *Qu'est-ce que la Propriété?*, 1840, translated by
Benjamin Tucker, 1876)

What is to be the form of government in the future? I hear
some of my younger readers reply: 'Why, how can you ask
such a question? You are a republican.' 'A republican! Yes;
but that word specifies nothing. *Res publica*; that is, the
public thing. Now, whoever is interested in public affairs – no
matter under what form of government – may call himself a
republican. Even kings are republicans.' – 'Well! you are a
democrat?' – 'No.' – 'What! you would have a monarchy?' –
'No.' – 'A constitutionalist?' – 'God forbid!' – 'You are then
an aristocrat?' – 'Not at all.' – 'You want a mixed government?' – 'Still less.' – 'What are you, then?' – 'I am an anarchist.' . . .

Man, in order to procure as speedily as possible the most
thorough satisfaction of his wants, seeks *rule*. In the beginning,
this rule is to him living, visible, and tangible. It is his father,
his master, his king. The more ignorant man is, the more
obedient he is, and the more absolute in his confidence in his
guide. But, it being a law of man's nature to conform to
rule, – that is, to discover it by his powers of reflection and
reason, – man reasons upon the commands of his chiefs. Now,
such reasoning as that is a protest against authority, – a
beginning of disobedience. At the moment that man inquires
into the motives which govern the will of his sovereign, – at
that moment man revolts. If he obeys no longer because the
king commands, but because the king demonstrates the wisdom
of his commands, it may be said that henceforth he will recognize no authority, and that he has become his own king.
Unhappy he who shall dare to command him, and shall offer,
as his authority, only the vote of the majority; for, sooner or
later, the minority will become the majority, and this im-

prudent despot will be overthrown, and all his laws annihilated.

In proportion as society becomes enlightened, royal authority diminishes. That is a fact to which all history bears witness. At the birth of nations, men reflect and reason in vain. Without methods, without principles, not knowing how to use their reason, they cannot judge of the justice of their conclusions. Then the authority of kings is immense, no knowledge having been acquired with which to contradict it. But, little by little, experience produces habits, which develop into customs; then the customs are formulated in maxims, laid down as principles, – in short, transformed into laws, to which the king, the living law, has to bow. There comes a time when customs and laws are so numerous that the will of the prince is, so to speak, entwined by the public will; and that, on taking the crown, he is obliged to swear that he will govern in conformity with established customs and usages; and that he is but the executive power of a society whose laws are made independently of him.

Up to this point, all is done instinctively, and, as it were, unconsciously; but see where this movement must end.

By means of self-instruction and the acquisition of ideas, man finally acquires the idea of science, – that is, of a system of knowledge in harmony with the reality of things, and inferred from observation. He searches for the science, or the system, of inanimate bodies, – the system of organic bodies, the system of the human mind, and the system of the universe: why should he not also search for the system of society? But, having reached this height, he comprehends that political truth, or the science of politics, exists quite independently of the will of sovereigns, the opinion of majorities, and popular beliefs, – that kings, ministers, magistrates, and nations, as wills, have no connection with the science, and are worthy of no consideration. He comprehends, at the same time, that if man is born a sociable being, the authority of his father over him ceases on the day when, his mind being formed and his education finished, he becomes the associate of his father; that his true chief and his king is the demonstrated truth; that politics is a science, not a stratagem; and that the function of the legislator is reduced, in the last analysis, to the methodical search for truth.

Thus, in a given society, the authority of man over man is inversely proportional to the stage of intellectual development which that society has reached; and the probable duration of that authority can be calculated from the more or less general desire for a true government, – that is, for a scientific government. And justice as the right of force and the right of artifice retreat before the steady advance of justice, and must finally be extinguished in equality, so the sovereignty of the will yields to the sovereignty of the reason, and must at last be lost in scientific socialism. Property and royalty have been crumbling to pieces ever since the world began. As man seeks justice in equality, so society seeks order in anarchy.

Anarchy, – the absence of a master, of a sovereign, – such is the form of government to which we are every day approximating, and which our accustomed habit of taking man for our rule, and his will for law, leads us to regard as the height of disorder and the expression of chaos . . .

Then, no government, no public economy, no administration, is possible, which is based on property.

Communism seeks *equality* and *law*. Property, born of the sovereignty of reason, and the sense of personal merit, wishes above all things *independence* and *proportionality*.

But communism, mistaking uniformity for law, and levelism for equality, becomes tyrannical and unjust. Property, by its despotism and encroachments, soon proves itself oppressive and anti-social.

The objects of communism and property are good – their results are bad. And why? Because both are exclusive, and each disregards two elements of society. Communism rejects independence and proportionality; property does not satisfy equality and law.

Now, if we imagine a society based upon these four principles, – equality, law, independence, and proportionality, – we find: –

1. That *equality,* consisting only in *equality of conditions,* that is, *of means,* and not in *equality of comfort,* – which it is the business of the labourers to achieve for themselves, when provided with equal means, – in no way violates justice and *equité.*

2. That *law*, resulting from the knowledge of facts, and consequently based upon necessity itself, never clashes with independence.

3. That individual *independence*, or the autonomy of the private reason, originating in the difference of talents and capacities, can exist without danger within the limits of the law.

4. That *proportionality*, being admitted only in the sphere of intelligence and sentiment, and not as regards material objects, may be observed without violating justice or social equality.

This third form of society, the synthesis of communism and property, we will call *liberty*.

In determining the nature of liberty, we do not unite communism and property indiscriminately; such a process would be absurd eclecticism. We search for analysis for those elements in each which are true, and in harmony with the laws of Nature and society, disregarding the rest altogether; and the result gives us an adequate expression of the natural form of human society, – in one word, liberty.

Liberty is equality, because it does not admit the government of the will, but only the authority of the law; that is, of necessity.

Liberty is infinite variety, because it respects all wills within the limits of the law.

Liberty is proportionality, because it allows the utmost latitude to the ambition for merit, and the emulation of glory.

We can now say, in the words of M. Cousin: 'Our principle is true; it is good, it is social; let us not fear to push it to its ultimate.'

Man's social nature being justice through reflection, *equité* through the classification of capacities, and having *liberty* for its formula, is the true basis of morality, the principle and regulator of all our actions. This is the universal motor, which philosophy is searching for, which religion strengthens, which egotism supplants, and whose place pure reason never can fill. *Duty* and *right* are born of *need*, which, when considered in connection with others, is a *right*, and when considered in connection with ourselves, a *duty*.

We need to eat and sleep. It is our right to procure those

things which are necessary to rest and nourishment. It is our duty to use them when Nature requires it.

We need to labour in order to live. To do so is both our right and our duty.

We need to love our wives and children. It is our duty to protect and support them. It is our right to be loved in preference to all others. Conjugal fidelity is justice. Adultery is high treason against society.

We need to exchange our products for other products. It is our right that this exchange should be one of equivalents; and since we consume before we produce, it would be our duty, if we could control the matter, to see to it that our last product shall follow our last consumption. Suicide is fraudulent bankruptcy.

We need to live our lives according to the dictates of our reason. It is our right to maintain our freedom. It is our duty to respect that of others.

We need to be appreciated by our fellows. It is our duty to deserve their praise. It is our right to be judged by our works.

Liberty is not opposed to the rights of succession and bequest. It contents itself with preventing violations of equality. 'Choose,' it tells us, 'between two legacies, but do not take both.' All our legislation concerning transmission, entailments, adoptions, and, if I may venture to use such a word, *coadjutoreries*, requires remodelling.

Liberty favours emulation, instead of destroying it. In social equality, emulation consists in accomplishing under like conditions; it is its own reward. No one suffers by the victory.

Liberty applauds self-sacrifice, and honours it with its votes, but it can dispense with it. Justice alone suffices to maintain the social equilibrium. Self-sacrifice is an act of supererogation. Happy, however, the man who can say, 'I sacrifice myself'.

Liberty is essentially an organizing force. To insure equality between men and peace among nations, agriculture and industry, and the centres of education, business and storage, must be distributed according to the climate and the geographical position of the country, the nature of the products, the character and natural talents of the inhabitants, etc., in proportions so just, so wise, so harmonious, that in no place shall there ever be either an excess or a lack of population, consumption, and products. There commences the science of public and private right, the true political economy. It is for the writers on jurisprudence, henceforth unembarrassed by the false principle of property, to describe the new laws, and bring peace upon earth. Knowledge and genius they do not lack; the foundation is now laid for them.

I have accomplished my task; property is conquered, never again to arise. Wherever this book is read and discussed, there will be deposited the germ of death to property; there, sooner or later, privilege and servitude will disappear, and the despotism of will will give place to the reign of reason. What sophisms, indeed, what prejudices (however obstinate) can stand before the simplicity of the following propositions?

I. Individual *possession* is the condition of social life; five thousand years of property demonstrate it. *Property* is the suicide of society. Possession is a right; property is against right. Suppress property while maintaining possession, and, by this simple modification of the principle, you will revolutionize law, government, economy, and institutions; you will drive evil from the face of the earth.

II. All having an equal right of occupancy, possession varies with the number of possessors; property cannot establish itself.

III. The effect of labour being the same for all, property is lost in the common prosperity.

IV. All human labour being the result of collective force, all property becomes, in consequence, collective and unitary. To speak more exactly, labour destroys property.

V. Every capacity for labour being, like every instrument of labour, an accumulated capital, and a collective property, inequality of wages and fortunes (on the grounds of inequality of capacities) is, therefore, injustice and robbery.

VI. The necessary conditions of commerce are the liberty of the contracting parties and the equivalent of the products exchanged. Now, value being expressed by the amount of time and outlay which each product costs, and liberty being inviolable, the wages of labourers (like their rights and duties) should be equal.

VII. Products are bought only by products. Now, the condition of all exchange being equivalence of products, profit is impossible and unjust. Observe this elementary principle of economy, and pauperism, luxury, oppression, vice, crime, and hunger will disappear from our midst.

VIII. Men are associated by the physical and mathematical law of production, before they are voluntarily associated by choice. Therefore, equality of conditions is demanded by justice; that is, by strict social laws: esteem, friendship, gratitude, admiration, all fall within the domain of *equitable* or *proportional* law only.

IX. Free association, liberty – whose sole function is to maintain equality in the means of production and equivalence in exchanges – is the only possible, the only just, the only true form of society.

X. Politics is the science of liberty. The government of man by man (under whatever name it be disguised) is oppression. Society finds its highest perfection in the union of order with anarchy.

The old civilization has run its course; a new sun is rising, and will soon renew the face of the earth. Let the present generation perish, let the old prevaricators die in the desert! The holy earth shall not cover their bones. Young man, exasperated by the corruption of the age, and absorbed in your zeal for justice! – if your country is dear to you, and if you have the interests of humanity at heart, have the courage to espouse the cause of liberty! Cast off your old selfishness, and plunge into the rising flood of popular equality! There your regenerated soul will acquire new life and vigour; your enervated genius will recover unconquerable energy; and your heart, perhaps already withered, will be rejuvenated! Everything will wear a different look to your illuminated vision; new sentiments will engender new ideas within you; religion, morality, poetry, art, language will appear before you in nobler and fairer forms; and thenceforth, sure of your faith, and thoughtfully enthusiastic, you will hail the dawn of universal regeneration!

And you, sad victims of an odious law! you, whom a jesting world despoils and outrages! – you, whose labour has always been fruitless, and whose rest has been without hope, – take courage! your tears are numbered! The fathers have sown in affliction, the children shall reap in rejoicings!

DISOBEDIENCE:
MAN'S ORIGINAL VIRTUE

OSCAR WILDE
(From *The Soul of Man under Socialism*, 1891)

. . . The virtues of the poor may be readily admitted, and are much to be regretted. We are often told that the poor are grateful for charity. Some of them are, no doubt, but the best amongst the poor are never grateful. They are ungrateful, discontented, disobedient, and rebellious. They are quite right to be so. Charity they feel to be a ridiculously inadequate mode of partial restitution, or a sentimental dole, usually accompanied by some impertinent attempt on the part of the sentimentalist to tyrannize over their private lives. Why should they be grateful for the crumbs that fall from the rich man's table? They should be seated at the board and are beginning to know it. As for being discontented, a man who would not be discontented with such surroundings, and such a low mode of life, would be a perfect brute. Disobedience, in the eyes of anyone who has read history, is man's original virtue. It is through disobedience that progress has been made, through disobedience and through rebellion. Sometimes the poor are praised for being thrifty. But to recommend thrift to the poor is both grotesque and insulting. It is like advising a man who is starving to eat less. For a town or country labourer to practice thrift would be absolutely immoral. Man should not be ready to show that he can live like a badly fed animal. He should decline to live like that, and should either steal or go on the rates, which is considered by many to be a form of stealing. As for begging, it is safer to beg than to take, but it is finer to take than to beg. No: a poor man who is ungrateful, unthrifty, discontented and rebellious, is probably a real personality, and has much in him. He is at any rate a healthy protest. As for the virtuous poor, one can pity them, of course, but one cannot possibly admire them. They have made private terms with the enemy, and sold their birthright for very bad pottage. They must also be extraordinarily stupid. I can quite understand a man accepting laws that protect private property, and admit of its accumulation, as long as he himself is able under those conditions to realize some form of beautiful and intellectual life. But it is almost incredible to me how a man whose life is marred and made hideous by such laws can possibly acquiesce in their continuance.

However, the explanation is not really difficult to find. It is simply this. Misery and poverty are so absolutely degrading, and exercise such a paralysing effect over the nature of men, that no class is ever really conscious of its own suffering. They have to be told of it by other people, and they often entirely disbelieve them. What is said by great employers of labour against agitators is unquestionably true. Agitators are a set of interfering, meddling people, who come down to some perfectly contented class of the community, and sow the seeds of discontent amongst them. That is the reason why agitators are so abundantly necessary. Without them, in our incomplete state, there would be no advance towards civilization. Slavery was put down in America, not in consequence of any action on the part of the slaves, or even expressed desire on their own part that they should be free. It was put down entirely through the grossly illegal conduct of certain agitators in Boston and elsewhere, who were not slaves themselves, nor owners of slaves, nor had anything to do with the question really. It was, undoubtedly, the Abolitionists who set the torch alight, who began the whole thing. And it is curious to note that from the slaves themselves they received, not merely very little assistance, but hardly any sympathy even; and when at the close of the war the slaves found themselves free, found themselves indeed so absolutely free that they were free to starve, many of them bitterly regretted the new state of things. To the thinker, the most tragic fact in the whole of the French Revolution is not that Marie Antoinette was killed for being a queen, but that the starved peasant of the Vendée voluntarily went out to die for the hideous cause of feudalism.

ANARCHISM AND THE RELIGIOUS IMPULSE

HERBERT READ
(From *The Philosophy of Anarchism*, 1940, reprinted in *Anarchy and Order*, 1954)

Admittedly a system of equity, no less than a system of law, implies a machinery for determining and administering its principles. I can imagine no society which does not embody some method of arbitration. But just as the judge in equity is supposed to appeal to universal principles of reason, and to ignore statutory law when it comes into conflict with these principles, so the arbiter in an anarchist community will appeal to these same principles, as determined by philosophy or common sense; and will do so unimpeded by all those legal and economic prejudices which the present organization of society entails.

It will be said that I am appealing to mystical entities, to idealistic notions which all good materialists reject. I do not deny it. What I do deny is that you can build any enduring society without some such mystical ethos. Such a statement will shock the Marxian socialist, who, in spite of Marx's warnings, is usually a naive materialist. Marx's theory – as I think he himself would have been the first to admit – was not a universal theory. It did not deal with all the facts of life – or dealt with some of them only in a very superficial way. Marx rightly rejected the unhistorical methods of the German metaphysicians, who tried to make the facts fit a pre-conceived theory. He also, just as firmly, rejected the mechanical materialism of the eighteenth century – rejected it on the grounds that though it could explain the existing nature of things, it ignored the whole process of historical development – the universe as organic growth. Most Marxians forget the first thesis on Feuerbach, which reads: 'The chief defect of all hitherto existing materialism – that of Feuerbach included – is that the object, reality, sensuousness, is conceived only in the form of the *object* but not as *human sensuous activity, practice*, not subjectivity.' Naturally, when it came to interpreting the history of religion, Marx would have treated it as a social product; but that is far from treating it as an illusion. Indeed, the historical evidence must tend altogether in the opposite direction, and compel us to recognize in religion a social necessity. There has never been a civilization without its corresponding religion, and the appearance of rationalism and scepticism is always a symptom of decadence.

Admittedly there is a general fund of reason to which all civilizations contribute their share and which includes an attitude of comparative detachment from the particular religion of one's epoch. But to recognize the historical evolution of a phenomenon like religion does not explain it away. It is far more likely to give it a scientific justification, to reveal it as necessary 'human sensuous activity', and therefore to throw suspicion on any social philosophy which arbitrarily excludes religion from the organization it proposes for society.

It is already clear, after twenty years of socialism in Russia, that if you do not provide your society with a new religion, it will gradually revert to the old one. Communism has, of course, its religious aspects, and apart from the gradual readmission of the Orthodox Church, the deification of Lenin (sacred tomb, effigies, creation of a legend – all the elements are there) is a deliberate attempt to create an outlet for religious emotions. Still more deliberate attempts to create the paraphernalia of a new creed were made by the Nazis in Germany, where the necessity for a religion of some kind has never been officially denied. In Italy Mussolini was far too wily to do anything but come to terms with the Catholic Church, and a deep and frustrating ambiguity exists in the minds of many Italian communists. Far from scoffing at these irrational aspects of communism and fascism, we should rather criticize these political creeds for lack of any real sensuous and aesthetic content, for the poverty of their ritual, and above all for a misunderstanding of the function of poetry and imagination in the life of the community.

It is possible that out of the ruins of our capitalist civilization a new religion will emerge, just as Christianity emerged from the ruins of the Roman civilization. Civilizations monotonously repeat certain patterns of belief in the course of their history, elaborate parallel myths. Socialism, as conceived by its pseudo-historical materialists, is not such a religion, and never will be. And though, from this point of view, it must be conceded that fascism has shown more imagination, it is in itself such a phenomenon of decadence – the first defensive awareness of the fate awaiting the existing social order – that its ideological superstructure is not of much permanent interest. For a religion is never a synthetic creation – you cannot select your legends and saints from the mythical past and combine them with some kind of political or radical policy to make a nice convenient creed. A prophet, like a poet, is born. But even granted a prophet, we are still far from the establishment of a religion. It needed five centuries to build the religion of Christianity on the message of Christ. That message had to be moulded, enlarged, and to a considerable extent distorted until it conformed with what Jung has called the archetypes of the collective unconscious – those complex psychological factors which give cohesion to a society. Religion, in its later stages, may well become the opium of the people; but whilst it is vital it is the only force which can hold a people together – which can supply them with a natural authority to appeal to when their personal interests clash.

I call religion a natural authority, but it has usually been conceived as a supernatural authority. It is natural in relation to the morphology of society; supernatural in relation to the morphology of the physical universe. But in either aspect it is in opposition to the artificial authority of the State. The State only acquires its supreme authority when religion begins to decline, and the great struggle between Church and State, when, as in modern Europe, it ends so decisively in favour of the State, is from the point of view of the organic life of society, eventually fatal. It is because modern socialism has been unable to perceive this truth and has instead linked itself to the dead hand of the State, that everywhere socialism is meeting its defeat. The natural ally of socialism was the Church, though admittedly in the actual historical circumstances of the nineteenth century it was difficult to see this. The Church was so corrupted, so much a dependency of the ruling classes, that only a few rare spirits could see through appearances to the realities, and conceived socialism in the terms of a new religion, or more simply as a new reformation of Christianity.

Whether, in the actual circumstances of today, it is still possible to find a path from the old religion to a new religion is doubtful. A new religion can arise only on the basis of a new society, and step by step with such a society – perhaps in Russia, perhaps in Spain, perhaps in the United States: it is impossible to say where, because even the germ of such a new society is nowhere evident and its full information lies deeply buried in the future.

I am not a revivalist – I have no religion to recommend and none to believe in. I merely affirm, on the evidence of the history of civilizations, that a religion is a necessary element in any organic society. And I am so conscious of the slow process of spiritual development that I am in no mood to look for a new religion, and have no hope of finding one. I would only venture one observation. Both in its origins and development, up to its zenith, religion is closely associated with art. Religion and art are, indeed, if not alternative modes of expression, modes intimately associated. Apart from the essentially aesthetic nature of religion ritual; apart, too, from the dependence of religion on art for the visualization of its subjective concepts; there is, besides, an identity of the highest forms of poetic and mystic expression. Poetry, in its intensest and most creative moments, penetrates to the same level of the unconscious as mysticism. Certain writers – and they are among the greatest – Saint Francis, Dante, Saint Teresa, Saint John of the Cross, Blake – rank equally as poets and as mystics. For this reason it may well happen that the origins of a new religion will be found if not in mysticism, then in art rather than in any form of moralistic revivalism.

What has all this to do with anarchism? Merely this: socialism of the Marxist tradition, that is to say, state socialism, has so completely cut itself off from religious sanctions and has been driven to such pitiful subterfuges in its search for substitutes for religion, that by contrast anarchism, which is not without its mystic strain, is a religion itself. It is possible, that is to say, to conceive a new religion developing out of anarchism. During the Spanish Civil War many observers were struck by the religious intensity of the anarchists. In that country of potential renaissance anarchism has inspired, not only heroes but even saints – a new race of men whose lives are devoted, in sensuous imagination *and in practice*, to the creation of a new type of human society.

Part 2
The Anarchists Accuse

The anarchist indictment of existing society has been thorough and many-faceted, based on the libertarian assumption that power-oriented institutions are unnatural as well as restrictive, and on the realization that authority in overt or hidden forms permeates our lives at every level and at every stage from the schoolroom to the home for the aged.

In the selection that follows the intimate link between political government and organized religions is recognized equally strongly by Michael Bakunin the collectivist and by Max Stirner the individualist, and, while Bakunin insists in a way Stirner would have rejected that human freedom only exists within a community, Stirner makes a point Bakunin would have accepted when he draws out the relationship between punishment and the idea of the sacred and shows how rebellion becomes associated in the minds of rulers with crime.

Most anarchists prefer to avoid using the word political (which for them has connotations of power relationships) in describing their ideas of social and economic relations, but Paul Goodman sees politics in the original sense of any kind of organization of the community; he suggests that the pre-occupation with gaining and holding power is in fact hostile to the 'normal politics' of localized communities. By implication he is opposing anarchist decentralization to the pyramidical politics of the national state.

This area of the perils of massive governmental structures is one which Americans like Goodman have been inclined to explore deeply, perhaps because their own system is at least nominally federalist. Another of them, Randolph Bourne, demonstrates how intimate and fatal is the relationship between the State and militarism, while Lysander Spooner, a contemporary of the Abolitionists, attacks the idea that a fixed constitution can be a guarantee of freedom or anything else but a bulwark of tyranny and imposition.

The illusion that representative government actually gives any power to the ordinary people who cast their votes every few years for men over whose actions they have no subsequent control has often been exposed by the anarchists, as Michael Bakunin here does as he looks at Swiss cantonal politics, while Proudhon sharply recollects his own sense of powerlessness on the other side of the electoral fence when he became a parliamentarian with the frustrated intent of achieving results that might be beneficial to the people.

Laws are the forms that give sanction to coercion applied by authoritarian governments, and the anarchists have long argued, not only that law itself is a form of violence, but also that, once property and government were abolished there would, as Kropotkin demonstrates, be no need for laws to control occasional outbursts of aberrant behaviour.

If laws in themselves are abstract formulae, their concrete manifestations are punishment, including prisons. For their defiance of authority and law, anarchists have often suffered imprisonment and other punishments, so that when they speak bitter experience often inspires their words, as it did those of Kropotkin when he wrote of the effects of prisons; he had spent years in Russian and French jails before he settled down in the freedom of Victorian England. But the experience of punishment is not necessary for a libertarian to recognize not only its injustice but also its futility in preventing crime, and William Godwin, who experienced merely the threat of punishment during the anti-Jacobin hysteria of the 1790s, condemned it as thoroughly and effectively as any of the anarchists who had actually suffered.

Godwin was also one of the first libertarians (though Winstanley had preceded him in this) to recognize the interdependence of government and 'accumulated property', by which he meant the kind of property that comes from exploiting the labour of others. One of the results of such exploitation is, of course, the transformation of useful and enjoyable work into forms of toil that are not merely burdensome and superfluous but also physically and mentally unhealthy,

as Tolstoy shows very clearly in his criticism of that phenomenon praised by Victorian economists and developed by
Victorian industrialists, the division of labour.

Authority, which turns potentially pleasant work into joyless
toil, penetrates even more intimate regions of our lives. Even
our way of assessing the tempo of our lives is conditioned by
the clock-oriented patterns of authoritarian systems, as George
Woodcock shows in his essay on 'The Tyranny of the Clock'.
Wherever the anarchist looks, he sees the dead hand of
power strangling the potentialities of life and he is impelled to
reject it.

CHURCH AND STATE

MICHAEL BAKUNIN
(From *Oeuvres*, Vol. IV, 1910, translated by
George Woodcock)

It is obvious that freedom will not be restored to humanity,
and that the true interests of society – whether of groups, of
local organizations or of all the individuals who compose
society – will find true satisfaction only when there are no
more States. It is obvious that all the so-called general interests
which the State is reputed to represent, and which in reality
are nothing else than the general and continuing negation
of the positive interests of regions, communes, associations
and the vast majority of individuals subjected to the State,
are in fact an abstraction, a fiction, a lie, and that the State
is like a vast shambles or an enormous graveyard in which,
under the shadow and pretext of that abstraction, all the true
aspirations and all the living forces of a country, generously
and beatifically allow themselves to be buried. Since no
abstraction ever exists by or for itself, since it has neither
legs to walk with nor arms to create nor stomach to digest
this mass of victims which are given it to devour, it is just as
obvious that the religious and celestial abstraction, God
Himself, represents in reality the very positive and real
interests of a privileged caste, the clergy; in the same way His

earthly complement, the political abstraction of the State, represents the no less positive and real interests of the class which is today the principal if not the only agent of exploitation and which into the bargain tends to absorb all other classes, the bourgeoisie. Just as the clergy has always been divided and nowadays tends to be even more divided between a rich and powerful minority and a subordinate and rather impoverished majority, so the bourgeoisie and its various organizations, both social and political, in industry, agriculture, banking and commerce, as well as in all the administrative, financial, judiciary, academic, police and military functions of the State, tends to split up more and more into a truly dominant oligarchy and an innumerable mass of snobbish and decayed individuals living in a perpetual illusion, inevitably and increasingly pushed down into the proletariat by the irresistible force of present-day economic developments, and reduced to serve as the blind instruments of that all-powerful oligarchy.

The abolition of the Church and the State must be the first and indispensable condition of the true liberation of society; only after this can society be organized in another manner, but not from the top downwards and according to an ideal plan, dreamed up by a few sages or scholars, and certainly not by decrees issued by some dictatorial power or even by a national assembly elected by universal suffrage. As I have already shown, such a system would lead inevitably to the creation of a new state, and consequently to the formation of a governmental aristocracy, that is to say a whole class of individuals having nothing in common with the mass of the people, which would immediately begin to exploit and subdue that people in the name of the commonwealth or in order to save the State.

The future organization of society should be carried out entirely from below upwards, by the free association and federation of the workers, in associations first of all, then in communes, in regions, in nations, and, finally, in a great international and universal federation. It is then only that the true and invigorating order of liberty and general happiness will be established, that order which, far from denying either of them, affirms and brings into harmony the interests of individuals and of society.

Some declare that the harmonization and universal solidarity of the interests of individuals and society can never in fact be realized because these interests, since they are contradictory, can never come into equilibrium or even reach the slightest mutual understanding. To objections of this kind I answer that if up to the present these interests have been nowhere and never in accord, it is because of the State, which has sacrificed the interests of the majority to the profit of a privileged minority. In other words that famous incompatibility, that struggle between personal interests and those of society, is no more than a trickery and a political lie, born of a theological lie, which invented the doctrine of original sin to dishonour man and destroy his inner consciousness of his own worth. This same false idea of the antagonism of interests was also spawned by the dreams of metaphysics, which, as everyone knows, is the close cousin of theology. Failing to understand the sociability of human nature, metaphysics regarded society as a mechanical and purely artificial aggregate of individuals, abruptly brought together under the blessing of some formal and secret treaty, concluded either freely or under the influence of some superior power. Before entering into society, these individuals, endowed with some sort of immortal soul, enjoyed total freedom.

But if the metaphysicians, above all those who believe in the immortality of the soul, affirm that outside society men are free beings, we arrive inevitably at the conclusion that men can unite in society only at the price of renouncing their liberty, their natural independence, and of sacrificing their interests, first the personal and then the local ones. Such a renunciation, such a sacrifice of the self, must by that token be all the more imperative where the society is more populous and its organization more complex. In such a case, the State is the expression of all individual sacrifices. Existing in such an abstract and at the same time violent form, the State continues – it goes without saying – more and more to hinder individual liberty in the name of the lie which it calls 'public good', even though quite obviously it represents exclusively the interests of the dominant class. In this way the State appears before us as an inevitable negation, an annihilation of all liberty, of all interests, individual as well as general.

Thus it appears that all metaphysical and theological systems are linked together in such a way that they are mutually explanatory. This is why, with a clear conscience, the logical defenders of these systems can and must continue to exploit the popular masses by means of Church and State. Stuffing their pockets and satisfying all their filthy lusts, they can console themselves at the same time with the thought that they are labouring for the glory of God, for the victory of civilization and for the eternal bliss of the proletariat.

But the others of us, who believe neither in God nor in the immortality of the soul, nor in individual free will, affirm that freedom must be understood in its fullest and widest sense as the destination of man's historic progress. By a strange and yet logical contrast, our adversaries, the idealist theologians and metaphysicians, take the principle of liberty as the foundation and basis of their theories and arrive quite simply at the indispensability of human slavery. We others, who are theoretically materialist, tend in practice to create and make lasting a rational and noble idealism. Our enemies, divine and transcendental idealists, fall in practice into a materialism that is vile and bloody, and they do it in the name of the same logic, according to which each development is a negation of the basic principle. We are convinced that all the richness of human intellectual, moral and material development, as well as man's apparent independence, is the product of life in society. Outside society, man would not only be unfree, but he would not even have developed into a true man, that is to say a self-conscious being who feels, thinks and talks. Only the combination of intelligence and collective work could force man out of the stage of savagery and brutishness which constituted his first nature, or rather his first point on the way of development. We are profoundly convinced of the truth that all human life – interests, tendencies, needs, illusions, even stupidities, as well as acts of violence and injustice and every action that has the appearance of being voluntary – is only a consequence of the fatal forces of life in society. One cannot admit the idea of mutual independence without denying the reciprocal influence of the correlation of manifestations of external nature.

In nature itself, that marvellous correlation and filiation of phenomena is not attained, admittedly, without struggle. On the contrary, the harmony of natural forces appears only as the veritable result of that continual struggle, which is the very condition of life and movement. In nature and in society as well, order without struggle is death.

If order is natural and possible in the universe, it is entirely because that universe is not governed by any system thought up in advance and imposed by a supreme will. The theological hypothesis of a divine legislation leads to an evident absurdity, and to the negation not only of all order, but of nature itself. Natural laws are real only in so far as they are inherent in nature, that is to say in so far as they are fixed by no authority. These laws are only simple manifestations or rather continual modalities of the development of things and of the combinations of varied, transitory but real facts. Together, this constitutes what we call 'nature'. Human intelligence and science observed these facts and controlled them experimentally, and then reassembled them into a system and called them laws. But nature itself knows no laws. It acts unconsciously, representing in itself the infinite variety of phenomena, appearing and repeating themselves according to necessity. That is why, thanks to this inevitability of action, universal order can exist and in fact does exist.

Such an order also emerged in human society, which appeared to evolve in a so-called anti-natural manner, but in reality submits to the natural and inevitable march of events. It was only man's superiority over other animals and his ability to think that brought into his development a special element, which, we may say in passing, was entirely natural in the sense that, like everything that exists, man is the material product of the union and interaction of forces. The special element is the power of reasoning, or rather the faculty of generalization and abstraction thanks to which man can project himself by means of thought, examine himself and observe himself as an alien and external object. Raising himself above himself by the means of ideas, and in this way raising himself above the surrounding world, he arrives at the representation of perfect abstraction, which is absolute nothingness. That final limit of the highest abstraction of thought, that absolute nothing, is God.

That is the meaning and the historic basis of all theological dogma. Understanding neither nature nor the material causes of their own thoughts, taking no account of the conditions of natural laws that are peculiar to them, the first men in society could not know that their absolutes were only the result of the faculty of conceiving abstract ideas. That is why they considered these ideas, drawn from nature, as real objects before which nature itself ceased to have any significance. They then set about worshipping their own fictions, their impossible notions of the absolute, and to bestow honour upon them. But it was necessary, in some way or another, to embody and make palpable the abstract idea of nothingness or God. With this aim, they exalted the idea of divinity and endowed it with all the qualities and powers, both good and evil, which they had encountered only in nature and society.

Such were the origin and the historic development of all religions, beginning with fetishism and ending with Christianity.

We have little intention of embarking on the history of religious absurdities, whether theological or metaphysical, and even less of discussing the successive unfolding of all the divine incarnations and visions created by the centuries of barbarism. Everyone knows that superstition has always given birth to frightful misfortunes and has ended in streams of blood and tears. We will be content to say that all these revolting aberrations of poor humanity were inevitable historical circumstances in the normal growth and evolution of social organisms. Such aberrations engendered in society that fatal notion, which came to dominate the human imagination, that the universe is governed by a supernatural power and will. Century followed century, and societies grew so used to this idea, that finally they killed within themselves all inclinations towards further progress and all capacity to attain it.

The ambition first of all of a few individuals, and later of whole social classes, raised slavery and conquest into vital principles, and planted deeper than ever that terrible idea of divinity. From that time, all society became impossible without, as its foundation, the two institutions of Church and State.

These two social scourges are still defended by all the dogmatists.

Hardly had these institutions appeared in the world when two castes were immediately organized: that of the priests and that of the aristocrats, which, with no loss of time, took care to implant deeply in the enslaved people the indispensability, utility and sanctity of Church and State.

All this had for its aim to change a brutal slavery into a legal and assured slavery, consecrated by the will of the Supreme Being.

But the priests and aristocrats – did they believe sincerely in these institutions, which they maintained with all their power and in their own interests? Were they only liars and deceivers? No, I believe they were at one and the same time believers and imposters . . .

But how, even so, can we reconcile two such apparently incompatible roles: dupers and duped, liars and believers? Logically it seems difficult, yet in fact, in everyday life, these qualities are often associated.

The vast majority of people live in contradiction with themselves and under continual misapprehension. They are generally unaware of it until some extraordinary event draws them out of their habitual somnambulism and forces them to look at themselves and to look around them.

In politics, as in religion, men are only machines in the hands of exploiters. But robbers and robbed, oppressors and oppressed, live beside each other, governed by a handful of individuals whom one must regard as the real exploiters. These are always the same kind of people, free of all political and religious prejudices, who maltreat and oppress almost as a matter of conscience. In the seventeenth and eighteenth centuries up to the explosion of the Great Revolution, as in our day, they have commanded in Europe and have had things almost entirely their own way. We must believe that their domination cannot be long extended.

While these principal leaders deceive and mislead the people quite deliberately, their servants, the tools of Church and State, zealously apply themselves to upholding the sanctity and integrity of these odious institutions. If the Church is necessary for the salvation of the soul, as the priests and most of the statesmen tell us, the State in its turn is just as necessary for the conservation of peace, order and justice; and the dogmatists of all schools cry out: 'Without the Church and Government, there would be neither civilization nor progress.'

There is no need to discuss the problem of eternal salvation, since we do not believe in the immortality of the soul. We are convinced that the most harmful of all things, for humanity and for truth and progress, is the Church. Could it be otherwise? Does it not fall on the Church to pervert the younger generations and especially the women? Is it not She who by her dogmas, her lies, her stupidity and her ignominy, seeks to destroy logical thinking and science? Does She not menace the dignity of man by perverting his notions of right and justice? Does She not turn what is living into a corpse, cast aside freedom, and preach the eternal slavery of the masses for the benefit of tyrants and exploiters? Is it not this implacable Church that tends to perpetuate the reign of shadows, of ignorance, of poverty and of crime?

If the progress of our century is not to be a lying dream, it must make an end to the Church.

THE STATE AND THE SACRED

Max Stirner
(From *The Ego and His Own*, translated by
Steven T. Byington, 1907)

The best State will clearly be that which has the most loyal citizens, and the more the devoted mind for *legality* is lost, so much the more will the State, this system of morality, this moral life itself, be diminished in force and quality. With the 'good citizens' the good State too perishes and dissolves into anarchy and lawlessness. 'Respect for the law!' By this cement the total of the State is held together. 'The law is *sacred*, and he who affronts it is a *criminal*.' Without crime no State: the moral world – and this the State is – is crammed full of scamps, liars, thieves, etc. Since the State is the 'lordship of law', its hierarchy, it follows that the egoist, in all cases where *his* advantage runs against the State's, can satisfy himself only by crime.

The State cannot give up the claim that its *laws* and ordin- ances are *sacred*. At this the individual ranks as the *unholy* (barbarian, natural man, 'egoist') over against the State, exactly as he was once regarded by the Church; before the individual the State takes on the nimbus of a saint. Thus it issues a law against duelling. Two men who are both in one in this, that they are willing to stake their life for a cause (no matter what), are not to be allowed this, because the State will not have it; it imposes a penalty on it. Where is the liberty of self- determination then? It is at once quite another situation if, as, e.g., in North America, society determines to let the duellists bear certain evil *consequences* of their act, e.g., with- drawal of credit hitherto enjoyed. To refuse credit is every- body's affair, and, if a society wants to withdraw it for this or that reason, the man who is hit cannot therefore complain of encroachment on his liberty: the society is simply availing itself of its own liberty. That is no penalty for sin, no penalty for a *crime*. The duel is no crime there, but only an act against which the society adopts countermeasures, resolves on a *defence*. The State, on the contrary, stamps the duel as a crime, i.e., as an injury to its sacred law: it makes it a *criminal case*. The society leaves it to the individual's decision whether he will draw upon himself evil consequences and in- conveniences by his mode of action, and thereby recognizes his free decision; the State behaves in exactly the reverse way, denying all right to the individual's decision and, instead, ascribing the sole right to its own decision, the law of the State, so that he who transgresses the State's commandment is looked upon as if he were acting against God's command- ment – a view which likewise was once maintained by the Church. Here God is the Holy in and of Himself, and the commandments of the Church, as of the State, are the com- mandments of this Holy One, which he transmits to the world through his anointed and Lords-by-the-Grace-of-God. If the Church has *deadly sins*, the State has *capital crimes*; if the one has heretics, the other has traitors; the one *ecclesi- astical penalties*, the other *criminal penalties*; the one *in-*

quisitorial processes, the other *fiscal*; in short, there sins, here crimes, there sinners, here criminals, there inquisition and here – inquisition. Will the sanctity of the State not fall like the Church's? The awe of its laws, the reverence for its highness, the humility of its 'subjects', will this remain? Will the 'saint's' face not be stripped of its adornment?

What a folly, to ask the State's authority that it should enter into an honourable fight with the individual, and, as they express themselves in the matter of freedom of the Press, share sun and wind equally! If the State, this thought, is to be a *de facto* power, it simply must be a superior power against the individual. The State is 'sacred' and must not expose itself to 'impudent attacks' of individuals. If the State is *sacred*, there must be censorship. The political liberals admit the former and dispute the interference. But in any case they concede repressive measures to it, for – they stick at this, that State is more than the individual and exercises a justified revenge, called punishment.

Punishment has a meaning only when it is to afford expiation for the injuring of a *sacred thing*. If something is sacred to anyone, he certainly deserves punishment when he acts as its enemy. A man who lets a man's life continue in existence *because* to him it is sacred and he has a dread of touching it is simply a – *religious* man.

Weitling lays crime at the door of 'social disorder', and lives in the expectation that under communistic arrangements crimes will become impossible, because the temptations to them, e.g., money, fall away. As, however, his organized society is also exalted as a sacred and inviolable one, he miscalculates in that good-hearted opinion. Such as with their mouth professed allegience to the communistic society, but worked underhand for its ruin, would not be lacking. Besides, Weitling has to keep in with 'curative means against the natural remainder of human diseases and weaknesses,' and 'curative means' already announce to begin with that individuals will be looked upon as 'called' to a particular 'salvation' and hence treated according to the requirements of this 'human calling'. *Curative means* or *healing* is only the reverse side of *punishment,* the *theory of cure* runs parallel to the *theory of punishment*; if the latter sees in an action a sin against right, the former takes it for a sin of the man *against himself*, as a decadence from his health. But the correct thing is that I regard it either as an action that *suits me* or as one that *does not suit me*, as hostile or friendly to me, i.e., that I treat it as my *property*, which I cherish or demolish. 'Crime' or 'disease' are not either of them an *egoistic* view of the matter, i.e., a judgment *starting from me*, but starting from *another* – to wit, whether it injures *right*, general right, or the *health* partly of the individual (the sick one), partly of the generality (society). 'Crime' is treated inexorably, 'disease' with 'loving gentleness, compassion', and the like.

Punishment follows crime. If crime falls because the sacred vanishes, punishment must not less be drawn into its fall; for it too has significance only over against something sacred. Ecclesiastical punishments have been abolished. Why? Because how one behaves toward the 'holy God' is his own affair. But, as this one punishment, *ecclesiastical punishment*, has fallen, so all *punishments* must fall. As sin against the so-called God is a man's own affair, so is that against every kind of the so-called sacred. According to our theories of penal law, with whose 'improvement in conformity to the times' people are tormenting themselves in vain, they want to *punish* men for this or that 'inhumanity'; and therein they make silliness of these theories especially plain by their consistency, hanging the little thieves and letting the big ones run. For injury to property they have the house of correction, and for 'violence of thought', suppression of 'natural rights of man', only – representation and petitions.

The criminal code has continued existence only through the sacred and perishes of itself if punishment is given up. Now they want to create everywhere a new penal law, without indulging in a misgiving about punishment itself. But it is exactly punishment that must make room for satisfaction, which, again, cannot aim at satisfying right or justice, but at procuring *us* a satisfactory outcome. If one does to us what we *will not put up with*, we break his power and bring our own to bear; we satisfy *ourselves* on him, and do not fall into the folly of wanting to satisfy right (the spook). It is not the *sacred* that is to defend itself against man, but man against man; as *God* too, you know, no longer defends himself against man,

God to whom formerly (and in part, indeed, even now) all the 'servants of God' offered their hands to punish the blasphemer, as they still at this very day lend their hands to the sacred. This devotion to the sacred brings it to pass also that, without lively participation of one's own, one only delivers misdoers into the hands of the police and courts: a nonparticipating making over to the authorities, 'who, of course, will best administer sacred matters'. The people are quite crazy for hounding the police on against everything that seems to it to be immoral, often only unseemly, and this popular rage for the moral protects the police institution more than the government could in any way protect it.

In crime the egoist has hitherto asserted himself and mocked the sacred; the break with the sacred, or rather of the sacred, may become general. A revolution never returns, but a mighty, reckless, shameless, conscienceless, proud – *crime*, does it not rumble in distant thunders, and do you not see how the sky grows presciently silent and gloomy?

NORMAL POLITICS AND THE PSYCHOLOGY OF POWER

Paul Goodman
(From *People and Personnel*, 1965)

Living functions, biological, psychosociological, or social, have very little to do with abstract, preconceived 'power' that manages or coerces from outside the specific functions themselves. Indeed, it is commonplace that abstract power – in the form of 'will power', 'training', 'discipline', 'bureaucracy', 'reform schooling', 'scientific management', etc. – uniformly *thwarts* normal functioning and debases the persons involved. (It has a natural use, in emergencies, when not high-grade but minimal low-grade behaviour is required.) Normal activities do not need extrinsic motivations, they have their own intrinsic energies and ends-in-view; and decisions are continually made by the ongoing functions themselves, adjusting to the environment and one another.

We may then define the subject of normal politics. It is the constitutional relations of functional interests and interest groups in the community in which they transact. This is the bread and butter of ancient political theory and obviously has nothing to do with sovereignty or even power – for the ancients the existence of power implied unconstitutionality, tyranny. But even modern authors who move in a theory of 'sovereignty', like Spinoza, Locke, Adam Smith, Jefferson, or Madison, understand that the commonwealth is strongest when the functional interests can seek their own level and there is the weakest exercise of 'power'. For instance, Spinoza tries to play power like a fish, Jefferson to de-energize it, Madison to balance it out, Smith to make it an umpire.

Let us now quickly sketch the meaning of the recent transcendant importance of 'power' and getting into 'power', as if otherwise communities could not function.

First, and least important, there is the innocuous, nonviolent and rather natural development of a kind of abstract power in an indigenous (non-invaded) society. The functions of civilization include production, trade and travel, the bringing up of the young in the mores; also subtle but essential polarities like experimentation and stability; also irrational and superstitious fantasies like exacting revenge for crime and protecting taboos. Different interests in the whole will continually conflict, as individuals or as interested groups; yet, since all require the commonwealth, there is also a strong functional interest in adjudication and peace, in harmonizing social invention or at least compromise. It is plausible that in the interests of armistice and adjudication, there should arise a kind of abstract institution above the conflicts, to settle them or obviate them by plans and laws; this would certainly be power. (This derivation is plausible but I doubt that it is historical, for in fact it is just this kind of thing that lively primitive communities accomplished by quick intuition, tone of voice, exchange of glance, and suddenly there is unanimity, to the anthropologist's astonishment.) Much more likely, and we know historically, abstract power is invented in simple societies in emergencies of danger, of enemy attack or divine wrath. But such 'dictatorship' is *ad hoc* and surprisingly lapses. Surprisingly, considering that power corrupts;

yet it makes psychological sense, for emergency is a negative function, to meet a threat to the pre-conditions of the interesting functions of life; once the danger is past, the 'power' has no energy of function, no foreground interest, to maintain it. To give a very late example: it seemed remarkable to the Europeans, but not to the Americans, that Washington, like Cincinnatus, went home to his farm; and even the Continental Congress languished. There were no conditions of 'power'.

(Indeed – and this is why I have chosen the example – in the last decades of the eighteenth century, in many respects the Americans lived in a kind of peaceful community anarchy, spiced by mutinies that were hardly punished. The Constitution, as Richard Lee pointed out, was foisted on them by trickery, the work of very special interest groups; it would have been quite sufficient simply to amend the Articles.)

Altogether different from this idyll is the universal history of most of the world, civilized or barbarian. Everywhere is invasion, conquest, and domination, involving for the victors the necessity to keep and exercise power, and for the others the necessity to strive for power, in order to escape suffering and exploitation. This too is entirely functional. The conqueror is originally a pirate; he and his band do not share in the commonwealth, they have interests apart from the community preyed on. Subsequently, however, piracy becomes government, the process of getting people to perform by extrinsic motivations, of penalty and blackmail, and later bribery and training. But it is only the semblance of a commonwealth, for activity is not voluntary. Necessarily, such directed and extrinsically motivated performance is not so strong, efficient, spontaneous, inventive, well-constructed, or lovely as the normal functioning of a free community of interests. Very soon society becomes lifeless. The means of community action, initiative, decision, have been pre-empted by the powerful. But the slaveholders, exploiters, and governors share in that same society and are themselves vitiated. Yet they never learn to get down off the people's back and relinquish their power; others are striving to achieve it; and most are sunk in resignation. Inevitably, as people become stupider and more careless, administration increases in size and power, and conversely. By and large, the cultures

that we study in the melancholy pages of history are pathetic
mixtures, with the ingredients often still discernible: There is
a certain amount of normal function surviving or reviving –
bread is baked, arts and sciences are pursued by a few, etc.;
mostly we see the abortions of lively social functioning
saddled, exploited, prevented, perverted, drained dry, pater-
nalized by an adopted system of power and management that
pre-empts the means and makes decisions *ab extra*. And the
damnable thing is that, of course, everybody believes that
except in this pattern nothing could possibly be accomplished:
if there were no marriage license and no tax, none could
properly mate and no children be born and raised; if there
were no tolls there would be no bridges; if there were no
university charters, there would be no higher learning; if
there were no usury and no Iron Law of Wages, there would
be no capital; if there were no markup of drug prices, there
would be no scientific research. Once a society has this style
of thought, that every activity requires licensing, underwriting,
deciding by abstract power, it becomes inevitably desirable for
an ambitious man to seek power and for a vigorous nation to
try to be a Great Power. The more some have the power drive,
the more it seems to be necessary to the others to compete, or
submit, just in order to survive. (And importantly they are
right.) Many are ruthless and most live in fear.

Even so, this is not the final development of the belief in
'power'. For that occurs when to get into power, to be
prestigious and in a position to make decisions, is taken to be
the social good itself, apart from any functions that it is
thought to make possible. The pattern of dominance – and
submission has then been internalized and, by its clinch, fills
up the whole experience. If a man is not continually proving his potency, his mastery of others and of himself, he
becomes prey to a panic of being defeated and victimized.
Every vital function must therefore be used as a means of
proving or it is felt as a symptom of weakness. Simply
to enjoy, produce, learn, give or take, love or be angry
(rather than cool), is to be vulnerable. This is different, and
has different consequences, from the previous merely external domination and submission. A people that has life but
thwarted functions will rebel when it can, against feudal dues,

clogs to trade, suppression of thought and speech, taxation without representation, insulting privilege, the Iron Law of Wages, colonialism. But our people do not rebel against poisoning, genetic deformation, imminent total destruction.

Rather, people aspire to be top-managers no matter what the goods or services produced. One is a promoter, period; or a celebrity, period. The Gross National Product must increase without consideration of the standard of life. There is no natural limit, so the only security is in deterrence. The environment is rife with projected enemies. There is a huddling together and conforming to avoid vulnerability of any idiosyncrasy, at the same time as each one has to be one-up among his identical similars. Next, there is excitement in identifying the 'really' powerful, the leaders, the Great Nations, the decision-makers, dramatized on the front page. But these leaders, of course, feel equally powerless in the face of the Great Events. For it is characteristic of the syndrome that as soon as there is occasion for any practical activity, toward happiness, value, spirit, or even simple safety, everyone suffers from the feeling of utter powerlessness; the internalized submissiveness now has its innings. Modern technology is too complex; there is a population explosion; the computer will work out the proper war game for us; they've got your number, don't stick your neck out; 'fallout is a physical fact of our nuclear age, it can be faced like any other fact' (*Manual of Civil Defence*); 'I'm strong, I can take sex or leave it' (eighteen-year-old third-offender for felonious assault). In brief, the underside of the psychology of power is that Nothing Can Be Done; and the resolution of the stalemate is to explode. This is the Cold War.

I have frequently explored this psychology of proving, resignation and catastrophic explosion (Wilhelm Reich's 'primary masochism'), and I shall not pursue it again. It is filling the void of vital function by identifying with the agent that has frustrated it; with, subsequently, a strongly defended conceit, but panic when any occasion calls for initiative, originality, or even animal response. Here I have simply tried to relate this psychology to the uncritical unanimous acceptance of the idea of 'getting into power in order to . . .' or just 'getting into power' as an end in itself. There is a vicious circle, for (except in emergencies) the very exercise of abstract power, managing and coercing, itself tends to stand in the way and alienate, to thwart function and diminish energy, and so to increase the psychology of power. But of course the consequence of the process is to put us in fact on a continual emergency, so power creates its own need. I have tried to show how, historically, the psychology has been exacerbated by the miserable system of extrinsic motivation by incentives and punishments (including profits, wages, unemployment), reducing people to low-grade organisms no different from Professor Skinner's pigeons; whereas normal function is intrinsically motivated towards specific ends-in-view, and leads to growth in inventiveness and freedom. Where people are not directly in feelingful contact with what is to be done, nothing is done well and on time; they are always behind and the emergency becomes chronic. Even with good intentions, a few managers do not have enough *mind* for the needs of society – not even if their computers gallop through the calculations like lightning. I conclude that the consensus of recent political scientists that political theory is essentially the study of power-manoeuvres, is itself a neurotic ideology. Normal politics has to do with the relations of specific functions in a community; and *such a study would often result in practical political inventions that would solve problems* – it would not merely predict elections and solve nothing, or play war games and destroy humanity.

Let me sum up these remarks in one homely and not newsy proposition: Throughout the world, it is bad domestic politics that creates the deadly international politics. Conversely, pacifism is revolutionary: we will not have peace unless there is a profound change in social structure, including getting rid of national sovereign power.

A.R.

WAR IS THE HEALTH OF THE STATE

RANDOLPH BOURNE
(From 'The State', 1919)

War is the health of the State. It automatically sets in motion throughout society those irresistible forces for uniformity, for passionate co-operation with the Government in coercing into obedience the minority groups and individuals which lack the larger herd sense. The machinery of government sets and enforces the drastic penalties, the minorities are either intimidated into silence, or brought slowly around by a subtle process of persuasion which may seem to them really to be converting them. Of course the ideal of perfect loyalty, perfect uniformity is never attained. The classes upon whom the amateur work of coercion falls are unwearied in their zeal, but often their agitation, instead of converting, merely serves to stiffen their resistance. Minorities are rendered sullen, and some intellectual opinion bitter and satirical. But in general, the nation in war-time attains a uniformity of feeling, a hierarchy of values, culminating at the undisputed apex of the State ideal, which could not possibly be produced through any other agency than war. Other values such as artistic creation, knowledge, reason, beauty, the enhancement of life, are instantly and almost unanimously sacrificed, and the significant classes who have constituted themselves the amateur agents of the State are engaged not only in sacrificing these values for themselves but in coercing all other persons into sacrificing them.

War – or at least modern war waged by a democratic republic against a powerful enemy – seems to achieve for a nation almost all that the most inflamed political idealist could desire. Citizens are no longer indifferent to their Government, but each cell of the body politic is brimming with life and activity. We are at least on the way to full realization of that collective community in which each individual somehow contains the virtue of the whole. In a nation at war, every citizen identifies himself with the whole, and feels immensely strengthened in that identification. The purpose and desire of the collective community live in each person who throws himself whole-heartedly into the cause of war. The impeding distinction between society and the individual is almost blotted out. At war, the individual becomes almost identical with his society. He achieves a superb self-assurance, an intuition of the rightness of all his ideas and emotions, so that in the suppression of opponents or heretics he is invincibly strong; he feels behind him all the power of the collective community. The individual as social being in war seems to have achieved almost his apotheosis. Not for any religious impulse could the American nation have been expected to show such devotion *en masse*, such sacrifice and labour. Certainly not for any secular good, such as universal education or the subjugation of nature, would it have poured forth its treasure and its life, or would it have permitted such stern coercive measures to be taken against it, such as conscripting its money and its men. But for the sake of a war of offensive self-defence, undertaken to support a difficult cause to the slogan of 'democracy', it would reach the highest level ever known of collective effort.

For these secular goods, connected with the enhancement of life, the education of man and the use of the intelligence to realize reason and beauty in the nation's communal living, are alien to our traditional ideal of the State. The State is intimately connected with war, for it is the organization of the collective community when it acts in a political manner, and to act in a political manner towards a rival group has meant, throughout all history – war.

There is nothing invidious in the use of the term, 'herd', in connection with the State. It is merely an attempt to reduce closer to first principles the nature of this institution in the shadow of which we all live, move and have our being. Ethnologists are generally agreed that human society made its first appearance as the human pack and not as a collection of individuals or of couples. The herd is in fact the original unit, and only as it was differentiated did personal individuality develop. All the most primitive surviving types of men are

shown to live in a very complex but very rigid social organization where opportunity for individuation is scarcely given.
These tribes remain strictly organized herds, and the difference between them and the modern State is one of degree of
sophistication and variety of organization, and not of kind.

Psychologists recognize the gregarious impulse as one of
the strongest primitive pulls which keeps together the herds
of the different species of higher animals. Mankind is no
exception. Our pugnacious evolutionary history has prevented
the impulse from ever dying out. This gregarious impulse
is the tendency to imitate, to conform, to coalesce together,
and is most powerful when the herd believes itself threatened
with attack. Animals crowd together for protection, and
men become most conscious of their collectivity at the threat
of war. Consciousness of collectivity brings confidence and
a feeling of massed strength, which in turn arouses pugnacity
and the battle is on. In civilized man, the gregarious impulse
acts not only to produce concerted action for defence, but
also to produce identity of opinion. Since thought is a form
of behaviour, the gregarious impulse floods up into its realms
and demands that sense of uniform thought which wartime
produces so successfully. And it is in this flooding of the
conscious life of society that gregariousness works its havoc.

For just as in modern societies the sex-instinct is enormously
over-supplied for the requirements of human propagation, so
the gregarious impulse is enormously over-supplied for the
work of protection which it is called upon to perform. It
would be quite enough if we were gregarious enough to enjoy
the companionship of others, to be able to co-operate with
them, and to feel a slight malaise at solitude. Unfortunately,
however, this impulse is not content with these reasonable
and healthful demands, but insists that like-mindedness shall
prevail everywhere, in all departments of life. So that all
human progress, all novelty, and non-conformity, must be
carried against the resistance of this tyrannical herd-instinct
which drives the individual into obedience and conformity
with the majority. Even in the most modern and enlightened
societies this impulse shows little sign of abating. As it is
driven by inexorable economic demand out of the sphere of

utility, it seems to fasten itself even more fiercely in the realm of feeling and opinion, so that conformity comes to be a thing aggressively desired and demanded.

The gregarious impulse keeps its hold all the more virulently because when the group is in motion or is taking any positive action, this feeling of being with and supported by the collective herd very greatly feeds that will to power, the nourishment of which the individual organism so constantly demands. You feel powerful by conforming, and you feel forlorn and helpless if you are out of the crowd. While even if you do not get any access of power by thinking and feeling just as everybody else in your group does, you get at least the warm feeling of obedience, the soothing irresponsibility of protection.

Joining as it does to these very vigorous tendencies of the individual – the pleasure in power and the pleasure in obedience – this gregarious impulse becomes irresistible in society. War stimulates it to the highest possible degree, sending the influences of its mysterious herd-current with its inflations of power and obedience to the farthest reaches of the society, to every individual and little group that can possibly be affected. And it is these impulses which the State – the organization of the entire herd, the entire collectivity – is founded on and makes use of.

There is, of course, in the feeling towards the State a large element of pure filial mysticism. The sense of insecurity, the desire for protection, sends one's desire back to the father and mother, with whom is associated the earliest feeling of protection. It is not for nothing that one's State is still thought of as Fatherland or Motherland, that one's relation towards it is conceived in terms of family affection. The war has shown that nowhere under the shock of danger have these primitive childlike attitudes failed to assert themselves again, as much in this country as anywhere. If we have not the intense Father-sense of the German who worships his Vaterland, at least in Uncle Sam we have a symbol of protecting, kindly authority, and in the many Mother-posts of the Red Cross, we see how easily in the more tender functions of war service, the ruling organization is conceived in family terms. A people at war have become in the most literal sense obedient, respectful, trustful children again, full of that naive faith in the all-wisdom and all-power of the adult who takes care of them, imposes his mild but necessary rule upon them and in whom they lose their responsibility and anxieties. In this recrudescence of the child, there is great comfort, and a certain influx of power. On most people the strain of being an independent adult weighs heavily, and upon none more than those members of the significant classes who have had bequeathed to them or have assumed the responsibilities of governing. The State provides the most convenient of symbols under which these classes can retain all the actual pragmatic satisfaction of governing, but can rid themselves of the psychic burden of adulthood. They continue to direct industry and government and all the institutions of society pretty much as before, but in their own conscious eyes and in the eyes of the general public, they are turned from their selfish and predatory ways, and have become loyal servants of society, or something greater than they – the State. The man who moves from the direction of a large business in New York to a post in the war management industrial service in Washington does not apparently alter very much his power or his administrative technique. But psychically, what a transformation has occurred! His is now not only the power but the glory! And his sense of satisfaction is directly proportional not to the genuine amount of personal sacrifice that may be involved in the change but to the extent to which he retains his industrial prerogative and sense of command.

From members of this class a certain insuperable indignation arises if the change from private enterprise to State service involves any real loss of power and personal privilege. If there is to be pragmatic sacrifice, let it be, they feel, on the field of honour, in the traditionally acclaimed deaths by battle, in that detour of suicide, as Nietzsche calls war. The State in wartime supplies satisfaction for this very craving, but its chief value is the opportunity it gives for this regression to infantile attitudes. In your reaction to an imagined attack in your country or an insult to its government, you draw closer to the herd for protection, you conform in word and deed, and you insist vehemently that everybody else shall think, speak and act together. And you fix your adoring gaze upon the State, with a truly filial look, as upon the Father of the flock, the quasi-personal symbol of the strength of the herd, and the leader and determinant of your definite action and ideas.

THE INDEFENSIBLE CONSTITUTION

LYSANDER SPOONER
(From *No Treason*, 1870)

The Constitution has no inherent authority or obligation. It has no authority or obligation at all, unless as a contract between man and man. And it does not so much as even purport to be a contract between persons now existing. It purports, at most, to be only a contract between persons living eighty years ago. And it can be supposed to have been a contract then only between persons who had already come to years of discretion, so as to be competent to make reasonable and obligatory contracts. Furthermore, we know, historically, that only a small portion even of the people then existing were consulted on the subject, or asked, or permitted to express either their consent or dissent in any formal manner. Those persons, if any, who did give their consent formally, are all dead now. Most of them have been dead forty, fifty, sixty, or seventy years. *And the Constitution, so far as it was their contract, died with them.* They had no natural power or right to make it obligatory upon their children. It is not only plainly impossible, in the nature of things, that they *could* bind their posterity, but they did not even attempt to bind them. That is to say, the instrument does not purport to be an agreement between anybody but 'the people' *then* existing; nor does it, either expressly or impliedly, assert any right, power, or disposition, on their part, to bind anybody but themselves. Let us see. Its language is:

We, the people of the United States [that is, the people

then existing in the United States], in order to form a more perfect union, insure domestic tranquillity, provide for the common defense, promote the general welfare, and secure the blessings of liberty to ourselves *and our prosperity*, do ordain and establish this Constitution for the United States of America.

It is plain, in the first place, that this language, *as an agreement*, purports to be only what it at most really was, viz., a contract between the people then existing; and, of necessity, binding, as a contract, only upon those then existing. In the second place, the language neither expresses nor implies that they had any intention or desire, nor that they imagined they had any right or power, to bind their 'posterity' to live under it. It does not say that their 'posterity' will, shall or must live under it. It only says, in effect, that their hopes and motives in adopting it were that it might prove useful to their posterity, as well as to themselves, by promoting their union, safety, tranquillity, liberty, etc.

Suppose an agreement were entered into, in this form:

We, the people of Boston, agree to maintain a fort on Governor's Island, to protect ourselves and our posterity against invasion.

This agreement, as an agreement, would clearly bind nobody but the people then existing. Secondly, it would assert no right, power, or disposition, on their part, to compel their 'posterity' to maintain such a fort. It would only indicate that the supposed welfare of their posterity was one of the motives that induced the original parties to enter into an agreement.

When a man says he is building a house for himself and his posterity, he does not mean to be understood as saying that he has any thought of binding them, nor is it to be inferred that he is so foolish as to imagine that he has any right or power to bind them, to live in it. So far as they are concerned, he only means to be understood as saying that his hopes and motives, in building it, are that they, or at least some of them, may find it for their happiness to live in it.

So when a man says he is planting a tree for himself and his posterity, he does not mean to be understood as saying that he has any thought of compelling them, nor is it to be inferred that he is such a simpleton as to imagine that he has any right or power to compel them, to eat fruit. So far as they are concerned, he only means to say that his hopes and motives, in planting the tree, are that its fruit may be agreeable to them.

So it was with those who originally adopted the Constitution. Whatever may have been their personal intentions, the legal meaning of their language, so far as their 'posterity' was concerned, simply was, that the hopes and motives, in entering into the agreement, were that it might promote their union, safety, tranquillity, and welfare; and that it might tend 'to secure to them the blessings of liberty'. The language does not assert nor at all imply, any right, power, or disposition, on the part of the original parties to the agreement, to compel their 'posterity' to live under it. If they had intended to bind their posterity to live under it, they should have said that their object was, not 'to secure to them the blessings of liberty', but to make slaves of them; for if their 'posterity' are bound to live under it, they are nothing less than the slaves of their foolish, tyrannical, and dead grandfathers.

It cannot be said that the Constitution formed 'the people of the United States', for all time, into a corporation. It does not speak of 'the people' as a corporation, but as individuals. A corporation does not describe itself as 'we', nor as 'people', nor as 'ourselves'. Nor does a corporation, in legal language, have any 'posterity'. It supposes itself to have, and speaks of itself as having, perpetual existence, as a single individuality.

Moreover, no body of men, existing at any one time, have the power to create a perpetual corporation. A corporation can become practically perpetual only by the voluntary accession of new members, as the old ones die off. But for this voluntary accession of new members, the corporation necessarily dies with the death of those who originally composed it.

Legally speaking, therefore, there is, in the Constitution, nothing that professes or attempts to bind the 'posterity' of those who established it . . .

The Constitution itself, then, being of no authority, on what authority does our government practically rest? On what ground can those who pretend to administer it, claim the right to seize men's property, to restrain them in their natural liberty of action, industry and trade, and to kill all those who deny their authority to dispose of men's properties, liberties and lives at their pleasure or discretion?

The most they can say, in answer to this question, is, that some half, two-thirds, or three-quarters, of the male adults of the country have a *tacit understanding* that they will maintain a government under the Constitution; that they will select, by ballot, the persons to administer it; and that those persons who may receive a majority, or a plurality, of their ballots, shall act as their representatives, and administer the Constitution in their name, and by their authority.

But this tacit understanding (admitting it to exist) cannot at all justify the conclusion drawn from it. A tacit understanding between A, B, and C, that they will, by ballot, depute D as their agent, to deprive me of my property, liberty, or life, cannot at all authorize D to do so. He is none the less a robber, tyrant, and murderer, because he claims to act as their agent, than he would be if he avowedly acted on his own responsibility alone.

Neither am I bound to recognize him as their agent, nor can he legitimately claim to be their agent, when he brings no written *authority* from them accrediting him as such. I am under no obligation to take his word as to who his principals may be, or whether he has any. Bringing no credentials, I have a right to say he has no such authority even as he claims to have; and that he is therefore intending to rob, enslave or murder me on his own account.

This tacit understanding, therefore, among the voters of the country, amounts to nothing as an authority to their agents. Neither do the ballots by which they select their agents, avail any more than does their tacit understanding; for their ballots are given in secret, and therefore in a way to avoid any personal responsibility for the acts of their agents.

No body of men can be said to authorize a man to act as their agent, to the injury of a third person, unless they do it in so open and authentic a manner as to make themselves personally responsible for his acts. None of the voters in this country appoint their political agents in any open, authentic manner, or in any manner to make themselves responsible for their acts. Therefore these pretended agents cannot legitimately claim to be really agents. Somebody must be responsible for the acts of these pretended agents; and if they cannot show any open and authentic credentials from their principals, they cannot, by law or reason, be said to have any principals. The maxim applies here, that what does not appear, does not exist. If they can show no principals, they have none.

But even these pretended agents do not themselves know who their pretended principals are. These latter act in secret; for acting by secret ballot is acting in secret as much as if they were to meet in secret conclave in the darkness of the night. And they are personally as much unknown to the agents they select, as they are to others. No pretended agent therefore can ever know by whose ballot he is selected, or consequently who his real principals are. Not knowing who his principals are, he has no right to say that he has any. He can, at most, say only that he is the agent of a secret band of robbers and murderers, who are bound by that faith which prevails among confederates in crime, to stand by him, if his acts, done in their name, shall be resisted.

Men honestly engaged in attempting to establish justice in the world, have no occasion thus to act in secret; or to appoint agents for which they (the principals) are not willing to be responsible.

The secret ballot makes a secret government; and a secret government is a secret band of robbers and murderers. Open despotism is better than this. The single despot stands out in the fact of all men, and says, I am the State: My will is law; I am your master: I take the responsibility of my acts: The only arbiter I acknowledge is the sword: If anyone denies my right, let him try conclusions with me.

But a secret government is little less than a government of assassins. Under it, a man knows not who his tyrants are, until they have struck, and perhaps not then. He may *guess,* beforehand, as to some of his immediate neighbours. But he really knows nothing. The man to whom he would most naturally fly for protection, may prove an enemy, when the time of trial comes.

This is the kind of government we have; and it is the only one we are likely to have, until men are ready to say: We will consent to no Constitution, except such a one as we are neither ashamed nor afraid to sign; and we will authorize no government to do anything in our name which we are not willing to be personally responsible.

THE ILLUSION OF
UNIVERSAL SUFFRAGE

MICHAEL BAKUNIN
(From *Oeuvres*, Vol. II, 1907, translated by
George Woodcock)

Men once believed that the establishment of universal suffrage would guarantee the freedom of the peoples. That, alas, was a great illusion, and the realization of that illusion has led in many places to the downfall and demoralization of the radical party. The radicals did not wish to deceive the people – or so the liberal papers assure us – but in that case they were certainly themselves deceived. They were genuinely convinced when they promised the people freedom through universal suffrage, and inspired by that conviction they were able to arouse the masses and overthrow the established aristocratic governments. Today, having learnt from experience and power politics, they have lost faith in themselves and in their own principles and in that way they have sunk into defeat and corruption.

Yet the whole thing seemed so natural and so simple; once legislative and executive power emanated directly from a popular election, must it not become the pure expression of the people's will, and could that will produce anything other than freedom and well-being among the populace?

The whole deception of the representative system lies in

the fiction that a government and a legislature emerging out of a popular election must or even can represent the real will of the people. Instinctively and inevitably the people expect two things: the greatest possible material prosperity combined with the greatest freedom of movement and action: that means the best organization of popular economic interests, and the complete absence of any kind of power or political organization – since all political organization is destined to end in the negation of freedom. Such are the basic longings of the people.

The instincts of the rulers, whether they legislate or execute the laws, are – by the very fact of their exceptional position – diametrically opposite. However democratic may be their feelings and their intentions, once they achieve the elevation of office they can only view society in the same way as a schoolmaster views his pupils, and between pupils and masters equality cannot exist. On one side there is the feeling of superiority that is inevitably provoked by a position of superiority; on the other side, there is the sense of inferiority which follows from the superiority of the teacher, whether he is exercising an executive or a legislative power. Whoever talks of political power talks of domination; but where domination exists there is inevitably a somewhat large section of society that is dominated, and those who are dominated quite naturally detest their dominators, while the dominators have no choice but to subdue and oppress those they dominate.

This is the eternal history of political power, ever since that power has appeared in the world. This is what also explains why and how the most extreme of democrats, the most raging rebels, become the most cautious of conservatives as soon as they attain to power. Such recantations are usually regarded as acts of treason, but that is an error; their main cause is simply the change of position and hence of perspective . . .

In Switzerland, as elsewhere, the ruling class is completely different and separate from the mass of the governed. Here, as everywhere, no matter how egalitarian our political constitution may be, it is the bourgeoisie who rule, and it is the people – workers and peasants – who obey their laws. The people have neither the leisure nor the necessary education to occupy themselves with government. Since the bourgeoisie have both, they have, in fact if not by right, exclusive privilege. Thus, in Switzerland as elsewhere, political equality is merely a puerile fiction, a lie.

But how, separated as they are from the people by all the economic and social circumstances of their existence, can the bourgeoisie express, in laws and in government, the feelings, ideas and wishes of the people? It is impossible, and daily experience in fact proves that, in legislation as well as government, the bourgeoisie is mainly directed by its own interests and prejudices, without any great concern for those of the people.

It is true that all our legislators, as well as all the members of cantonal governments, are elected, directly or indirectly, by the people. It is true that on election day even the proudest of bourgeoisie, if they have any political ambitions, are obliged to pay court to Her Majesty, the Sovereign People . . . But once the elections are over, the people return to their work and the bourgeoisie to their profitable businesses and political intrigues. They neither meet nor recognize each other again. And how can one expect the people, burdened by their work and ignorant for the most part of current problems, to supervise the political actions of their representatives? In reality, the control exercised by voters on their elected representatives is a pure fiction. But since, in the representative system, popular control is the only guarantee of the people's freedom, it is quite evident that such freedom in its turn is no more than a fiction.

PARLIAMENTARY ISOLATION

PIERRE-JOSEPH PROUDHON
(From *Les Confessions d'un Révolutionnaire*, 1849)

I entered the National Assembly with the timidity of a child, with the ardour of a neophyte. Assiduous, from nine o'clock in the morning, at the meetings of bureaux and committees, I did not quit the Assembly until the evening, and then I was exhausted with fatigue and disgust. As soon as I set foot in the parliamentary Sinai, I ceased to be in touch with the masses; because I was absorbed by my legislative work, I entirely lost sight of the current of events. I knew nothing, either of the situation of the national workshops, or the policy of the government, or of the intrigues that were growing up in the heart of the Assembly. One must have lived in that isolator which is called a National Assembly to realize how the men who are most completely ignorant of the state of the country are almost always those who represent it . . . Most of my colleagues of the left and the extreme left were in the same perplexity of mind, the same ignorance of daily facts. One spoke of the national workshops only with a kind of terror, for fear of the people is the sickness of all those who belong to authority; the people, for those in power, are the enemy.

THE USELESSNESS OF LAWS

PETER KROPOTKIN
(From *Law and Authority*, 1886)

The millions of laws which exist for the regulation of humanity appear upon investigation to be divided into three principal categories: protection of property, protection of persons, protection of government. And by analysing each of these three categories, we arrive at the same logical and necessary conclusion: *the uselessness and hurtfulness of law.*

Socialists know what is meant by protection of property. Laws on property are not made to guarantee either to the individual or to society the enjoyment of the produce of their own labour. On the contrary, they are made to rob the producer of a part of what he has created, and to secure to certain other people that portion of the produce which they have stolen either from the producer or from society as a whole. When, for example, the law establishes Mr So-and-So's right to a house, it is not establishing his right to a cottage he has built for himself, or to a house he has erected with the

help of some of his friends. In that case no one would have
disputed his right. On the contrary, the law is establishing
his right to a house which is not the product of his labour;
first of all because he has had it built for him by others to
whom he has not paid the full value of their work, and next
because that house represents a social value which he could
not have produced for himself. The law is establishing his
right to what belongs to everybody in general and to nobody
in particular. The same house built in the midst of Siberia
would not have the value it possesses in a large town, and,
as we know, that value arises from the labour of something
like fifty generations of men who have built the town,
beautified it, supplied it with water and gas, fine promenades,
colleges, theatres, shops, railways and roads leading in all
directions. Thus, by recognizing the rights of Mr So-and-So
to a particular house in Paris, London, or Rouen, the law
is unjustly appropriating to him a certain portion of the produce of the labour of mankind in general. And it is precisely
because this appropriation and all other forms of property
bearing the same character are a crying injustice, that a whole
arsenal of laws and a whole army of soldiers, policemen
and judges are needed to maintain it against the good sense
and just feeling inherent in humanity.

Half our laws, – the civil code in each country, – serve no
other purpose than to maintain this appropriation, this monopoly for the benefit of certain individuals against the whole of
mankind. Three-quarters of the causes decided by the tribunals are nothing but quarrels between monopolists – two
robbers disputing over their booty. And a great many of our
criminal laws have the same object in view, their end being
to keep the workman in a subordinate position towards his
employer, and thus affording security for exploitation.

As for guaranteeing the product of his labour to the producer, there are no laws which even attempt such a thing. It is
so simple and natural, so much a part of the manners and
customs of mankind, that law has not given it so much as a
thought. Open brigandage, sword in hand, is no feature of
our age. Neither does one workman ever come and dispute
the produce of his labour with another. If they have a misunderstanding they settle it by calling in a third person, with-

out having recourse to law. The only person who exacts from another what that other has produced, is the proprietor, who comes in and deducts the lion's share. As for humanity in general, it everywhere respects the right of each to what he has created, without the interposition of any special laws.

As all the laws about property which make up thick volumes of codes and are the delight of our lawyers have no other object than to protect the unjust appropriation of human labour by certain monopolists, there is no reason for their existence, and, on the day of the revolution, social revolutionists are thoroughly determined to put an end to them. Indeed, a bonfire might be made with perfect justice of all laws bearing upon the so-called 'rights of property', all title-deeds, all registers, in a word, of all that is in any way connected with an institution which will soon be looked upon as a blot in the history of humanity, as humiliating as the slavery and serfdom of past ages.

The remarks just made upon laws concerning property are quite as applicable to the second category of laws; those for the maintenance of government, i.e., constitutional law.

It again is a complete arsenal of laws, decrees, ordinances, orders in council, and what not, all serving to protect the diverse forms of representative government, delegated or usurped, beneath which humanity is writhing. We know very well – anarchists have often enough pointed out in their perpetual criticism of the various forms of government – that the mission of all governments, monarchical, constitutional, or republican, is to protect and maintain by force the privileges of the classes in possession, the aristocracy, clergy and traders. A good third of our laws – and each country possesses some tens of thousands of them – the fundamental laws on taxes, excise duties, the organization of ministerial departments and their offices, of the army, the police, the Church, etc., have no other end than to maintain, patch up, and develop the administrative machine. And this machine in its turn serves almost entirely to protect the privileges of the possessing classes. Analyze all these laws, observe them in action day by day, and you will discover that not one is worth preserving.

About such laws there can be no two opinions. Not only

anarchists, but more or less revolutionary radicals also, are agreed that the only use to be made of laws concerning the organization of government is to fling them into the fire.

The third category of law still remains to be considered; that relating to the protection of the person and the detection and prevention of 'crime'. This is the most important because most prejudices attach to it; because, if law enjoys a certain amount of consideration, it is in consequence of the belief that this species of law is absolutely indispensable to the maintenance of security in our societies. These are laws developed from the nucleus of customs useful to human communities, which have been turned to account by rulers to sanctify their own domination. The authority of the chiefs of tribes, of rich families in towns, and of the king, depended upon their judicial functions, and even down to the present day, whenever the necessity of government is spoken of, its function as supreme judge is the thing implied. 'Without a government, men would tear one another to pieces,' argues the village orator. 'The ultimate end of all government is to secure twelve honest jurymen to every accused person,' said Burke.

Well, in spite of all the prejudices existing on this subject, it is quite time that anarchists should boldly declare this category of law as useless and injurious as the preceding ones.

First of all, as to so-called 'crimes' – assaults upon persons, it is well known that two-thirds, and often as many as three-quarters, of such 'crimes' are instigated by the desire to obtain possession of someone's wealth. This immense class of so-called 'crimes and misdemeanours' will disappear on the day on which private property ceases to exist. 'But,' it will be said, 'there will always be brutes who will attempt the lives of their fellow citizens, who will lay their hands to a knife in every quarrel, and revenge the slightest offence by murder, if there are no laws to restrain and punishments to withhold them.' This refrain is repeated every time the right of society *to punish* is called in question.

Yet there is one fact concerning this head which at the present time is thoroughly established; the severity of punishment does not diminish the amount of crime. Hang, and, if you like, quarter murderers, and the number of murders will not decrease by one. On the other hand, abolish the penalty of death, and there will not be one murder more; there will be fewer. Statistics prove it. But if the harvest is good, and bread cheap, and the weather fine, the number of murders immediately decreases. This again is proved by statistics. The amount of crime always augments and diminishes in proportion to the price of provisions and the state of the weather. Not that all murderers are actuated by hunger. That is not the case. But when the harvest is good, and provisions are at an obtainable price, and when the sun shines, men, lighter-hearted and less miserable than usual, do not give way to gloomy passions, do not from trivial motives plunge a knife into the bosom of a fellow creature.

Moreover, it is also a well known fact that the fear of punishment has never stopped a single murderer. He who kills his neighbour for revenge or misery does not reason much about consequences; and there have been few murderers who were not firmly convinced that they should escape prosecution.

Without speaking of a society in which a man will receive a better education, in which the development of all his faculties, and the possibility of exercising them, will procure him so many enjoyments that he will not seek to poison them by remorse – even in our society, even with those sad products of misery whom we see today in the public houses of great cities – on the day when no punishment is inflicted upon murderers, the number of murders will not be augmented by a single case. And it is extremely probable that it will be, on the contrary, diminished by all those cases which are due at present to habitual criminals, who have been brutalized in prisons.

We are continually being told of the benefits conferred by law, and the beneficial effect of penalties, but have the speakers ever attempted to strike a balance between the benefits attributed to laws and penalties, and the degrading effects of these penalties upon humanity? Only calculate all the evil passions awakened in mankind by the atrocious punishments formerly inflicted in our streets! Man is the cruelest animal upon earth. And who has pampered and developed the cruel instincts unknown, even among monkeys, if it is not the king, the judge, and the priests, armed with law, who caused flesh to be torn off in strips, boiling pitch to be poured into wounds, limbs to be dislocated, bones to be crushed, men to be sawn asunder to maintain their authority? Only estimate the torrent of depravity let loose in human society by the 'informing' which is countenanced by judges, and paid in hard cash by governments, under pretext of assisting in the discovery of 'crime'. Only go into the jails and study what man becomes when he is deprived of freedom and shut up with other depraved beings, steeped in the vice and corruption which oozes from the very walls of our existing prisons. Only remember that the more these prisons are reformed, the more detestable they become. Our model modern penitentiaries are a hundred-fold more abominable than the dungeons of the Middle Ages. Finally, consider what corruption, what depravity of mind is kept up among men by the idea of obedience, the very essence of law; of chastisement; of authority having the right to punish, to judge irrespective of our conscience and the esteem of our friends; of the necessity for executioners, jailers, and informers – in a word, by all the attributes of law and authority. Consider all this, and you will assuredly agree with us in saying that a law inflicting penalties is an abomination which should cease to exist.

Peoples without political organization, and therefore less depraved than ourselves, have perfectly understood that the man who is called 'criminal' is simply unfortunate; that the remedy is not to flog him, to chain him up, or to kill him on the scaffold or in prison, but to help him by the most brotherly care, by treatment based on equality, by the usages of life among honest men. In the next revolution we hope that this cry will go forth:

'Burn the guillotines; demolish the prisons; drive away the judges, policemen and informers – the impurest race upon the face of the earth; treat as a brother the man who has been led by passion to do ill to his fellow; above all, take from the ignoble products of middle-class idleness the possibility of displaying their vices in attractive colours; and be sure that but few crimes will mar our society.'

The main supports of crime are idleness, law and authority; laws about property, laws about government, laws about penalties and misdemeanours; and authority, which takes upon itself to manufacture these laws and to apply them.

No more laws! No more judges! Liberty, equality, and practical human sympathy are the only effective barriers we can oppose to the anti-social instincts of certain among us.

THE VIOLENCE OF LAWS

LEO TOLSTOY
(From *The Slavery of Our Times*, 1900, translated by Aylmer Maude)

Many constitutions have been devised, beginning with the English and American and ending with the Japanese and the Turkish, according to which people are to believe that all laws established in their country are established at their desire. But everyone knows that not in despotic countries only, but in the countries nominally most free – England, America, France, and others – laws are made not by the will of all, but by the will of those who have power, and therefore always and everywhere are such as are profitable to those who have power: be they many, or few, or only one man. Everywhere and always the laws are enforced by the only means that has compelled, and still compels, some people to obey the will of others, i.e., by blows, by deprivation of liberty, and by murder. There can be no other way.

It cannot be otherwise. For laws are demands to execute certain rules; and to compel some people to obey certain rules (*i.e.* to do what other people want of them) can only be effected by blows, by deprivation of liberty, and by murder. If there are laws, there must be the force that can compel people to obey them. And there is only one force that can compel people to obey rules (*i.e.* to obey the will of others) – and that is violence; not the simple violence which people use to one another in moments of passion, but the organized violence used by people who have power, in order to compel others to obey the laws they (the powerful) have made – in other words, to do their will.

And so the essence of legislature does not lie in Subject or Object, in rights, or in the idea of the dominion of the collective will of the people, or in other such indefinite and confused conditions; but it lies in the fact that people who wield organized violence have power to compel others to obey them and do as they like.

So that the exact and irrefutable definition of legislation, intelligible to all, is that: *Laws are rules, made by people who govern by means of organized violence, for non-compliance with which the non-complier is subjected to blows, to loss of liberty, or even to being murdered.*

ON PUNISHMENT

WILLIAM GODWIN
(From *Enquiry Concerning Political Justice*, 1793)

Let us proceed to consider the three principal ends that punishment proposes to itself, restraint, reformation and example. Under each of these heads the arguments on the affirmative side must be allowed to be cogent, not irresistible. Under each of them considerations will occur, that will oblige us to doubt universally of the propriety of punishment.

The first and most innocent of all the classes of coercion, is that which is employed in repelling actual force. This has but little to do with any species of political institution, but may nevertheless deserve to be first considered. In this case I am employed (suppose, for example, a drawn sword is pointed at my own breast or that of another, with threats of instant destruction) in preventing a mischief that seems about inevitably to ensue. In this case there appears to be no time for experiments. And yet, even here, a strict research will suggest to us important doubts. The powers of reason and truth are yet unfathomed. The truth which one man cannot communicate in less than a year, another can communicate in a fortnight. The shortest term may have an understanding commensurate to it. When Marius said, with a stern look, and a commanding countenance, to the soldier, that was sent down into his dungeon to assassinate him, 'Wretch, you have the temerity to kill Marius!' and with these few words drove him to flight; it was, that the grandeur of the idea conceived in his own mind, made its way with irresistible force to the mind of his executioner. He had no arms for resistance; he had no vengeance to threaten; he was debilitated and deserted; it was by the force of sentiment only, that he disarmed his destroyer. If there were falsehood and prejudice mixed with the idea communicated, in this case, can we believe that truth is not still more powerful? It would be well for the human species, if they were all, in this respect, like Marius, all accustomed to place an intrepid confidence in the single energy of intellect. Who shall say what there is that would be impossible to men thus bold, and actuated only by the purest sentiments? Who shall say how far the whole species might be improved, did they cease to respect force in others, and did they refuse to employ it for themselves?

The difference however, between this species of coercion, and the species which usually bears the denomination of punishment, is obvious. Punishment is employed against an individual whose violence is over. He is, at present, engaged in no hostility, against the community, or any of its members. He is quietly pursuing, it may be, those occupations which are beneficial to himself, and injurious to none. Upon what pretence is this man to be the subject of violence?

For restraint. Restraint from what? 'From some future injury which it is to be feared he will commit.' This is the very argument which has been employed to justify the most execrable tyrannies. By what reasoning have the inquisition, the employment of spies, and the various kinds of public censure directed against opinion, been vindicated? By recollecting that there is an intimate connection between men's opinions and their conduct; that immoral sentiments lead, by a very probable consequence, to immoral actions. There is not more reason, in many cases at least, to apprehend that the man who has once committed robbery, will commit it again, than the man who has dissipated his property at the gaming table or who is accustomed to profess that, upon any emergency, he will not scruple to have recourse to this expedient. Nothing can be more obvious than that, whatever precautions may be allowable with respect to the future, justice will reluctantly class among these precautions a violence to be committed on my neighbour. Nor is it oftener unjust, than it is superfluous. Why not arm myself with vigilance and energy, instead of locking up every man whom my imagination may bid me fear, that I may spend my days in undisturbed inactivity? If communities, instead of aspiring, as they have hitherto done, to embrace a vast territory, and glut their vanity with ideas of empire, were contented with a small district, with a proviso of confederation in cases of necessity, every individual would then live under the public eye; and the disapprobation of his neighbours, a species of coercion, not derived from the caprice of men, but from the system of the universe, would inevitably oblige him, either to reform, or to emigrate. – The sum of the argument under this head is, that all punishment for the sake of restraint, is punishment upon suspicion, a species of punishment, the most abhorrent to reason, and arbitrary in its application, that can be devised.

The second object which punishment may be imagined to propose to itself, is reformation. We have already seen various objections that may be offered to it from this point of view. Coercion cannot convince, cannot conciliate, but on the contrary alienates the mind of him against whom it is employed. Coercion has nothing in common with reason, and therefore can have no proper tendency to the cultivation of virtue. It is true that reason is nothing more than a collation and comparison of various emotions and feelings; but they must be the feelings originally appropriate to the question, not those which an arbitrary will, stimulated by the possession of power, may annex to it. Reason is omnipotent: if my conduct be wrong, a very simple statement, flowing from a clear and comprehensible view, will make it appear to be such; nor is it probable that there is any perverseness that would persist in vice, in the face of all the recommendations with which virtue might be invested, and all the beauty in which it might be displayed.

But to this it may be answered, 'that this view of the subject may indeed be abstractedly true, but that it is not true relative to the present imperfection of human faculties. The grand requisite for the reformation and improvement of the human species, seems to consist in the rousing of the mind. It is for this reason that the school of adversity has so often been considered as the school of virtue. In an even course of easy and prosperous circumstances, the faculties sleep. But, when great and urgent occasion is presented, it should seem that the mind rises to the level of the occasion. Difficulties awaken vigour, and engender strength; and it will frequently happen that, the more you check and oppress me, the more will my faculties swell, till they burst all the obstacles of oppression.'

The opinion of the excellence of adversity, is built upon a very obvious mistake. If we divest ourselves of paradox and singularity, we shall perceive that adversity is a bad thing, but that there is something else that is worse. Mind can neither exist, nor be improved, without the reception of ideas. It will improve more in a calamitous, than a torpid state. A man will sometimes be found wiser at the end of his career, who has been treated with severity, than with neglect. But, because severity is one way of generating thought, it does not follow that it is the best.

It has already been shown that coercion, absolutely considered, is injustice. Can injustice be the best mode of disseminating principles of equity and reason? Oppression, exercised to a certain extent, is the most ruinous of all things. What is it but this, that has habituated mankind to so much ignorance and vice for so many thousand years? Is it probable, that that which has been thus terrible in its consequences, should, under any variation of circumstances, be made a source of eminent good? All coercion sours the mind. He that suffers it, is practically persuaded of the want of a philanthropy sufficiently enlarged, in those with whom he has intercourse. He feels that justice prevails only with great limitations, and that he cannot depend upon being treated with justice. The lesson which coercion reads to him is, 'Submit to force, and abjure reason. Be not directed by the convictions of your understanding, but by the basest part of your nature, the fear of personal pain, and a compulsory awe of the injustice of others.' It was thus Elizabeth of England and Frederick of Prussia were educated in the school of adversity. The way in which they profited by this discipline, was by finding resources in their own minds, enabling them to regard, with an unconquered spirit, the violence employed against them. Can this be the best mode of forming men to virtue? If it be, perhaps it is further requisite, that the coercion we use should be flagrantly unjust, since the improvement seems to lie, not in submission, but resistance.

But it is certain that truth is adequate to excite the mind, without the aid of adversity. By truth is here understood a just view of all the attractions of industry, knowledge and benevolence. If I apprehend the value of any pursuit, shall I not engage in it? If I apprehend it clearly, shall I not engage in it zealously? If you would awaken my mind in the most effectual manner, speak to the genuine and honourable feelings of my nature. For that purpose, thoroughly understand yourself that which you would recommend to me, impregnate your mind with evidence, and speak from the clearness of your view, and the fullness of conviction. Were we accustomed to an education, in which truth was never neglected from indolence, or told in a way treacherous to its excellence, in which the preceptor subjected himself to the perpetual discipline of finding the way to communicate it with brevity and force, but without prejudice and acrimony, it cannot be believed, but that such an education, would be more effectual for the improvement of the mind, than all the modes of angry or benevolent coercion that ever were devised.

The last object which punishment proposes, is example. Had legislators confined their views to reformation and restraint, their exertions of power, though mistaken, would still have borne the stamp of humanity. But, the moment vengeance presented itself as a stimulus to the one side, or the exhibition of a terrible example on the other, no barbarity was thought too great. Ingenious cruelty was busied to find new means of torturing the victim, or rendering the spectacle impressive and horrible.

It has long since been observed, that this system of policy constantly fails of its purpose. Further refinements in barbarity, produce a certain impression, so long as they are new; but this impression soon vanishes, and the whole scope of a gloomy invention is exhausted in vain. The reason of this phenomenon, is that, whatever may be the force with which novelty strikes the imagination, the inherent nature of the situation speedily recurs, and asserts its indestructible empire. We feel the emergencies to which we are exposed, and we feel, or think we feel, the dictates of reason inciting us to their relief. Whatever ideas we form to the mandates of law, we draw, with sincerity, though it may be with some mixture of mistake, from the essential conditions of our existence. We compare them with the despotism which society exercises in its corporate capacity; and, the more frequent is our comparison, the greater are our murmurs and indignation against the injustice to which we are exposed. But indignation is not a sentiment that conciliates; barbarity possesses none of the attributes of persuasion. It may terrify; but it cannot produce in us candour and docility. Thus ulcerated with injustice, our distresses, our temptations, and all the eloquence of feeling present themselves again and again. Is it any wonder they should prove victorious?

Punishment for example, is liable to all the objections which are urged against punishment for restraint or reformation, and to certain other objections peculiar to itself. It is employed against a person not now in the commission of offence, and of whom we can only suspect that he ever will offend. It supersedes argument, reason and conviction, and requires us to think such a species of conduct our duty, because such is the good pleasure of our superiors, and because, as we are taught by the example in question, they will make us rue our stubbornness if we think otherwise. In addition to this it is to be remembered that, when I am made to suffer as an example to others, I am myself treated with supercilious neglect, as if I were totally incapable of feeling and morality. If you inflict pain upon me, you are either just or unjust. If you be just, it should seem necessary that there should be something in me that makes me fit the subject of pain, either absolute desert, which is absurd, or mischief I may be expected to perpetuate, or lastly, a tendency in what you do, to produce my reformation. If any of these be the reason why the suffering I undergo is just, then example is out of the question: it may be an incidental consequence of the procedure, but it forms no part of its principle. It must surely be a very artificial and injudicious scheme for guiding the sentiments of mankind, to fix upon an individual as a subject of torture or death, respecting whom this treatment has no direct fitness, merely that we may bid others to look, and derive instruction from his misery.

PRISON AND ITS EFFECTS

Peter Kropotkin
(From *In Russian and French Prisons*, 1887)

In a prisoner's greyish life, which flows without passion and emotions, all those best feelings which may improve human character soon die away. Even those workmen who like their trade and find some aesthetic satisfaction in it, lose their taste for work. Physical energy is very soon killed in prison. I remember the years passed in prison in Russia. I entered my cell in the fortress with the firm resolution not to succumb. To maintain my bodily energy, I regularly every day walked my five miles in my cell, and twice a day I performed some gymnastics with my heavy oak chair. And, when pen and ink were allowed to enter my cell, I had before me the task of recasting a large work – a great field to cover – that of submitting to a systematic revision the Indices of Glaciation. Later on, in France, another passion inspired me – the elaboration of the bases of what I consider a new system of philosophy – the bases of Anarchy. But, in both cases, I soon felt lassitude overtaking me. Bodily energy disappeared by-and-by. And I can think of no better comparison for the state of a prisoner than that of wintering in the Arctic regions. Read reports of Arctic expeditions – the old ones, those of the good-hearted Parry, or of the elder Ross. When going through them you feel a note of physical and mental depression pervading the whole diary, and growing more and more dreary, until sun and hopes reappear on the horizon. That is the state of a prisoner. The brain has no longer the energy for sustained attention; thought is less rapid, or, rather, less persistent: it loses its depth. An American report mentioned last year that while the study of languages usually prospers with the prisoners, they are mostly unable to persevere in mathematics; and so it is.

It seems to me that this depression of healthy nervous energy can be best accounted for by the want of impressions. In ordinary life thousands of sounds and colours strike our senses; thousands of small, varied facts come within our knowledge, and spur the activity of the brain. Nothing of the kind strikes the prisoner; his impressions are few, and always the same. Therefore – the eagerness of the prisoners for anything new, for any new impression. I cannot forget the eagerness with which I observed, when taking a walk in the fortress yard, the changes of colour on the gilt needle of the fortress, its rosy tints at sunset, its bluish colours in the morning, its changing aspects on cloudy and bright days, in the morning and evening, winter and summer. It was the only thing which changed its aspect. The appearance of a parrot in the yard was a great event. It was a new impression. This is probably also the reason that all prisoners are so fond of illustrations; they convey new impressions in a new way. All impressions received by the prisoner, be they from his reading or from his own thoughts, pass through the medium of his imagination. And the brain, already poorly fed by a less active heart and impoverished blood, becomes tired, worried. It loses its energy.

This circumstance probably explains also the striking want of energy, of ardour, in prison work. In fact, each time I saw at Clairvaux the prisoners lazily crossing the yards, lazily followed by a lazy warder, my imagination always transported me back to my father's house and his numerous serfs. Prison-work is slavish work; and slavish work cannot inspire a human being with the best inspiration of man – the need to work and to create. The prisoner may learn a handicraft, but he will never learn to love his work. In most instances he will learn to hate it.

There is another important cause of demoralization in prisons which cannot be too much insisted upon, as it is

common to all prisons and inherent in the system of deprivation of liberty itself. All transgressions against the established
principles of morality can be traced to a want of firm Will.
Most of the inmates of our prisons are people who have not
had firmness enough to resist the temptations that surrounded
them, or to master a passionate impulse that momentarily
overpowered them. Now, in prison, as in a monastery, the
prisoner is secluded from all temptations of the outer world;
and his intercourse with other men is so limited and so
regulated that he seldom feels the influence of strong passions.
But, precisely in consequence of that he has almost no opportunity for exercising and reinforcing the firmness of his Will.
He is a machine. He has no choice between two courses of
action; the very few opportunities of free choice which he
has, are of no moment. All his life he has been regulated
and ordered beforehand; he has only to follow the current,
to obey under the fear of cruel punishment. In these conditions such firmness of Will as he may have had before entering
the prison, disappears. And, where shall he find the strength
to resist the temptations which will suddenly arise before him,
as by enchantment, as soon as he has stepped outside the
walls? Where will he find the strength to resist the first impulse of a passionate character, if, during many years, everything has been done to kill in him the interior force of
resistance, to make him a docile tool in the hands of those
who govern him?

This fact, in my opinion – and it seems to me that there can
be no two opinions in the matter – is the strongest condemnation of all systems based on depriving the condemned man of
his liberty. The origin of the systematic suppression of all
individual will in the prisoners, the systematic reduction of
men to the level of unreasoning machines, carried on throughout the long years of imprisonment, is easily explained. It
grew from the desire of preventing any breaches of discipline,
and of keeping the greatest number of prisoners with the
least possible amount of warders. And we may see throughout
the bulky literature of 'prison-discipline' that the greatest
admiration is bestowed precisely on those systems which
have obtained the results of discipline with the least possible
number of warders. The ideal of our prisons would be a

thousand automatons, rising and working, eating and going to bed, by electric currents transmitted to them from a single warder. But our modern and perfected system of prisons, although realizing perhaps some immediate economies for the State Budget, are also the most appropriate for bringing *récidive* to the strikingly high figures it attains now. The less prisons approximate to their present ideal, the less the *récidive*. And it is not to be wondered at that men accustomed to be mere machines do not prove to be the men whom society needs.

As soon as the prisoner is released, the comrades of his former life wait upon him. They receive him in brotherly guise, and, as soon as liberated, he is taken up by the current which already once has brought him to a prison. Guardians and Prisoners' Aid Societies cannot help. All they can do is to undo the bad work done by the prison, to counterbalance its bad effects in some of the released prisoners. While the influence of honest men who could have tendered a brotherly hand to the man *before* he was brought into the prisoner's dock, would have prevented him from committing the faults he has committed, now, after he has undergone the prison education, their efforts will remain fruitless in most cases.

And what a contrast between the fraternal reception of the brotherhood of 'magsmen' and the reception on behalf of 'respectable people', who conceal under a Christian exterior a Pharisaic egotism! For them the liberated prisoner is something plague-stricken. Who of them would invite him into his own house, and merely say, 'Here is a room, there is work for you; sit at this table, and be one of our family'? He needs most fraternal support, he is most in need of a brotherly hand stretched out to him. But, after having done all in our power to make him a foe of society, after having inoculated him with the vices which characterize prisons, who will tender him the brotherly hand he is in need of?

ON PROPERTY

WILLIAM GODWIN
(From *Enquiry Concerning Political Justice*, 1793)

The subject of property is the keystone that completes the fabric of political justice. According as our ideas respecting it are crude or correct, they will enlighten us as to the consequences of a *simple form of society without government*, and remove the prejudices that attach us to complexity. There is nothing that more powerfully tends to distort our *judgement* and *opinions*, than erroneous notions concerning the goods of fortune. Finally, the period that must put an end to the system of *coercion* and *punishment*, is intimately connected with the circumstances of property's being placed upon an equitable basis . . .

Of property there are three degrees.

The first and simplest degree, is that of my permanent right in those things, the use of which being attributed to me, a greater sum of benefit or pleasure will result, than could have arisen from their being otherwise appropriated. It is of no consequence, in this case, how I came into possession of them, the only necessary condition being, their superior usefulness to me, and that my title to them is such as is generally acquiesced in, by the community in which I live. Every man is unjust, who conducts himself in such a manner respecting those things, as to infringe, in any degree, upon my power of using them, at the time when the using them will be of real importance to me.

It has already appeared that one of the most essential of the rights of man, is my right to the forbearance of others; not merely that they shall refrain from everything that may, by direct consequence, affect my life, or the possession of my powers, but that they shall refrain from usurping upon my understanding, and shall leave me a certain equal sphere for the exercise of my private judgment. This is necessary, because it is possible for them to be wrong, as well as for me to be so, because the exercise of the understanding is essential to the improvement of man, and because the pain and interruption I suffer, are as real, when they infringe, in my conception only, upon what is of importance to me, as if the infringement had been, in the utmost degree, palpable. Hence it follows, that no man may, in ordinary cases, make use of my apartment, furniture, garments, or my food, in the way of barter or loan, without having first obtained my consent.

The second degree of property, is the empire to which every man is entitled, over the produce of his own industry, even that part of it the use of which ought not to be appropriated to himself . . . He has no right of option in the general disposal of anything which may fall into his hands. Every shilling of his property, and even every, the minutest, exertion of his powers, have received their destination from the degrees of justice. He is only the steward. But still he is the steward. These things must be trusted to his award, checked only by the censorial power that is vested, in the general sense, and favourable or unfavourable opinion, of that portion of mankind among whom he resides. Man is changed, from the capable subject of illimitable excellence, into the vilest and most despicable thing that imagination can conceive, when he is restrained from acting upon the dictates of his understanding . . .

It will readily be perceived, that this second species of property, is in a less rigorous sense fundamental, than the first. It is, in one point of view, a sort of usurpation. It vests in me the preservation of that, which in point of complete and absolute right, belongs to you.

The third degree of property, is that which occupies the most vigilant attention in the civilized states of Europe. It is a system, in whatever manner established, by which one man enters into the faculty of disposing of the produce of another man's industry. There is scarcely any species of wealth, expenditure or splendour, existing in any civilized country, that is not, in some way, produced, by the express manual labour, and corporeal industry, of the inhabitants of that country. The spontaneous productions of the earth are few, and contribute little to wealth, expenditure or splendour. Every man may calculate, in every glass of wine he drinks, and every ornament he annexes to his person, how many individuals have been condemned to slavery and sweat, incessant drudgery, unwholesome food, continual hardships, deplorable ignorance, and brutal insensibility, that he may be supplied with these luxuries. It is a gross imposition, that men are accustomed to put upon themselves, when they talk of the property bequeathed to them by their ancestors. The property is produced by the daily labour of men who are now in existence. All that their ancestors bequeathed to them, was a mouldy patent, which they show, as a title to extort from their neighbours what the labour of those neighbours has produced.

It is clear therefore that the third species of property, is in direct contradiction to the second.

The most desirable state of human society would require, that the quantity of manual labour and corporeal industry to be exerted, and particularly that part of it which is not the uninfluenced choice of our own judgment, but is imposed upon each individual by the necessity of his affairs, should be reduced within as narrow limits as possible. For any man to enjoy the most trivial accommodation, while, at the same time, a similar accommodation is not accessible to every other member of the community is, absolutely speaking, wrong. All refinements of luxury, all inventions that tend to give employment to a great number of labouring hands, are directly adverse to the propagation of happiness. Every additional tax that is laid on, every new channel that is opened for the expenditure of the public money, unless it be compensated (which is scarcely ever the case) by an equivalent deduction from the luxuries of the rich, is so much added to the general stock of ignorance, drudgery and hardship . . .

The fruitful source of crimes consists in this circumstance, one man's possessing in abundance, that of which another man is destitute. We must change the nature of mind, before we can prevent it from being powerfully influenced by this circumstance, when brought strongly home to its situation. Man must cease to have senses, the pleasures of appetite and vanity must cease to gratify, before he can look on tamely at the monopoly of these pleasures. He must cease to have a sense of justice, before he can clearly and fully approve this mixed scene of superfluity and want. It is true, that the proper method of curing this inequality, is by reason and not violence. But the immediate tendency of the established administration, is to persuade men that reason is impotent. The injustice of which they complain, is upheld by force; and they are too easily induced, by force to attempt its correction. All they endeavour, is the partial correction of an injustice, which education tells them is necessary, but more powerful reason affirms to be tyrannical.

Force grows out of monopoly. It might accidentally have occurred among savages, whose appetites exceeded their supply, or whose passions were inflamed by the presence of the object of their desire; but it would gradually have died away, as reason and civilization advanced. Accumulated property has fixed its empire; and henceforth all is an open contention, of the strength and cunning of one party, against the strength and cunning of the other. In this case, the violent and premature struggles of the necessitous, are undoubtedly an evil. They tend to defeat the very cause in the success of which they are most deeply interested; they tend to procrastinate the triumph of justice. But the true crime, in every instance, is in the selfish and partial propensities of men, thinking only of themselves, and despising the emolument of others; and, of these, the rich have their share.

The spirit of oppression, the spirit of servility, and the spirit of fraud, these are the immediate growth of the established administration of property. They are alike hostile to intellectual and moral improvement. The other vices of envy, malice and revenge, are their inseparable companions. In a state of society, where men lived in the midst of plenty, and where all shared alike the bounties of nature, these sentiments would inevitably expire. The narrow principle of selfishness would vanish. No man being obliged to guard his little store, or provide, with anxiety and pain, for his restless wants, each would lose his individual existence, in the thought of the general good. No man would be an enemy to his neighbour, for they would have no subject of contention: and of consequence, philanthropy would resume the empire which reason assigns her. Mind would be delivered from perpetual anxiety about corporal support, and free to expiate in the field of thought which is congenial to her. Each would assist the enquiries of all.

THE TYRANNY OF THE CLOCK

GEORGE WOODCOCK
(From *The Rejection of Politics*, 1972)

In no characteristic is existing society in the West more sharply distinguished from the earlier societies, whether of Europe or the East, than in its conception of time. To the ancient Chinese or Greek, to the Arab herdsman or Mexican peon of today, time is represented by the cyclic processes of nature, the alternation of day and night, the passage from season to season. The nomads and farmers measured and still measure their day from sunrise to sunset, and their years in terms of seedtime and harvest, of the falling leaf and the ice thawing on the lakes and rivers. The farmer worked according to the elements, the craftsman for as long as he felt it necessary to perfect his product. Time was seen as a process of natural change, and men were not concerned in its exact measurement. For this reason civilizations highly developed in other respects had the most primitive means of measuring time: the hour glass with its trickling sand or dripping water, the sun dial, useless on a dull day, and the candle or lamp whose unburnt remnant of oil or wax indicated the hours. All these devices were approximate and inexact, and were often rendered unreliable by the weather or the personal laziness of the tender. Nowhere in the ancient or medieval world were more than a tiny minority of men concerned with time in the terms of mathematical exactitude.

Modern, Western man, however, lives in a world which runs according to the mechanical and mathematical symbols of clock time. The clock dictates his movements and inhibits his actions. The clock turns time from a process of nature into a commodity that can be measured and bought and sold like soap or sultanas. And because, without some means of exact time keeping, industrial capitalism could never have developed and could not continue to exploit the workers, the clock represents an element of mechanical tyranny in the lives of modern men more potent than any individual exploiter or than any other machine. It is therefore valuable to trace the historical process by which the clock influenced the social development of modern European civilization.

It is a frequent circumstance of history that a culture or civilization develops the device that will later be used for its destruction. The ancient Chinese, for example, invented gunpowder, which was developed by the military experts of the West and eventually led to the Chinese civilization itself being destroyed by the high explosives of modern warfare. Similarly, the supreme achievement of the craftsmen of the medieval cities of Europe was the invention of the clock which, with its revolutionary alteration of the concept of time, materially assisted the death of the Middle Ages.

There is a tradition that the clock first appeared in the eleventh century, as a device for ringing bells at regular intervals in the monasteries which, with the regimented life they imposed on their inmates, were the closest social approximation in the Middle Ages to the factory of today. The first authenticated clock, however, appeared in the thirteenth century, and it was not until the fourteenth century that clocks became common as ornaments of the public buildings in German cities.

These early clocks, operated by weights, were not particularly accurate, and it was not until the sixteenth century that any great reliability was attained. In England, for instance, the clock at Hampton Court, made in 1540, is said to have been the first accurate clock in the country. And even the accuracy of the sixteenth-century clocks is relative, for they were equipped only with hour hands. The idea of measuring time in minutes and seconds had been thought out by the early mathematicians as far back as the fourteenth century, but it was not until the invention of the pendulum in 1657 that sufficient accuracy was attained to permit the addition of a minute hand, and the second hand did not appear until the eighteenth century. These two centuries, it should be observed, were those in which capitalism grew to such an extent that it was able to take advantage of the techniques of the industrial revolution to establish its economic domination over society.

The clock, as Lewis Mumford has pointed out, is the key machine of the machine age, both for its influence on technics and for its influence on the habits of men. Technically, the clock was the first really automatic machine that attained any importance in the life of man. Previous to its invention, the common machines were of such a nature that their operation depended on some external and unreliable force, such as human or animal muscles, water or wind. It is true that the Greeks had invented a number of primitive machines, but these were used, like Hero's steam engine, either for obtaining 'supernatural' effects in the temples, or for amusing the tyrants of Levantine cities. But the clock was the first automatic machine that attained public importance and a social function. Clock-making became the industry from which men learnt the elements of machine-making and gained the technical skill that was to produce the complicated machinery of the Industrial Revolution.

Socially the clock had a more radical influence than any other machine, in that it was the means by which the regularization and regimentation of life necessary for an exploiting system of industry could best be assured. The clock provided a means by which time – a category so elusive that no philosophy has yet determined its nature – could be measured concretely in the more tangible terms of space provided by the circumference of a clock dial. Time as duration became disregarded, and men began to talk and think always in 'lengths' of time, just as if they were talking in lengths of calico. And time, being now measurable in mathematical symbols, was regarded as a commodity that could be bought and sold in the same way as any other commodity.

The new capitalists, in particular, became rabidly time-conscious. Time, here symbolizing the labour of the workers, was regarded by them almost as if it were the chief raw material of industry. 'Time is money' was one of the key slogans of capitalist ideology, and the timekeeper was the most significant of the new types of official introduced by the capitalist dispensation.

In the early factories the employers went so far as to manipulate their clocks or sound their factory whistles at the wrong times in order to defraud the workers of a little of this valuable new commodity. Later such practices became less frequent, but the influence of the clock imposed a regularity on the lives of the majority of men that had previously been known only in monasteries. Men actually became like clocks, acting with a repetitive regularity which had no resemblance to the rhythmic life of a natural being. They became, as the Victorian phrase put it, 'as regular as clockwork'. Only in the country districts where the natural lives of animals and plants and the elements still dominated existence, did any large portion of the population fail to succumb to the deadly tick of monotony.

At first this new attitude to time, this new regularity of life, was imposed by the clock-owning masters on the unwilling poor. The factory slave reacted in his spare time by living with a chaotic irregularity which characterized the gin-sodden slums of early nineteenth-century industrialism. Men fled to the timeless worlds of drink or Methodist inspiration. But gradually the idea of regularity spread downwards and among the workers. Nineteenth-century religion and morality played their part in proclaiming the sin of 'wasting time'. The introduction of mass-produced watches and clocks in the 1850s spread time-consciousness among those who had previously merely reacted to the stimulus of the knocker-up or the factory whistle. In the church and the school, in the office and the workshop, punctuality was held up as the greatest of the virtues.

Out of this slavish dependence on mechanical time which spread insidiously into every class in the nineteenth century, there grew up the demoralizing regimentation which today still characterizes factory life. The man who fails to conform faces social disapproval and economic ruin – unless he drops out into a nonconformist way of life in which time ceases to be of prime importance. Hurried meals, the regular morning and evening scramble for trains or buses, the strain of having to work to time schedules, all contribute, by digestive and nervous disturbances, to ruin health and shorten life.

Nor does the financial imposition of regularity tend, in the long run, to greater efficiency. Indeed, the quality of the product is usually much poorer, because the employer, regarding time as a commodity which he has to pay for, forces the operative to maintain such a speed that his work must necessarily be skimped. Quantity rather than quality becoming the criterion, the enjoyment is taken out of the work itself, and the worker in his turn becomes a 'clock-watcher', concerned only with when he will be able to escape to the scanty and monotonous leisure of industrial society, in which he 'kills time' by cramming in as much time-scheduled and mechanical enjoyment of cinema, radio and newspaper as his wage packet and his tiredness will allow. Only if he is willing to accept the hazards of living by his faith or his wits can the man without money avoid living as a slave to the clock.

The problem of the clock is, in general, similar to that of the machine. Mechanized time is valuable as a means of coordinating activities in a highly developed society, just as the machine is valuable as a means of reducing unnecessary labour to a minimum. Both are valuable for the contribution they make to the smooth running of society, and should be used in so far as they assist men to co-operate efficiently and to eliminate monotonous toil and social confusion. But neither should be allowed to dominate men's lives as they do today.

Now the movement of the clock sets the tempo of men's lives – they become the servants of the concept of time which they themselves have made, and are held in fear, like Frankenstein by his own monster. In a sane and free society such an arbitrary domination of man by man-made machines is even more ridiculous than the domination of man by man. Mechanical time would be relegated to its true function as a means of reference and co-ordination, and men would return again to a balanced view of life no longer dominated by time-regulation and the worship of the clock. Complete liberty implies freedom from the tyranny of abstractions as well as from the rule of men.

Part 3
The Wrong Road of Change

If, for almost two centuries, the anarchists have been constant in their insistence that existing society must be radically changed, for more than a century they have been equally constant in their rejection of the means proposed by their rivals on the left, the authoritarian socialists. When Marx and his successors followed more avowedly reactionary political tacticians in arguing that the end justifies any means, the anarchists almost invariably replied that the means conditions any end. In other words, to proceed through the use of power towards the abolition of power, as the Marxists implied in their theory of a transitional dictatorship of the proletariat, is an impossibility, a paradox that refuses to resolve itself.

The conflict is more than a mere struggle between Marxists and anarchists: it is a conflict between all socialists who propose to proceed to the just society through enlarging the powers of the State, and all libertarians who believe that the very use of the State dooms to failure any attempt to achieve even a modest increase in libertarian equality.

As we have seen the conflict of views emerged even before there were movements to project the rival attitudes. Proudhon as an individual wrote in 1846 a letter to Marx as an individual, which is reproduced here and in which the whole basis of the argument is laid out; Marx never replied, at least directly.

Later on, at the height of the rift within the First International between the anarchists and the authoritarians, Michael Bakunin delineated with extraordinary prophetical insight the perils of the Marxist state and the threat of heartless technocratic control in such a society. The theme was developed further by the American individualist anarchist, Benjamin Tucker, when in the 1880s he examined the claims of the two sides and reiterated Bakunin's warning.

Anarchists returning to Russia after the revolutions of 1917 were doomed to see Bakunin's prophecies coming true, to such an extent that when one reads Emma Goldman's account of her disillusionment (a disillusionment that nearly sixty years of history has amply justified), it is with an amazing sense of *déjà vu*; the early anarchists had seen it all, had prophesied accurately, and nothing proved more completely or more agonizingly than the Russian Revolution how rightly they had emphasized the corrupting quality of power acquired and retained. What makes Emma Goldman's account especially interesting is the Nietzschean touch that is evident in her conclusion; only through transvaluing our values – i.e., providing ourselves with a new morality equal to the occasion – can we hope to secure and fulfil the victories of any revolution. Anything less plunges us back into the old morass of tyranny and corruption, as has certainly happened in the Communist world. Some anarchists gave the Bolsheviks the benefit of the doubt and disagreed with Emma Goldman in the 1920s; none would do so now.

TO KARL MARX, 1846

PIERRE-JOSEPH PROUDHON
(From *Correspondence*, 1874-5)

Lyon, 17 May 1846

My dear Monsieur Marx,

I gladly agree to become one of the recipients of your correspondence, whose aims and organization seem to me most useful. Yet I cannot promise to write often or at great length: my varied occupations, combined with a natural idleness, do not favour such epistolary efforts. I must also take the liberty of making certain qualifications which are suggested by various passages of your letter.

First, although my ideas in the matter of organization and realization are at this moment more or less settled, at least as regards principles, I believe it is my duty, as it is the duty of all socialists, to maintain for some time yet the critical or dubitive form; in short, I make profession in public of an almost absolute economic anti-dogmatism.

Let us seek together, if you wish, the laws of society, the manner in which these laws are realized, the process by which we shall succeed in discovering them; but, for God's sake, after having demolished all the *a priori* dogmatisms, do not let us in our turn dream of indoctrinating the people; do not let us fall into the contradiction of your compatriot Martin Luther, who, having overthrown Catholic theology, at once set about, with excommunication and anathema, the foundation of a Protestant theology. For the last three centuries Germany has been mainly occupied in undoing Luther's shoddy work; do not let us leave humanity with a similar mess to clear up as a result of our efforts. I applaud with all my heart your thought of bringing all opinions to light; let us carry on a good and loyal polemic; let us give the world an example of learned and far-sighted tolerance, but let us not, merely because we are at the head of a movement, make ourselves the leaders of a new intolerance, let us not pose as the apostles of a new religion, even if it be the religion of logic, the religion of reason. Let us gather together and encourage all protests, let us brand all exclusiveness, all mysticism; let us never regard a question as exhausted, and when we have used our last argument, let us begin again, if need be, with eloquence and irony. On that condition, I will gladly enter your association. Otherwise – no!

I have also some observations to make on this phrase of your letter: *at the moment of action.* Perhaps you still retain the opinion that no reform is at present possible without a *coup de main*, without what was formerly called a revolution and is really nothing but a shock. That opinion, which I understand, which I excuse, and would willingly discuss, having myself shared it for a long time, my most recent studies have made me abandon completely. I believe we have no need of it in order to succeed; and that consequently we should not put forward *revolutionary action* as a means of social reform, because that pretended means would simply be an appeal to force, to arbitrariness, in brief, a contradiction. I myself put the problem in this way: *to bring about the return to society, by an economic combination, of the wealth which was withdrawn from society by another economic combination.* In other words, through Political Economy to turn the theory of Property against Property in such a way as to engender what you German socialists call *community* and what I will limit myself for the moment to calling *liberty* or *equality*. But I believe that I know the means of solving this problem with only a short delay; I would therefore prefer to burn Property by a slow fire, rather than give it new strength by making a St Bartholomew's night of the proprietors ...

Your very devoted
Pierre-Joseph Proudhon

PERILS OF THE MARXIST STATE

MICHAEL BAKUNIN
(From *Oeuvres*, Vol. IV, 1910, translated by
George Woodcock)

It is natural for the State to break apart the solidarity of mankind and in this way to deny humanity. The State can preserve itself in its integrity and in its full strength only if it establishes itself as the supreme and absolute end, for its own citizens (or, to speak more brutally, for its own sub-jects) at least, since it cannot impose itself on the yet un-conquered subjects of other States. This leads inevitably, through the birth of State morality and 'reasons of State', to a breach with human morality in its universal manifesta-tions and with human reason. The principle of political or State morality is very simple. Since the State is the supreme end, everything favourable to the development of its power is good; everything contrary to it, even the most humane thing in the world, is bad. Such morality is called patriotism. The International is the negation of patriotism and conse-quently it is the negation of the State. And so, if Marx and his friends of the German Socialist Democratic Party were to succeed in introducing the State principle into our programme, they would kill the International.

For its self-preservation, the State must necessarily be ex-ternally powerful, but if it is so in its relations with the outer world, it must equally certainly be powerful internally. Every

State has to be inspired and guided by a special morality conforming to the particular conditions of its existence, a morality which is a negation of human and universal morality. The State must make sure that all its subjects, in thought and above all in deed, are inspired only by the principles of this patriotic and particular morality, and that they remain deaf to the teachings of a purely human or universal morality. Hence the need for State censorship, since too much liberty of thought and opinion is – as Marx believes with good reason if one accepts his eminently political point of view – incompatible with that unanimous adherence which security of the State demands. That such is indeed Marx's opinion is sufficiently proved by the attempts he has made to introduce under plausible pretexts a veiled censorship into the International.

Yet however vigilant such censorship may be, even if the government takes into its own hands all education and all popular instruction, as Mazzini desires and as Marx now wishes, the State can never be sure that forbidden and perilous thought are not insinuated like contraband into the consciousness of the peoples it governs. Forbidden fruit is so attractive to men, and the demon of revolt, that eternal enemy of the State, awakens so easily in their hearts when they are not sufficiently brutalized, that neither education nor instruction, nor even censorship, can effectively guarantee the tranquillity of the State. It still needs a police of devoted agents who will secretly and unobtrusively supervise and steer the current of popular opinions and passions. We have seen that Marx himself has been so convinced of this need that he has thought it necessary to infiltrate with his secret agents all the regions of the International and, above all, Italy, France and Spain.

Yet however perfect from the viewpoint of State security the organization of education and popular instruction, of police and censorship may be, the State cannot be sure of survival unless it has an armed force to defend it against its *internal enemies.*

The State is the government from above downwards, by a minority, of an immense mass of men, extremely varied in their social positions, occupations, interests and aspirations. The ruling minority, even if it were elected a thousand times by universal suffrage and supervised in its acts by popular institutions, could not possibly – unless it were endowed with the omniscience, omnipresence and omnipotence credited by the theologians to God – understand and anticipate the needs or satisfy with an even justice the legitimate and pressing interests of everyone. There will always be malcontents because there will always be people who are sacrificed.

In any case, like the Church, the State is by its very nature a great sacrificer of living men. It is itself an arbitrary being, in whose heart all the positive, living, individual as well as local interests of the people come together, do battle and destroy each other, to become absorbed into that abstraction called the Common interest, the *public good*, the *public safety* and where all individual wills cancel each other out in that further abstraction which is called the *will of the people*. In fact, this so-called will of the people is never anything other than the sacrifice and negation of all those actual and individual wills, in the same way as the so-called public good is merely the sacrifice of their interests. But for such an omnivorous abstraction to impose itself on millions of men, it must be represented and supported by some actual being, some living force. And this being, this force – they have always existed in the Church as the clergy, and in the State as the ruling or governing class.

But in Mr Marx's popular State, we are told, there will be no privileged class at all. All will be equal, not only from the juridical and political but also from the economic point of view. At least we are promised that, though I doubt very much, considering the means of approach and the course that is projected, whether that promise can ever be kept. Perhaps there will no longer be a privileged class as such, but there will be a government and, let me emphasize, an extremely complex government, which will not be content with ruling and administering the masses politically, as all governments now do, but will also administer them economically, concentrating in its own hands production and the 'just' division of wealth, agriculture, the establishment and development of factories, the organization and operation of commerce, and, above all, the application of capital to production by the only banker, the State. All of this will call for an immense development of science, and for the presence in government of many 'heads overflowing with brains'. It will be the reign of *scientific intelligence*, the most aristocratic, despotic, arrogant and scornful of all regimes. There will be a new class, a new hierarchy of real and pretended scholars, and the world will be divided into a majority that rules in the name of science and a vast ignorant majority. Then, let the mass of the ignorant look out!

Such a regime cannot fail to arouse formidable discontent among that mass, and in order to bridle it, the enlightening and liberating government of Mr Marx will need a no less formidable armed force. For government must be strong, says Mr Engels, to keep in order those millions of illiterates whose brutal uprising could destroy and overthrow everything, even a government directed by heads overflowing with brains.

One can well see how, beneath all the democratic and socialistic phrases and promises of Mr Marx's programme, there survives in his State everything that contributes to the truly despotic and brutal nature of all States, whatever their forms of government, and that in the last resort, the People's State so strongly recommended by Mr Marx, and the aristocratic-monarchic State maintained with such skill and power by Mr Bismarck, are completely identical in the nature of both their internal and external aims. Externally there is the same deployment of military power, which means conquest; internally, there is the same employment of armed forces, the last argument of all threatened political powers, against the masses who, tired of always believing, hoping, accepting and obeying, rise in rebellion.

STATE SOCIALISM AND ANARCHISM

BENJAMIN TUCKER
(From *State Socialism and Anarchism*, 1888)

Probably no agitation has ever achieved the magnitude, either in the number of its recruits or the area of its influence, which has been attained by Modern Socialism, and at the same time been so little understood, not only by the hostile and the indifferent, but by the friendly, and even by the great mass of its adherents themselves. This unfortunate and highly danger-ous state of things is due partly to the fact that the human relationships which this movement – if anything so chaotic can be called a movement – aims to transform involve no special class or classes, but literally all mankind; partly to the fact that these relationships are infinitely more varied and complex in their nature than those with which any special reform has ever been called upon to deal; and partly to the fact that the great moulding forces of society, the channels of information and enlightenment, are well nigh exclusively in control of those whose immediate pecuniary interests are antagonistic to the bottom claim of Socialism that labour should be put in possession of its own.

Almost the only persons who may be said to comprehend even approximately the significance, principles, and purposes of Socialism are the chief leaders of the extreme wings of Socialist forces, and perhaps a few of the money kings them-selves. It is a subject of which it has lately been quite the fashion for preacher, professor, and penny-a-liner to treat, and, for the most part, woeful work they have made of it, exciting the derision and pity of those competent to judge. That those prominent in the intermediate Socialistic divisions do not fully understand what they are about is evident from the positions they occupy. If they did; if they were consistent, logical thinkers; if they were what the French call *consequent* men, – their reasoning faculties would long since have driven them to one extreme or the other.

For it is a curious fact that the two extremes of the vast army now under consideration, though united, as has been hinted above, by the common claim that labour shall be put in possession of its own, are more diametrically opposed to each other in their fundamental principles of social action and their methods of reaching the ends aimed at than either is to their common enemy, the existing society. They are based on two principles, the history of whose conflict is almost equivalent to the history of the world since man came into it; and all intermediate parties, including that of the upholders of the existing society, are based upon a compromise between them. It is clear, then, that any intelligent, deep-rooted opposition to the prevailing order of things must come from one or other of these extremes, for anything from any other source, far from being revolutionary in character, could be only in the nature of superficial modification, such as would be utterly unable to concentrate upon itself the degree of attention and interest now bestowed upon Modern Socialism.

The two principles referred to are *Authority* and *Liberty*, and the names of the two schools of Socialistic thought which fully and unreservedly represent one or other of them are, respectively, State Socialism and Anarchism. Whoso knows what these two schools want, and how they propose to get it, understands the Socialistic movement. For, just as it has been said that there is no half-way house between Rome and Reason, so it may be said that there is no half-way house between State Socialism and Anarchism . . .

First, then, State Socialism, which may be described as *the doctrine that all the affairs of men should be managed by the government regardless of individual choice.*

Marx, its founder, concluded that the only way to abolish the class monopolies was to centralize and consolidate all industrial and commercial interests, all productive and distributive agencies, in one vast monopoly in the hands of the State. The government must become banker, manufacturer, farmer, carrier, and merchant, and in these capacities must suffer no competition. Land, tools, and all instruments of production must be wrested from individual hands, and made the property of the collectivity. To the individual can belong only the products to be consumed, not the means of producing them. A man may own his clothes and his food, but not the sewing-machine which makes his shirts or the spade which digs his potatoes. Product and capital are essentially different things; the former belongs to the individuals, the latter to society. Society must seize the capital which belongs to it, by the ballot if it can, by revolution if it must. Once in possession of it, it must administer it on the majority principle, through its organ, the State, utilize it in production and distribution, fix all prices by the amount of labour involved, and employ the whole people in its workshops, farms, stores, etc. The nation must be transformed into a vast bureaucracy, and every individual into a State official. Everything must be done on the cost principle, the people having no motive to make a profit out of themselves. Individuals not being allowed to own capital, no one can employ another or even himself. Every man will be a wage-receiver, and the State the only wage-payer. He who will not work for the State must starve or, more likely, go to prison. All freedom of trade must disappear. Competition must be utterly wiped out. All industrial and commercial activity must be centred in one vast, enormous all-inclusive monopoly. The remedy for *monopolies* is MONOPOLY . . .

What other applications this principle of Authority, once adopted in the economic sphere, will develop is very evident. It means the absolute control by the majority of all individual conduct. The right of such control is already admitted by the State Socialists, though they maintain that, as a matter of fact, the individual would be allowed a much larger liberty than he now enjoys. But he would only be allowed it; he could not claim it as his own. There would be no foundation of society upon a guaranteed equality of the largest possible liberty. Such liberty as might exist would exist by sufferance, and could be taken away at any moment. Constitutional guarantees would be of no avail. There would be but one article in the constitution of a State Socialistic country: 'The right of the majority is absolute.'

The claim of the State Socialists, however, that this right would not be exercised in matters pertaining to the individual in the more intimate and private relations of his life is not borne out by the history of governments. It has ever been the tendency of power to add to itself, to enlarge its sphere, to encroach beyond the limits set for it; and where the habit of resisting such encroachment is not fostered, and the individual is not taught to be jealous of his rights, individuality gradually disappears and the government or State becomes the all-in-all. Control naturally accompanies responsibility. Under the system of State Socialism, therefore, which holds the community responsible for the health, wealth and wisdom of the individual, it is evident that the community, through its majority expression, will insist more and more on prescribing the conditions of health, wealth, and wisdom, thus impairing and finally destroying individual independence, and with it all sense of individual responsibility . . .

Such is the ideal of the logical State Socialist, such the goal which lies at the end of the road that Karl Marx took. Let us now follow the fortunes of Warren and Proudhon, who took the other road, – the road of Liberty.

This brings us to Anarchism, which may be described as *the doctrine that all the affairs of men should be managed by individuals or voluntary associations, and that the State should be abolished.*

When Warren and Proudhon, in prosecuting their search for justice to labour, came face to face with the obstacle of class monopolies, they saw that these monopolies rested upon Authority, and concluded that the thing to be done was, not to strengthen this Authority and thus make monopoly universal, but to utterly uproot Authority and give full sway to the opposite principle, Liberty, by making competition, the antithesis of monopoly, universal. They saw in competition the great leveller of prices to the labour cost of production. In this they agreed with the political economists. The query then naturally presented itself why all prices do not fall to labour cost; why there is any room for incomes acquired otherwise than by labour; in a word, why the usurer, the receiver of interest, rent, and profit, exists. The answer was found in the present one-sidedness of competition. It was discovered that capital had so manipulated legislation that unlimited competition is allowed in supplying productive labour, thus keeping wages down to the starvation point, or as near it as practicable; that a great deal of competition is always allowed in supplying productive labour, or the labour of the mercantile classes, thus keeping, not the prices of goods, but the merchant's actual profits on them, down to a point somewhat approximating equitable wages for the merchant's work; but that almost no competition at all is allowed in supplying capital, upon the aid of which both productive and distributive labour are dependent for their power of achievement, thus keeping the rate of interest on money and of house-rent and ground-rent at as high a point as the necessities of the people will bear.

On discovering this, Warren and Proudhon charged the political economists with being afraid of their own doctrine. The Manchester men were accused of being inconsistent. They believed in liberty to compete with the labourer in order to reduce his wages, but not in liberty to compete with the capitalist in order to reduce his usury. *Laissez faire* was very good sauce for the goose, labour, but very poor sauce for the gander, capital. But how to correct this inconsistency, how to serve this gander with this goose, how to put capital at the service of business men and labourers at cost, or free of usury, – that was the problem.

Marx, as we have seen, solved it by declaring capital to be a different thing from product, and maintaining that it belonged to society and should be seized by society and employed for the benefit of all alike. Proudhon scoffed at this distinction between capital and product. He maintained that capital and product are not different kinds of wealth; that all wealth undergoes an incessant transformation from capital into product and from product into capital, the process repeating itself interminably; . . . and that the same laws of equity govern the possession of the one that govern the possession of the other.

For these and other reasons Proudhon and Warren found themselves unable to sanction any such plan as the seizure of capital by society. But, though opposed to socializing the ownership of capital, they aimed, nevertheless, to socialize its effects by making its use beneficial to all instead of a means of impoverishing the many to enrich the few. And when the light burst in upon them, they saw that this could be done by subjecting capital to the natural law of competition, thus bringing the price of its use down to cost, – that is, to nothing beyond the expenses incidental to handling and transferring it. So they raised the banner of Absolute Free Trade; free trade at home, as well as with foreign countries; the logical carrying out of the Manchester doctrine; *laissez faire* the universal rule. Under this banner they began their fight upon monopolies, whether the all-inclusive monopoly of the State Socialists, or the various class monopolies that now prevail.

Of the latter they distinguished four of principal importance: the money monopoly, the land monopoly, the tariff monopoly, and the patent monopoly.

First in the importance of its evil influence they considered the money monopoly, which consists of the privilege given by the government to certain individuals, or to individuals holding certain kinds of property, of issuing the circulating medium, a privilege which is now enforced in this country by a national tax of ten per cent upon all other persons who attempt to furnish a circulating medium, and by State laws making it a criminal offence to issue notes as currency. It is claimed that the holders of this privilege control the rate of interest, the rate of rent of houses and buildings, and the prices in goods, the first directly, and the second and third indirectly. For, say Proudhon and Warren, if the business of banking were made free to all, more and more persons would enter into it until the competition should become sharp enough to reduce the price of lending money to the labour cost, which statistics show to be less than three-quarters of one per cent. In that case the thousands of people who are now deterred from going into business by the ruinously high rates which they must pay for capital with which to start and carry on business would find their difficulties removed. If they have property which they do not desire to convert into money by sale, a bank will take it as collateral for a loan of a certain proportion of its market value at less than one per cent discount. If they have no property, but are industrious, honest and capable, they will generally be able to get their individual notes endorsed by a sufficient number of known and solvent parties; and on such business paper they will be able to get a loan at a bank on similar favourable terms. Thus interests will fall at a blow. The banks will really not be lending capital at all, but will be doing business on the capital of their customers, the business consisting in an exchange of the known and widely available credits of the banks for the unknown and unavailable, but equally good, credits of the customers, and a charge therefore of less than one per cent, not as interest for the use of capital, but as pay for the labour of running the banks. This facility of acquiring capital will give an unheard-of impetus to business, and consequently create an unprecedented demand for labour, – a demand which will always be in excess of the supply, directly the contrary of the present condition of the labour market . . . Labour will then be in a position to dictate its wages, and will thus secure its natural wage, its entire product. Thus the same blow that strikes interest down will send wages up. But this is not all. Down will go profits also. For merchants, instead of buying at high prices on credit, will borrow money of the banks at less than one per cent, buy at low prices for cash and correspondingly reduce the prices of their goods to their customers. And with the rest will go house-rent. For no one who can borrow capital at one per cent with which to build a house of his own will consent to pay rent to a landlord at a higher rate than that. Such is the vast claim made by Proudhon and Warren as to the results of the simple abolition of the money monopoly.

Second in importance comes the land monopoly, the evil effects of which are seen principally in exclusively agricultural countries, like Ireland. This monopoly consists in the enforcement by government of land titles which do not rest upon personal occupancy and cultivation. It was obvious to Warren and Proudhon that, as soon as individuals should no longer be protected by their fellows in anything but personal occupancy and cultivation of land, ground-rent would disappear, and so usury have one less leg to stand on . . .

Third, the tariff monopoly, which consists in fostering production at high prices under favourable conditions by visiting with the penalty of taxation those who patronize production at low prices and under favourable conditions. The evil to which this monopoly gives rise might more properly be called *mis*usury than usury, because it compels labour to pay, not exactly for the use of capital, but rather for the misuse of capital. The abolition of this monopoly would result in a great reduction in the price of all articles taxed, and this saving to the labourers who consume these articles would be another step toward securing the labourer his natural wage, his entire product . . .

Fourth, the patent monopoly, which consists in protecting inventors and authors against competition for a period long enough to enable them to extort from the people a reward enormously in excess of the labour measure of their services,

– in other words, in giving certain people a right of property for a term of years in laws and facts of nature, and the power to exact tribute from others for the use of this natural wealth, which should be open to all. The abolition of this monopoly would fill its beneficiaries with a wholesome fear of competition which should cause them to be satisfied with pay for their services equal to that which other labourers get for theirs, and to secure it by placing their products and works on the market at the outset at prices so low that their lines of business would be no more tempting to competitors than any other lines.

The development of the economic programme which consists in the destruction of these monopolies and the substitution for them of the freest competition led its authors to a perception of the fact that all their thought rested on a very fundamental principle, the freedom of the individual, his right to sovereignty over himself, his products, and his affairs, and of rebellion against the dictation of external authority. Just as the idea of taking capital away from individuals and giving it to the government started by Marx in a path which ends in making the government everything and the individual nothing, so the idea of putting it within easy reach of all individuals started Warren and Proudhon in a path which ends in making the individual everything and the government nothing. If the individual has a right to govern himself, all external government is tyranny. Hence the necessity of abolishing the State. This was the logical conclusion to which Warren and Proudhon were forced, and it became the fundamental article of their political philosophy. It is the doctrine which Proudhon named An-archism, a word derived from the Greek, and meaning, not necessarily absence of order, as is generally supposed, but absence of rule. The Anarchists are simply unterrified Jeffersonian Democrats. They believe that 'the best government is that which governs least', and that which governs least is no government at all. Even the simple police function of protecting persons and property they deny to government supported by compulsory taxation . . . Compulsory taxation is to them the life principle of all the monopolies, and passive, but organized, resistance to the tax-collector they contemplate, when the proper time comes, as one of the most effective methods of accomplishing their purposes . . .

Nor does the Anarchist scheme furnish any code of morals to be imposed upon the individual. 'Mind your own business' is its only moral law. Interference with another's business is a crime, the only crime, and as such properly to be resisted. In accordance with this view the Anarchists look upon attempts to arbitrarily suppress vice as in themselves crimes. They believe liberty and the resultant social well-being to be a sure cure for all vices. But they recognize the right of the drunkard, the gambler, the rake and the harlot to live their lives until they shall freely choose to abandon them.

In the matter of the maintenance and rearing of children, the Anarchists would neither institute the communistic nursery which the State Socialists favour, or keep the communistic school system which now prevails. The nurse and teacher, like the doctor and the preacher, must be selected voluntarily, and their services must be paid for by those who patronize them. Parental rights must not be taken away, and parental responsibilities must not be foisted upon them.

Even in so delicate a matter as that of the relations of the sexes the Anarchists do not shrink from the application of their principle. They acknowledge and defend the right of any man and woman, or any men and women, to love each other for as long or as short a time as they can, will, or may. To them legal marriage and legal divorce are equal absurdities. They look forward to the time when every individual, whether man or woman, shall be self-supporting, and when each shall have an independent home of his or her own, whether it be a separate house or rooms in a house with others: when the love relations between these independent individuals shall be as varied as are individual inclinations and attractions; and when the children born of these relations shall belong exclusively to the mothers until old enough to belong to themselves.

Such are the main features of the Anarchistic social ideal. There is wide difference of opinion among those who hold it as to the best method of obtaining it. Time forbids the treatment of that phase of the subject here. I will simply call attention to the fact that it is an ideal utterly inconsistent with that of those Communists who falsely call themselves Anarchists while at the same time advocating a *régime* of Archism fully as despotic as that of the State Socialists themselves. And it is an ideal that can be as little advanced by the forcible expropriation recommended by John Most and Prince Kropotkin as retarded by the brooms of those Mrs Partingtons of the bench who sentence them to prison; an ideal which the martyrs of Chicago did far more to help by their glorious death upon the gallows for the common cause of Socialism than by their unfortunate advocacy during their lives, in the name of Anarchism, of force as a revolutionary agent and authority as a safeguard of the new social order. The Anarchists believe in liberty both as ends and means, and are hostile to anything that antagonizes it.

THE FAILURE OF THE
RUSSIAN REVOLUTION

Emma Goldman
(From *My Further Disillusionment with Russia*, 1924)

It is now clear why the Russian Revolution, as conducted by the Communist Party, was a failure. The political power of the party, organized and centralized in the State, sought to maintain itself by all means at hand. The central authorities attempted to force the activities of the people into forms corresponding with the purposes of the party. The sole aim of the latter was to strengthen the State and monopolize all economical, political and social activities – even all cultural manifestations. The revolution had an entirely different object, and in its very character it was the negation of authority and centralization. It strove to open ever-larger fields for proletarian expression and to multiply the phases of individual and collective effort. The aims and tendencies of the Revolution were diametrically opposed to those of the ruling political party.

Just as diametrically opposed were the *methods* of the Revolution and of the State. Those of the former were inspired by the spirit of the Revolution itself: that is to say, by emancipating from all oppressive and limiting forces; in short, *by libertarian principles*. The methods of the State, on the contrary – of the Bolshevik State as of every government – were based on *coercion*, which in the course of things necessarily developed into systematic violence, oppression and terrorism. Thus two opposing tendencies struggled for supremacy: the Bolshevik State against the Revolution. That struggle was a life-and-death struggle. The two tendencies, contradictory in aims and methods, could not work harmoniously: the triumph of the State meant the defeat of the Revolution.

It would be an error to assume that the failure of the Revolution was due entirely to the character of the Bolsheviki. Fundamentally, it was the result of the principles and methods of Bolshevism. It was the authoritarian spirit and principles of the State which stifled the libertarian and liberating aspirations. Were any other political party in control of the government in Russia the result would have been essentially the same. It is not so much the Bolsheviki who killed the Russian Revolution as the Bolshevik idea. It was Marxism, however modified; in short, fanatical governmentalism . . . The Russian Revolution reflects on a small scale the century-old struggle of the libertarian principle against the authoritarian. For what is progress if not the more general acceptance of the principles of liberty as against those of coercion? The Russian Revolution was a libertarian step defeated by the Bolshevik Party, by the temporary victory of the reactionary, the governmental idea . . .

The libertarian principle was strong in the initial days of the Revolution, the need for free expression all-absorbing. But when the first wave of enthusiasm receded into the ebb of everyday prosaic life, a firm conviction was needed to keep the fires of liberty burning. There was only a comparative handful in the great vastness of Russia to keep those fires lit – the Anarchists, whose number was small and whose efforts, absolutely suppressed under the Tsar, had had no time to bear fruit. The Russian people, to some extent instinctive Anarchists, were yet too unfamiliar with true libertarian principles and methods to apply them effectively to life. Most of the Russian Anarchists were unfortunately still in the meshes of limited group activities and of individual endeavour as against the more important social and collective efforts . . .

But the failure of the Anarchists in the Russian Revolution – in the sense just indicated – does by no means argue the defeat of the libertarian idea. On the contrary, the Russian Revolution has demonstrated beyond doubt that the State idea, State Socialism, in all its manifestations (economic, political, social, educational) is entirely and hopelessly bankrupt. Never before in all history has authority, government, the State, proved so inherently static, reactionary and even counter-revolutionary in effect. In short, the very antithesis of revolution.

It remains true, as it has through all progress, that only the libertarian spirit and method can bring man a step further in his eternal striving for the better, finer, and freer life . . . all political tenets and parties notwithstanding, no revolution can be truly and permanently successful unless it puts its emphatic veto upon all tyranny and centralization, and determinedly strives to make the revolution a real revaluation of all economic, social, and cultural values. Not mere substitution of one political party for another in control of the Government, not the masking of autocracy by proletarian slogans, not political scene shifting of any kind, but the complete reversal of all these authoritarian principles will alone serve the revolution.

In the economic field this transformation must be in the hands of the industrial masses: the latter have the choice between an industrial State and anarcho-syndicalism. In the case of the former the menace to the constructive development of the new social structure would be as great as from the political State. It would become a dead weight upon the growth of the new forms of life. For that very reason syndicalism (or industrialism) alone is not, as its exponents claim, sufficient unto itself. It is only when the libertarian spirit permeates the economic organizations of the workers that the manifold creative energies of the people can manifest themselves and the revolution be safeguarded and defended. Only free initiative and popular participation in the affairs of the revolution can prevent the terrible blunders committed in Russia. For instance, with fuel only a hundred versts from

Petrograd there would have been no necessity for that city to suffer from cold had the workers' economic organizations of Petrograd been free to exercise their initiative for the common good. The peasants of the Ukraine would not have been hampered in the cultivation of their land had they had access to the farm implements stacked up in the warehouses of Kharkov and other industrial centres awaiting orders from Moscow for their distribution. These are characteristic examples of Bolshevik governmentalism and centralization, which should serve as a warning to the workers of Europe and America of the destructive effects of Statism.

The industrial power of the masses, expressed through their libertarian associations – anarcho-syndicalism – is alone able to organize successfully the economic life and carry on production. On the other hand, the co-operatives, working in harmony with the industrial bodies, serve as the distributing and exchange media between city and country, and at the same time link in fraternal bond the industrial and agrarian masses. A common tie of mutual service and aid is created which is the strongest bulwark of the revolution – far more effective than compulsory labour, the Red Army, or terrorism. In that way alone can revolution act as a leaven to quicken the development of new social forms and inspire the masses to greater achievements.

But libertarian industrial organizations and the co-operatives are not the only media in the interplay of the complex phases of social life. There are the cultural forces which, though closely related to the economic activities, have yet their own functions to perform . . . In Russia this was made impossible almost from the beginning of the October Revolution, by the violent separation of the intelligentsia and the masses. It is true that the original offender in this case was the intelligentsia, which in Russia tenaciously clung – as it does in other countries – to the coat-tails of the bourgeoisie. This element, unable to comprehend the significance of revolutionary events, strove to stem the tide by wholesale sabotage. But in Russia there was also another kind of intelligentsia – one with a glorious revolutionary past of a hundred years. That part of the intelligentsia kept faith with the people, though it could not unreservedly accept the new dictatorship. The fatal error of the Bolsheviki was that they made no distinction between the two elements. They met sabotage with wholesale terror against the intelligentsia as a class, and inaugurated a campaign of hatred more intensive that the persecution of the bourgeoisie itself – a method which created an abyss between the intelligentsia and the proletariat and reared a barrier against constructive work.

Lenin was the first to realize that criminal blunder. He pointed out that it was a grave error to lead the workers to believe that they could build up the industries and engage in cultural work without the aid and co-operation of the intelligentsia. The proletariat had neither the knowledge nor the training for the task, and the intelligentsia had to be restored in the direction of industrial life. But the recognition of one error never safeguarded Lenin and his party from immediately committing another. The technical intelligentsia was called back on terms which added disintegration to the antagonism against the regime.

While the workers continued to starve, engineers, industrial experts, and technicians received high salaries, special privileges, and the best rations. They became the pampered employees of the State and the new slave drivers of the masses. The latter, fed for years on the fallacious teachings that muscle alone is necessary for a successful revolution and that only physical labour is productive, and incited by the campaign of hatred which stamped every intellectual a counterrevolutionist and speculator, could not make peace with those they had been taught to scorn and distrust.

Unfortunately Russia is not the only country where this proletarian attitude against the intelligentsia prevails. Everywhere political demagogues play upon the ignorance of the masses, teach them that education and culture are bourgeois prejudices, that the workers can do without them, and that they alone are able to rebuild society. The Russian Revolution has made it very clear that both brain and muscle are indispensable to the work of social regeneration. Intellectual and physical labour are closely related in the social body as brain and hand in the human organism. One cannot function without the other . . .

*   *   *   *   *

In previous pages I have tried to point out why Bolshevik principles, methods, and tactics failed, and that similar principles and methods applied in any other country, even of the highest industrial development, must fail. I have further shown that it is not only Bolshevism that failed, but Marxism itself. That is to say, the STATE IDEA, the *authoritarian principle*, has been proven bankrupt by the experience of the Russian Revolution. If I were to sum up my whole argument in one sentence I should say: The inherent tendency of the State is to concentrate, to narrow, and monopolize all social activities; the nature of revolution is, on the contrary, to grow, to broaden, and disseminate itself in ever-wider circles. In other words, the State is institutional and static; revolution is fluent, dynamic. These two tendencies are incompatible and mutually destructive. The State idea killed the Russian Revolution and it must have had the same result in all other revolutions, unless *the libertarian idea prevails.*

Yet I go much further. It is not only Bolshevism, Marxism, and Governmentalism which are fatal to revolution as well as to all vital human progress. The main cause of the defeat of the Russian Revolution lies much deeper. It is to be found in the whole Socialist conception of revolution itself.

The dominant, almost general, idea of revolution – particularly the Socialist idea – is that revolution is a violent change of social conditions through which one social class, the working class, becomes dominant over another class, the capitalist class. It is the conception of a purely physical change, and as such it involves only political scene shifting and institutional rearrangements. Bourgeois dictatorship is replaced by the 'dictatorship of the proletariat' – or by that of its 'advance guard', the Communist Party; Lenin takes the seat of the Romanovs, the Imperial Cabinet is rechristened Soviet of People's Commissars, Trotsky is appointed Minister of War, and a labourer becomes the Military Governor-General of Moscow. That is, in essence, the Bolshevik conception of revolution, as translated into actual practice. And with a few minor alterations it is also the idea of revolution held by all other Socialist parties.

This conception is inherently and fatally false. Revolution

is indeed a violent process. But if it is to result only in a change of dictatorship, in a shifting of names and political personalities, then it is hardly worth while. It is surely not worth all the struggle and sacrifice, the stupendous loss in human life and cultural values that result from every revolution. If such a revolution were even to bring social well-being (which has not been the case in Russia) then it would also not be worth the terrific price paid: mere improvement can be brought about without bloody revolution. It is not palliatives or reforms that are the real aim and purpose of revolution, as I conceive it.

In my opinion – a thousandfold strengthened by the Russian experience – the great mission of revolution, of the SOCIAL REVOLUTION, is a *fundamental transvaluation of values.* A transvaluation not only of social, but also of human values. The latter are even pre-eminent, for they are the basis of all social values. Our institutions and conditions rest upon deep-seated ideas. To change those conditions and at the same time leave the underlying ideas and values intact means only a superficial transformation, one that cannot be permanent or bring real betterment. It is a change of form only, not of substance, as so tragically proved by Russia.

It is at once the great failure and the great tragedy of the Russian Revolution that it attempted (in the leadership of the ruling political party) to change only institutions and conditions while ignoring entirely the human and social values involved in the Revolution. Worse yet, in its mad passion for power, the Communist State even sought to strengthen and deepen the very ideas and conceptions which the Revolution had come to destroy. It supported and encouraged all the worst antisocial qualities and systematically destroyed the already awakened conception of the new revolutionary values. The sense of justice and equality, the love of liberty and of human brotherhood – these fundamentals of the real regeneration of society – the Communist State suppressed to the point of extermination. Man's instinctive sense of equity was branded as weak sentimentality; human dignity and liberty became a bourgeois superstition; the sanctity of life, which is the very essence of social reconstruction, was condemned as unrevolutionary, almost counter-revolutionary. This fearful perversion

of fundamental values bore within itself the seed of destruction. With the conception that the Revolution was only a
means of securing political power, it was inevitable that all
revolutionary values should be subordinate to the needs of
the Socialist State; indeed, exploited to further the security
of the newly acquired governmental power. 'Reasons of State',
masked as the 'interests of the Revolution and of the People'.
became the sole criterion of action, even of feeling. Violence,
the tragic inevitability of revolutionary upheavals, became an
established custom, a habit, and was presently enthroned as the
most powerful and 'ideal' institution. Did not Zinoviev himself canonize Dzerzhinsky, the head of the bloody Tcheka,
as the 'saint of the Revolution'? Were not the greatest public
honours paid by the State to Uritsky, the founder and sadistic
chief of the Petrograd Tcheka?

This perversion of the ethical values soon crystallized into
the all-dominating slogan of the Communist Party: THE
END JUSTIFIES ALL MEANS. Similarly in the past the
Inquisition and Jesuits adopted this motto and subordinated
to it all morality. It avenged itself upon the Jesuits as it did
upon the Russian Revolution. In the wake of this slogan
followed lying, deceit, hypocrisy and treachery, murder, open
and secret. It should be of utmost interest to students of social
psychology that two movements as widely separated in time
and ideas as Jesuitism and Bolshevism *reached exactly similar
results* in the evolution of the principle that the end justifies
all means. The historic parallel, almost entirely ignored so
far, contains a most important lesson for all coming revolutions and for the whole future of mankind.

There is no greater fallacy than the belief that aims and
purposes are one thing, while methods and tactics are another.
This conception is a potent menace to social regeneration. All
human experience teaches that methods and means cannot be
separated from the ultimate aim. The means employed become,
through individual habit and social practice, part and parcel
of the final purpose; they influence it, modify it, and presently
the aims and means become identical. From the day of my
arrival in Russia I felt it, at first vaguely, then ever more
consciously and clearly. The great and inspiring aims of the
Revolution became so clouded with and obscured by the

methods used by the ruling political power that it was hard to distinguish what was temporary means and what final purpose. Psychologically and socially the means necessarily influence and alter the aims. The whole history of man is continuous proof of the maxim that to divest one's methods of ethical concepts means to sink into the depths of utter demoralization. In that lies the real tragedy of the Bolshevik philosophy as applied to the Russian Revolution. May this lesson not be in vain.

No revolution can ever succeed as a factor of liberation unless the MEANS used to further it be identical in spirit and tendency with the PURPOSES to be achieved. Revolution is the negation of the existing, a violent protest against man's inhumanity to man with all the thousand and one slaveries it involves. It is the destroyer of dominant values upon which a complex system of injustice, oppression, and wrong has been built up by ignorance and brutality. It is the herald of NEW VALUES, ushering in a transformation of the basic relations of man to man, and of man to society. It is not a mere reformer, patching up some social evils; not a mere changer of forms and institutions; not only a re-distributor of social well-being. It is all that, yet more, much more. It is, first and foremost, the TRANSVALUATOR, the bearer of *new* values. It is the great TEACHER of the NEW ETHICS, inspiring man with a new concept of life, and its manifestations in social relationships. It is the mental and spiritual regenerator.

Its first ethical precept is the identity of means used and aims sought. The ultimate end of all revolutionary social change is to establish the sanctity of human life, the dignity of man, the right of every human being to liberty and well-being. Unless this be the essential aim of revolution, violent social changes would have no justification. For *external* social alterations can be, and have been, accomplished by the normal processes of evolution. Revolution, on the contrary, signifies not merely *external* change, but *internal*, basic, fundamental change. That internal change of concepts and ideas, permeating ever-larger social strata, finally culminates in the violent upheaval known as revolution. Shall that climax reverse the process of transvaluation, turn against it, betray it? That is what happened in Russia. On the contrary, the revolution itself must quicken and further the process of which it is the cumulative expression; its main mission is to inspire it, to carry it to greater heights, give it fullest scope•for expression. Only thus is revolution true to itself.

Applied in practice it means that the period of the actual revolution, the so-called transitory stage, must be the introduction, the prelude to the new social conditions. It is the threshold to the NEW LIFE, the new HOUSE OF MAN AND HUMANITY. As such it must be of the spirit of the new life, harmonious with the construction of the new edifice.

Today is the parent of tomorrow. The present casts its shadow far into the future. That is the law of life, individual and social. Revolution that divests itself of ethical values thereby lays the foundation of injustice, deceit and oppression for the future society. The means used to *prepare* the future become its *cornerstone*. Witness the tragic condition of Russia. The methods of State centralization have paralysed individual initiative and effort; the tyranny of the dictatorship has cowed the people into slavish submission and all but extinguished the fires of liberty; organized terrorism has depraved and brutalized the masses and stifled every idealistic life, and all sense of dignity of man and the value of life has been eliminated; coercion at every step has made effort bitter, labour a punishment, has turned the whole of existence into a scheme of mutual deceit, and has revived the lowest and most brutal instincts of man. A sorry heritage to begin a new life of freedom and brotherhood.

It cannot be sufficiently emphasized that revolution is in vain unless inspired by its ultimate ideal. Revolutionary methods must be in tune with revolutionary aims. The means used to further the revolution must harmonize with its purposes. In short, the ethical values which the revolution is to establish in the new society must be *initiated* with the revolutionary activities of the so-called transitional period. The latter can serve as a real and dependable bridge to the better life only if built of the same material as the life to be achieved. Revolution is the mirror of the coming day . . .

Part 4
Revolution? Rebellion? Insurrection?

By no means all those who can be described as Anarchists would regard themselves as revolutionaries, despite the fact that all of them look forward to a fundamental transformation of society and its goals. It is largely a question of semantics. Godwin, Tolstoy, Gandhi, would have objected to the suggestion of violent cataclysm which the myth of the Revolution has implanted in the popular mind. Max Stirner, in the passage quoted in this section, makes a distinction (similar to those made in later years by Herbert Read and Albert Camus) between revolution and insurrection, favouring the latter. But in fact when we examine what he says it seems clear that he conceived the Revolution as a re-arrangement of power relationships, and that what he meant by insurrection has in fact a great deal in common with the general uprising of which the revolutionary Bakunin used to talk when he contemplated inciting the peasants to insurrection. Kropotkin always argued that revolution was merely a speeding-up of evolution, and was inclined to downplay – though he never disowned – its violent aspects, while Proudhon, though he talked incessantly of revolution, meant by this term a peaceful but sweeping social transformation rather than any cataclysmic act, and foresaw its achievement by a grassroots change in economic relations – what he called 'the war of the workshops'.

At the same time, most anarchists have given thought to the practical means by which they might overthrow the existing order or undermine it by beginning to build the new order within its structure. In 'Anarchist Action' the contemporary British writer Nicolas Walter provided a useful summary of the varying approaches of different kinds of anarchist to the problem of achieving the transition from the old order to the new, and Murray Bookchin's 'Affinity Groups' is an interesting footnote on the anarchist organization of groups for action – a kind of organization very different from that of the ordinary political parties. In 'Revolution and Social Reality' Alex Comfort presents a criticism of the traditional revolutionary scenario, and suggests anarchist alternatives more in keeping with modern reality.

The debate over the morality and the practicality of violent methods has continued among anarchists for over a century and it still leaves them divided. Probably the majority have been willing rather than eager to use violence, though they have been inclined, as Kropotkin is in the passage we reproduce, to point out that they are very far from holding a monopoly in this respect.

Anarchist violence came into particular prominence at the turn of the century, when a small number of mainly individualist anarchists assassinated a series of prominent political figures and also a number of uninvolved people. The acts of these men, and the enormous publicity that attended them, undoubtedly did the anarchist cause a great deal of harm at the time, but the terrorists had and expressed a point of view of their own, and to gain a full understanding of anarchist attitudes they must be heard. Alexander Berkman made an attempt on the life of the American steel magnate Henry Clay Frick in 1892, and we include his own description of the attempt, which reveals much about his feelings at the time; we also reproduce the impressive attack he made many years later on the violence that permeates the lawful world; clearly, like many other anarchists of his kind, Berkman thought that his deeds might help break a way through to an era of trust and peacefulness. This dichotomous view is revealed dramatically in the statement of Emile Henry to the court that tried him: there is a repellent precision and collectedness about Henry's statement, particularly when one remembers that the bomb he threw into the Café Terminus was meant to kill people whom individually he had no reason to condemn, but still, behind the cold and audacious assassin, there lurks a generous vision of a happy future into which he knows he cannot survive, yet which he anticipates with his own grim kind of joy.

The diametrical opposite in terms of anarchist method to the acts of terrorists is the kind of radical non-violent civil disobedience recommended by the anarchists who are also pacifists; Thoreau's 'Civil Disobedience' is the classic text on this kind of peaceful withdrawal of co-operation, and Tolstoy's 'Resistance to Military Service' not merely states the case for the conscientious objectors in all wars, but also looks forward to Gandhi's great campaigns of *Satyagraha*, through which the British were persuaded to leave India in peace.

Anarcho-syndicalism – the organization of the workers in unions that will serve as fighting formations in achieving revolutionary gains in the general strike and then as the infra-structures of liberated industry – has enjoyed much prestige among anarchists for the past eighty years, and it was considered by many as the ideal solution to the problem of revolutionary victory. Though they were inclined to disown each other, there was in fact a great deal in common between the revolutionary syndicalists and the advocates of civil disobedience, since both placed great value in the universal withdrawal of co-operation. In the three extracts which follow on this subject, George Woodcock defines anarcho-syndicalism in a pamphlet of the 1940s; the speeches by Monatte and Malatesta form the substance of the debate at the Amsterdam Anarchist Congress of 1907 between those who were willing to accept the syndicates as the main instruments of anarchist struggle and those, like Malatesta, who wished to retain the essential anarchist goal of struggling for the liberation of all men rather than for that of the working class alone, and who feared that the syndicates might become ossified class institutions.

THE PRINCIPLE OF THE REVOLUTION

PIERRE-JOSEPH PROUDHON
(From *Les Confessions d'un Révolutionnaire*, 1849)

All men are equal and free; society, by nature and destination, is therefore autonomous and ungovernable. If the sphere of activity of each citizen is determined by the natural division of work and by the choice he makes of a profession, if the social functions are combined in such a way as to produce a harmonious effect, order results from the free activity of all men; there is no government. Whoever puts his hand on me to govern me is an usurper and a tyrant; I declare him my enemy.

But social physiology does not immediately allow that egalitarian organization; the idea of providence, which was one of the first to appear in society, has been in opposition to it. Equality comes to us by a succession of tyrannies and governments, in which liberty is continually at grips with absolutism, like Israel and Jehovah. Thus equality is born continually for us out of inequality; liberty has government for its point of departure . . . authority was the first social idea of the human race. And the second was to work immediately for the abolition of authority, each wishing to use it as the instrument of his liberty against the liberty of others . . .

The principle of the revolution, we know it still, is Liberty. Liberty! That is to say: 1. political enfranchisement, by the organization of universal suffrage, by the independent centralization of social functions, by the incessant and perpetual revision of the Constitution; 2. industrial enfranchisement, by the mutual guarantee of credit and sale. In other words: no more government of man by man, by means of the accumulation of powers; no more exploitation of man by man by means of the accumulation of capital.

REVOLUTION AND INSURRECTION

MAX STIRNER
(From *The Ego and His Own*, 1907, translated by
Steve Byington)

Revolution and insurrection must not be looked upon as
synonymous. The former consists in an overturning of conditions, of the established condition or status, the State or
society, and is accordingly a *political* or *social* act; the latter
has indeed for its unavoidable consequence a transformation
of circumstances, yet does not start from it but from men's
discontent with themselves, is not an armed rising, but a
rising of individuals, a getting up, without regard to the
arrangements that spring from it. The Revolution aimed at
new *arrangements*; insurrection leads us no longer to *let* ourselves be arranged, but to arrange ourselves, and sets no
glittering hopes on 'institutions'. It is not a fight against the
established, since, if it prospers, the established collapses of
itself; it is only a working forth of me out of the established. If I leave the established, it is dead and passes into
decay. Now, as my object is not the overthrow of an established order by my elevation above it, my purpose and deed
are not a political or social but (as directed toward myself
and my ownness alone) an *egoistic* purpose and deed.

ANARCHIST ACTION

NICOLAS WALTER
(From *About Anarchism*, 1969)

The change from theorizing about anarchism to putting it
into practice means a change of organization. The typical discussion or propaganda group, which is open to easy participa-

tion by outsiders and easy observation by the authorities, and which is based on each member doing what he wants to do and not doing what he doesn't want to do, will become more exclusive and more formal. This is a moment of great danger, since an attitude which is too rigid leads to authoritarianism and sectarianism, while one which is too lax leads to confusion and irresponsibility. It is a moment of even greater danger, since when anarchism becomes a serious matter anarchists become a serious threat to the authorities, and real persecution begins.

The most common form of anarchist action is for agitation over an issue to become participation in a campaign. This may be reformist, for something which would not change the whole system, or revolutionary, for a change in the system itself; it may be legal or illegal or both, violent or non-violent or just un-violent. It may have a chance of success, or it may be hopeless from the start. The anarchists may be influential or even dominant in the campaign, or they may be only one of many groups taking part. It does not take long to think of a wide variety of possible fields of action, and for a century anarchists have tried them all. The form of action with which anarchists have been happiest and which is most typical of anarchism is direct action.

The idea of direct action is also often misunderstood, by anarchists as well as their enemies again. When the phrase was first used (during the 1890s) it meant no more than the opposite of 'political' – that is, parliamentary action; and in the context of the labour movement it meant 'industrial' action, especially strikes, boycotts and sabotage, which were thought of as preparations for and rehearsals of revolution. The point was that the action is applied not indirectly through representatives but directly by the people most closely involved in a situation and directly on the situation, and it is intended to win some measure of success rather than mere publicity.

This would seem clear enough, but direct action has in fact been confused with propaganda by deed and especially with civil disobedience. The technique of direct action was actually developed in the French syndicalist movement in reaction against the more extreme techniques of propaganda by deed;

instead of getting side-tracked into dramatic but ineffective gestures, the trade-unionists got on with the dull but effective work – that at least was the theory. But as the syndicalist movement grew and came into conflict with the system in France, Spain, Italy, the United States and Russia, and even Britain, the high points of direct action began to take on the same function as acts of propaganda by deed. Then, when Gandhi began to describe as direct action what was really a non-violent form of civil disobedience, all three phases were confused and came to mean much the same – more or less any form of political activity which is against the law or otherwise outside the accepted rules of constitutional etiquette.

For most anarchists, however, direct action still has its original meaning, though as well as its traditional forms it also takes new ones – invading military bases or taking over universities, squatting in houses or occupying factories. What makes it particularly attractive to anarchists is that it is consistent with libertarian principles and also with itself. Most forms of political action by opposition groups are mainly designed to win power; some groups use the techniques of direct action, but as soon as they win power they not only stop using such techniques, but prevent any other groups using them either. Anarchists are in favour of direct action at all times; they see it as normal action, as action which reinforces itself and grows as it is used, as action which can be used to create and also sustain a free society.

But there are some anarchists who have no faith in the possibility of creating a free society, and their action varies accordingly. One of the strongest pessimistic tendencies in anarchism is nihilism. Nihilism was the word which Turgenev coined (in his novel *Fathers and Sons*) to describe the sceptical and scornful attitude of the young populists in Russia a century ago, but it came to mean the view which denies the value not only of the State or of prevailing morality, but of society and of humanity itself; for the strict nihilist nothing is sacred, not even himself – so nihilism is one step beyond the most thorough egoism.

An extreme form of action inspired by nihilism is terrorism for its own sake rather than for revenge or propaganda.

Anarchists have no monopoly of terror, but it has sometimes been fashionable in some sections of the movement. After the frustrating experience of preaching a minority theory in a hostile or often indifferent society, it is tempting to attack society physically. It may not do much about the hostility, but it will certainly end the indifference; let them hate me, so long as they fear me, is the terrorist's line of thought. But if reasoned assassination has been unproductive, random terror has been counter-productive, and it is not too much to say that nothing has done more damage to anarchism than the streak of psychopathic violence which always ran and still runs through it.

A milder form of action inspired by nihilism is bohemianism, which is a constant phenomenon though the name seems to change with each manifestation. This too has been fashionable in some sections of the anarchist movement, and of course far outside as well. Instead of attacking society, the bohemian drops out of it – though, while living without conforming to the values of society, he usually lives in and on society. A lot of nonsense is talked about this tendency. Bohemians may be parasites, but that is true of many other people. On the other hand they don't hurt anyone except themselves, which is not true of many other people. The best thing that can be said about them is that they can do some good by enjoying themselves and challenging received values in an ostentatious but harmless way. The worst thing that can be said about them is that they cannot really change society and may divert energy from trying to do this, which for most anarchists is the whole point of anarchism.

A more consistent and constructive way of dropping out of society is to leave it and set up a new self-sufficient community. This has at times been a widespread phenomenon, among religious enthusiasts during the Middle Ages, for instance, and among many kinds of people more recently, especially in North America and of course in Palestine. Anarchists have been affected by this tendency in the past, but not much nowadays; like other left-wing groups, they are more likely to set up their own informal community, based on a network of people living and working together within society, than to secede from society. This may be thought of as the nucleus of a new form of society growing inside the old forms, or else as a viable form of refuge from the demands of authority which is not too extreme for ordinary people.

Another form of action which is based on a pessimistic view of the prospects for anarchism is permanent protest. According to this view, there is no hope of changing society, of destroying the State system, and of putting anarchism into practice. What is important is not the future, the strict adherence to a fixed ideal and the careful elaboration of a beautiful utopia, but the present, the belated recognition of a bitter reality and the constant resistance to an ugly situation. Permanent protest is the theory of many former anarchists who have not given up their beliefs but no longer hope for success; it is also the practice of many active anarchists who keep their beliefs intact and carry on as if they still hoped for success but who know – consciously or unconsciously – that they will never see it. What most anarchists have been involved in during the last century may be described as permanent protest when it is looked at with hindsight; but it is just as dogmatic to say that things will never change as to say that things are bound to change, and no one can tell when protest might become effective and the present might suddenly turn into the future. The real distinction is that permanent protest is thought of as a rearguard action in a hopeless cause, while most anarchist activity is thought of as the action of a vanguard or at least of scouts in a struggle which we may not win and which may never end but which is still worth fighting.

The best tactics in this struggle are all those which are consistent with the general strategy of the war for freedom and equality, from guerilla skirmishes in one's private life to set battles in major social campaigns. Anarchists are almost always in a small minority, so they have little choice of battlefield but have to fight wherever the action is. In general the most successful occasions have been those when anarchist agitation has led to anarchist participation in wider left-wing movements – especially in the labour movement, but also in anti-militarist or even pacifist movements in countries preparing for or fighting in wars, anti-clerical and humanist movements in religious countries, movements for national or colonial liberation, for radical or sexual equality, for legal or penal reform, or for civil liberties in general.

Such participation inevitably means alliance with non-anarchist groups and some compromise of anarchist principles, and anarchists who become deeply involved in such action are always in danger of abandoning anarchism altogether. On the other hand, refusal to take such a risk generally means sterility and sectarianism, and the anarchist movement has tended to be influential only when it has accepted a full part. The particular anarchist contribution to such occasions is twofold – to emphasize the goal of a libertarian society, and to insist on libertarian methods of achieving it. This is in fact a single contribution, for the most important point we can make is not just that the end does not justify the means, but that the means determines the end – that means *are* ends in most cases. We can be sure of our own actions, but not of the consequences.

A good opportunity for anarchists to give society a push towards anarchism seems to be active participation on these lines in such non-sectarian movements as the Committee of 100 in Britain, the March 22 Movement in France, the SDS in Germany, the Provos in Holland, the Zengakuren in Japan, and the various civil rights, draft resistance, and student power groups in the United States. In the old days the greatest opportunity for really substantial movement towards anarchism was of course in militant syndicalist episodes in France, Spain, Italy, the United States and Russia, and above all in the revolutions of Russia and Spain; nowadays it is not so much in the violent and authoritarian revolutions of Asia, Africa and South America as in insurrectionary upheavals such as those of Hungary in 1956 and France in 1968 – and Britain when?

AFFINITY GROUPS

MURRAY BOOKCHIN
(From *Post-Scarcity Anarchism*, 1974)

The term 'affinity group' is the English translation of the Spanish *grupo de afinidad*, which was the name of an organizational form devised in pre-Franco days as the basis of the redoubtable Federacion Anarquista Iberica, the Iberian Anarchist Federation. (The FAI consisted of the most idealistic militants in the CNT, the immense anarcho-syndicalist labour union.) A slavish imitation of the FAI's forms of organization and methods would be neither possible nor desirable. The Spanish anarchists of the thirties were faced with entirely different social problems from those which confront American anarchists today. The affinity group form, however, has features that apply to any social situation, and these have often been intuitively adopted by American radicals, who call the resulting organizations 'collectives', 'communes' or 'families'.

The affinity group could easily be regarded as a new type of extended family, in which kinship ties are replaced by deeply empathetic human relationships – relationships nourished by common revolutionary ideas and practice. Long before the word 'tribe' gained popularity in the American counter-culture, the Spanish anarchists called their congresses *asambleas de las tribus*, – assemblies of the tribes. Each affinity group is deliberately kept small to allow for the greatest degree of intimacy between those who compose it. Autonomous, communal and directly democratic, the group combines revolutionary theory with revolutionary lifestyle in its everyday behaviour. It creates a free space in which revolutionaries can remake themselves individually, and also as social beings.

Affinity groups are intended to function as catalysts within the popular movement, not as 'vanguards'; they provide initiative and consciousness, not a 'general staff' and a source of 'command'. The groups proliferate on a molecular level and they have their own 'Brownian movement'. Whether they link together or separate is determined by living situations, not by bureaucratic fiat from a distant centre. Under conditions of political repression, affinity groups are highly resistant to police infiltration. Owing to the intimacy of the relationships between the participants, the groups are often difficult to penetrate and, even if penetration occurs, there is no centralized apparatus to provide the infiltrators with an overview of the movement as a whole. Even under such demanding conditions, affinity groups can still retain contact with each other through their periodicals and literature.

During periods of heightened activity, on the other hand, nothing prevents affinity groups from working together closely on any scale required by a living situation. They can easily federate by means of local, regional or national assemblies to formulate common policies and they can create temporary action committees (like those of the French students and workers in 1968) to coordinate specific tasks. Affinity groups, however, are always rooted in the popular movement. Their loyalties belong to the social forms created by the revolutionary people, not to an impersonal bureaucracy. As a result of their autonomy and localism, the groups can retain a sensitive appreciation of new possibilities. Intensely experimental and variegated in lifestyles, they act as a stimulus to each other as well as on the popular movement. Each group tries to acquire the resources needed to function largely on its own. Each group seeks a rounded body of knowledge and experience in order to overcome the social and psychological limitations imposed by bourgeois society on individual development. Each group, as a nucleus of consciousness and experience, tries to advance the spontaneous revolutionary movement of the people to a point where the group can finally disappear into the organic social forms created by the revolution.

REVOLUTION AND
SOCIAL REALITY

ALEX COMFORT
(From *Authority and Delinquency in the Modern State*, 1950)

This is an age of discouraged revolutionaries. The nineteenth-century pattern of violent social change from below commands the full allegiance of serious sociologists only in those countries which lagged behind in the pattern of centralization – the Balkan States, Spain and Italy, the Communist States and the emergent nationalist movements of the East. Revolution in its original liberal and radical significance is revolution towards, rather than against, centralization. It takes over all the assumptions concerning the function of the state which exist in the parliamentary tradition – its object is, in fact, the capture of institutions to redress grievances.

Part of the discomfiture of English revolutionary bodies of all complexions comes from the appreciation that the nineteenth-century notion of a *levée-en-masse* against class oppressors had little reality; revolutions which have succeeded have invariably been organized around a rival government, a closely knit directing body which has depended upon popular feeling for its support, but which has been concerned primarily to take over the existing legislative and enforcement mechanism. Another unfavourable factor is that the inevitable progress of urban population towards discontented insurrection, foreseen by the early socialists, has been decisively halted in some societies by the palliation of the worst features of industrialism and a distinct increase in material comfort. The centralized society no longer invariably provides a militantly revolutionary proletariat. The chief threat to this superficial stability comes from the boom-to-slump oscillation of centralized economies, but the manifestations of discontent, when they do appear, are directed by the whole pattern of urban social life into channels which lead towards aggravations of the centralized pattern. If social-democratic governments are violently overthrown under these conditions, it is by more extreme forms of hierarchy based on exaggerations of their own irrational attitudes – Fascism, Nazism, or totalitarian Communism. Revolution under these conditions is generally a final stabilization of the pattern of the permanent war economy as a solution to outstanding difficulties. Like war, it gains its support by creating a sense of civic purpose, and directing attention to stereotype enemies. The first task of any revolutionary administration is to ensure that the change of control does not seriously derange the detailed working of the community – the second is to provide itself with an enforcement executive capable of interposing between itself and the public at large.

Of the revolutionary movements in Europe, only the Anarchists differ from the preconceived ideas of state function which existing governments uphold. The earliest theorists of anarchism, such as William Godwin and Kropotkin, strikingly anticipate the findings of sociology in their estimate of human behaviour and the means of modifying conduct. The quaintness of Godwin's suggestion that a free individual should not deign to play in an orchestra under a conductor is less obvious if we state it in terms of the restriction of art to professionals which is one of the many types of vicarious living in modern society. Godwin did not foresee the wide availability of this type of centralized art which technology has provided, and might not have accepted its value if he had. Kropotkin profoundly influenced human biology by his theory of mutual aid, propounded as a counterblast to the social conclusions drawn from the Darwinian 'struggle for existence'. He was one of the first systematic students of animal communities, and may be regarded as the founder of modern social ecology.

The actual and visible tendency towards central organization as a requisite for technological progress weighted the balance heavily against the anarchist wing of the radical movement. As a potential mass movement, anarchism retains its strength only in Spain, where an anarchist community was set up during the Civil War, and in Italy. It retains its nineteenth-century ideology only in cultures where industrialism did not fully disrupt the pattern of rural communal life, and where the idea of local self-sufficiency has never appeared chimerical or retrogressive.

The forces which mould the individual revolutionary are at least as complex as those which mould governments. Psychopaths of the power-acquisition type, schizophrenics, and theorists taking refuge in utopian schemes may all participate: some at least are people who, in a different context, would be institutional rulers . . .

It is, however, as groundless to identify all revolutionary thought with psychopathy as it is to detect signs of insanity in all institutional rulers. Whatever irrational attitudes emerge in the course of revolutions are evoked by real defects in society. The psychiatry which identifies all discontent with society as a manifestation of ill-health, calling for 'readjustment', denies its own vocation . . . We can allow at least as much recognition of the part of unconscious process in the psychology of social agitation as in the psychology of government without losing sight of the fact that the merit of adaptation depends on the circumstances to which the patient is being asked to adapt. The redirection of aggressive impulses produced by asocial living against the pattern of asociality, rather than against external stereotypes, is no more than the counterpart of the mechanism by which humanity has overcome smallpox and cholera, and is an eminently acceptable outlet for such impulses, provided that it takes the form of rational and fully conscious disobedience by intelligent individuals towards irresponsible institutions. That the material of such a revolution exists is evident from clinical practice. Whenever the social psychologist points out to the individual the reasons for his inability to find satisfaction in existing patterns of society, he is performing an obligatory and entirely necessary work of subversion.

We find the revolutionary obligations of psychiatry easier to accept in the context of Fascism or Communism than in our own system. Few if any psychotherapists would wish to 'readjust' the SS man or the *Totenkommando* leader to his occupation. Both science and the public of centralized order underestimate their own power to restrain group delinquency by individual action. It has been repeatedly suggested that the concentration of military power in the hands of the state renders effective resistance impossible. In terms of the actionist fantasy of nineteenth-century radicals, this is undoubtedly true, but the centralized war-state is probably more vulnerable to individual disobedience than any previous type of culture, by reason of its dependence upon technology and acquiescence. We have seen the precarious balance which such states maintain whenever they engage in war or in civil persecution. Defensive and offensive wars conducted by large states, by means of civilian armies, are wholly at the mercy of individual morale, and military powers devote immense energy to its maintenance. The threat of domination by external enemies has done much to obscure the fact that defensive war is itself a conscious governmental choice – the legislature which has to face a thoroughly unreliable public is likely to display a diplomatic caution similar to that of states which possess no reasonable chance of resisting aggression by arms. Under present conditions, where defensive as well as offensive war is compatible with individual and national survival, such an attitude may be held to provide a valuable safeguard . . .

It has been suggested that the growth of social sense may render nations unfit to withstand the attacks of their less-scrupulous neighbours. The process, however, is not one which can be reversed. We cannot have it both ways. Either social psychology will devote itself to cultivating positive attitudes based on human responsibility, whatever the consequences, or it must cease to exist as an independent science and accept a purely veterinary status. Like the effects of atomic energy, we cannot select and reject certain consequences of knowledge – we can only accommodate ourselves to the whole pattern of our results. The irrelevance of military victory in terms of total war, and the knowledge of the nature of the consequences of defence on economical and cultural life, provided added grounds for declining to abandon the struggle.

To a great extent, the idea of the indefensibility of social cultures is true only if we think in terms of military and institutional defences of the kind advocated by the state. Such cultures are highly resistant to outside interference, and this resistance is all the more effective because it is not dependent on organization. Centralized societies like our own have no cultural defence in depth; their defeat is always total. Once the crust of military protection is broken, the state has exhausted its resources, and may regard it as an obligation to hand over the executive to the victors in the interests of law and order. Predominantly social societies depend for their integrity on the patterns of life and belief of individuals and small groups. One of the essential weaknesses of asociality is that it has no adequate defences against tyrants, domestic or foreign – by inculcating patterns of life which may express themselves in independence and in resistance to central authority when this appears necessary, we are actually creating a public which is better able to look after itself than the society of conformists on which military defence depends. If resistance to outside aggression by these means involves the acceptance of loss, risk, suffering, and a partial retrogression of society, it may be held that such risks are not greater than those of successful defensive war at the present time. The features of national life – political sovereignty, institutions, the state itself, which military leaders aim to defend, are less significant in the value scale of civilization than sociality, stability, and individual judgment.

Responsible sociology must recognize, however, a sense of urgency in conducting its propaganda: the stage of transition, in which individuals are disgusted and distrustful towards the existing pattern, without having had time to form a stable new one, is particularly likely to produce catastrophes. In view of the mechanisms by which attitudes are formed, the transition cannot occupy much less than a generation, and if we are to stabilize our culture in the modern world we should clearly devote more time to practical and educational work outside the existing pattern and based on first principles.

Whether revolution takes place suddenly or gradually is more a matter of circumstance and event than of choice. The historical 'revolution' is usually only the coming to a head of such a process of gradual attitude-change. Decisive action may be required, but not as an element in a revolution-fantasy. The transition from asocial to social living takes place at a level which religious apostles term 'life changing' rather than at the barricades, and any violence which it involves is more likely to come from the exponents of older patterns, who still regard institutional coercion as a means of 'saving the Republic', than from the revolutionaries themselves.

By far the most serious criticism of the orthodox and Marxist conception of revolution . . . arises from the extent of the change which such a revolution is expected to produce by mainly institutional methods. That revolutionary governments can infuse a new social integration into their publics is not in question; to this extent, revolution does modify and improve individual adjustment in cultures where lack of objectivity is a cause of ill-health. This, however, can occur without reference to the social objectives of the movement. Nazism was largely successful in revivifying German group feeling. The methods of the revolutionaries are almost always, however, identical with those used by asocial ruling groups in wartime – projection, mobilization of group resentment against stereotypes, and a political or geographical nationalism of class or state. Even where, as in the early internationalist days of Communism, projection is confined to a class enemy, it is difficult to re-interpret Marxist revolutionary ideas in any terms which coincide with modern anthropological work. Any fundamental change in the pattern of a culture depends upon changes in the character-structure of its members, both as cause and as effect. It has been repeatedly shown that such changes depend less upon public and political institutions than upon relatively inconspicuous environmental forces in childhood. It would be perfectly possible to make a case that the changes in a given culture which might follow a shift in the pattern of infant-feeding behaviour are likely to be more extensive than those arising from a revolution in the distribution of economic and political power.

This view does not suggest that economic change is impracticable, but only that it must be conducted with a different type of social change, and not merely affixed to an existing culture. The adversary of 'revolution' today is not human nature but the necessity for modifying cultural patterns as a whole by scientific means. No such modification can be brought about through the interplay of aggressions and projections which makes up almost the whole of traditional political thought, both governmental and revolutionary. *The status of power-mechanisms as a means of self-expression for delinquents and for aggressive impulses effectively limits their use as a means of social change based upon observational research.*

To this extent, modern sociology would seem to uphold the libertarian-anarchist rather than the totalitarian-institutional conception of social change, though it does so with marked reservations. Repudiation of authority may spring equally from maturity and immaturity, and in a proportion of agitators it is in itself a psychopathic trait. Yet the basic tenets of many of the earlier anarchist writers, fundamental human sociality, the inappropriateness of coercive means to modify cultural patterns, and the basing of political change upon the assumption of personal responsibility by individuals, through 'mutual aid' and 'direct action', retained general validity in terms of the new conception of sociology which does not depend on the unconscious forces which may have prompted those who stated them.

Anarchism, though it shows some of the actionistic fantasy that is common to the radical thought of the nineteenth century, is based not so much on a utopian future as on a return to a primitive naturalism which shall free men from the political state and economic exploitation. In this sense anarchism has much in common with the mythology of the return to an Arcadian past.
(Kimball Young, *Handbook of Social Psychology*, 1946)

The Golden Age, however, like the 'state of nature', has faded out of the currency of social thought, and the actionist fantasies with it. The profound transformation of the original myths of Godwin or Shelley through the systematic study of man has brought them more into line with the realities of experience. Like other myths, they are not programmes of action, but glimpses of possibilities, to be followed or rejected in terms of reality and experience. If there is or was a Golden Age, its existence is in the human mind rather than in concrete societies. To this extent, the myth of human sociality, like the myth of human health, is one of the aspirations which humanity has perpetually attempted to reconcile with reality, first by magic and by prayer, later by empirical action, and later still by planned investigation and applied science. Revolutions which give too great or too literal credit to their myths in the historical sense, and which aim at concrete retrogressions in society, by abandoning machinery and technical progress, are contradictions of the entire tendency of human values. If society fails to fit the known requirements of man, we can modify it in one direction only, towards increased control over ourselves and our environment. This type of revolution stands in sharp contrast to the policy of revolutionaries who wish to plunge forward empirically, and revolutionaries who are obsessed with a largely illusory past.

> A somewhat curious prescription has been suggested for 'our present discontent'. Unfortunately it is not based upon scientific aetiology but is a manifestation of psychopathology. Its plan is to scrap the whole modern industrial set-up and return to the pre-industrialized form of society. This was seriously put forward as a line of action some years ago by Gandhi in India, and also found favour in the Irish Free State. Life, however, is set in a one-dimensional time track. Neither in the individual nor in the group can it turn back, and in times of difficulty the impulse to regress may be attended by fantasy notions leading into even greater difficulty those who attempt to put them into practice.
>
> (J. Halliday, *Lancet*, 10 August 1946)

The mystical and regressive substitutes for the centralized state passed out of the currency of scientific thought with the end of the last century. The opponents of the institutional approach today are to this extent upon psychologically securer ground. In the words of a twentieth-century anarchist:

> We are not a primitive society, and there is no need to become primitive in order to secure the essentials of demo-

cratic liberty. We want to retain all our scientific and industrial triumphs – electric power, machine tools, mass production and the rest. We do not propose to revert to the economy of the hand-loom and the plough . . . The fundamental truth about economics is that the methods and instruments of production, freely used and fairly used, are capable of giving every human being a decent standard of living.

(Herbert Read, *To Hell with Culture*, 1943)

Our criticism of centralization or of institutional society is not a proper ground for the rejection of the methods which have made our enquiry into it possible, but only for further efforts to select the favourable and eliminate the harmful in its fabric. The only serious prospect of de-industrialization lies in the catastrophic destruction of Western society by war, famine, or exhaustion, and such a revolution would restore government indefinitely to the jungle and the bacilli.

If the word 'anarchism', as a name for the attempt to effect changes away from the centralized and institutional to-wards the social and 'life-orientated' society, carries irrational implications, or suggests a preconceived ideology either of man or of society, we may hesitate to accept it. No branch of science can afford to ally itself with revolutionary fantasy, with emotionally determined ideas of human conduct, or with psychopathic attitudes. On the other hand suggested alterna-tives – 'biotechnic civilization' (Mumford), 'para-primitive society' (G. R. Taylor) – have little advantage beyond their novelty, and acknowledge none of the debts which we owe to pioneers. 'Free society' is equally undesirable for its importation of an emotive and undefinable idea of free-dom.

If, therefore, the intervention of sociology in modern affairs tends to propagate a form of anarchism, it is an anarchism based on observational research, which has little in common with the older revolutionary theory beside its objectives. It rests upon standards of scientific assessment to which the propagandist and actionist elements in nineteenth-century revolutionary thought are highly inimical. It is also experimental and tentative rather than dogmatic and Messianic. As a theory of revolution it recognizes the revolutionary process as one to which no further limit can be imposed – revolution of this kind is not a single act of redress or vengeance followed by a golden age, but a continuous human activity whose objectives recede as it progresses.

ANARCHISM AND VIOLENCE

PETER KROPOTKIN
(From a speech at the Commune celebration in London, quoted by Woodcock and Avakumovic in *The Anarchist Prince*)

Anarchism is represented as *the* party of violence. But when I look back to the acts of violence which I have lived through during the last twenty years, I see the 35,000 Paris workers exterminated by the French property owners in May 1871; the attempt of the Social-Democrat Hoedel and the Republican Nobiling against the German Emperor, the attempt of the Socialist Otero in Spain, and in Italy that of Passanante, who was a Mazzinian more than anything else; thirty-two gallows in Russia and upon them not one Anarchist; the Irish Nationalists' violence; and the Anarchists' acts of violence during the last few years; and I maintain that violence belongs to *all* parties, and that they all have recourse to it when they lose confidence in other means and are brought to despair.

Of all parties I now see only one party – the Anarchist – which respects human life, and loudly insists upon the abolition of capital punishment, prison torture and punishment of man by man altogether. All other parties teach every day their utter disrespect of human life. Killing the foe, torturing him to death in prison, is their principle. For the interest of bondholders they will massacre the miners in the mine, kill passengers in a train, or bombard Alexandria, slaughtering women and children in the streets. They only ripen the fruit of their own teachings. The sacredness of human life! Yes, by all means; but society itself must first learn to recognize the sacredness of human life, and not teach the opposite.

THE VIOLENCE OF THE LAWFUL WORLD

ALEXANDER BERKMAN
(From *What is Anarchist Communism?*, 1929)

Wherever you turn you will find that our entire life is built on violence or the fear of it. From earliest childhood you are subjected to the violence of parents or elders. At home, in school, in the office, factory, field, or shops, it is always someone's *authority* which keeps you obedient and compels you to do his will.

The right to compel you is called authority. Fear of punishment has been made into duty and is called obedience.

In this atmosphere of force and violence, of authority and obedience, of duty, fear and punishment we all grow up; we breathe it through our lives. We are so steeped in the spirit of violence that we never stop to ask whether violence is right or wrong. We only ask if it is legal, whether the law permits it.

You don't question the right of the government to kill, to confiscate and imprison. If a private person should be guilty of the things the government is doing all the time, you'd brand him a murderer, thief and scoundrel. But as long as the violence committed is 'lawful', you approve of it and submit to it. So it is not really violence that you object to, but people using violence 'unlawfully'.

This lawful violence and the fear of it dominate our whole existence, individual and collective. Authority controls our lives from the cradle to the grave – authority parental, priestly and divine, political, economic, social and moral. But whatever the character of that authority, it is always the same executioner wielding power over you through your fear of

punishment in one form or another. You are afraid of God
and the devil, of the priest and the neighbour, of your
employer and boss, of the politician and policeman, of the
judge and the jailer, of the law and the government. All your
life is a long chain of fears – fears which bruise your body
and lacerate your soul. On those fears is based the authority
of God, of the Church, of parents, of capitalist and ruler.

Look into your heart and see if what I say is not true.
Why, even among children the ten-year-old Johnny bosses
his younger brother or sister by the authority of his greater
physical strength, just as Johnny's father bosses him by his
superior strength, and by Johnny's dependence on his support. You stand for the authority of priest and preacher
when you think they can 'call down the wrath of God upon
your head'. You submit to the domination of boss, judge,
and government because of their power to deprive you of
work, to ruin your business, to put you in prison – a power,
by the way, that you yourself have given into their hands.

So authority rules your whole life, the authority of the
past and the present, of the dead and the living, and your
existence is a continuous invasion and violation of yourself,
a constant subjection to the thoughts and will of someone
else.

And as you are invaded and violated, so you subconsciously
revenge yourself by invading and violating others over whom
you have authority or can exercise compulsion, physical or
moral. In this way all life has become a crazy quilt of
authority, of domination and submission, of command
and obedience, of coercion, and subjection, of rulers and
ruled, of violence and force in a thousand and one forms.

Can you wonder that even idealists are still held in the
meshes of this spirit of authority and violence, and are often
impelled by their feelings and environment to invasive acts
entirely at variance with their ideas?

We are all still barbarians who resort to force and violence
to settle our debts, difficulties and troubles. Violence is the
method of ignorance, the method of the weak. The strong of
heart and brain need no violence, for they are irresistible in
their consciousness of being right. The further we get away
from primitive man and the hatchet age, the less recourse

we shall have to force and violence. The more enlightened man will become, the less he will employ compulsion and coercion. He will rise from the dust and stand erect; he will bow to no tsar in heaven or on earth. He will become fully human when he will scorn to rule and refuse to be ruled. He will be truly free only when there shall be no more masters.

Anarchism is the ideal of such a condition; of a society without force and compulsion, where all men shall be equals; and live in freedom, peace and harmony.

AN ASSASSIN'S ATTEMPT

ALEXANDER BERKMAN
(From *Prison Memoirs of an Anarchist*, 1912)

The door of Frick's private office, to the left of the reception-room, swings open as the coloured attendant emerges, and I catch a flitting glimpse of a black-bearded, well-knit figure at a table at the back of the room.

'Mistah Frick is engaged. He can't see you now, sah,' the Negro says, handing me back my card.

I take the pasteboard, return it to my case, and walk slowly out of the reception-room. But quickly retracing my steps, I pass through the gate separating the clerks from the visitors, and, brushing the astounded attendant aside, I step into the office on the left, and find myself facing Frick.

For an instant the sunlight, streaming through the windows, dazzles me. I discern two men at the further end of the long table. 'Fr –,' I begin. The look of terror on his face strikes me speechless. It is the dread of the conscious presence of death. 'He understands,' it flashes through my mind. With a quick motion I draw the revolver. As I raise the weapon, I see Frick clutch with both hands the arm of the chair, and attempt to rise. I aim at his head. 'Perhaps he wears armour,' I reflect. With a look of horror he quickly averts his face, as I pull the trigger. There is a flash, and the high-ceilinged room reverberates as with the booming

of cannon. I hear a sharp, piercing cry, and see Frick on his
knees, his head against the arm of the chair. I feel calm
and possessed, intent upon every movement of the man. He
is lying head and shoulders under the large armchair, without
sound or motion. 'Dead?' I wonder. I must make sure. About
twenty-five feet separate us. I take a few steps towards him,
when suddenly the other man, whose presence I had quite
forgotten, leaps upon me. I struggle to loosen his hold.
He looks slender and small. I would not hurt him; I have
no business with him. Suddenly I hear the cry. 'Murder!
Help!' My heart stands still as I realize that it is Frick
shouting. 'Alive?' I wonder. I hurl the stranger aside and
fire at the crawling figure of Frick. The man struck my hand,
– I have missed! He grapples with me, and we wrestle across
the room. I try to throw him, but spying an opening between
his arm and body, I thrust the revolver against his side and
aim at Frick, cowering behind the chair. I pull the trigger.
There is a click – but no explosion! By the throat I catch the
stranger, still clinging to me, when suddenly something heavy
strikes me on the back of the head. Sharp pains shoot through
my eyes. I sink to the floor, vaguely conscious of the weapon
slipping from my hands.

'Where is the hammer? Hit him, carpenter!' Confused
voices ring in my ears. Painfully I strive to rise. The weight
of many bodies is pressing on me. Now – it's Frick's voice!
Not dead? . . . I crawl in the direction of the sound, dragging
the struggling men with me. I must get the dagger from my
pocket – I have it! Repeatedly I strike with it at the legs of
the man near the window. I hear Frick cry out in pain –
there is much shouting and stamping – my arms are pulled
and twisted, and I am lifted bodily from the floor.

Police, clerks, workmen in overalls, surround me. An officer
pulls my head back by the hair, and my eyes meet Frick's.
He stands in front of me, supported by several men. His
face is ashen grey; the black beard is streaked with red, and
blood is oozing from his neck. For an instant a strange feeling, as of shame, comes over me; but the next moment I am
filled with an anger at the sentiment, so unworthy of a
revolutionist. With defiant hatred I look him full in the
face.

'Mr Frick, do you identify this man as your assailant?'
Frick nods weakly.

The street is lined with a dense, excited crowd. A young man in civilian dress, who is accompanying the police, inquires, not unkindly:

'Are you hurt? You're bleeding.'

I pass my hand over my face. I feel no pain, but there is a peculiar sensation about my eyes.

'I've lost my glasses,' I remark, involuntarily.

'You'll be damn lucky if you don't lose your head,' an officer retorts.

A TERRORIST'S DEFENCE

EMILE HENRY
(From *Gazette des Tribunaux*, 27-8 April 1894; translated by George Woodcock)

It is not a defence that I present to you. I am not in any way seeking to escape the reprisals of the society I have attacked. Besides, I acknowledge only one tribunal – myself, and the verdict of any other is meaningless to me. I wish merely to give you an explanation of my acts and to tell you how I was led to perform them.

I have been an anarchist for only a short time. It was as recently as the middle of the year 1891 that I entered the revolutionary movement. Up to that time, I had lived in circles entirely imbued with current morality. I had been accustomed to respect and even to love the principles of fatherland and family, of authority and property.

For teachers in the present generation too often forget one thing; it is that life, with its struggles and defeats, its injustices and iniquities, takes upon itself indiscreetly to open the eyes of the ignorant to reality. This happened to me, as it happens to everyone. I had been told that life was easy, that it was wide open to those who were intelligent and energetic; experience showed me that only the cynical and the servile were able to secure good seats at the banquet.

I had been told that our social institutions were founded on justice and equality; I observed all around me nothing but lies and impostures.

Each day I shed an illusion. Everywhere I went, I witnessed the same miseries among some, and the same joys among others. I was not slow to understand that the grand words I had been taught to venerate: honour, devotion, duty, were only the mask that concealed the most shameful basenesses.

The manufacturer who created a colossal fortune out of the toil of workers who lacked everything was an honest gentleman. The deputy and the minister, their hands ever open for bribes, were devoted to the public good. The officer who experimented with a new type of rifle on children of seven had done his duty, and, openly in parliament, the president of the council congratulated him! Everything I saw revolted me, and my intelligence was attracted by criticism of the existing social organization. Such criticism has been made too often for me to repeat it. It is enough to say that I became the enemy of a society that I judged to be criminal.

Drawn at first to socialism, I was not slow in separating myself from that party. I have too much love of freedom, too much respect for individual initiative, too much repugnance for military organization, to assume a number in the ordered army of the fourth estate. Besides, I realized that basically socialism changes nothing in the existing order. It maintains the principle of authority, and, whatever self-styled free-thinkers may say about it, that principle is no more than the antiquated survival of faith in a superior power.

Scientific studies gradually made me aware of the play of natural forces in the universe. I became materialist and atheist; I came to realize that modern science discards the hypothesis of God, of which it has no need. In the same way, religious and authoritarian morality, which are based on false assumptions, should be allowed to disappear. What then, I asked myself, was the new morality in harmony with the laws of nature that might regenerate the old world and give birth to a happy humanity?

It was at this moment that I came into contact with a group of anarchist comrades whom I consider, even today, among the best I have ever known. The character of these men immediately captivated me. I discerned in them a great sincerity, a total frankness, a searching distrust of all prejudices, and I wanted to understand the idea that produced men so different from anyone I had encountered up to that point.

The idea – as soon as I embraced it – found in my mind a soil completely prepared by observation and personal reflection to receive it. It merely gave precision to what already existed there in vague and wavering form. In my turn I became an anarchist.

I do not need to develop on this occasion the whole theory of anarchism. I merely wish to emphasize its revolutionary aspect, the destructive and negative aspect that brings me here before you.

At this moment of embittered struggle between the middle class and its enemies, I am almost tempted to say, with Souvarine in *Germinal*: 'All discussions about the future are criminal, since they hinder pure and simple destruction and slow down the march of the revolution . . .'

I brought with me into the struggle a profound hatred which every day was renewed by the spectacle of this society where everything is base, everything is equivocal, everything is ugly, where everything is an impediment to the outflow of human passions, to the generous impulses of the heart, to the free flight of thought.

I wanted to strike as strongly and as justly as I could. Let us start then with the first attempt I made, the explosion in the Rue des Bon-Enfants. I had followed closely the events at Carmaux. The first news of the strike had filled me with joy. The miners seemed at last to have abandoned those useless pacific strikes in which the trusting worker patiently waits for his few francs to triumph over the company's millions. They seemed to have entered on a way of violence which manifested itself resolutely on the 15th August 1892. The offices and buildings of the mine were invaded by a crowd of people tired of suffering without reprisals; justice was about to be wrought on the engineer whom his workers so deeply hated, when the timorous ones chose to interfere.

Who were these men? The same who cause the miscarriage of all revolutionary movements because they fear

that the people, once they act freely, will no longer obey their
voices; those who persuade thousands of men to endure
privations month after month so as to beat the drum over
their sufferings and create for themselves a popularity that
will put them into office: such men – I mean the socialist
leaders – in fact assumed the leadership of the strike movement.

Immediately a wave of glib gentlemen appeared in the
region; they put themselves entirely at the disposition of the
struggle, organized subscriptions, arranged conferences and
appealed on all sides for funds. The miners surrendered all
initiative into their hands, and what happened, everyone
knows.

The strike went on and on, and the miners established
the most intimate acquaintance with hunger, which became
their habitual companion; they used up the tiny reserve fund
of their syndicate and of the other organizations which
came to their help, and then, at the end of two months, they
returned crestfallen to their pit, more wretched than ever
before. It would have been so simple in the beginning to
have attacked the Company in its only sensitive spot, the
financial one; to have burnt the stocks of coal, to have
broken the mining machines, to have demolished the drain-
age pumps.

Then, certainly, the Company would have very soon
capitulated. But the great pontiffs of socialism would not
allow such procedures because they are anarchist procedures. At such games one runs the risk of prison and – who
knows? – perhaps one of those bullets that performed so
miraculously at Fourmies? That is not the way to win seats on
municipal councils or in legislatures. In brief, having been
momentarily troubled, order reigned once again at Carmaux.

More powerful than ever, the Company continued its
exploitation, and the gentlemen shareholders congratulated
themselves on the happy outcome of the strike. Their dividends would be even more pleasant to gather in.

It was then that I decided to intrude among that concert
of happy tones a voice the bourgeois had already heard
but which they thought had died with Ravachol: the voice
of dynamite.

I wanted to show the bourgeoisie that henceforward their pleasures would not be untouched, that their insolent triumphs would be disturbed, that their golden calf would rock violently on its pedestal until the final shock that would cast it down among filth and blood.

At the same time I wanted to make the miners understand that there is only one category of men, the anarchists, who sincerely resent their sufferings and are willing to avenge them. Such men do not sit in parliament like Monsieur Guesde and his associates, but they march to the guillotine.

So I prepared a bomb. At one stage the accusation that had been thrown at Ravachol came to my memory. What about the innocent victims? I soon resolved that question. The building where the Carmaux Company had its offices was inhabited only by bourgeois; hence there would be no innocent victims. The whole of the bourgeoisie lives by the exploitation of the unfortunate, and should expiate its crimes together. So it was with absolute confidence in the legitimacy of my deed that I left my bomb before the door to the Company's offices.

I have already explained my hope, in case my device was discovered before it exploded, that it would go off in the police station, where those it harmed would still be my enemies. Such were the motives that led me to commit the first attempt of which I have been accused.

Let us go on to the second incident, of the Café Terminus. I had returned to Paris at the time of the Vaillant affair, and I witnessed the frightful repression that followed the explosion at the Palais-Bourbon. I saw the draconian measures which the government decided to take against the anarchists. Everywhere there were spies, and searches, and arrests. A crowd of individuals were indiscriminately rounded up, torn from their families, and thrown into prison. Nobody was concerned about what happened to the wives and children of these comrades while they remained in jail.

The anarchist was no longer regarded as a man, but as a wild beast to be hunted everywhere while the bourgeois Press, which is the vile slave of authority, loudly demands his extermination.

At the same time, libertarian papers and pamphlets were

A.R.

seized and the right of meeting was abrogated. Worse than that: when it seemed desirable to get one comrade completely out of the way, an informer came and left in his room a packet which he said contained tannin; the next day a search was made, on a warrant dated the previous day, a box of suspicious powders was found, the comrade was taken to court and sentenced to three years in gaol. If you wish to know the truth of that, ask the wretched spy who found his way into the home of comrade Mérigeaud!

But all such procedures were good because they struck at an enemy who had spread fear, and those who had trembled wanted to display their courage. As the crown of that crusade against the heretics, we heard M. Reynal, Minister of the Interior, declare in the Chamber of Deputies that the measures taken by the government had thrown terror into the camp of the anarchists. But that was not yet enough. A man who had killed nobody was condemned to death. It was necessary to appear brave right to the end, and one fine morning he was guillotined.

But, gentlemen of the bourgeoisie, you have reckoned a little too much without your host. You arrested hundreds of men and women, you violated scores of homes, but still outside the prison walls there were men unknown to you who watched from the shadows as you hunted the anarchists, and waited only for the moment that would be favourable for them in their turn to hunt the hunters.

Reynal's words were a challenge thrown before the anarchists. The gauntlet was taken up. The bomb in the Café Terminus is the answer to all your violations of freedom, to your arrests, to your searches, to your laws against the Press, to your mass transportations, to your guillotinings. But why, you ask, attack these peaceful café guests, who sat listening to music and who, no doubt, were neither judges nor deputies nor bureaucrats? Why? It is very simple. The bourgeoisie did not distinguish among the anarchists. Vaillant, a man on his own, threw a bomb; nine-tenths of the comrades did not even know him. But that meant nothing; the persecution was a mass one, and anyone with the slightest anarchist links was hunted down. And since you hold a whole party responsible for the actions of a single man, and strike indiscriminately, we also strike indiscriminately.

Perhaps we should attack only the deputies who make laws against us, the judges who apply those laws, the police who arrest us? I do not agree. These men are only instruments. They do not act in their own name. Their functions were instituted by the bourgeoisie for its own defence. They are no more guilty than the rest of you. Those good bourgeois who hold no office but who reap their dividends and live idly on the profits of the workers' toil, they also must take their share in the reprisals. And not only they, but all those who are satisfied with the existing order, who applaud the acts of the government and so become its accomplices, those clerks earning three or five hundred francs a month who hate the people even more violently than the rich, that stupid and pretentious mass of folk who always choose the strongest side – in other words, the daily clientele of Terminus and the other great cafés!

That is why I struck at random and did not choose my victims! The bourgeoisie must be brought to understand that those who have suffered are tired at last of their sufferings; they are showing their teeth and they will strike all the more brutally if you are brutal with them. They have no respect for human life, because the bourgeoisie themselves have shown they have no care for it. It is not for the assassins who were responsible for the bloody week and for Fourmies to regard others as assassins.

We will not spare the women and children of the bourgeois, for the women and children of those we love have not been spared. Must we not count among the innocent victims those children who die slowly of anaemia in the slums because bread is scarce in their houses; those women who grow pale in your workshops, working to earn forty sous a day and fortunate when poverty does not force them into prostitution; those old men whom you have made production machines all their lives and whom you cast on to the waste heap or into the workhouse when their strength has worn away?

At least have the courage of your crimes, gentlemen of the bourgeoisie, and grant that our reprisals are completely legitimate.

Of course, I am under no illusions. I know my deeds will not yet be understood by the masses who are unprepared for them. Even among the workers, for whom I have fought, there will be many, misled by your newspapers, who will regard me as their enemy. But that does not matter. I am not concerned with anyone's judgment. Nor am I ignorant of the fact that there are individuals claiming to be anarchists who hasten to disclaim any solidarity with the propagandists of the deed. They seek to establish a subtle distinction between the theoreticians and the terrorists. Too cowardly to risk their own lives, they deny those who act. But the influence they pretend to wield over the revolutionary movement is nil. Today the field is open to action, without weakness or retreat.

Alexander Herzen, the Russian revolutionary, once said: 'Of two things one must be chosen: to condemn and march forward, or to pardon and turn back half way.' We intend neither to pardon nor to turn back, and we shall always march forward until the revolution, which is the goal of our efforts, finally arrives to crown our work with the creation of a free world.

In that pitiless war which we have declared on the bourgeoisie, we ask for no pity. We give death, and we know how to endure it. So it is with indifference that I await your verdict. I know that my head is not the last you will cut off; yet others will fall, for the starving are beginning to know the way to your great cafés and restaurants, to the Terminus and Foyot. You will add other names to the bloody list of our dead.

You have hanged in Chicago, decapitated in Germany, garotted in Jerez, shot in Barcelona, guillotined in Montbrison and Paris, but what you will never destroy is anarchy. Its roots are too deep. It is born in the heart of a society that is rotting and falling apart. It is a violent reaction against the established order. It represents all the egalitarian and libertarian aspirations that strike out against authority. It is everywhere, which makes it impossible to contain. It will end by killing you.

CIVIL DISOBEDIENCE

HENRY DAVID THOREAU
(From 'Resistance to Civil Government', 1849)

I heartily accept the motto – 'That government is best which governs least'; and I should like to see it acted up to more rapidly and systematically. Carried out, it finally amounts to this, which I also believe – 'That government is best which governs not at all'; and when men are prepared for it, that will be the kind of government which they will have. Government is at best but an expedient; but most governments are usually, and all governments are sometimes, inexpedient. The objections which have been brought against a standing army, and they are many and weighty, and deserve to prevail, may also at last be brought against a standing government. The standing army is only an arm of the standing government. The government itself, which is the only mode which the people have chosen to execute their will, is equally liable to be abused and perverted before the people can act through it. Witness the present Mexican war, the work of comparatively a few individuals using the standing government as their tool; for, in the outset, the people would not have consented to this measure.

This American government – what is it but a tradition, though a recent one, endeavouring to transmit itself unimpaired to posterity, but each instant losing some of its integrity? It has not the vitality and force of a single living man; for a single man can bend it to his will. It is a sort of wooden gun to the people themselves. But it is not the less necessary for this; for the people must have some complicated machinery or other, and hear its din, to satisfy that idea of government which they have. Governments show thus how successfully men can be imposed on, even impose on themselves, for their own advantage. It is excellent, we must all allow. Yet this government never of itself furthered any enterprise, but by the alacrity with which it got out of its way.

It does not keep the country free. *It* does not settle the West. *It* does not educate. The character inherent in the American people has done all that has been accomplished; and it would have done somewhat more, if the government had not sometimes got in its way . . .

But, to speak practically and as a citizen, unlike those who call themselves no-government men, I ask for, not at once no government, but *at once* a better government. Let every man make known what kind of government would command his respect, and that will be one step toward obtaining it.

After all, the practical reason why, when the power is once in the hands of the people, a majority are permitted, and for a long time continue, to rule is not because they are most likely to be in the right, nor because this seems fairest to the minority, but because they are physically the strongest. But a government in which the majority rule in all cases cannot be based on justice, even as far as men understand it. Can there not be a government in which majorities do not virtually decide right and wrong, but conscience? – in which majorities decide only those questions to which the rule of expediency is applicable? Must the citizen ever for a moment, or in the least degree, resign his conscience to the legislator? Why has every man a conscience, then? I think that we should be men first, and subjects afterwards. It is not desirable to cultivate a respect for the law, as much as for the right. The only obligation which I have a right to assume is to do at any time what I think right. It is truly enough said, that a corporation has no conscience; but a corporation of conscientious men is a corporation *with* a conscience. Law never made men a whit more just; and by means of their respect for it, even the well-disposed are daily made the agents of injustice. A common and natural result of an undue respect for the law is, that you may see a file of soldiers, colonel, captain, corporal, privates, powder-monkeys, and all, marching in admirable order over hill and dale to the wars, against their wills, ay, against their common sense and consciences, which makes it very steep marching indeed, and produces a palpitation of the heart . . .

The mass of men serve the state thus, not as men mainly, but as machines, with their bodies. They are the standing army, and the militia, jailers, constables, posse comitatus, etc. In most cases there is no free exercise whatever of the judgment or of the moral sense; but they put themselves on a level with wood and earth and stones; and wooden men can perhaps be manufactured that will serve the purpose as well. Such command no more respect than men of straw or a lump of dirt. They have the same sort of worth only as horses and dogs. Yet such as these even are commonly esteemed as good citizens . . .

How does it become a man to behave toward this American government today? I answer, that he cannot without disgrace be associated with it. I cannot for an instant recognize that political organization as *my* government which is the *slave's* government also.

All men recognize the right of revolution; that is, the right to refuse allegiance to, and to resist, the government, when its tyranny or its inefficiency are great and unendurable. But almost all say that such is not the case now. But such was the case, they think, in the Revolution of '75. If one were to tell me that this was a bad government because it taxed certain foreign commodities brought to its ports, it is most probable that I should not make an ado about it, for I can do without them. All machines have their friction; and possibly this does enough good to counterbalance the evil. At any rate, it is a great evil to make a stir about it. But when the friction comes to have its machine, and oppression and robbery are organized, I say, let us not have such a machine any longer. In other words, when a sixth of the population of a nation which has undertaken to be the refuge of liberty are slaves, and a whole country is unjustly overrun and conquered by a foreign army, and subjected to military law, I think that it is not too soon for honest men to rebel and revolutionize. What makes this duty the more urgent is the fact that the country is not our own, but ours is the invading army.

Paley, a common authority with many on moral questions, in his chapter on the 'Duty of Submission to Civil Government', resolves all civil obligation into expediency; and he proceeds to say, 'that so long as the interest of the whole society requires it, that is, so long as the established government be obeyed, and no longer . . . This principle being admitted, the justice of every particular case of resistance is reduced to a computation of the quantity of the danger and grievance on the one side, and of the probability and expense of redressing it on the other.' Of this, he says, every man shall judge for himself. But Paley appears never to have contemplated those cases to which the rule of expediency does not apply, in which a people, as well as an individual, must do justice, cost what it may. If I have unjustly wrested a plank from a drowning man, I must restore it to him though I drown myself. This, according to Paley, would be inconvenient. But he that would save his life, in such a case, shall lose it. Thus people must cease to hold slaves, and to make war on Mexico, though it cost them their existence as a people . . .

All voting is a sort of gaming, like checkers or back-gammon, with a slight moral tinge to it, a playing with right and wrong, with moral questions; and betting naturally accompanies it. The character of the voters is not staked. I cast my vote, perchance, as I think right; but I am not vitally concerned that that right should prevail. I am willing to leave it to the majority. Its obligation, therefore, never exceeds that of expediency. Even voting *for the right* is *doing* nothing for it. It is only expressing to men feebly your desire that it should prevail. A wise man will not leave the right to the mercy of chance, nor wish it to prevail through the power of the majority. There is but little virtue in the action of masses of men. When the majority shall at length vote for the abolition of slavery, it will be because they are indifferent to slavery, or because there is but little slavery left to be abolished by their vote. *They* will then be the only slaves. Only *his* vote can hasten the abolition of slavery who asserts his own freedom by his vote.

I hear of a convention to be held at Baltimore, or else-where, for the selection of a candidate for the Presidency, made up chiefly of editors, and men who are politicians by profession; but I think, what is it to any independent, intelligent and respectable man what decision they may come to? Shall we not have the advantages of his wisdom and honesty nevertheless? Can we not count upon some independent votes? Are there not many individuals in the country who do not attend conventions? But no: I find that the respectable man, so called, has immediately drifted from his position, and despairs of his country, when his country has more reason to despair of him. He forthwith adopts one of the candidates thus selected as the only *available* one, thus proving that he is himself *available* for any purpose of the demagogue. His vote is of no more worth than that of any unprincipled foreigner or hireling native, who may have been bought. O for a man who is a *man*, and, as my neighbour says, has a bone in his back which you cannot pass your hand through! Our statistics are at fault: the population has been returned too large. How many *men* are there to a square thousand miles in this country? Hardly one. Does not America offer any inducement for men to settle here? The American has dwindled into an Odd Fellow – one who may be known by the development of his organ of gregariousness, and a manifest lack of intellect and cheerful self-reliance; whose first and chief concern, on coming into this world, is to see that the almshouses are in good repair; and, before yet he has lawfully donned the virile garb, to collect a fund for the support of the widows and orphans that may be; who, in short, ventures to live only by the aid of the Mutual Insurance Company, which has promised to bury him decently.

It is not a man's duty, as a matter of course, to devote himself to the eradication of any, even the most enormous wrong; he may still properly have other concerns to engage him; but it is his duty, at least, to wash his hands of it, and, if he gives it no thought longer, not to give it practically his support. If I devote myself to other pursuits and contemplations, I must first see, at least, that I do not pursue him, sitting upon another man's shoulders. I must get him off first, that he may pursue his contemplations too. See what gross inconsistency is tolerated. I have heard some of my townsmen say, 'I should like to have them order me out to help put down an insurrection of the slaves, or to march to Mexico; – see if I would go'; and yet these very men have each, directly by their allegiance, and so indirectly, at least, by their money, furnished a substitute. The soldier is applauded who refuses to serve in an unjust war by those who do not refuse to sustain the government which makes the war; is applauded by those whose act and authority he disregards and sets at naught; as if the state were penitent but not to that degree that it left off sinning for a moment. Thus, under the name of Order and Civil Government, we are all made at least to pay homage to and support our own meanness. After the first blush of sin comes its indifference; and from immoral it becomes, as it were, *un*moral, and quite unnecessary to that life which we have made.

The broadest and most prevalent error requires the most disinterested virtue to sustain it. The slight reproach to which the virtue of patriotism is commonly liable, the noble are most likely to incur. Those who, while they disapprove of the character and measures of a government, yield to it their allegiance and support are undoubtedly its most conscientious supporters, and so frequently the most serious obstacles to reform. Some are petitioning that state to dissolve the Union, to disregard the requisitions of the President. Why do they not dissolve it themselves – the union between themselves and the state – and refuse to pay their quota into its treasury? Do not they stand in the same relation to the state that the state does to the Union? And have not the same reasons prevented the state from resisting the Union which have prevented them from resisting the state?

How can a man be satisfied to entertain an opinion merely, and enjoy *it*? Is there any enjoyment in it, if his opinion is that he is aggrieved? If you are cheated out of a single dollar by your neighbour, you do not rest satisfied with knowing that you are cheated, or with saying that you are cheated, or even with petitioning him to pay you your due; but you take effectual steps at once to obtain the full amount, and see that you are never cheated again. Action from principle, the perception and the performance of right, changes things and relations; it is essentially revolutionary, and does not consist wholly with anything which was. It not only divides states and churches, it divides families; ay, it divides the *individual*; separating the diabolical in him from the divine.

Unjust laws exist: shall we be content to obey them, or shall we endeavour to amend them, and obey them until we have succeeded, or shall we transgress them at once? Men generally, under such a government as this, think that they ought to wait until they have persuaded the majority to alter them. They think that, if they should resist, the remedy would be worse than the evil. But it is the fault of the government itself that the remedy is worse than the evil. *It* makes it worse. Why does it not cherish its wise minority? Why does it cry and resist before it is hurt? Why does it not encourage its citizens to be on the alert to point out its faults, and *do* better than it would have them? Why does it always crucify Christ and excommunicate Copernicus and Luther, and pronounce Washington and Franklin rebels?

One would think, that a deliberate and practical denial of its authority was the only offence never contemplated by government; else, why has it not assigned its definite, its suitable and proportionate penalty? If a man who has no property refuses but once to earn nine shillings for the state, he is put in prison for a period unlimited by any law that I know, and determined only by the discretion of those who placed him there; but if he should steal ninety times nine shillings from the state, he is soon permitted to go at large again.

If the injustice is part of the necessary fiction of the machine of government, let it go, let it go: perchance it will wear smooth – certainly the machine will wear out. If the injustice has a spring, or a pulley, or a rope, or a crank, the remedy will not be worse than the evil; but if it is of such a nature that it requires you to be the agent of injustice to another, then, I say, break the law. Let your life be a counter friction to stop the machine. What I have to do is to see, at any rate, that I do not lend myself to the wrong which I condemn.

As for adopting the ways which the state has provided for remedying the evil, I know not of such ways. They take too much time, and a man's life will be gone. I have other affairs to attend to. I came into this world, not chiefly to make this a good place to live in, but to live in it, be it good or bad. A man has not everything to do, but something; and because he cannot do *everything*, it is not necessary that he should do *something* wrong. It is not my business to be petitioning the Governor or the Legislature any more than it is theirs to petition me; and if they should not hear my petition, what should I do then? But in this case the state has provided no way: its very constitution is the evil. This may seem to be harsh and stubborn and unconciliatory; but it is to treat with the utmost kindness and consideration the only spirit that can appreciate or deserves it. So is all change for the better, like birth or death, which convulses the body.

I do not hesitate to say, that those who call themselves Abolitionists should at once effectually withdraw their support, both in person and property, from the government of Massachusetts, and not wait till they constitute a majority of one, before they suffer the right to prevail through them. I think that it is enough if they have God on their side, without waiting for that other one. Moreover, any man more right than his neighbours constitutes a majority of one already.

RESISTANCE TO MILITARY SERVICE

LEO TOLSTOY
(From *The Kingdom of God is Within You*, 1893, translated by Aylmer Maude)

Governments were to free men from the cruelty of individual strife, to give them security in the permanence of a group life. But instead of that they subject men to the same necessity of strife, merely substituting strife with other States for strife with individual neighbours, and the danger of destruction both for the individual and for the State they leave just as it was.

The establishment of general military service resembles what happens when a man wants to prop up a rotten house. The walls bend inwards and he inserts supports, the roof sags down and other supports are put up, boards give way between the supports and still more supports are erected. And it comes to this, that though the supports hold the house they render it impossible to live in it.

It is the same with universal military service. It destroys all the benefits of the social order of life which it was employed to maintain.

The advantages of the social form of life consist in the security given to property and labour, and in associated action for the general welfare, but general military service destroys all this.

The taxes collected from the people for war preparations consume most of the production of labour that the army was intended to protect.

The tearing away of all men from their customary course of life infringes the possibility of labour itself.

The threat of war, ready to break out at any moment, renders all reforms of social life vain and useless.

In former times if a man were told that if he did not acknowledge the authority of the State he would be exposed to the attacks of evil men – domestic and foreign enemies – and would have to fight them himself and be liable to be murdered, and that therefore it was to his advantage to put up with some hardships to secure himself from such evils, he might well believe it, since the sacrifices he made for the State were only private sacrifices and afforded him the hope of a tranquil existence in a permanent State. But now when the sacrifices have been increased tenfold, and not only this, but the promised advantages have disappeared, it is natural for anyone to conclude that submission to authority is quite useless.

But the fatal significance of universal military service as a manifestation of the contradiction inherent in the social conception of life is not seen in that alone. The chief manifestation of this contradiction is contained in the fact that under universal military service every citizen, on being made a soldier, becomes a prop of the governmental organization and a participant in all the things the government does – the rightness of which he does not admit.

Governments assert that armies are chiefly needed for external defence, but that is not true. They are needed first

of all against their own subjects, and every man who performs military service involuntarily becomes an accomplice
in all the acts of violence the government inflicts on its subjects . . .

Universal military service is the last stage of violence that
governments need for the maintenance of the whole structure,
and it is the extreme limit to which submission on the part of
their subjects can go. It is the keystone of the arch holding up the edifice, and its removal would bring down the
whole building . . .

If most men choose to submit rather than refuse, that is
not the result of a sober balancing of advantages and disadvantages, but because they are induced to submit by the
hypnotization to which they are subjected. When submitting
they simply yield to the demands of the State without having
to reflect or make any effort of will. Resistance calls for
independent thought, and an effort of will of which not everyone is capable. But apart from the moral significance of com-
pliance or non-compliance, and considering it merely from
the standpoint of personal advantage, refusal will generally
be more advantageous for a man than submission.

Whoever I may be, whether I belong to the well-to-do
dominating class or to the oppressed labouring class, the disadvantages of non-submission are less and its advantages
greater than those of submission.

If I belong to the dominating minority, the disadvantages
of non-submission to the government's demands will consist
in my being tried for refusing to comply and at best I shall
be discharged, or (as is done with the Mennonites in Russia)
I shall be obliged to serve my time at some non-military
work. At worst I shall be condemned to exile or imprisonment for two or three years (I speak from examples that have
occurred in Russia), or possibly to an even longer term, or to
death – though the probability of such a penalty is very
small.

These are the disadvantages of non-submission. But the
disadvantages of submission are these: at best I shall escape
being sent to kill people and shall escape being myself exposed to the danger of being maimed or killed, and shall
merely be enrolled into military slavery. I shall be dressed

up like a clown and domineered over by every man above me in rank from a corporal to a field-marshal. I shall be forced to contort my body as they please, and after being kept from one to five years I shall for another ten years have to hold myself in readiness to be called up at any moment to go through all these things again. In the worst case I shall, in addition to all these conditions of slavery, be sent to war, where I shall be compelled to kill men of other nations who have done me no harm, and where I may be maimed or killed or (as happened in Sevastopol and as happens in every war) sent to certain death, or (most terrible of all) be sent against my own countrymen and compelled to kill my brothers for dynastic or other reasons quite alien to me.

Such are the comparative disadvantages.

The comparative advantages of submission and non-submission are these:

For a man who submits, the advantages are that after enduring all the humiliations and performing all the cruelties demanded of him, he may if he is not killed receive a gaudy red or gold decoration for his clown's dress, and may even, if he is very fortunate, obtain command of hundreds of thousands of men as brutalized as himself, and be called field-marshal and receive a lot of money.

The advantages of a man who refuses are the preservation of his human dignity, the respect of good men, and above all the certainty that he is doing God's work and so is indubitably doing good to his fellow-man.

Such are the advantages and disadvantages on both sides for a man of the oppressing, wealthy classes. For a man of the poor working class the advantages and disadvantages are the same, but with an important addition to the disadvantages. The disadvantages for a man of the labouring classes who has not refused military service comprise also this, that by entering the military service he by his participation and apparent approval, confirms the oppression to which he himself is subject.

But the question of the necessity of the State or its abolition will not be decided by reflections as to how necessary or unnecessary to men is the government they are called on to support by their participation in military service, still less will

it be decided by consideration of the advantages and disadvantages to each man of his submission or rejection of State
demands. That question will be decided irrevocably and
beyond appeal by the religious consciousness or conscience
of every man who in connection with military service has involuntarily to face the question of whether the State is to continue to exist or not.

SYNDICALISM DEFINED

GEORGE WOODCOCK
(From *Railways and Society*, 1943)

Syndicalism is a method of industrial organization which
goes away from all the traditional conceptions of authority
and government, of capitalism and the State. While communism, in abolishing individual capitalism, creates a worse
monster in its place in the form of the economic state,
syndicalism leaves all the patterns of administration which in
the past have resulted only in the oppression and exploitation of man by man, and sets out to build an organizational
form based on the natural needs of men rather than on the
interests of the ruling classes, based not on the dictates
of authority, but on the voluntary co-operation of free and
equal individuals in satisfying the economic needs of the
men who form society.

Syndicalism is the industrial manifestation of anarchism
. . . Anarchism advocates, instead of the governmental coercion of the individual, which exists in the most democratic
society that still retains the State, a society based on the
free co-operation of individual men and women for the
fulfilment of their social and economic needs. Organization,
on a voluntary basis, is necessary for the operation of the
means of production and the desirable public services, but
no kind of superior body of authority, with its parliaments,
police, bureaucracies, codes of law, taxes, armies and secretive
intrigues in internal and foreign politics, has any place or
value in a society based on justice and reason. In anarchy,

once he has fulfilled his contractual economic functions, an individual can live as he will, provided he does not interfere with the freedom of his fellows.

Anarchists believe that the means of production should be the property of society, held in common, and that only by such an arrangement will the restricting influence of private property be removed and the resources of nature and science be used to their full extent for the benefit of humanity. In order that there may be no possibility of such private interest arising, they advocate that, once the means of production have been taken out of the hands of their usurping controllers, they shall be run not by any authority or elite of leaders, but by the people who are themselves concerned in production, i.e. by the workers in each industry.

Syndicalism, as I have already said, is the method by which such control by the workers would be organized. It is, moreover, the method by which the workers under a property society would organize themselves for the attainment of the free classless society.

The syndicate is a form of union which differs from the ordinary trade union in that it aims, not only at the gaining of improvements in wages and conditions under the present system, but also at the overthrow of that system by a social revolution based on the economic direct action of the workers. This is not to say that it ignores the day-to-day struggle, but its members recognize that only by a complete destruction of the structure of property and authority can justice and security ever be attained by the workers.

The syndicate differs also from the ordinary trade union in its method of organization. The ordinary trade union follows the pattern of governmental society in that it has a centralized form, with authority at the centre and a permanent bureaucracy who, like any other bureaucracy, rapidly gain privilege and power and rise into a class with an economic position considerably higher than that of the workers who pay them and whom they are supposed to serve. The syndicate, on the other hand, is based on the organization of the workers by industry at the place of work. The workers of each factory or depot or farm are an autonomous unit, who govern their own affairs and who make all the decisions as to the work they will do. These units are joined federally in a syndicate which serves to co-ordinate the actions of the workers in each industry. The federal organization has no authority over the workers in any branch, and cannot impose a veto on action like a trade union executive. It has no permanent bureaucracy, and the few voluntary officials are chosen on a short term basis, have no privileges which raise their standard of living above that of the workers, and wield no authority of any kind.

Being governed from below and untainted by the ideas or institutions of authority, the syndicate represents more truly than any other type of organization the will of the workers and the good of society. Its lack of centralization and bureaucracy, of any kind of privilege or vested interest in the present order of society, give it a flexibility of action and a real solidarity which make it the ideal instrument for canalizing and influencing in the right way the spontaneous revolutionary activity of the people.

In the social revolution the syndicates will play their part by organizing the economic direct action of the workers. On the railways, for example, they would lead the workers in the expropriation of lines, stations and rolling stock, and their use for the purposes of the revolutionary movement and not for those of the dispossessed masters.

After the revolution the syndicates will form the framework on which the first phase of the free society will be built. Anarchists do not make any plans for the free society in its maturity, as they believe in the open and continual growth of social institutions, and recognize that any hard-and-fast plan of development will create only a rigid and sterile society. Nevertheless, they recognize that after the old society has been abolished some kind of social structure should be built immediately to take over the means of production and change the economic basis of society from that of a class order to one more appropriate to a free world. This means of organization they find in the syndicate.

The organization of industry, transport and farming under the syndicates will follow the same lines as the organization of the workers in the days before the end of the property society, except that now, instead of organizing for struggle, the workers will organize for the construction of an economic basis compatible with freedom and justice. Each working unit, a factory or a railway yard, will be run by the workers who actually operate it. There will be no authority, no management, and each worker will be jointly and equally responsible with the rest for the proper functioning of the industrial unit in which he works.

It should not be assumed from this that the syndicalist regards the operation of industry as a simple matter. On the contrary, he knows from experience its complexity, and regards a bureaucracy divorced from the actual work as being incapable of operating to its maximum efficiency so involved an organization as that of a railway. The workers are the men who have the knowledge of the actual operating of the railways, and if they were to study the problems of operation and co-ordination of their functions, they would be able to work the railways far more efficiently than the bureaucrats. The opportunity of gaining this knowledge is, of course, kept from the ordinary railway workers. In this connection I am using the word 'worker' in a broad sense, to include technical staff associated with civil engineering and locomotive construction, and also the clerical staff concerned with co-ordinating train operating, as these are both vitally necessary for the proper working of the railways and upon their direct co-operation with their fellow workers, eliminating the bureaucrats, will come a real workers' control of railways. It is therefore vitally necessary that such men should be brought into any industrial movement among the railwaymen.

In each industry the various units or sections will be joined in federations so as to co-ordinate operations throughout a country. The industrial federations or syndicates will in turn be united in a national federation of industry, which will co-ordinate activities in the various fields of work – of production and distribution and service.

The old motives of profit and self-interest will cease to dominate economic life. Instead, the incentive will be the good of the members of society, without distinction. In such circumstances there will be no impediment in the exploitation of the resources of nature and science to the full extent to which men and women desire it. People will decide the standard of life they desire and will work to attain it. It is hardly to be supposed that they will be content with what they endure today, and the possibility of better circumstances combined with the natural human inclination to work will serve to ensure that, left to themselves, the workers will find the means to operate industry a good deal more efficiently than has been the case under capitalism . . .

Hierarchical management, of course, would cease. Instead, administration would be vested in the workers themselves and, wherever it was impossible for all the workers to participate directly in administration, in delegates who would administer the functioning of the various services in accordance with the wishes of the workers who chose them. These delegates would have no authority, nor would they make any decision on questions of policy. Their task would be merely to co-ordinate work carried out entirely on a voluntary basis.

Such delegates would be in no way superior to their fellow workers, in power, privilege or position. Under anarchism the wages system, one of the prime means by which the rulers coerce the workers, would be abolished, and the workers, giving the labour necessary to carry on the functions of society, would in turn receive the goods they needed for a sufficient and happy life. No worker would get more than his mate because tradition said that his craft was worth twice as much a week, and there would be no directors or managers to live in high luxury while their lower-paid employees starved. Men would get, not according to their worth, for social worth cannot be estimated, but according to their need, which is the only just means of sharing the goods of society.

SYNDICALISM: AN ADVOCACY

PIERRE MONATTE
(From *Congrès anarchiste tenu à Amsterdam, Août 1907*,
1908, translated by George Woodcock)

What I want is not so much to give you a theoretical exposition of revolutionary syndicalism as to show it at work and in
this way to let the facts speak. Revolutionary syndicalism, unlike the forms of socialism and anarchism that preceded it,
manifests itself less through theories than through deeds,
and you must look for it in action rather than in books.

One would have to be blind not to see what there is in
common between anarchism and syndicalism. Both seek to
root out capitalism and the wage system by means of the
social revolution. Syndicalism exists as the proof of a reawakening of the working-class movement, and it revives in anarchism
a consciousness of its origins among the workers; on the other
hand, the anarchists have contributed not a little towards
bringing the working-class movement into the revolutionary
path and towards popularizing the idea of direct action. In
such ways syndicalism and anarchism have influenced each
other to their mutual benefit.

It is in France, among the militants of the Confédération
Générale du Travail, that the ideas of revolutionary socialism
emerged and were developed. The Confédération occupies
an entirely unique place in the international working-class
movement. It is the only organization that, in declaring itself
entirely revolutionary, has no attachments to any of the
political parties, not even the most advanced of them.
In most countries other than France, social-democracy plays
the leading role. In France, the CGT leaves far behind it,
both in terms of numerical strength and of the influence
it exercises, the Socialist party; claiming to represent *only*
the working class, it has firmly repulsed all the advances
that have been made to it over the past years. Autonomy

has been its strength and it intends to remain autonomous.

This stand of the CGT, its refusal to have dealings with the political parties, has earned it the title of 'anarchist' in the mouths of its exasperated adversaries. Yet nothing could be more false. The CGT, a vast grouping of syndicates and labour unions, has no official doctrine. All doctrines are represented within it and enjoy equal tolerance. A number of anarchists serve on the confederal committee; there they meet and work with socialists the majority of whom – it should be noted in passing – are no less hostile than the anarchists to any idea of an alliance between the syndicates and the Socialist party.

The structure of the CGT deserves some attention. Unlike those of so many other working-class organizations, it is neither centralist nor authoritarian. The confederal committee is not, as the editors and reporters of bourgeois papers imagine, a directive committee uniting in its hands both the legislative and executive functions; it is deprived of all authority. The CGT is controlled from below upwards; each syndicate has no master but itself; it is free to act or not to act; no will outside itself can inhibit or liberate its activity. At the base of the Confédération then is the syndicate. But this does not adhere directly to the Confédération; it can only do it through the intermediacy of its corporative federation on the one hand and its Bourses de travail on the other. It is the union of federations and the union of Bourses that together constitute the CGT.

Confederal activities are co-ordinated by the confederal committee which consists of delegates from both Bourses and federations. Besides the confederal committee there exist commissions which are drawn from its membership. These are the publication commission (for *La Voix du Peuple*), the membership commission, the budget commission, the commission for strikes and for the general strike.

In the regulation of collective affairs, the congress is entirely sovereign. Any syndicate, no matter how small it may be, has the right to be represented by a delegate chosen by itself.

The Confédération's budget is modest in the extreme. It does not exceed 30,000 francs a year. The continued agitation which climaxed in the great movement of May 1906 for the eight-hour day cost no more than 60,000 francs. Such a paltry figure, when it was divulged, created astonishment among the journalists. What! With these few thousand francs the Confédération could sustain, month after month, such an intense working-class agitation! It was because, though poor in money, French syndicalism is rich in energy, in devotion, in enthusiasm, and to such riches there is no risk of becoming a slave!

It is neither without effort nor in a short time that the French working-class movement has become what we see today. For thirty-five years – since the Paris Commune – it has been passing through multiple phases. The idea of making the proletariat, organized in 'resistance societies', the agent of social revolution was the basic idea, the seminal idea of the Great International Workingmen's Association, founded in London in 1864. The motto of the International, as you will all remember, was: 'The emancipation of the workers shall be the task of the workers themselves', and it is still our motto, the motto of all of us who are partisans of direct action and adversaries of parliamentarianism. The ideas of autonomy and federation which are so honoured among us, inspired in the past all those in the International who rebelled against the abuses of power by the General Council and, after the Hague Congress, openly took the side of Bakunin. More important, the idea of the general strike itself, which is today so popular, is an idea of the International, which first understood the power of its embraces.

The defeat of the Commune let loose a terrible reaction in France. The working-class movement was stopped dead, and its militants were murdered or forced into exile. Yet after a few years it reconstituted itself, feeble and timid at first; it would strengthen itself later . . . [when the proletariat], justly indifferent to the quarrels of the sects, recreated its unions which acquired a new name, the *syndicates*. Abandoned to itself and ignored because of its own weakness and the jealousies of rival groups, the syndicalist movement gradually acquired strength and confidence. It grew. The Fédération des Bourses was founded in 1892, the Confédération Générale du Travail, which from the beginning was careful to affirm its political neutrality, in 1895. In the meantime a workers' congress at Nantes in 1894 had voted to accept the principle of the revolutionary general strike. It was round about this time that a number of anarchists, realizing at last that philosophy is not enough to make a revolution, entered into a working-class movement which gave rise – among those who knew how to observe it, to the highest of hopes. Fernand Pelloutier was the man who at that period best incarnated this evolution among the anarchists.

All the subsequent congresses have accentuated increasingly the divorce between the organized working class and politics. At Toulouse, in 1897, our comrades Delesalle and Pouget obtained the adoption of the tactics of boycott and sabotage. In 1900, the *Voix du Peuple* was founded, with Pouget as chief editor. Emerging from the difficult period of its foundation, the CGT gives witness every day to its growing strength. It has become a power with which the government on the one hand and the socialist parties on the other must henceforward count.

From the government, supported by all the reformist socialists, the new movement suffered a terrible assault. Millerand, who had become a minister, attempted to national-ize the syndicates and to make each Bourse into a branch of his ministry. Agents in his pay worked for him in the various organizations, and an effort was made to corrupt the faithful militants. The danger was great, but it was exorcized thanks to the accord which was then reached between all the revolutionary factions, between anarchists, Guesdists and Blanquists. That accord was sustained, and the danger passed. The Confédération – strengthened from 1902 onward by the entry of the Fédération des Bourses, which meant the realization of *working-class unity* – takes its strength today from that accord, out of which was born revolutionary syndicalism, the doctrine which sees the syndicate as the organ of social transformation and the general strike its means.

But – and I ask our non-French comrades to give full attention to this very important point – neither the realiza-tion of working-class unity, nor the coalition of revolu-tionaries would have been able on its own to lead the CGT to its present level of prosperity and influence, if we had not remained faithful, in our syndicalist practice, to the fundamental principle which in fact excludes syndicates based on opinions: *only one syndicate for each profession and town.* The consequence of this principle is the political neutralization of the syndicate, which neither can nor should be either anarchist, or Guesdist, or Allemanist, or Blanquist, but simply working-class. In the syndicate divergences of opinion, which are often so subtle and artificial, take second place, and in this way agreement is possible. In practical life, interests come before ideas; in spite of all the quarrels between the schools and the sects, the interests of the workers, by the very fact that they are all subject to the law of wages, are identical. And that is the secret of the accord that was established between them, the accord that made the strength of syndicalism and allowed it last year, at the Congress of Amiens, proudly to affirm its self-sufficiency.

I would be gravely lacking if I did not show you the means on which revolutionary syndicalism counts in order to arrive at the emancipation of the working class. These means can be summed up in two words: *direct action.* What is this direct action? Long ago, under the influence of the socialist schools and principally of the Guesdist school, the workers confided to the state the task of settling their demands. How one remembers those processions of workers, headed by socialist deputies, carrying to the powers that be the accounts of the fourth estate! This form of action having led merely to deep disappointments, we came gradually to realize that the workers would never obtain any reforms that they could not impose *by themselves*; in other words, that the maxim of the International which I have just quoted should be understood and applied in the strictest manner. To act for oneself, to count only on oneself, that is direct action. But direct action, needless to say, can assume the most various forms.

Its principal form, or rather its most striking form, is the strike. A two-edged weapon, it was once said: we say, a solid and well-tempered weapon, which, wielded capably by the worker, can strike to the heart of capitalism. It is by means of the strike that the working mass enters into the class struggle and becomes familiar with the notions that emerge from it; it is by the strike that the masses receive their revolutionary education, that they understand their true strength and that of the enemy, that they take confidence in their power and learn to be audacious.

Sabotage is hardly less valuable. It can be formulated in this way: *For bad pay, bad work.* Like the strike, it has always been employed, but only in the last few years has it acquired a truly revolutionary significance. The results produced by sabotage are already considerable. On occasions when a strike has been powerless, sabotage has broken the resistance of management. A recent example is given by the sequence to a defeated strike of the building workers of Paris in 1906: the masons returned to the worksites with the resolution to give the management a peace that would be worse than war: and, by a unanimous tacit agreement, they began to slow down the rate of daily production: as if by chance, sacks of plaster or cement were found to be slashed, etc., etc. The war continues right to the present moment, and, I repeat, the results have been excellent. Not only has management given way on many occasions, but out of this campaign lasting for several months the building worker has emerged more conscious, more independent, and more rebellious.

But if I consider syndicalism as a whole, without lingering further over its particular manifestations, what apology need I make for it? The revolutionary spirit was dying in France, languishing from year to year. The revolutionarism of Guesde, for example, was no more than verbal or, even worse, electoral and parliamentary; the revolutionarism of Jaurès went even further in the same direction; it was simply, and even frankly, ministerial and governmental. As to the anarchists, their revolutionarism has taken superb retreat in the ivory tower of philosophic speculation. Among so many falterings, perhaps even because of them, syndicalism was born; the revolutionary spirit was reanimated and renewed by its contact, and the bourgeoisie – for the first time since the great voice of anarchist dynamite was silenced – the bourgeoisie trembled.

It is important that the proletarians of all countries should

profit from the syndicalist experience of the French proletariat. And it is the task of the anarchists to make sure
that the experience is repeated everywhere that there is a
working class working towards its emancipation. To that
partisan unionism which has produced, in Russia for example,
anarchist unions, and in Belgium and Germany Christian
and social-democratic unions, the anarchists should oppose a
syndicalism in the French style, a syndicalism that is neutral
or, more exactly, independent. In the same way as there is
only one working class, there should be, in each industry and
each town, no more than one working-class organization, a
single syndicate. Only on that condition can the class struggle
– ceasing to be hindered at every moment by the squabbles
of rival schools and sects – develop in all its breadth and
achieve its maximum effect.

Syndicalism, as the Congress of Amiens proclaimed in 1906,
is sufficient unto itself. That statement, I know, has never been
fully understood, even by the anarchists. It means that the
working class, having at last attained majority, means to
be self-sufficient and to rely on no-one else for its emancipation. What fault can an anarchist find with a will to action so
finely expressed?

Syndicalism does not waste time promising to the workers
an earthly paradise. It calls on them to conquer it, assuring
them that their actions will never be entirely in vain. It is a
school of will, of energy, and of fertile thinking. It opens
to anarchism, which has been too long closed in upon itself,
new perspectives and new hopes. Let all anarchists then come
to syndicalism; their work will be all the more fertile for
it, their blows against the social regime all the more decisive.

SYNDICALISM:
AN ANARCHIST CRITIQUE

ERRICO MALATESTA
(From *Congrès anarchiste tenu à Amsterdam, Août 1907*, 1908, translated by George Woodcock)

The conclusion Monatte has reached is that syndicalism is a necessary and sufficient means of social revolution. In other words, Monatte has proclaimed *that syndicalism is sufficient unto itself.* And that, in my view, is a radically false doctrine, to combating which I shall devote this discourse.

Syndicalism, or more exactly the working-class movement (for the working-class movement is a *fact* nobody can ignore, while syndicalism is a doctrine, a system, and we should avoid confounding the two), the working-class movement, I say, has always found in me a resolute but unblinded defender. I see it as particularly promising soil for our revolutionary propaganda, and also as a point of contact between the masses and ourselves. I have no need to insist on that. You must do me the justice of granting that I have never been one of those intellectual anarchists who, when the old International was dissolved, benevolently withdrew into the ivory tower of pure speculation; that wherever I have encountered it, in Italy, in France, in England and elsewhere, I have never ceased to combat that attitude of haughty isolation, and have never ceased to urge the comrades into that direction which the syndicalists, forgetting the past, call *new,* even though it was already glimpsed and followed, in the International, by the first of the anarchists.

Today, as in the past, I would like to see the anarchists entering the working-class movement. Today, as yesterday, I am a syndicalist in the sense that I am an upholder of the syndicates. I do not ask for anarchist syndicates, which would immediately give legitimacy to social-democratic, republican, royalist and all other kinds of syndicates, and which would divide the working class more than ever against itself. I do not even want to see *red* syndicates, because I do not want to see *yellow* syndicates. I would like far more to see syndicates wide open to all workers without regard for opinions, syndicates that are absolutely *neutral*.

Therefore I favour the most active participation in the working-class movement. But I do so above all in the interests of our propaganda whose scope in this way will be greatly widened. But in no way should that participation be considered as tantamount to a renunciation of our most cherished ideas. Within the syndicate we must remain anarchists, in all the strength and breadth of that definition. The working-class movement, in my eyes, is no more than a means – though doubtless it is the best of all the means that are available to us. But I refuse to take that means as an end, and in the same way I would not want us to lose sight of the totality of anarchist conceptions, or, to put it more simply, our other means of propaganda and agitation.

The syndicalists, on the other hand, are inclined to turn the means into an end, to regard the part as the whole. And in this way, in the minds of some of our comrades, syndicalism is in the process of becoming a new doctrine and of threatening the very existence of anarchism.

Yet, even if it fortifies itself with the somewhat useless epithet of revolutionary, syndicalism is no more – and will never be more – than a legalitarian and even conservative movement, with no other accessible end but the amelioration of the conditions of work. I need not look for any further proof than that which is offered to us by the great North American unions. Having shown themselves, when they were still weak, as imbued with the most radical revolutionism, these unions have become, in so far as they have gained power and wealth, completely conservative organizations, entirely concerned with making their members into the aristocrats of the factory, the workshop or the mine, and far less hostile to paternalistic capitalism than they are to non-organized workers, to that proletariat in rags so condemned by the social democrat! But that ever-growing unemployed proletariat, which is of no account to syndicalism, or which – rather – is merely an obstacle to it, we – the other anarchists – cannot forget, and it is our duty to defend it because its members have most to suffer.

Let me repeat: the anarchists must enter the working-class unions, first of all to carry on anarchist propaganda there, and then because it is the only way in which – on the day we all hope for – we may have at our disposition groups who are capable of taking over the direction of production; we must enter the unions, finally, to struggle energetically against that detestable state of mind that makes the syndicates disinclined to defend anything but special interests.

In my view, the basic error of Monatte and of all the revolutionary syndicalists arises from a much too simplistic conception of the class struggle. It is the conception according to which the economic interests of all the workers – of the working-class – are identical, the conception according to which it is enough for workers to take in hand the defence of their own interests, and the interests of the whole proletariat will be at the same time defended against capitalism.

I suggest that the reality is quite different. Like the bourgeoisie, like everyone else, the workers are subject to that law of universal competition which derives from the existence of government and private property and which will only disappear when they are extinguished. Thus, in the true sense of the word, there are no classes because there are no class interests. In the heart of the working 'class', as in the heart of the bourgeoisie, competition and struggle continue. The economic interests of one category of workers will be irrevocably opposed to those of another category. And everywhere one sees workers who both economically and morally are far nearer to the bourgeoisie than they are to the proletariat. Cornelissen has given us examples of this taken from this very country of Holland, and there are plenty of others. I don't need to remind you how often in strikes the workers employ violence – against the police and the managers? Not in the least, but against the *blacklegs* who nevertheless are workers just as exploited as themselves and even more humiliated, while the true enemies of the workers, the real obstacles to social equality, are still the police and the employers.

Nevertheless, moral solidarity is possible among the workers even in the absence of economic solidarity. The workers who isolate themselves in the defence of their corporate interests may not be aware of it, but it will emerge on the day when a common will towards social transformation turns them into new men. In present-day society, solidarity can only result from a communion that develops under the aegis of a shared ideal. It is the role of the anarchists to awaken the syndicates to that ideal, to orient them gradually towards the social revolution – at the risk of harm to those 'immediate advantages' to which at the present they seem so partial.

One cannot deny that syndicalist action involves us in certain perils. The greatest of these perils undoubtedly lies in the acceptance by the militant of office in the syndicates, particularly when it is paid office. Let us take it as a general rule: the anarchist who becomes a permanent and paid official in a syndicate is lost to propaganda, lost to anarchism! Henceforward he is under obligation to those who pay him and, since these are not all anarchists, the salaried official – placed between his conscience and his interest – must either follow his conscience and lose his position, or follow his interest – and then, goodbye to anarchism!

The presence of the official in the working-class movement is a danger comparable only to that of parliamentarism: both of them lead to corruption, and from corruption to death is not a very long step.

And now, let us consider the general strike. Personally, I accept the principle and for years I have been propagating it to the best of my powers. The general strike has always seemed to me an excellent means for starting the social revolution. Yet we must be on our guard against falling into the disastrous illusion that the general strike makes armed insurrection unnecessary.

We are told that by means of halting production abruptly the workers will succeed in a few days in starving out the bourgeoisie who, dying with hunger, will be obliged to surrender. I can think of no more grandiose absurdity. The first to die of hunger during a general strike would not be the bourgeois, who dispose of all the stores, but the workers who have only their toil on which to live.

The general strike as it is foretold to us is a pure utopia.

Either the worker, dying with hunger after three days of striking, will go back with bowed head to the workshop, and we can chalk up yet another defeat. Or he will seek to take over production by main force. Who will he find waiting to stop him? Soldiers, policemen, apart from the bourgeois themselves, and then the matter cannot help resolving into shooting and bombs. It will be insurrection, and victory will be to the strongest.

Let us therefore prepare for that inevitable insurrection instead of limiting ourselves to looking forward to the general strike as a panacea for all ills. And do not let anyone argue that governments are armed to the teeth and always stronger than those who rebel. In Barcelona in 1902 the soldiers were not very numerous. But nobody was ready for armed struggle and the workers, failing to understand that the political power was the real adversary, sent their delegates to the governor to ask him to force the employers to give in.

But even if we consider it in realistic terms, the general strike is still one of the weapons with two edges which it is necessary to employ with great caution. The provision of subsistence cannot be suspended indefinitely. Sooner or later it will be necessary to seize the means of feeding people, and for that we cannot wait until the strike has developed into an insurrection.

It is not so much to cease work that we should call on the workers, but rather to continue it for their own benefit. Without that, the general strike will soon be transformed into a general famine, even though one might have been energetic enough to seize hold immediately of all the produce accumulated in the shops. Basically, the idea of the general strike emerges from a totally erroneous belief: the belief that by taking over the products accumulated by the bourgeoisie, humanity can continue consuming, without producing, for no-one knows how many months and years. Such a belief inspired the authors of two propaganda pamphlets published twenty years ago and entitled *Les Produits de la Terre* and *Les Produits d'Industrie*, and these pamphlets, in my view, have done far more harm than good. Existing society is not in fact so rich as many believe. Kropotkin has shown somewhere or other that in the event of an abrupt cessation of production England would have no more than a month's produce; London would have only enough for three days. I know all about the phenomenon known as over-production. But over-production has its immediate corrective in the crises that quickly establish order in industry. Over-production is never more than temporary and relative.

I must now end. In the past I deplored that the comrades isolated themselves from the working-class movement. Today I deplore that many of us, falling into the contrary extreme, let themselves be swallowed up in the same movement. Once again, working-class organization, the strike, the general strike, direct action, boycott, sabotage and armed insurrection itself, are only *means*. Anarchy is the *end*. The anarchist revolution which we desire far exceeds the interests of a single class: it proposes the complete liberation of enslaved humanity, from the triple viewpoint, economic, political and moral. And let us therefore be on our guard against any unilateral and simplistic plan of action. Syndicalism is an excellent means of action by reason of the working-class forces which it puts at our disposition, but it cannot be our sole means. Even less must we lose sight of the one end that is worth our effort: Anarchy!

A.R.

Part 5
Flowers for the Rebels who Failed

There has never been a completely anarchist revolution or an anarchist society, but there have been insurrectionary situations approximating quite closely to the anarchist model, and over brief periods there have been local and partial experiments in anarchist organization. These occasions have taken on in the minds of anarchists a certain mythical quality, so that they celebrate their memory – the memory of the revolutions which, as an anarchist character in Malraux's *L'Espoir* remarked, are 'the holidays of life'.

The Paris Commune is the first of these occasions. The Commune was not the work of anarchists, and even less of Marxists. But Mutualist members of the International and disciples of Proudhon, including the painter Gustave Courbet, took an active part, as did associates of Bakunin like Eugène Varlin and Elisée Reclus. The idea of the Commune, of decentralized local government, was an anarchist idea, but – as Kropotkin's discussion of events of 1871 makes clear – later anarchists criticized the Communards for not having wrought more radical changes in social and economic relations.

In Russia, despite the great international reputation of Bakunin and Kropotkin, and despite a considerable Bakuninist influence on the Russian populist parties, the actual anarchist movement was always small, so that it played a minor part in the revolution of 1917 and, though for the most part its members fought beside the Bolsheviks in October because they believed in the soviets as free councils of workers and peasants, they were among the first of the dissidents proscribed and eliminated by the Cheka. Only in the Ukraine, as

an insurrectionary movement of peasants led by Nestor
Makhno, was anarchism a real force in Russia, and Makhno's
triumphs were mainly those of an inspired guerilla leader,
fighting against both Reds and Whites for local autonomy.
The very circumstances of constant warfare made it difficult
for any substantial advance to be made towards creating a
non-governmental society, but, as Peter Arshinov's account
suggests, the Makhnovists did sustain as far as lay in
their power the libertarian way of social organization.

Much more was achieved in Spain during the early months
of the Civil War, when the anarchists found themselves in
virtual control of large areas of Catalonia, Aragon and
Andalusia. In Barcelona most industries were collectivized
and run by the syndicates of the CNT, the anarchist-domin-
ated federation of unions. In the rural areas thousands of
villages transformed themselves into free communes following
the preachings of the wandering libertarian teachers who
had been moving through the countryside for two generations with their message of liberty. The extracts we have
included are George Orwell's powerful impression of Barcelona as a revolutionary city, two accounts of village communes by Borkenau (a critical observer) and Gaston Leval
(a supporter) respectively, a poem by Herbert Read which
transforms the Spanish communes into a symbol of social
integration, and a celebrated newspaper interview with that
formidable man of action, Buenaventura Durutti, whose
anarchist column achieved notable victories in Aragon;
Durutti's refusal to place his trust in governments must be
seen in the context of the fact that some anarchist leaders
did enter the republican government, an error that had
serious consequences in sapping anarchist strength, which lies
precisely in a realm of action outside that of government.
The best discussions of this question are too long to reproduce here, but Vernon Richards's *Lessons of the Spanish
Revolution* makes an excellent examination of the issues.

Most recently, anarchists have seen the Paris insurrection
of 1968, which sprang up with such spontaneous fury, as a
kind of pre-anarchist uprising. Certainly anarchists and
anarchistic groups played a more active role than most of
the rigidly political party formations which joined by after-

thought, and the strange unorganized order of the whole occasion made it especially appealing to anarchists, as Murray Bookchin's *Paris 1968* reveals. Perhaps most important, the Paris insurrection showed that highly organized authoritarian governments may be even more vulnerable than their predecessors to libertarian methods used effectively.

THE PARIS COMMUNE, 1871

PETER KROPOTKIN
(From *The Commune of Paris*, 1895)

On March 18 1871, the people of Paris rose against a despised and detested government, and proclaimed the city independent, free, belonging to itself.

This overthrow of the central power took place without the usual stage effects of revolution, without the firing of guns, without the shedding of blood upon barricades. When the armed people came out into the streets, the rulers fled away, the troops evacuated the town, the civil functionaries hurriedly retreated to Versailles carrying everything they could with them. The government evaporated like a pond of stagnant water in a spring breeze, and on the nineteenth the great city of Paris found herself free from the impurity which had defiled her, with the loss of scarcely a drop of her children's blood.

Yet the change thus accomplished began a new era in that long series of revolutions whereby the people are marching from slavery to freedom. Under the name 'Commune of Paris' a new idea was born, to become the starting point for future revolutions.

As is always the case, this fruitful idea was not the product of some one individual's brain, of the conceptions of some philosopher; it was born of the collective spirit, it sprang from the heart of a whole community. But at first it was vague, and many of those who acted upon and gave their lives for it did not look at it in the light in which we see it today; they

did not realize the full extent of the revolution they inaugurated or the fertility of the new principle they tried to
put into practice. It was only after they had begun to apply it
that its future bearing slowly dawned upon them; it was only
afterwards, when the new principle came to be thought out,
that it grew definite and precise and was seen in all its
clearness, in all its beauty, its justice and the importance of
its results.

During the five or six years that came before the Commune, socialism had taken a new departure in the spread and
rapid growth of the International Workingmen's Association.
In its local branches and general congresses the workers of
Europe met together and took counsel with one another
upon the social question as they had never done before.
Among those who saw that social revolution was inevitable
and were actively busy in making ready for it, one problem
above all others seemed to press for solution. 'The existing
development of industry will force a great economic revolution upon our society; this revolution will abolish private
property, will put in common all the capital piled up by
previous generations; but, what form of political grouping
will be most suited to these changes in our economic
system?'

'The grouping must not be merely national,' answered
the International Workingmen's Association, 'it must extend
across all artificial frontiers and boundary lines.' And soon
this grand idea sunk into the hearts of the peoples and took
fast hold of their minds. Though it has been hunted down
ever since by the united efforts of every species of reactionary,
it is alive nevertheless, and when the voice of the peoples in
revolt shall melt the obstacles to its development, it will reappear stronger than ever.

But it still remained to discover what should be the component parts of this vast association.

To this question two answers were given, each the expression of a distinct current of thought. One said the popular
state; the other said anarchy.

The German socialists advocated that the state should
take possession of all accumulated wealth and give it over
to associations of workers, and, further, should organize

production and exchange, and generally watch over the life and activities of society.

To them the socialists of the Latin race, strong in revolutionary experience, replied that it would be a miracle if such a state could ever exist; but if it could, it would surely be the worst of tyrannies. This ideal of the all-powerful and beneficient state is merely a copy from the past, they said; and they confronted it with a new ideal: an-archy, that is, the total abolition of the state, and social organization from the simple to the complex by means of the free federation of popular groups of producers and consumers.

It was soon admitted, even by the more liberal-minded state socialists, that anarchy certainly represented a much better sort of organization than that aimed at by the popular state. But, they said, the anarchist ideal is so far off that just now we cannot trouble about it.

At the same time, it was true that the anarchist theory did need some short, clear mode of expression, some formula at once simple and practical, to show plainly its point of departure and embody its conceptions, to indicate how it was supported by an actually existing tendency among the people. A federation of workers' unions and groups of consumers regardless of frontiers and quite independent of existing states seemed too vague; and, moreover, it was easy to see that it could not fully satisfy all the infinite variety of human requirements. A clearer formula was wanted, one more easily grasped, one which had a firm foundation in the realities of actual life.

If the question had merely been how best to elaborate a theory, we should have said theories, as theories, are not of so very much importance. But as long as a new idea has not found a clear, precise form of statement, growing naturally out of things as they actually exist, it does not take hold of men's minds, does not inspire them to enter into the unknown without some positive and clearly formulated idea to serve them, so to say, as a springboard when they reach the starting point.

As for the starting point, they must be led up to it by life itself.

For five whole months Paris had been isolated by the

German besiegers; for five whole months she had to draw upon her own vital resources, and moral strength which she possessed. She had caught a glimpse of her own force of initiative and realized what it meant. At the same time she had seen that the prating crew who seized power had no idea how to organize either the defence of France or its internal development. She had seen the central government at cross purposes with every manifestation of the intelligence of the mighty city. Finally, she had come to realize that any government must be powerless to guard against great disasters or to smooth the path of rapid evolution. During the siege her defenders, her workers, had suffered the most frightful privations, while her idlers revelled in insolent luxury, and thanks to the central government she had seen the failure of every attempt to put an end to these scandals. Each time that her people had showed signs of a desire for a free scope, the government had added weight to their chains. Naturally such experiences gave birth to the idea that Paris must make herself an independent commune, able to realize within her walls the wishes of her citizens.

The Commune of 1871 could be nothing but a first attempt. Beginning at the close of a great war, hemmed in between two armies ready to join hands and crush the people, it dared not unhesitatingly set forth upon the path of economic revolution. It neither boldly declared itself socialist nor proceeded to the expropriation of capital nor the organization of labour. It did not even take stock of the general resources of the city.

Nor did it break with the tradition of the state, of representative government. It did not seek to effect *within* the Commune the very organization from the simple to the complex which is inaugurated *without*, by proclaiming the independence and free federation of communes.

Yet it is certain that if the Commune of Paris could have lived a few months longer, it would have been inevitably driven by the force of circumstances toward both these revolutions. Let us not forget that the French middle class spent altogether four years (from 1789 to 1793) in revolutionary action before they changed a limited monarchy into a republic. Ought we then to be astonished that the people of Paris did not cross with one bound the space between an anarchist commune and the government of the spoilers? But let us also bear in mind that the next revolution, which in France and Spain at least will be communal, will take up the work of the Commune of Paris where it was interrupted by the massacres of the Versailles soldiery.

The Commune was defeated, and too well we know how the middle class avenged itself for the scare given it by the people when they shook their rulers' yoke loose upon their necks. It proved that there really are two classes in our modern society; on one side, the man who works and yields up to the monopolists of property more than half of what he produces and yet lightly passes over the wrong done him by his masters; on the other, the idler, the spoiler, hating his slave, ready to kill him like game, animated by the most savage instincts as soon as he is menaced in his possession.

After having shut in the people of Paris and closed all means of exit, the Versailles government let loose soldiers upon them; soldiers brutalized by drink and barrack life, who had been publicly told to make short work of 'the wolves and their cubs' . . .

And after this mad orgy, these piles of corpses, this whole-sale extermination, came the petty revenge, the cat-o-nine-tails, the irons in the ship's hold, the blows and insults of the jailers, the semi-starvation, all the refinements of cruelty. Can the people forget those base deeds?

Overthrown, but not conquered, the Commune in our days is born again. It is no longer a dream of the vanquished, caressing in imagination the lovely mirage of hope. No! the 'commune' of today is becoming the visible and definite aim of the revolution rumbling beneath our feet. The idea is sinking deep into the masses, it is giving them a rallying cry. We count on the present generation to bring about the social revolution *within* the commune, to put an end to the ignoble system of middle-class exploitation, to rid the people of the tutelage of the State, to inaugurate a new era of liberty, equality, solidarity in the evolution of the human race.

*   *   *   *   *

Ten years already separate us from the day when the people of Paris overthrew the traitor government which raised itself to power at the downfall of the empire; how is it that the oppressed masses of the civilized world are still irresistibly drawn toward the movement of 1871? Why is the idea represented by the Commune of Paris so attractive to the workers of every land, of every nationality?

The answer is easy. The revolution of 1871 was above all a popular one. It was made by the people themselves, it sprang spontaneously from the midst of the mass, and it was among the great masses of the people that it found its defenders, its heroes, its martyrs. It is just because it was so thoroughly 'low' that the middle class can never forgive it. And at the same time its moving spirit was the idea of a social revolution; vague certainly, perhaps unconscious, but still the effort to obtain at last, after the struggle of many centuries, true freedom, true equality for all men. It was the revolution of the lowest of the people marching forward to conquer their rights.

Attempts have been and are made to change the sense of this revolution, to represent it as a mere effort to regain the independence of Paris and thus to constitute a tiny state within France. But nothing could be more untrue. Paris did not seek to isolate herself from France, any more than to conquer it by force of arms; she did not care to shut herself within her walls like a nun in a convent; she was not inspired by the narrow spirit of the cloister. If she claimed her independence, if she tried to hinder the interference of the central power in her affairs, it was because she saw in that independence a means of quietly elaborating the bases of future organization and bringing about within herself a social revolution; a revolution which would have completely transformed the whole system of production and exchange by basing them on justice; which would have completely modified human relations by putting them on a footing of equality; which would have formed our social morality anew by founding it upon equality and solidarity. Communal independence was then but a means for the people of Paris; the social revolution was their end.

And this end might have been attained if the revolution

of March 18 had been able to take its natural course, if the people of Paris had not been cut to pieces by the assassins from Versailles. To find a clear, precise idea, comprehensible to all the world and summing up in a few words what was needed to accomplish the revolution, this was really the pre-occupation of the people of Paris from the earliest days of their independence. But a great idea does not germinate in a day, however rapid the elaboration and propagation of ideas during periods of revolution. It always needs a certain time to develop, to spread throughout the masses, to trans-late itself into action, and this time the Commune of Paris failed. It failed mostly because, as we have before observed, socialism ten years ago was passing through a period of transition. The authoritative and semi-religious communism of 1848 had no longer any hold over the practical, free-thinking minds of our epoch. The collectivism which attempted to yoke together the wage system and collective property, was incomprehensible, unattractive, and bristling with difficulties in practical application. Free communism, anarchist communism, was only beginning to dawn upon the minds of the workers and scarcely ventured to provoke the attacks of the worshipper of government. Minds were undecided. Socialists themselves, having no definite end in view, did not dare to lay hands upon private property; they deluded themselves with the argument which has lulled the activities of many an age: 'Let us first make sure of victory, and then see what can be done.'

Make sure of victory! As if there were any way of form-ing a free commune without laying hands upon property! As if there were any way of conquering the foe while the great mass of the people is not directly interested in the tri-umph of the revolution, by seeing that it will bring material, moral and intellectual well-being to everybody! They tried to consolidate the Commune first and defer the social revolu-tion until afterward, whereas the only way to go about it was *to consolidate the Commune by means of the social revolution.*

The same thing happened with regard to the principle of government. By proclaiming the free Commune, the people of Paris proclaimed an essential anarchist principle, which was the breakdown of the state. But as the idea of anarchism had then but faintly dawned upon men's minds, it was checked half way, and in the midst of the Commune the ancient principle of authority cropped up and the people gave themselves a council of the Commune, on the model of municipal councils elsewhere.

And yet, if we admit that a central government to regulate the relations of communes between themselves is quite needless, why should we admit its necessity to regulate the mutual relations of the groups which make up each commune? And if we leave the business of coming to a common understanding with regard to enterprises which concern several cities at once to the free initiative of the communes concerned, why refuse this same free initiative to the groups composing a single commune? There is no more reason for a government inside the commune than for a government outside.

But in 1871, the people of Paris, who have overthrown so many governments, were only making their first attempt to revolt against the governmental system itself; consequently they let themselves be carried away by the fetish worship of governments and set up one of their own.

The result is a matter of history. Paris sent her devoted sons to the town hall. There, shelved in the midst of files of old papers, obliged to rule when their instincts prompted them to be and to act among the people, obliged to discuss when it was needful to act, to compromise when no compromise was the best policy, and, finally, losing the inspiration which only comes from continual contact with the masses, they saw themselves reduced to impotence. Being paralysed by their separation from the people – the revolutionary centre and heart – they themselves paralysed the popular initiative.

The Commune of Paris, the child of a period of transition, born beneath the Prussian guns, was doomed to perish. But by its eminently popular character it began a new series of revolutions, by its ideas it was the forerunner of the social revolution. Its lesson has been learned, and when France once more bristles with communes in revolt, the people are not likely to give themselves a government and expect that government to initiate revolutionary measures. When they have rid themselves of the parasites who devour them, they will take possession of all social wealth to share according to the principles of anarchist communism. And when they have entirely abolished property, government, and the state, they will form themselves freely, according to the necessities indicated by life itself. Breaking its chains, overthrowing its idols, humanity will march onward to a better future, knowing neither masters nor slaves, keeping its veneration for the noble martyrs who bought with their blood and suffering those first attempts at emancipation which have enlightened our march toward the conquest of liberty.

MAKHNO'S ANARCHISM IN PRACTICE

PETER ARSHINOV
(From *History of the Makhnovist Movement* (*1918-1921*), 1923, translated by Lorraine and Fredy Perlman, 1974)

It is necessary to emphasize the historic fact that the honour of having annihilated the Denikinist counter-revolution in the autumn of 1919 belongs almost entirely to the Makhnovists. If the insurgents had not won the decisive victory at Peregonovka, and had not destroyed the Denikinist supply lines for artillery, food and ammunition, the Whites would probably have entered Moscow in December 1919. The battle between the Whites and the Reds near Orel was relatively insignificant. In fact, Denikin's southern retreat had already begun before this battle, having been provoked precisely by the defeat of his rearguard. All the subsequent military operations of the Denikinists had the sole purpose of protecting their rear and evacuating their munitions and supplies. Along the whole length of the route from Orel through Kursk to the shores of the Black Sea and the Sea of Azov, the Red Army advanced almost without resistance. Its entry into the Ukraine and the Caucasus was carried out in exactly the same way as its entry had been carried out a year earlier, at the time of the fall of the Hetman – along paths that were already cleared.

Purely military concerns absorbed nearly all the forces of the Makhnovists at this time. The state of war in the region was absolutely unfavourable to internal creative activities. Even so, the Makhnovists demonstrated the necessary initiative and diligence in this domain as well. First of all, wherever they went they undertook to prevent an important misunderstanding: the possibility of being taken for a new power or party. As soon as they entered a city, they declared that they did not represent any kind of authority, that their armed forces obliged no one to any sort of obligation and had no other aim than to protect the freedom of the working people. The freedom of the peasants and workers, said the Makhnovists, resided in the peasants and workers themselves and might not be restricted. In all fields of their lives it was up to the workers and peasants to construct what they considered necessary. As for the Makhnovists, they could only assist them with advice, and by putting at their disposal the intellectual or military forces they needed, but under no circumstances could the Makhnovists in any way prescribe for them.

Alexandrovsk and the surrounding region were the first places where the Makhnovists remained for a fairly long time. They immediately invited the working population to participate in a general conference of the workers of the city. When the conference met, a detailed report was given on the military situation in the region and it was proposed that the workers organize the life of the city and the functioning of the factories with their own forces and their own organizations, basing themselves on the principles of labour and equality. The workers enthusiastically acclaimed all these suggestions; but they hesitated to carry them out, troubled by their novelty, and troubled mainly by the nearness of the front, which made them fear that the situation of the city was uncertain and unstable. The first conference was followed by a second. The problems of organizing life according to the principles of self-management by the workers were examined and discussed with animation by the masses of workers, who all welcomed this idea with the greatest enthusiasm, but who only with difficulty succeeded in giving it concrete forms. Railroad workers took the first step in this direction. They formed a committee charged with organizing the railway network of the region, establishing a detailed plan for the movement of trains, the transport of passengers, the system of payments, etc. From this point on, the proletariat of Alexandrovsk began to turn systematically to the problem of creating organs of self-management.

Shortly after the workers' meetings, a regional congress of peasants and workers was called at Alexandrovsk for October 20 1919. More than 200 delegates took part, among whom 180 were peasants, and the rest workers. The congress dealt with: a) military questions (the struggle against Denikin; reinforcement and maintenance of the insurrectionary army); b) questions dealing with the constructive activity in the region.

The congress continued for nearly a week and was characterized by a remarkable spirit on the part of those present. This was largely due to specific circumstances. First of all, the return of the victorious Makhnovist army to its own region was an extremely important event for the peasants, since nearly every family had one or two of its members among the insurgents. But still more important was the fact that the congress met in conditions of absolute freedom. There was no influence emanating from above. Besides all this, the congress had an excellent militant and speaker in the anarchist Voline, who, to the amazement of the peasants, lucidly expressed their own thoughts and wishes. The idea of free soviets genuinely functioning in the interests of the working population; the question of direct relations between peasants and city workers, based on mutual exchange of the products of their labour; the launching of a stateless and egalitarian social organization in the cities and the country – all these ideas which Voline developed in his lectures, represented the very ideas of the peasantry. This was precisely the way the peasants conceived the revolution and creative revolutionary work . . .

When the peasants left, they emphasized the need to put the decisions of the congress into practice. The delegates took away with them copies of the resolutions in order to make them known all over the countryside . . . Unfortunately, the freedom of the working masses is continually threatened by its worst enemy – authority. The delegates hardly had time to return to their homes when many of their villages were again occupied by Denikin's troops, coming by forced marches from the northern front. To be sure, this time the invasion was only of short duration; it was the death agony of a dying enemy. But it halted the constructive work of the peasants at the most vital moment, and since another authority, equally hostile to the freedom of the masses – Bolshevism – was approaching from the north, this invasion did irreparable harm to the workers' cause: not only was it impossible to assemble a new congress, but even the decisions of the first could not be put into practice.

In the city of Ekaterinoslav, which was occupied by the insurgent army at the time of the congress, conditions were even less favourable for constructive activity in the economic sphere. Denikin's troops, who were driven out of the city, managed to dig in on the left bank of the Dnieper River. Daily, for a whole month, they bombarded the city from their numerous armoured trains. Each time the cultural section of the insurrectionary army managed to call a meeting of the city's workers, the Denikinists, who were well informed, fired great numbers of shells, especially in the places where the sessions were held. No serious work, no systematic organization was possible. It was possible to hold only a few meetings in the centre and in the suburbs of the city. The Makhnovists did, however, succeed in publishing their daily newspaper . . .

Throughout the liberated region, the Makhnovists were the only organization powerful enough to impose its will on the enemy. But they never used this power for the purpose of domination or even to gain political influence; they never used it against their purely political or ideological opponents. The military opponents, the conspirators against the freedom of action of the workers and peasants, the state apparatus, the prisons – these were the elements against which the efforts of the Makhnovist army were directed.

Prisons are the symbol of the servitude of the people. They are always built to subjugate the people, the workers and peasants. Throughout the centuries, the bourgeoisie in all countries crushed the spirit of rebellion or resistance of the masses by means of execution and imprisonment. And in our time, in the Communist and Socialist State, prisons devour mainly the proletariat of the city and the country-side. Free people have no use for prisons. Wherever prisons exist, the people are not free. Prisons represent a constant threat to the workers, an encroachment on their conscious-ness and will, and a visible sign of their servitude. This is how the Makhnovists defined their relationship to prisons. In keeping with this attitude, they demolished prisons wherever they went. In Berdyansk the prison was dynamited in the presence of an enormous crowd, which took an active part in its destruction. At Alexandrovsk, Krivoi-Rog, Ekaterino-slav and elsewhere, prisons were demolished or burned by the Makhnovists. Everywhere the workers cheered this act.

It gives us great satisfaction to be able to state that the Makhnovists fully applied the revolutionary principles of freedom of speech, of thought, of the Press, and of political association. In all the cities and towns occupied by the Makhnovists, they began by lifting all the prohibitions and repealing all the restrictions imposed on the Press and on political organizations by one or another power. Complete freedom of speech, Press, assembly, and association of any kind and for everyone was immediately proclaimed. During the few weeks that the Makhnovists spent at Ekaterinoslav, five or six newspapers of various political orientations appeared: the right Socialist-Revolutionary paper, *Narodov-lastie* (*The People's Power*), the left Socialist-Revolution-ary paper, *Znamya Vosstanya* (*The Standard of Revolt*), the Bolshevik *Zvezda* (*Star*), and others. However, the Bolsheviks hardly had the right to freedom of the Press and association because they had destroyed, wherever they had been able to, the freedom of the Press and association of the working class, and also because their organization at Ekaterinoslav had taken a direct part in the criminal invasion of the Gulyai-Polye region in June 1919; it would only have been just to inflict a severe punishment on them. But, in order not to injure the great principles of freedom of speech and assembly, the Bolsheviks were not disturbed and could enjoy, along with all the other political tendencies, all the rights inscribed on the banner of the proletarian revolution.

The only restriction that the Makhnovists considered necessary to impose on the Bolsheviks, the left-Socialist-Revolu-
tionaries, and other statists was a prohibition on the formation
of those 'revolutionary committees' which sought to impose
a dictatorship over the people. In Alexandrovsk, right after
the occupation of these cities by the Makhnovists, the
Bolsheviks hastened to organize *Revkoms* (*Revolutionary
Committees*), seeking through them to establish their political
power and govern the population. At Alexandrovsk, the members of the *Revkom* went so far as to propose to Makhno
a division of spheres of action, leaving Makhno the military
power and reserving for the Committee full freedom of action
and all political and civil authority. Makhno advised them to
go and take up some honest trade instead of seeking to
impose their will on the workers; he even threatened to put
to death the members of the *Revkom* if they undertook any
authoritarian measures against the working population. At
Ekaterinoslav, a similar *Revkom* was dissolved in the same
way. In this context the Makhnovists' attitude was completely
justified and consistent. To protect the full freedom of speech,
Press organization, they had to take measures against formations which sought to stifle this freedom, to suppress other
organizations, and to impose their will and dictatorial
authority on the workers. And when, in November, 1919, the
commander of the Makhnovist Third (Crimean) insurrectional Regiment, Polonsky, was implicated in the activities
of an authoritarian organization of this type, he was executed
along with other members of the organization.

Here is the Makhnovists' text regarding freedom of the
Press and of association:

1. All socialist political parties, organizations and tendencies
have the right to propagate their ideas, theories, views and
opinions freely, both orally and in writing. No restriction
of socialist freedom of speech and Press will be allowed,
and no persecution will take place in this domain.

Remark. Military communiqués may not be printed
unless they are supplied by the editors of the central organ
of the revolutionary insurgents, *Put' k Svobode.*

2. In allowing all political parties and organizations full and complete freedom to propagate their ideas, the Makhnovist insurgent army wishes to inform all the parties that any attempt to prepare, organize and impose a political authority over the working people will not be permitted by the revolutionary insurgents, such an act having nothing in common with the free dissemination of ideas.

Ekaterinoslav. November 5, 1919.
Revolutionary Military Council of
the Makhnovist Insurgent Army

In the course of the whole Russian Revolution, the period of the Makhnovschina was the only period in which the freedom of the working masses found full expression. However painful and unstable the situation in Alexandrovsk, and especially in Ekaterinoslav, where shells from the armoured trains of Denikin's army fell daily, the workers of these two cities could for the first time in their history say and do anything they wanted, and as they wanted. In addition, they at last held in their own hands the tremendous possibility to organize their life and their work themselves, according to their own judgments and their own understanding of justice and truth.

At the end of the month, the Makhnovists were forced to leave Ekaterinoslav. But they had time to demonstrate to the working masses that true freedom resides in the hands of the workers themselves, and that it begins to radiate and develop as soon as statelessness and equality are established among them.

ANARCHISTS IN THE SPANISH CIVIL WAR

Buenaventura Durutti in an interview with
Pierre Van Paasen
(*Toronto Star*, September 1936)

For us it is a question of crushing fascism once and for all. Yes, and in spite of government.

No government in the world fights fascism to the death. When the bourgeoisie sees power slipping from its grasp it has recourse to fascism to maintain itself. The liberal government of Spain could have rendered the fascist elements powerless long ago. Instead it temporised and compromised and dallied. Even now at this moment, there are men in this government who want to go easy with the rebels. You can never tell, you know – the present government might yet need these rebellious forces to crush the workers' movement . . .

We know what we want. To us it means nothing that there is a Soviet Union somewhere in the world, for the sake of whose peace and tranquillity the workers of Germany and China were sacrificed to fascist barbarism by Stalin. We want the revolution here in Spain, right now, not maybe after the next European war. We are giving Hitler and Mussolini far more worry today with our revolution than the whole Red Army of Russia. We are setting an example to the German and Italian working class how to deal with fascism.

I do not expect any help for a libertarian revolution from any government in the world. Maybe the conflicting interests in the various imperialisms might have some influence on our struggle. That is quite possible. Franco is doing his best to drag Europe into the conflict. He will not hesitate to pitch Germany in against us. But we expect no help, not even from our government in the last analysis.

[Pierre Van Paasen interjects: 'You will be sitting on a pile of ruins if you are victorious.']

We have always lived in slums and holes in the wall. We

will know how to accommodate ourselves for a time. For you must not forget, we can also build. It is we who built those palaces and cities here in Spain and America and everywhere. We, the workers, can build others to take their place. And better ones. We are not in the least afraid of ruins. We are going to inherit the earth. There is not the slightest doubt about that. The bourgeoisie might blast and ruin its own world before it leaves the stage of history. We carry a new world, here in our hearts. That world is growing this minute.

BARCELONA, 1936

GEORGE ORWELL
(From *Homage to Catalonia*, 1938)

This was in late December 1936, less than seven months ago as I write, and yet it is a period that has already receded into enormous distance. Later events have obliterated it much more completely than they have obliterated 1935, or 1905, for that matter. I had come to Spain with some notion of writing newspaper articles, but I had joined the militia almost immediately, because at that time and in that atmosphere it seemed the only conceivable thing to do. The Anarchists were still in virtual control of Catalonia and the revolution was still in full swing. To anyone who had been there since the beginning it probably seemed even in December or January that the revolutionary period was ending; but when one came straight from England the aspect of Barcelona was something startling and overwhelming. It was the first time that I had ever been in a town where the working class was in the saddle. Practically every building of any size had been seized by the workers and was draped with red flags or with the red and black flag of the Anarchists; every wall was scrawled with the hammer and sickle and with the initials of the revolutionary parties; almost every church had been gutted and its images burnt. Churches here and there were being systematically demolished by gangs of workmen. Every shop and café had an inscription saying that it had been collectivized; even the bootblacks had been collectivized and their boxes painted red and black. Waiters and shop-walkers looked you in the face and treated you as an equal. Servile and even ceremonial forms of speech had temporarily disappeared. Nobody said 'Señor' or 'Don' or even 'Usted'; everyone called everyone else 'Comrade' and 'Thou', and said 'Salud!' instead of 'Buenos dias'. Tipping had been forbidden by law since the time of Primo de Rivera; almost my first experience was receiving a lecture from a hotel manager for trying to tip a lift-boy. There were no private motor cars, they had all been commandeered, and all the trams and taxis and much of the other transport were painted red and black. The revolutionary posters were everywhere, flaming from the walls in clean reds and blues that made the few remaining advertisements look like daubs of mud. Down the Ramblas, the wide central artery of the town where crowds of people streamed constantly to and fro, the loud-speakers were bellowing revolutionary songs all day and far into the night. And it was the aspect of the crowds that was the queerest thing of all. In outward appearance it was a town in which the wealthy classes had practically ceased to exist. Except for a small number of women and foreigners there were no 'well-dressed' people at all. Practically everyone wore rough working-class clothes, or blue overalls or some variant of the militia uniform. All this was queer and moving. There was much in it that I did not understand, in some ways I did not even like it, but I recognized it immediately as a state of affairs worth fighting for. Also I believed that things were as they appeared, that this was really a workers' State and that the entire bourgeoisie had either fled, been killed, or voluntarily come over to the workers' side; I did not realize that great numbers of well-to-do bourgeois were simply lying low and disguising themselves as proletarians for the time being.

Together with all this there was something of the evil atmosphere of war. The town had a gaunt untidy look, roads and buildings were in poor repair, the streets at night were dimly lit for fear of air-raids, the shops were mostly shabby and half-empty. Meat was scarce and milk practically unobtainable, there was a shortage of coal, sugar and petrol, and a really serious shortage of bread. Even at this period the bread-queues were often hundreds of yards long. Yet so far as one could judge the people were contented and hopeful. There was no unemployment, and the price of living was still extremely low; you saw very few conspicuously destitute people, and no beggars except the gipsies. Above all there was a belief in the revolution and the future, a feeling of having suddenly emerged into an era of equality and freedom. Human beings were trying to behave as human beings and not as cogs in the capitalist machine. In the barbers' shops were Anarchist notices (the barbers were mostly Anarchists) solemnly explaining that barbers were no longer slaves. In the streets were coloured posters appealing to prostitutes to stop being prostitutes. To anyone from the hard-boiled, sneering civilization of the English-speaking races there was something rather pathetic in the literalness with which these idealistic Spaniards took the hackneyed phrases of revolution. At that time revolutionary ballads of the naivest kind, all about the proletarian brotherhood and the wickedness of Mussolini, were being sold on the streets for a few centimes each. I have often seen an illiterate militiaman buy one of these ballads, laboriously spell out the words, and then, when he had got the hang of it, begin singing it to an appropriate tune.

AN ANDALUSIAN COMMUNE

FRANZ BORKENAU
(From *Spanish Cockpit*, 1937)

6 September
We passed the night at Pozoblanco, together with some Spanish journalists, who were in no doubt about the disastrous results of the day, in spite of the elegant and optimistic telegrams to their newspapers. One of them called my attention to the southern sector of the Cordova front, not from the military, but from the political and psychological point of view. I was well advised in following his hint. In the after-

noon, after a long and trying drive, we entered Castro del Rio.

Castro, a typically populous and wretched Andalusian *pueblo*, is one of the oldest anarchist centres in Andalusia. Its CNT group looks back upon an existence of twenty-six years, and, since the defeat of the guardia in Castro, the anarchists are the one existing organization. The beginning of the revolution in Castro was very similar to that in Pozo-blanco; revolt of the guardia together with the caziques and the rich against the republic, first successful, then leading to the siege of the village by its own inhabitants, the starving out of the guardia, their surrender, and finally the inevitable wholesale massacre. The insurgents, whose main lines run a few miles from the village, had attacked it twice since, but without success. All entries were heavily barricaded and watched with unusual technical competence. And so the local anarchists had had time to introduce their anarchist Eden, which, in most points, resembled closely the one introduced by the Anabaptists in Muenster in 1534.

The salient point of the anarchist régime in Castro is the abolition of money. Exchange is suppressed; production has changed very little. The land of Castro belonged to three of the greatest magnates of Spain, all of them absentees, of course; it has now been expropriated. The local *ayuntamiento* has not merged with the committee, as every-where else in Andalusia, but has been dissolved, and the committee has taken its place and introduced a sort of Soviet system. The committee took over the estates, and runs them. They have not even been merged, but are worked separately, each by the hands previously employed on its lands. Money wages, of course, have been abolished. It would be incorrect to say that they have been replaced by pay in kind. There is no pay whatever; the inhabitants are fed directly from the village stores.

Under this system, the provisioning of the village is of the poorest kind; poorer, I should venture to say, than it can possibly have been before, even in the wretched condi-tions in which Andalusian *brazeros* are wont to live. The *pueblo* is fortunate in growing wheat, and not only olives, as in many other *pueblos* of its kind; so there is at any rate

bread. Moreover, the village owns large herds of sheep, expropriated with the estates, so there is some meat. And they
still have a store of cigarettes. That's all. I tried in vain to
get a drink, either of coffee or wine or lemonade. The village
bar had been closed as nefarious commerce. I had a look at
the stores. They were so low as to foretell approaching
starvation. But the inhabitants seemed to be proud of this
state of things. They were pleased, as they told us, that
coffee-drinking had come to an end; they seemed to regard
this abolition of useless things as a moral improvement.
What few commodities they needed from outside, mainly
clothes, they hoped to get by direct exchange of their surplus
in olives (for which, however, no arrangement had yet been
made). Their hatred of the upper class was far less economic
than moral. They did not want to get the good living of those
they had expropriated, but to get rid of their luxuries, which
to them seemed to be so many vices. Their conception of
the new order which was to be brought about was thoroughly
ascetic.

A COMMUNE IN ARAGON

GASTON LEVAL
(From *Collectives in the Spanish Revolution*, 1971, translated
by Vernon Richards, 1975)

To the north of the province of Teruel, Mas de las Matas
is the chief village of the canton bearing its name, which
comprises 19 villages. It had 2300 inhabitants. The most
important of the surrounding localities were Aquaviva with
2000 inhabitants, Mirambel (1400), La Ginebrosa (1300).
Only six villages were entirely collectivized by May 1937,
four were almost completely, and for five others col-
lectivization was 50 per cent. Three others were about to
collectivize and only one village was hesitating. Very soon
all the villages were 100 per cent collectivized.

Here the libertarian movement preceded the syndicalist
movement. Smallholdings were widespread, and did not

favour the emergence of associations of wage earners. And in Mas de las Matas, where thanks to irrigation life was relatively comfortable compared with the surrounding villages, which were more or less without water and life was hard, libertarian ideas took root from the beginnings of the century, not so much on class issues as for reasons of human conscience. If groups were started to fight against the exploitation of man by man, for equality and social justice and against subjection by the State, their inspiration was above all humanity. It was the last generation of these men who were at the head of the collectivist organization of the canton.

Under the monarchy liberal tendencies predominated. The Republic of 1931 brought about some changes, so mild that they disappointed most of the population. The result was that they tended towards the revolutionary Left; in 1932 the first CNT Syndicate was created and on the 8th December of the same year, in an insurrectional coup which covered Aragon and a large part of Catalonia, libertarian communism was proclaimed. The Civil Guard, at the orders of the republic as it had previously been in the service of the monarchy, put down this first attempt in two days, and the Syndicate was closed until the eve of the legislative elections in February 1936 which gave victory to the Popular Front. The Syndicate was then immediately reconstituted.

Five months later the local fascists were defeated without a struggle and towards mid-September our comrades launched the idea of an agrarian Collective. The initiative was accepted unanimously at a meeting of the Syndicate. It was therefore necessary to set up a separate group. A list of those who had already joined of their own accord was circulated and within a fortnight 200 families had joined. At the time of my visit the number had risen to 550 out of a total of 600 families comprising the population of the village. The remaining 50 families belonged to the socialist UGT and obeyed the instructions issued by their leaders.

Throughout the canton the same principle was applied. One was free to join the Collective or to carry on cultivating the land individually. The various stages of socialization achieved by the different villages was proof of this freedom of choice.

In none of these villages was there a written list of rules. Simply each month the assembly of members of each Collective would indicate to the Commission consisting of five elected members, the general lines to follow on specific problems that had been openly discussed.

In spite of that, my recollection of Mas de las Matas is linked, quite unconsciously, to the happy Icaria to which the utopians, and especially Etienne Cabet, have often referred. The faces and the behaviour of the people, the attitude of the women seated on the thresholds of their homes, or knitting and talking outside their houses, were peaceful and happy. One guessed that underlying it was a good way of life. Let us seek to discover what it was.

In Mas de las Matas 32 groups of workers were set up; they were more or less of the same size, determined by the tasks to be undertaken, or the extent of the agricultural areas to be worked which were limited by their capricious encirclement by the mountains. Each group cultivated some of the irrigated land and some of the dry lands. Thus the pleasant and less pleasant, heavy, work was equitably shared by everybody.

The blessings of water made it possible to grow large quantities of vegetables and fruit. The other, less fortunate, villages could only grow cereals, mainly corn – nine quintals per hectare, perhaps less – and olives. In all the Collectives of the canton the groups of workers chose their delegates, and nominated their administrative Commissions. And just as the delegates in Mas de las Matas who always set the example, met weekly to organize the work to be done, a similar procedure was adopted in the other collectivized villages. As everywhere, efforts were constantly being co-ordinated.

At the time of my visit it had not been found possible to increase the area under cultivation. Full use was already being made of the irrigated lands. But the dry lands which had hitherto been used only for grazing livestock, were earmarked for growing cereals and to this end they had started to fold the sheep on the mountain slopes, now freely available, where there was enough vegetation to feed them. At the same time a start was made to get ready the land for sow-ing corn, oats and rye . . .

It was an easier matter to increase the herds. The numbers of sheep were increased by 25 per cent; breeding sows doubled from 30 to 60, and milch cows from 18 to 24 (there was no suitable pasture in the area for cattle). A large number of piglets were purchased in Catalonia and were distributed among the population, since there was no time or labour to construct collective piggeries, the work on which, however, was due to start at any moment. Meanwhile each family raised one or two pigs which would be slaughtered in one large operation and salted and then distributed on the basis of the needs of each household.

But production was not limited to agriculture and live-stock. In this chief village of the canton, as in all collectivized chief-villages and villages of any size, small industries sprang up: building, boot and shoe making, the manufacture of clothing and slippers, meat processing, etc. . . . As in Graus and many other places, these specialities constituted a section of what was called the 'general Collective' which operated for the general good.

If then the agrarian section needed to purchase certain tools it would apply, through its delegate, to the administrative Commission which would then issue him with a voucher for the delegate of the metal workers to whom their requirements were explained. The order was at the same time entered in the account book of the engineering section. If a family needed furniture they would also get in touch with the administrative section who would hand them an order voucher for the delegate of the cabinet makers, or the carpenters (woodworkers all belonged to a single Syndicate). Such was the mechanism by which the activities of each group of producers was checked as well as the expenditure by each family.

Neither official currency (pesetas) nor local money was used in any Collective in the canton.

Socialization of commerce was one of the first stages. But it was not complete. At the time of my visit there were still two recalcitrant grocers whose businesses were in a bad way because of a lack of supplies. But generally speaking municipal stores also replaced the former system of distribution.

Let us look more closely into the functioning of a collectivized village. It is difficult to describe adequately by the written word this large scale movement which comprises agrarian socialization. In Mas de las Matas as in every collectivized village one was confronted by red and black placards affixed not only to all the workshops, communal stores, hotels and so on but also to the cantonal warehouses for chemical products, cement, raw materials for the various industries, where the collectivists from other cantonal villages came to replenish their stocks in accordance with the norms established by their delegates at fraternal meetings. In the shop of a former well-to-do fascist tradesman who disappeared there were stacks of clothing intended for the inhabitants of the canton. Elsewhere was the section for general supplies where vouchers were supplied to individuals on request and also where requests by each family were entered on a card index.

In the cantonal distillery – a new initiative – they were extracting alcohol and tartaric acid from the residue of grapes sent there from all the villages. And those villages had set up an administrative Commission for the distillery which met periodically. When one visited the factory one would be shown the technical improvements introduced to produce 90° alcohol which was required in medicine and for surgical operations at the front.

In the tailor's workshop, men and women workers were engaged in cutting and making suits to measure for comrades who had ordered them. On the racks, wool or corduroy garments, each with its label bearing the name of the consignee were waiting to be dealt with on the sewing machines.*

Women bought their meat in a well appointed, marble lined establishment. Bread which was formerly baked at home by the overworked housewives was being kneaded and baked in the collective bakehouses.

At the café everybody was entitled to have two cups of roasted chicory (that was all there was), two refreshments,

---

* For a family consisting of mother and father and two children between the ages of 6 and 14, an annual clothes allowance of 280 pesetas was made. This represented twice or three times the amount a peasant family would have spent on clothes previously.

or two lemonades, daily.

On a visit to the surroundings one would discover a nursery where vegetable seedlings were being raised, in huge quantities for planting out throughout the canton, by a family who previously had prospered in this business but who had joined the Collective from the beginning.

In the dressmaking workshop not only were women's clothes made up but, as in many other villages, young women were learning to sew for themselves and their families to be.

A placard attracts one's attention. It reads: 'Popular Bookshop'. It is in fact a library. On its shelves were from six to ten copies of different works of sociology, literature, general works on cultural and scientific subjects made available to everybody, including the individualists. There were also to be found in large numbers text books for schools (history, geography, arithmetic), story books, novels and readers for the young and for adults; then there were exercise books, and excellent printed courses for learning how to draw, with excellent examples to follow based on the most modern teaching techniques.

Here too, though the spirit and practice of general solidarity inspired the conduct and behaviour of each and all, every family was allocated a small plot of land on which to grow vegetables and fruit and to raise rabbits. This supplemented the food supply arrangements which in any case were not rigid; things were so arranged that everybody had a choice. Thus rationing was not synonymous with bureaucratic conformity.

The scale for consumption – foodstuffs, clothing, footwear, etc. – had previously been marked on the family *carnet*. But following the resolution of the Congress in Caspe, it was thought preferable to use the standard booklet produced by the regional Federation of Collectives for all the Collectives, in order to avoid excessive differences depending on the relative prosperity or poverty of the villages and even of the cantons.

When therefore clothing was also rationed it was not because in this part of Aragon the Collectives lacked the necessary resources to buy them. They generally had enough goods, especially corn, to barter for cloth, machines and all that was produced in Catalonia, where manufacturing industries predominated. But things were strained by the war effort. And furthermore the value of the corn, meat, vegetables, and oil supplied without payment to support those on the fighting front was enormous. Supplies, without payment, were also sent to Madrid which was besieged by the Fascist armies. It was also a fact that some industrial regions badly socialized or lacking raw materials to produce certain goods, could not honour the barter arrangements made.

Medical care and pharmaceutical products were free. Furthermore, as well as the public library referred to, there was another, operated by the Syndicate and the Libertarian Youth. School attendance was compulsory up to the age of 14. In a group of *masias* (small farmhouses), built on the mountain slopes some distance from the village, a school was opened for older children who had never before sat at a school desk. And in Mas de las Matas two new classes had just been improvised, each to deal with 50 children whose education was entrusted to two young women who had taken a course in advanced studies in Saragossa and Valencia.*

Public entertainment was free both for collectivists and individualists.

On the basis of the agreements made throughout Aragon, as well as in Castile and the Levante, no Collective could conduct business on its own account. In this way any possibility of speculation that could arise in that agitated war period was avoided, as well as the kind of competition which so often manifested itself among the collectivized factories in Barcelona, especially in the textile industry.

These measures of a moral nature, ran parallel with the sense of organization which emerged in most of the socialized villages. Each village Collective communicated to the can-

---

* Fifty children seems a lot. But in view of the backwardness of the Spanish educational organization, this represented a step forward. What mattered was to teach people to read at any price. The writer (in the 1920s) had 52 pupils from 5 to 15 years of age in the 'rationalist' school in Corunna where he had to improvise as schoolteacher. He coped with his task until the time when Primo de Rivera ordered the closure of these establishments.

tonal *Comité* a list of its surplus goods and of those it needed. Thus each village in the canton of Mas de las Matas had a current account in the books kept in the chief village in which it was entered what it supplied and what it received. At the same time the cantonal *Comité* knew exactly what stocks of wine, meat, oil, corn, potatoes, sugar-beet – widely grown in Aragon – were available in each village.

Furthermore if the village which supplied the oil did not need the wine offered, it could ask for other goods. These would be supplied and that village's surpluses would be sent to Mas de las Matas where they would be held in reserve for eventual barter with other Collectives in the canton. It was a kind of clearing-house. Thus through the intermediary of the general Warehouse or the communal depot, barter within and outside the village was possible at all times.

This system of compensation was carried out without the least reticence for the spirit of speculation had disappeared. Any village which was going through particular difficulties and had nothing to barter was not thereby condemned to poverty or to having to raise loans on which the interest charges and repayments would grievously jeopardise its economic situation for years to come.

In the interdependent cantons the problem did not present itself in these terms. Thus for instance in that of Mas de las Matas the main economic resources of Seno and of La Ginebrosa had, that year, been destroyed by hailstorms. Under a capitalist regime it would have resulted in untold privations, even to emigration for several years for some of the men. In a regime of strict justice, loans secured with difficulty could be a permanent millstone round their necks. Under the regime of libertarian solidarity, the difficulty was shared by the effort of the whole canton. Foodstuffs, vegetable plants, seeds, were all supplied in a fraternal manner, without mortgages, and without contracting debts. The revolution had created a new civilization.

A SONG FOR THE
SPANISH ANARCHISTS

HERBERT READ
(From *Thirty-five Poems*, 1940)

> The golden lemon is not made
> but grows on a green tree:
> A strong man and his crystal eyes
> is a man born free.
>
> The oxen pass under the yoke
> and the blind are led at will:
> But a man born free has a path of his own
> and a house on the hill.
>
> And men are men who till the land
> and women are women who weave:
> Fifty men own the lemon grove
> and no man is a slave.

PARIS, 1968

MURRAY BOOKCHIN
(From *Post-Scarcity Anarchism*, 1974)

The Quality of Everyday Life

The 1968 May-June uprising was one of the most important
events to occur in France since the Paris Commune of 1871.
Not only did it shake the foundations of bourgeois society
in France, it raised issues and posed solutions of unprecedented importance for modern industrial society. It deserves
the closest study and the most thoroughgoing discussion by
revolutionaries everywhere.

The May-June uprising occurred in an industrialized, consumption-oriented country – less developed than the United States, but essentially in the same economic category. The uprising exploded the myth that the wealth and resources of modern industrial society can be used to absorb all revolutionary opposition. The May-June events showed that contradictions and antagonisms in capitalism are not eliminated by stratification and advanced forms of industrialism, but changed in form and character.

The fact that the uprising took everyone by surprise, including the most sophisticated theoreticians in the Marxist, Situationist and anarchist movements, underscores the importance of the May-June events and raises the need to re-examine the sources of revolutionary unrest in modern society. The graffiti on the walls of Paris – 'Power to the imagination', 'It is forbidden to forbid', 'Life without dead times', 'Never work' – represent a more probing analysis of these sources than all the theoretical tomes inherited from the past. The uprising revealed that we are at the end of an old era and well into the beginning of a new one. The motive forces of revolution today, at least in the industrialized world, are not simply scarcity and material need, but also *the quality of everyday life*, the demand *for the liberation of experience*, the attempt to gain *control over one's destiny*. It matters little that the graffiti on the walls of Paris were initially scrawled by a small minority. From everything I have seen, it is clear that the graffiti (which now form the content of several books) have captured the imagination of many thousands in Paris. They have touched the revolutionary nerve of the city.

The Spontaneous Majority Movement

The revolt was a majority movement in the sense that it cut across nearly all the class lines in France. It involved not only students and workers, but technicians, engineers and clerical people in nearly every stratum of the state, industrial and commercial bureaucracy. It swept in professionals and labourers, intellectuals and football players, television broadcasters and subway workers. It even touched the gendarmerie of Paris, and almost certainly affected the great mass of conscript soldiers in the French army.

The revolt was initiated primarily by the young. It was begun by university students, then it was taken up by young industrial workers, unemployed youths, and the 'leather jackets' – the so-called 'delinquent youth' of the cities. Special emphasis must be given to high school students and adolescents, who often showed more courage and determination than the university students. But the revolt swept in older people as well – blue- and white-collar workers, technicians and professionals. Although it was catalyzed by conscious revolutionaries, especially by anarchist affinity groups whose existence no one had even faintly supposed, the flow, the movement of the uprising was spontaneous. No one had 'summoned it forth'; no one had 'organized' it; no one succeeded in 'controlling' it.

A festive atmosphere prevailed throughout most of the May-June days, an awakening of solidarity, of mutual aid, indeed of a selfhood and self-expression that had not been seen in Paris since the Commune. People literally discovered themselves and their fellow human beings anew – or remade themselves. In many industrial towns, workers clogged the squares, hung out red flags, read avidly and discussed every leaflet that fell into their hands. A fever for life gripped millions, a reawakening of senses that people never thought they possessed, a joy and elation they never thought they could feel. Tongues were loosened, ears and eyes acquired a new acuity. There was singing, with new, and often ribald, verses added to old tunes. Many factory floors were turned into dance floors. The sexual inhibitions that had frozen the lives of so many young people in France were shattered in a matter of days. This was not a solemn revolt, a *coup d'état* bureaucratically plotted and manipulated by a 'vanguard' party; it was witty, satirical, inventive and creative – and therein lay its strength, its capacity for immense self-mobilization, its infectiousness.

Many people transcended the narrow limitations that had impeded their social vision. For thousands of students, the revolution had destroyed the prissy, tight-assed sense of 'studenthood' – that privileged, pompous state that is expressed

in America by the 'position paper' and by the stuffy sociolo-
gese of the 'analytical' document. The individual workers who
came to the action committees at Censier ceased to be
'workers' as such. They became revolutionaries. And it is
precisely on the basis of this new identity that people whose
lives had been spent in universities, factories and offices could
meet freely, exchange experiences and engage in common
actions without any self-consciousness about their social
'origins' or 'background'.

The revolt had created the beginnings of its own classless,
nonhierarchical society. Its primary task was to extend this
qualitatively new realm to the country at large – to every
corner of French society. Its hope lay in the extension of
self-management in all its forms – the general assemblies and
their administrative forms, the action committees, the factory
strike committees – to all areas of the economy, indeed to
all areas of life itself. The most advanced consciousness of
this task seems to have appeared not so much among the
workers in the more traditional industries, where the Com-
munist-controlled CGT exercises great power, as among those
in newer, more technically advanced industries, such as
electronics. (Let me emphasize that this is a tentative conclusion, drawn from a number of scattered but impressive
episodes that were related to me by young militants in the
student-worker action committees.)

Authority and Hierarchy

Of paramount importance is the light that the May-June
revolt cast on the problem of authority and hierarchy. In
this respect it challenged not only the conscious processes of
individuals, but also their most important unconscious,
socially conditioned habits. (It does not have to be argued at
any great length that the habits of authority and hierarchy
are instilled in the individual at the very outset of life – in
the family milieu of infancy, in childhood 'education' at
home and in school, in the organization of work, 'leisure'
and everyday life. This shaping of the character structure
of the individual by what seem like 'archetypal' norms of
obedience and command constitutes the very essence of what

we call the 'socialization' of the young.)

The mystique of bureaucratic 'organization', of imposed, formalized hierarchies and structures, pervades the most radical movements in nonrevolutionary periods. The remarkable susceptibility of the left to authoritarian and hierarchical impulses reveals the deep roots of the radical movement in the very society it professedly seeks to overthrow. In this respect, nearly every revolutionary organization is a potential source of counter-revolution. Only if the revolutionary organization is so 'structured' that its forms reflect the direct, decentralized forms of freedom initiated by the revolution, only if the revolutionary organization fosters in the revolutionist the lifestyles and personality of freedom, can this potential for counter-revolution be diminished. Only then is it possible for the revolutionary movement to dissolve into the revolution, to disappear into its new, directly democratic social forms like surgical thread into a healing wound.

The act of revolution rips apart all the tendons that hold authority and hierarchy together in the established order. The direct entry of the people into the social arena is the very essence of revolution. Revolution is the most advanced form of direct action. By the same token, direct action in 'normal' times is the indispensable preparation for revolutionary action. In both cases, there is a substitution of social action from below for political action within the established, hierarchical framework. In both cases, there are molecular changes of 'masses', classes and social strata into revolutionary individuals. This condition must become permanent if the revolution is to be successful – if it is not to be transformed into a counterrevolution masked by revolutionary ideology. Every formula, every organization, every 'tried-and-tested' programme, must give way to the demands of the revolution. There is no theory, programme or party that has greater significance than the revolution itself.

Among the most serious obstacles to the May-June uprising were not only de Gaulle and the police, but also the hardened organizations of the left – the Communist party that suffocated initiative in many factories and the Leninist and Trotskyist groups that created such a bad odour in the general assembly of the Sorbonne. I speak here not of the many individuals who romantically identified themselves with Che, Mao, Lenin or Trotsky (often with all four at once), but of those who surrendered their entire identity, initiative and volition to tightly disciplined, hierarchical organizations. However well-intended these people may have been, it became their task to 'discipline' the revolt, more precisely to de-revolutionize it by imbuing it with the habits of obedience and authority that their organizations have assimilated from the established order. These habits, fostered by participation in highly structured organizations – organizations modelled, in fact, on the very society the 'revolutionaries' profess to oppose – led to parliamentary manoeuvring, secret caucusing, and attempts to 'control' the revolutionary forms of freedom created by the revolution. They produced in the Sorbonne assembly a poisonous vapour of manipulation. Many students to whom I spoke were absolutely convinced that these groups were prepared to destroy the Sorbonne assembly if they could not 'control' it. The groups were concerned not with the vitality of the revolutionary forms, but with the growth of their own organizations. Having created authentic forms of freedom in which everyone could freely express his viewpoint, the assembly would have been perfectly justified to have banned all bureaucratically organized groups from its midst.

It remains to the lasting credit of the March 22nd Movement that it merged into the revolutionary assemblies and virtually disappeared as an organization, except in name. In its own assemblies, March 22nd arrived at all its decisions by the 'sense of the assembly', and it permitted all tendencies within its midst to freely test their views in practice. Such tolerance did not impair its 'effectiveness'; this anarchic movement, by the common agreement of nearly all observers, did more to catalyze the revolt than any other student group. What distinguishes March 22nd and groups such as the anarchists and Situationists from all others is that they worked not for the 'seizure of power' but for its dissolution.

The Dialectic of Modern Revolution

The French events of May and June reveal, vividly and

dramatically, the remarkable dialectic of revolution. The everyday misery of a society is highlighted by the possibilities for the realization of desire and freedom. The greater these possibilities, the more intolerable the everyday misery. For this reason, it matters little that French society has been more affluent in recent years than at any time in its history. Affluence in its highly distorted bourgeois form merely indicates that the material conditions for freedom have developed, that the technical possibilities for a new, liberated life are overripe.

It is plain, now, that these possibilities have haunted French society for a long time, even if unperceived by most people. The insensate consumption of goods graphs, in its own warped way, the tension between the shabby reality of French society and the liberatory possibilities of a revolution today, just as a sedating diet and extravagant obesity reveal the tension in an individual. A time is finally reached when the diet of goods becomes tasteless, when the social obesity becomes intolerable. The breaking point is unpredictable. In the case of France, it was the barricades of May 10, a day which shook the conscience of the entire country and posed a question to the workers: 'If the students, those 'children of the bourgeoisie', can do it, why can't we?' It is clear that a molecular process was going on in France, completely invisible to the most conscious revolutionaries, a process that the barricades precipitated into revolutionary action. After May 10, the tension between the mediocrity of everyday life and the possibilities of a liberated society exploded into the most massive general strike in history.

The scope of the strike shows that nearly all strata of French society were profoundly disaffected and that the revolution was anchored not in a particular class but in everyone who felt dispossessed, denied and cheated of life. The revolutionary thrust came from a stratum which, more than any other, should have 'accommodated' itself to the existing order – the young. It was the young who had been nourished on the pap of Gaullist 'civilization', who had not experienced the contrasts between the relatively attractive features of the pre-war civilization and the shabbiness of the new one. But the pap didn't work. Its power to co-opt and absorb, in fact, is weaker than was suspected by most critics of French society. The pap-fed society could not withstand the drive for life, particularly in the young.

No less important, the lives of young people in France, as in America, had never been burdened by the Depression years and the quest for material security that shaped the lives of their elders. The prevailing reality of French life was taken by the young people for what it is – shabby, ugly, egotistical, hypocritical and spiritually annihilating. This single fact – the revolt of the young – is the most damning evidence of the system's inability to prevail on its own terms.

The tremendous internal decay of Gaullist society, a decay long antedating the revolt itself, took forms that do not fit into any of the traditional, economically oriented formulas of 'revolution'. Much had been written about 'consumerism' in French society to the effect that it was a polluting form of social mobilization. The fact that objects, *commodities*, were replacing the traditional subjective loyalties fostered by the Church, the school, the mass media and the family, should have been seen as evidence of greater social decomposition than was suspected. The fact that traditional class consciousness was declining in the working class should have been evidence that conditions were maturing for a major *social* revolution, not a minority *class* revolution. The fact that 'lumpen' values in dress, music, art and lifestyle were spreading among French youth should have been evidence that the potential for 'disorder' and direct action was ripening behind the façade of conventional political protest.

By a remarkable twist of dialectic irony, a process of 'debourgeoisification' was going on precisely when France had attained unprecedented heights of material affluence. Whatever may have been the personal popularity of de Gaulle, a process of deinstitutionalization was going on precisely when state capitalism seemed more entrenched in the social structure than at any time in the recent past. The tension between drab reality and the liberatory possibilities was increasing precisely when French society seemed more quiescent than at any time since the 1920s. A process of alienation was going on precisely when it seemed that the verities of bourgeois society were more secure than at any time in the history of the republic.

The point is that the issues that make for social unrest had changed qualitatively. The problems of survival, scarcity and renunciation had changed into those of life, abundance and desire. The 'French dream', like the 'American dream', was eroding and becoming demystified. Bourgeois society had given all it could give on the only terms it was capable of 'giving' anything – a plethora of shabby material goods acquired by meaningless, deadening work. Experience itself (not 'vanguard parties' and 'tried-and-tested programmes') became the mobilizing agent and source of creativity for the May-June uprising. And this is as it should be. Not only is it natural that an uprising *breaks out* spontaneously – a feature of all the great revolutions in history – but it is also natural that it *unfolds* spontaneously. This hardly means that revolutionary groups stand mute before the events. If they have ideas and suggestions, it is their responsibility to present them. But to use the social forms created by the revolution for manipulatory purposes, to operate secretly behind the back of the revolution, to distrust it and try to replace it by the 'glorious party', is wantonly criminal and unforgivable. Either the revolution eventually absorbs *all* political organisms, or the political organisms become ends in themselves – the inevitable sources of bureaucracy, hierarchy and human enslavement.

To diminish the spontaneity of a revolution, to break the continuum between *self*-mobilization and *self*-emancipation, to remove the *self* from the process in order to mediate it with political organizations and institutions borrowed from the past, is to vitiate the revolution's liberatory goals. If the revolution does not start from below, if it does not enlarge the 'base' of society until it becomes the society itself, then it is a mere *coup d'état*. If it does not produce a society in which each individual controls his daily life, instead of daily life controlling each individual, then it is a counter-revolution. Social liberation can only occur if it is simultaneously self-liberation – if the 'mass' movement is a self-activity that involves the highest degree of individuation and self-awakening.

In the molecular movement below that prepares the condition for revolution, in the self-mobilization that carries the revolution forward, in the joyous atmosphere that consolidates the revolution – in *all* of these successive steps, we have a *continuum* of individuation, a process in which power is dissolved, an expansion of personal experience and freedom almost aesthetically congruent with the possibilities of our time. To see this process and articulate it, to catalyze the process and pose the next practical tasks, to deal unequivocally with the ideological movements that seek to 'control' the revolutionary process – these, as the French events have shown, are the primary responsibilities of the revolutionary today.

Part 6
Liberating Education

Education has always held a special place in the attention of
anarchists, partly at least because it has seemed to them one
of the areas in which they can initiate the process of social
change while awaiting the general transformation of society.
They recognize, as Godwin did when he wrote on 'The Evils
of National Education', how powerful an instrument it can
be in the hands of intelligent and determined rulers; they
recognize also how far it can foster the kind of free consciousness without which no fundamental change in society
can be expected.

Godwin was not merely a pioneer in recognizing the threat
implied in state-controlled education; he was also one of the
first theoreticians of a completely free education. He never
succeeded in establishing a school based on his ideas, though
he made the attempt, but he wrote extensively on the subject,
particularly in *The Enquirer*, and the extract we have entitled
'Education through Desire' is one of the earliest and best
accounts of how to teach by utilizing the student's inclinations.

Paul Goodman, in a more recent age, became involved
in teaching at many levels, and the suggestions he makes in the
extract entitled 'Alternatives to Miseducation' illustrate the
flexible view which many modern anarchists adopt towards
a liberating kind of education in a society that is still unfree.

Finally, in recent decades Herbert Read has been the best
known and most influential of all the anarchist theoreticians
of education. In his *Education through Art* he developed
the argument that the social virtues necessary in a liberated
life are best developed by the fostering of the aesthetic
faculties rather than by an early emphasis on informational

teaching, and he sees an education developed in this way as a potent agent of social change. The extract from *The Grass Roots of Art* which we publish is an effective summary of Read's views on this subject.

THE EVILS OF NATIONAL EDUCATION

WILLIAM GODWIN
(From *Enquiry Concerning Political Justice*, 1793)

The injuries that result from a system of national education are, in the first place, that all public establishments include in them the idea of permanence. They endeavour, it may be, to secure and to diffuse whatever advantage to society is already known, but they forget that more remains to be known. If they realized the most substantial benefits at the time of their introduction, they must inevitably become less and less useful as they increased in duration. But to describe them as useless, is a very feeble expression of their demerits. They actively restrain the flights of mind, and fix it in the belief of exploded errors. It has frequently been observed of universities, and extensive establishments for the purpose of education, that the knowledge taught there, is a century behind the knowledge which exists among the unshackled and unprejudiced members of the same political community. The moment any scheme of proceeding gains a permanent establishment, it becomes impressed, as one of its characteristic features, with an aversion to change. Some violent concussion may oblige its conductors to change an old system of philosophy for a system less obsolete; and they are then as pertinaciously attached to this second doctrine, as they were to the first. Real intellectual improvement demands, that mind should, as speedily as possible, be advanced to the height of knowledge already existing among the enlightened members of the community, and start from thence in the pursuit of further acquisitions. But public education has always expended its energies in the support of prejudice; it teaches its pupils, not the fortitude that shall bring every proposition to the test of examination, but the art of vindicating such tenets as may chance to be established. We study Aristotle, or Thomas Aquinas, or Bellarmine, or chief justice Coke, not that we may detect their errors, but that our minds may be fully impregnated with their absurdities. This feature runs through every species of public establishment; and, even in the petty institution of Sunday-schools, the chief lessons that are taught, are a superstitious veneration for the Church of England, and how to bow to every man in a handsome coat. All this is directly contrary to the true interest of mankind. All this must be unlearned, before we can begin to be wise.

It is the characteristic of mind to be capable of improvement. An individual surrenders the best attribute of man, the moment he resolves to adhere to certain fixed principles, for reasons not now present to his mind, but which formerly were. The instant in which he shuts upon himself the career of enquiry, is the instant of his intellectual decease. He is no longer a man; he is the ghost of departed man. There can be no scheme more egregiously stamped with folly, than that of separating a tenet from the evidence upon which its validity depends. If I cease from the habit of being able to recall this evidence, my belief is no longer a perception, but a prejudice: it may influence me like a prejudice; but cannot animate me like a real apprehension of truth. The difference between the man thus guided, and the man that keeps his mind permanently alive, is the difference between cowardice and fortitude. The man who is, in the best sense, an intellectual being, delights to recollect the reasons that have convinced him, to repeat them to others, that they may produce conviction in them, and stand more distinct and explicit in his own mind; and he adds to this a willingness to examine objections, because he takes no pride in consistent error. The man who is not capable of this salutary exercise, to what valuable purpose can he be employed? Hence it appears, that no vice can be more destructive, than that which teaches us to regard any judgment as final, and not open to review. The same principle that applies to individuals, applies to communities. There is no proposition at present apprehended to be true, so valuable, as to justify the introduction of an establishment for the purpose of inculcating it on mankind. Refer them to reading, to conversation, to meditation; but teach them neither creeds nor catechisms, either moral or political.

Secondly, the idea of national education, is founded in an inattention to the nature of mind. Whatever each man does for himself, is done well; whatever his neighbour or his country undertake to do for him, is done ill. It is our wisdom to incite men to act for themselves, not to retain them in a state of perpetual pupillage. He that learns, because he desires to learn, will listen to the instructions he receives, and apprehend their meaning. He that teaches, because he desires to teach, will discharge his occupation with enthusiasm and energy. But the moment political institution undertakes to assign every man his place, the functions of all will be discharged with supineness and indifference. Universities and extensive establishments have long been remarked for formal dullness. Civil policy has given me the power to appropriate my estate to certain theoretical purposes; but it is an idle presumption to think I can entail my views, as I can entail my fortune. Remove these obstacles, which prevent men from seeing, and which restrain them from pursuing, their real advantage; but do not absurdly undertake to relieve them from the activity which this pursuit requires. What I earn, what I acquire only because I desire to acquire it, I estimate at its true value; but what is thrust upon me, may make me indolent, but cannot make me respectable. It is an extreme folly, to endeavour to secure to others, independently of exertion on their part, the means of being happy. This whole proposition of a national education, is founded upon a supposition which has been repeatedly refuted in this work, but which has recurred upon us in a thousand forms, that unpatronized truth is inadequate to the purpose of enlightening mankind.

Thirdly, the project of a national education ought uniformly to be discouraged, on account of its obvious alliance with national government. This is an alliance of a more formidable nature, than the old and much contested alliance of church and state. Before we put so powerful a machine under the direction of so ambiguous an agent, it behoves us to consider well what it is that we do. Government will not fail to employ it, to strengthen its hands, and perpetuate its institutions. If we could even suppose the agents of government not to propose to themselves an object, which will be apt to appear in their eyes, not merely innocent, but meritorious; the evil would not the less happen. Their views as institutors of a system of education, will not fail to be analogous to their views in their political capacity: the data upon which their conduct as statesmen, is vindicated, will be the data upon which their instructions are founded. It is not true that our youth ought to be instructed to venerate the constitution, however excellent; they should be led to venerate truth; and the constitution only so far as it corresponds with their uninfluenced deductions of truth. Had the scheme of a national education been adopted when despotism was most triumphant, it is not to be believed that it could have for ever stifled the voice of truth. But it would have been the most formidable and profound contrivance for that purpose, that imagination can suggest. Still, in the countries where liberty chiefly prevails, it is reasonably to be assumed that there are important errors, and a national education has the most direct tendency to perpetuate these errors, and to form all minds upon one model.

EDUCATION THROUGH DESIRE

WILLIAM GODWIN
(*The Enquirer*, 1797)

Liberty is one of the most desirable of all sublunary advantages. I would willingly therefore communicate knowledge without infringing, or with as little as possible violence to, the volition and individual judgment of the person to be instructed.

Again; I desire to excite a given individual to the acquisition of knowledge. The only possible method in which I can excite a sensitive being to the performance of a voluntary action is by the exhibition of motive.

Motives are of two sorts, intrinsic and extrinsic. Intrinsic motives are those which arise from the inherent nature of the thing recommended. Extrinsic motives are those which have no constant and unalterable connection with the thing recommended, but are combined with it by accident or at the pleasure of some individual.

Thus I may recommend some species of knowledge by a display of the advantages which will necessarily attend upon its acquisition or flow from its possession. Or, on the other hand, I may recommend it despotically, by allurements or menaces, by showing that the pursuit of it will be attended with my approbation, and that the neglect of it will be regarded by me with displeasure.

The first of these classes of motives is unquestionably the best. To be governed by such motives is the pure and genuine condition of a rational being. By exercise it strengthens the judgment. It elevates us with a sense of independence. It causes a man to stand alone and is the only method by which he can be rendered truly an individual, the creature not of implicit faith but of his own understanding.

If a thing be really good, it can be shown to be such. If you cannot demonstrate its excellence, it may well be suspected that you are no proper judge of it. Why should not I be admitted to decide upon that which is to be acquired by the application of my labour?

Is it necessary that a child should learn a thing before it can have any idea of its value? It is probable that there is no one thing that is of eminent importance for a child to learn. The true object of juvenile education is to provide against the age of five-and-twenty a mind well regulated, active and prepared to learn. Whatever will inspire habits of industry and observation will sufficiently answer this purpose. Is it not possible to find something that will fulfill these conditions, the benefit of which a child shall understand, and the acquisition of which he may be taught to desire? Study with desire is real activity; without desire it is but the semblance and mockery of activity. Let us not, in the eagerness of our haste to educate, forget all the ends of education.

The most desirable mode of education, therefore, in all instances where it shall be found sufficiently practicable, is that which is careful that all the acquisitions of the pupil shall be preceded and accompanied by desire. The best motive to learn is a perception of the value of the thing learned. The worst motive, without deciding whether or not it be necessary to have recourse to it, may well be affirmed to be constraint and fear. There is a motive between these, less pure than the first but not so displeasing as the last, which is desire, not springing from the intrinsic excellence of the object, but from the accidental attractions which the teacher may have annexed to it . . .

Nothing can be more happily adapted to remove the difficulties of instruction, than that the pupil should first be excited to desire knowledge, and next that his difficulties should be solved for him, and his path cleared, as often and as soon as he thinks proper to desire it.

This plan is calculated entirely to change the fact of education. The whole formidable apparatus which has hitherto attended it is swept away. Strictly speaking, no such characters are left upon the scene as either preceptor or pupil. The boy, like the man, studies because he desires it. He proceeds upon a plan of his own invention, or which, by adopting, he has made his own. Everything bespeaks independence and equality. The man, as well as the boy, would be glad in cases of difficulty to consult a person more informed than himself. That the boy is accustomed almost always to consult the man, and not the man the boy, is to be regarded rather as an accident than anything essential. Much even of this would be removed if we remembered that the most inferior judge may often, by the varieties of his apprehension, give valuable information to the most enlightened. The boy, however, should be consulted by the man unaffectedly, not according to any preconcerted scheme, or for the purpose of persuading him that he is what he is not.

There are three considerable advantages that would attend upon this species of education.

First, liberty. Three-quarters of the slavery and restraint that are now imposed upon young persons would be annihilated at a stroke.

Secondly, the judgement would be strengthened by continual exercise. Boys would no longer learn their lessons after the manner of parrots. No one would learn without a reason, satisfactory to himself, why he learned; and it would perhaps be well, if he were frequently prompted to assign his reasons. Boys would then consider for themselves whether they understood what they read. To know when and how to ask a question is no contemptible part of learning. Sometimes they would pass over difficulties and neglect essential preliminaries, but then the nature of the thing would speedily recall them and induce them to return to examine the tracts which before had been overlooked. For this purpose it would be well that the subjects of their juvenile studies should often be discussed, and that one boy should compare his progress and his competence to decide in certain points with those of another. There is nothing that more strongly excites our enquiries than this mode of detecting our ignorance.

Thirdly, to study for ourselves is the true method of acquiring habits of activity. The horse that goes round in a mill, and the boy that is anticipated and led by the hand in all his acquirements, is not active. I do not call a wheel that turns around fifty times a minute active. Activity is a mental quality. If therefore you would generate habits of activity, turn the boy loose in the fields of science. Let him explore the path for himself. Without increasing his difficulties, you may venture to leave him for a moment and suffer him to ask the question before he receives the information. Far be it from the system here laid down to increase the difficulties of youth. No, it diminishes them a hundredfold. Its office is to produce inclination, and a willing temper makes every burden light.

Lastly, it is a tendency of this system to produce in the young, when they are grown up to the stature of men, a love of literature. The established modes of education produce the opposite effect, unless in a fortunate few, who, by the celerity of their progress, and the distinctions they obtain, perhaps escape from the general influence. But, in the majority of cases, the memory of our slavery becomes associated with the studies we pursued, and it is not till after repeated struggles, that those things can be rendered the objects of our choice, which were for so long a time the themes of compulsion.

ALTERNATIVES TO MISEDUCATION

PAUL GOODMAN
(From *Compulsory Miseducation*, 1962)

The compulsory system has become a universal trap, and it is no good. Very many of the youth, both poor and middle class, might be better off if the system simply did not exist, even if they then had no formal schooling at all. (I am extremely curious for a philosophic study of Prince Edward County in Virginia, where for some years schooling did not exist for Negro children.)

But what would become of these children? For very many, both poor and middle class, their homes are worse than the schools, and the city streets are worse in another way. Our urban and suburban environments are precisely not cities or communities where adults naturally attend to the young and educate to a viable life. Also, perhaps especially in the case of the overt drop-outs, the state of their body and soul is such that we must give them refuge and remedy, whether it be called school, settlement house, youth worker or work camp.

There are thinkable alternatives . . . Here are half a dozen directly relevant to the subject we have been discussing, the system as a compulsory trap. In principle, when a law begins to do more harm than good, the best policy is to alleviate it or try doing without it.

1. Have 'no school at all' for a few classes. These children should be selected from tolerable, though not necessarily cultured, homes. They should be neighbours and numerous enough to be a society for one another so that they do not feel merely 'different'. Will they learn the rudiments anyway? This experiment cannot do the children any academic harm, since there is good evidence that normal children will make up the first seven years school-work with four to seven months of good teaching.

2. Dispense with the school building for a few classes; provide teachers and use the city itself as the school – its streets, cafeterias, stores, movies, museums, parks and factories. Where feasible, it certainly makes more sense to teach using the real subject matter than to bring an abstraction of the subject matter into the school building as 'curriculum'. Such a class should probably not exceed ten children for one pedagogue. The idea – it is the model of Athenian education – is not dissimilar to youth-gang work, but not applied to delinquents and not playing to the gang ideology.

3. Along the same lines, but both outside and inside the school building, use appropriate *unlicensed* adults of the community – the druggist, the storekeeper, the mechanic – as the proper educators of the young into the grown-up world. By this means we can try to overcome the separation of the young from the grown-up world so characteristic in modern urban life, and to diminish the omnivorous authority of the professional school-people. Certainly it would be a useful and animating experience for the adults. (There is the beginning of such a volunteer programme in the New York and some other systems.)

4. Make class attendance not compulsory, in the manner of A. S. Neill's Summerhill. If the teachers are good, absence would tend to be eliminated; if they are bad, let them know it. The compulsory law is useful to get the children away from the parents, but it must not result in trapping the children. A fine modification of this suggestion is the rule used by Frank Brown in Florida; he permits the children to be absent for a week or a month to engage in any worthwhile enterprise or visit any new environment.

5. Decentralize an urban school (or do not build a new big building) into small units, twenty to fifty, in available storefronts or clubhouses. These tiny schools equipped with record-player and pin-ball machine, could combine play, socializing, discussion and formal teaching. For special events, the small units can be brought together into a common auditorium or gymnasium, so as to give the sense of the greater community. Correspondingly, I think it would be worthwhile to give the Little Red Schoolhouse a spin under modern urban conditions, and see how it works out: that is,

to combine all the ages in a little room for twenty-five to
thirty, rather than to grade by age.

6. Use a *pro rata* of the school money to send
children to economically marginal farms for a couple of
months of the year, perhaps six children from mixed backgrounds to a farmer. The only requirement is that the farmer
feed them and not beat them; best, of course, if they take
part in the farmwork. This will give the farmer cash, as part
of the generally desirable programme to redress the urban-
rural ratio to something nearer to 70 per cent to 30 per
cent. (At present, less than 8 per cent of families are rural.)
Conceivably, some of the urban children will take to the
other way of life, and we might generate a new kind of rural
culture . . .

*　　　*　　　*　　　*　　　*

Fundamentally, there is no right education except growing
up into a worthwhile world. Indeed, our excessive concern
with problems of education at present simply means that the
grownups do not have such a world. The poor youth of
America will *not* become equal by rising through the middle
class, going to middle-class schools. By plain social justice,
the Negroes, and other societies, have the right to, and must
get, equal opportunity for schooling with the rest, but the
exaggerated expectation for the schooling is a chimera – and,
I fear, will be shockingly disappointing. But also the middle-
class youth will not escape their increasing exploitation and
anomie in such schools. A decent education aims at, prepares
for, a more worthwhile future, with a different community
spirit, different occupations, and more real utility than attaining status and salary.

We are suffering from a bad style, perhaps a wrong religion.
Although it is pretty certain, as I have said, that the automated future will see less employment in the manufacture of
hardware and more employment in service occupations, as
well as more leisure, yet astoundingly the mass-production
and cash-accounting attitude towards the hardware is carried
over unchanged into the thinking about the services and
leisure! The lockstep regimentation and the petty-bourgeois

credits and competitive grading in the schooling are typical of all the rest . . .

My bias is that we maximize automation as quickly as possible, *where it is relevant* – taking care to cushion job dislocation and to provide adequate social insurance. But the spirit and method of automation, logistics, chains of command, and clerical work are *entirely irrelevant* to humane services, community service, communications, community culture, high culture, citizenly initiative, education and recreation. To give a rather special but not trivial example of what I mean, TV sets should be maximum-mass-produced with maximum automation, in a good standard model, as cheaply as possible; but TV programming should, except for a few national services, be as much decentralized, tailor-made, and reliant on popular and free-artist initiative as possible.

The dangers of the highly technological and automated future are obvious. We might become a brainwashed society of idle and frivolous consumers. We might continue in a rat-race of highly competitive, unnecessary busy-work with a meaninglessly expanding Gross National Product. In either case, there might still be an outcast group that must be suppressed. To countervail these dangers and make active, competent and initiating citizens who can produce a community culture and a noble recreation, we need a very different education than the schooling that we have been getting.

Large parts of it must be directly useful, rather than useless and merely aiming at status. Here we think of the spending in the public sector, advocated by Myrdal, Keyserling, Galbraith and many others, e.g. the money spent on town improvement, community service or rural rehabilitation can also provide educational occasions. (When these economists invariably list schooling as high – and often first – in the list of public expenditures, they fail to realize that such expense is probably wasted and perhaps even further dislocates the economy. I would say the same about Galbraith's pitch for new highways.)

On the whole, the education must be voluntary rather than compulsory, for no growth to freedom occurs except by intrinsic motivation. Therefore the educational opportunities must be various and variously administered. We must diminish rather than expand the present monolithic school system. I would suggest that, on the model of the GI Bill, we experiment, giving the school money directly to the high-school adolescents, for any plausible self-chosen educational proposals, such as purposeful travel or individual enterprise. This would also, of course, lead to the proliferation of experimental schools.

Unlike the present inflexible lockstep, our educational policy must allow for periodic quitting and easy return to the scholastic ladder, so that the young have time to find themselves and to study when they are themselves ready. This is Eric Erickson's valuable notion of the need for *moratoria* in the life-career; and the anthropological insistence of Stanley Diamond and others, that our society neglects the crises of growing up.

Education must foster independent thought and expression, rather than conformity. For example, to countervail the mass communications, we have an imperative social need, indeed a constitutional need to protect liberty, for many thousands of independent media; local newspapers, independent broadcasters, little magazines, little theatres, and these, under professional guidance, could provide remarkable occasions for the employment and education of adolescents of brain and talent . . .

Finally, contemporary education must inevitably be heavily weighted towards the sciences. But this does not necessarily call for school training of a relatively few technicians, or rare creative scientists (if such can indeed be trained in schools). Our aim must be to make a great number of citizens at home in a technological environment, not alienated from the machines we use, not ignorant as consumers, who can somewhat judge government scientific policy, who can enjoy the humanistic beauty of the sciences, and, above all, who can understand the morality of a scientific way of life.

AN AESTHETIC APPROACH
TO EDUCATION
HERBERT READ
(From *The Grass Roots of Art*, 1955)

I have repeatedly drawn attention to *sensibility* as the human quality underlying all processes involving skill, all achievements displaying taste, and I said that the first requirement in any civilization with pretensions to cultural values is a system of education or upbringing which not only preserves the innate sensibility of the child, but makes this the basis of mental development. I now return to that fundamental question.

In all our attempts to define the place of art in society we are continually struggling against the general notion that art is unnatural – that the artist is a rare and eccentric individual, having little or nothing in common with the common man. But it is only greatness that is uncommon, only genius that is eccentric. The appreciation of good form, the perception of rhythm and harmony, the instinct to make things shapely and efficient – these are normal human characteristics, innate rather than acquired, and certainly present in the child from its earliest years. We teach art to children – or perhaps we don't – but what we do not sufficiently realize is that children are artists in any case, just as inevitably as they are walkers or singers, talkers or players of games. Art is merely one method of human expression – the method which makes use of the expressive line, of expressive colour, of plastic form. There is an art of children, just as there is an art of savages or an art of adults. The mistake we make is to assume that this activity in children, the existence of which we can hardly deny, is merely a naive and clumsy attempt to imitate an adult activity. An imitative element is present in all childish activities, but the desire is never to imitate for the sake of imitation, but to communicate something in a common language. The drive behind all such childish efforts is an inner subjective need, not the monkey-like reflex, not an 'aping', as we say, of adult behaviour.

It is very important to admit the truth of this observation, for on such an admission depends the choice between teaching the child to imitate adult standards and recognizing that the child has standards of its own, appropriate to its age and expressive needs and gradually evolving to cope with widening circles of experience. This is a basic distinction in education generally, but for the moment I am only concerned with the effect it has on our attitude towards the aesthetic activity in children.

We are all prepared to admit that art is an affair of the emotions, perhaps also of intuitions and of the intelligence, and we ought therefore to realize that it is not merely a question of the simple growth of a separate faculty, the gradual maturation of a skill. Let us rather consider the analogy of love. The love of a child is one thing, and though the psycho-analysts have taken away our belief in its complete innocence, nevertheless we know that infancy, childhood, adolescence and maturity, represent so many stages in the development of the emotion of love which differ *in kind*. However much we may be deceived by the apparent thread of continuity represented by the uniqueness of each personality, we know that the transition from one stage of emotional development to another is often sudden and cataclysmic. The child of yesterday, attached to its parents by bonds of affection, is suddenly today the victim of a passion which makes it a new being.

The art of the child is the art of a human being with perceptions and emotions, reactions and fantasies, which differ in nature from the perceptions and emotions, reactions and fantasies of the adult. Instead, therefore, of judging the art of children by adult standards, we should be acting more scientifically if we were to compare it with the art of savages and of primitive man generally. Many of the observations which have been made about primitive art can be applied to the art of children. In both cases we are dealing with what Lévy-Bruhl has called a *pre-logical* state of mentality, and the many characteristics which are common to both types of art spring from this fact. The art of children must be studied, not as the child's feeble effort to imitate the plastic modes of expression practised by the civilized adults, but as the child's direct and unsophisticated expression of its own world of feeling. Once we have adopted this correct attitude towards the art of children, once we have an understanding of the place which plastic modes of expression occupy in the child's emotional life, then our methods of teaching children must change radically, and the place which art should occupy in the scheme of education takes on altogether new significance . . .

Let me begin by making clear what we do *not* claim. We do not claim that we are teaching children to observe external objects with exactness. We are not attempting to sharpen the child's powers of observation, of classification, of memory. All that is a pedagogical activity which we are content to leave to the science master, and we would agree that a certain type of drawing or design should be taught, like writing and numeration, in conjunction with scientific observation; it is a necessary form of notation or record. It is a skill which becomes appropriate at the secondary stage of education.

In the second place – and it is important to appreciate this point – we are *not* attempting to create professional artists. To become a competent painter or sculptor in the professional sense will require a long and arduous training in technique, and this vocational instruction should be given (as it is at present) in institutions specially devoted to the purpose. We teach children to speak, but we do not expect them all to be orators: we teach them to write, but we do not expect them all to be poets. In the same way, we teach them to draw and paint and model without any expectation that art will necessarily become their exclusive vocation in life.

What we do teach children by all these means is a particular medium of expression. Sounds, words, lines, colours – all these are the raw materials out of which the child has to learn to communicate with the outer world. He has also at his command certain gestures, which he combines with sounds, words, lines and colours. In his difficulty – for it is enormously difficult at first for the child to make himself understood – he will use everything that comes to hand: he makes a total effort to express himself, to express his inner feelings and desires.

Normally the parent and teacher make every effort to understand the *verbal* signs which the child makes: we listen to the first babblings of the baby and try to construe them into words. How patiently we guide and encourage the child in his efforts, first to talk and then to write!

But the child has also at his command this other language of line and colour, and he could often say by this means things for which he still lacks the words. He can express his emotions and desires, his perceptions and daydreams, by signs and symbols, by approximate representations. But more often than not his efforts in this direction receive no encouragement from the teacher, and even less from the parent. This activity, which should flourish as naturally as speech, is discouraged and becomes atrophied. The child is then visually dumb, a word which originally meant stupid.

But if we do encourage the child to develop his visual communications, his language of images, a new direction for expansion and growth is opened up for him. We might say that one of our aims, and perhaps the chief one, should be to give the child the necessary confidence and skill to develop a new but quite natural medium of expression – to make the language of symbols as much a trained habit as the language of signs, to give the pictograph the same significance as the phonetic alphabet. But our secondary aim is to encourage the child to reveal its personality, its innate characteristics. For the parent and the teacher a child's drawings become a new window into the child's mind.

But there is more to be discovered than the psychology of the individual child. As we gather and correlate this plastic imagery produced by children, we learn much about children in general, about their common characteristics and their mental development. And finally, but not in my opinion least important, we learn much about the nature of the aesthetic activity, about the place of art in life and in the evolution of mankind. For what these children produce is not merely line and colour, but line and colour (form, too, and cubic volume) which are significant and expressive, and which are significant and expressive quite naturally and instinctively. We learn, in short, that the primary elements of art – the factors which make it emotionally effective – are given to it by man's own nature and needs, and are not the creation of man's consciousness and intellect . . .

One thing that has been demonstrated beyond any doubt is that the aesthetic faculty is present in every child as a birthright, and that it can be made to blossom in the most unlikely surroundings – in gloomy industrial slums no less than in the beautiful precincts of a school like Eton or Winchester. Of course, as the child grows and its perceptions feed more or less consciously on its environment, this environment begins to be reflected in the subject matter of the child's art. But only in the subject matter. The style can develop independently of the content. It is not the environment which matters so much as the method of teaching.

If you now ask me: What is this method of teaching practised in schools which produce the paintings I have shown? My answer can only be in the most general terms. I am not myself a teacher, and I do not like to dictate to those who carry on this most difficult vocation. But I observe teachers and I note the results: I see that certain methods lead to results which I consider good, other methods to results which I consider bad, or to no results at all. It is easier to describe the methods which have bad results than those which have good results, the latter infinitely subtle and un- certain. The bad results are always produced by a method which is too conscious and deliberate, by a discipline which is imposed from without, which is the command of a drill- sergeant. The good results are produced apparently by no method at all, or by a system of hints and suggestions, and the discipline which undoubtedly exists and *must* exist, arises out of the activity itself, is in fact a kind of concentration on tools and materials, an absorption in concrete things. The good teacher is not a dictator, but rather a pupil more ad- vanced in technique than the others, more conscious of the aim to be achieved and the means that must be adopted, who works with the children, sympathizes with them and en- courages them, gives them that priceless possession which is self-confidence. It is only fear that prevents the child from being an artist – fear that its private world of fantasy will seem ridiculous to the adult, fear that its expressive signs and symbols will not be adequate. Cast out fear from the child, and you have then released all its potentialities for emotional growth and maturation.

That, of course, is not the final stage of education. You have liberated the child from fear, but beyond liberation there must be the more positive world of co-operation. You have liberated the child by means of sympathy and understanding, and the same faculties must be used to create human bonds, social bonds, until the individual child finds his fulfilment in the adult world of the community. That is the general purpose of education, but I know of no methods so effective for this purpose as those which are in a concrete sense *creative*. As individuals we create to communicate: we create a language out of sounds, we create a pictorial language out of line and colour. But every language, even the language of art, is a communal creation; it represents an agreed system of signs, to be used in common. Art is a bond. It is not a bond which should be the exclusive privilege of a class, of a tiny group of connoisseurs and artists. Art should be an integral part of our communal life, as it was in Ancient Greece, as it was in the Middle Ages: and it should enter our lives at their formative stage, as a natural function of human relationships, as the language of form and colour, as universal and as innocent as the language of words . . .

There is one further point to note: art is a natural discipline. In an obvious sense, art is a discipline imposed by the tool and the material – a child cannot use a pencil or a pen, a brush or a potter's wheel, without discovering that in order to be expressive, hand and eye must work in an instinctive unison. Art in this way produces an integration of the senses which we call *skill*, and which is one of the most fundamental purposes of any system of education . . . But art is also a discipline in another and more profound sense. There is in the very process of perception, and in this complementary process of expression, an instinctive tendency to *form*. The formal perfection of most primitive works of art, achieved without any system of instruction, has often been a subject for wonder and astonishment. The unsophisticated art of children, before any instruction is given, has the same tendency towards formal organization – not only balance of composition and selective emphasis of significant detail, but also towards expressive line and harmonious colour. Natural expression has its own instinctive form, and this would seem to suggest that the aim of education should be to seize on this innate sense of discipline, in order to develop and mature it, rather than to impose on the child a system of discipline which may be alien to its nature and harmful to its growth.

When the mental growth of the child has been impeded, and its psyche distorted (with results which are definitely neurotic and even delinquent), then there is much evidence which suggests that the practice of a creative art may have a therapeutic effect, gradually leading the child back to a balanced psychological disposition. The wider claims which are made for the place of art in education do not stop short at the achievement of a balanced personality for each individual child: that integration of the personality which is aimed at is an integration within the group or community to which the child belongs. We have never dared to trace the connections between the disordered state of our civilization and our traditional systems of education. If our schools were producing naturally and normally personalities which we could describe as balanced, integrated or harmonious, we should not be able to tolerate a condition of universal disunity and mutual distrust. We should therefore re-examine our whole tradition of education since the Renaissance and dare to ask ourselves whether it had been generally productive of individual serenity and social harmony. We might then have to confess that in our exclusive preoccupation with knowledge and science, we had omitted to educate those human faculties which are connected with the emotional and integrative aspects of human life – that we had carefully nurtured inhuman monsters, with certain organs of the intelligence gigantically enlarged, others completely atrophied. I am not making scientific assertions: I am merely pointing out that in certain directions we have not dared to question the presuppositions of our academic traditions and that at the same time these presuppositions have a clear connection with the character of our civilization.

I hope I have now made it clear that what I have called the development of a balanced aesthetic awareness is not an end in itself. Our aim is the same as Plato's – the moral and intellectual wholeness or health of mankind – and art is for me, as it was for Plato, a means to this end.

Part 7
Glimpses of a New World

One of the essential anarchist beliefs is that man, still bound
by mental chains, cannot chart the world where free men
will live; and there have, for this reason, been few anarchist
utopias. Perhaps Kropotkin's tentative sketches of the world
after the revolution, collected in *The Conquest of Bread*, are
the nearest direct approach, though William Morris's *News
from Nowhere* – written by a libertarian socialist – comes as
close as one could wish to the kind of society that most
anarchists would like to see.

Nevertheless, anarchists did discuss many aspects of the
world of the future, and out of their writings it is possible
to construct a fair vision of the kind of society most of them
would have accepted.

Proudhon, writing about the destinies of the revolution in
the passage titled 'The Old Society – and the New', shows
how the principles of a free society would differ from those of
the world he knew. Godwin delineates the kind of situation
that might ensue with the dissolution of government, seeing
a pattern of small parishes (or communes) united by the most
fragile of linking institutions. Basically he is saying, as
Tolstoy does in the fragment we reproduce, that men can
arrange their own lives better than governments can do it
for them. And Michael Bakunin analyses the role authority
should play in such a situation; essentially it is the authority
of superior knowledge, acknowledged after examination but
never allowed to transform itself into political power.

This new world, as Proudhon suggests in 'The Revolution
and the Nation', will mean the end of all states and all
divisions between them. But this cannot be achieved by some
super-government; rather it must come, as Colin Ward
suggests in 'Topless Federation' and George Woodcock in

'Reflections on Decentralism', through the breakdown of the political order into local units bearing prime responsibility and their arrangement on the basis of a true federalism.

Essentially, once the problems of power have been solved, the ordering of the new society must be seen in economic terms – how production is organized, how consumption is arranged. Generally, as the passages already reproduced on syndicalism will have shown, and as James Guillaume suggests in 'The Organization of Production', the anarchists favour a flexible arrangement by which some craftsmen work individually and others in associations or syndicates, controlling their places of work and distributing their products in agreement with other syndicates or with communes – the associations of men and women based on residential patterns. Favourite subjects of critics of such voluntary work patterns have been the questions of lazy men and dirty work, for which Alexander Berkman provides the anarchist answers, though it should be added, as William Morris makes clear, that in a well-planned society the work that now seems tedious will mainly be performed by machines, the new slaves.

Given a re-arrangement of priorities, existing technology leaves little doubt that production can be organized much more rationally than at present, so that essentials can be produced easily, and more leisure for creative work be secured. The problem of a just distribution remains. Early anarchists, like Proudhon and Josiah Warren, thought that it should relate to each man's productivity, and for this reason they arranged a system of exchange on the basis of labour notes which Warren – as he explains in 'The Time Store' – attempted to put into practice both in circumstances of city shopkeeping and in village communities.

James Guillaume, one of Bakunin's early anarchist disciples, writing on 'Exchange and Distribution' in 1876, thought that, to begin with, a Proudhonian system of exchange would be necessary, but that eventually it might evolve into a system of distribution by need. Kropotkin became a whole-hearted advocate of anarchist-communism, and in his famous pamphlet, 'The Wage System', he put the case for rejecting any system based on payments to the workers and insisted that free distribution was the only just and practicable system in a society that did not wish to slip back into inequality and authoritarianism.

To the problem of crime in a free society – which could only occur in the form of infringement on the person or liberty of individuals – Kropotkin brings the argument that there must be some self-protective restraint of violent men, but that friendly treatment remains the real cure.

Kropotkin – at least – among the early anarchists recognized the significance of man's position in the world of nature and the responsibilities it might involve. Unlike most socialists, the anarchists were never greatly attracted to the vaunted affluent society of the mid-twentieth century. There was always among them the feeling that it might be necessary to simplify the social and economic pattern and to accept lower standards of existence for the sake of a liberated life or even for survival, and Proudhon – like Paul Goodman after him – spoke up for honourable poverty. 'It is not good for man to live in ease,' Proudhon declared. 'We must, on the contrary, always feel the prick of need . . . Poverty is good, and we must think of it as being the source of all our joys. Reason demands that we should live with it – frugally, modifying our pleasures, labouring assiduously and subordinating all our appetites to justice.' (Translation by Elizabeth Fraser in *Selected Writings of P.-J. Proudhon*, edited by Stewart Edwards, 1969.)

It is this insight of the anarchists that Murray Bookchin develops when he declares in the extract we have entitled 'Anarchism and Ecology' that 'an anarchist society . . . has become the precondition for the practice of ecological principles'. For, in fact, anarchism is the only current in the modern world sufficiently detached from considerations of profit on the one hand and power on the other to look objectively and sensitively at man within the world of nature, different from other living beings, not unequal.

A.R.   K

THE OLD SOCIETY –
AND THE NEW

PIERRE-JOSEPH PROUDHON
(From *Idée Générale de la Révolution aux XIXé Siècle*,
1851, translated by John Beverley Robinson, 1923)

Given:
  Man, *The Family*, SOCIETY.

An individual, sexual and social being, endowed with
reason, love and conscience, capable of learning by experience, of perfecting himself by reflection, and of earning his
living by work.

The problem is to so organize the powers of this being,
that he may remain always at peace with himself, and may
extract from Nature, which is given to him, the largest
possible amount of well-being.

We know how previous generations have solved it.

They borrowed from the Family, the second component
part of Humanity, the principle which is proper to it alone,
AUTHORITY, and by the arbitrary use of this principle,
they constructed an artificial system, varied according to
periods and climates, which has been regarded as the natural
order and necessary for humanity.

This system, which may be called the system of order by
authority, was at first divided into spiritual and temporal
authority.

After a short period in which it preponderated, and long
centuries of struggle to maintain its supremacy, sacerdotal-
ism seems at last to have given up its claim to temporal
power; the Papacy, with all its soldiery, which the Jesuits
and lay brothers of today would restore, has been cast out
and set below matters of merely human interest.

For two years past the spiritual power has been in a way to
again seize supremacy. It has formed a coalition with the
secular power against the Revolution, and bargains with it
upon a footing of equality. Both have ended by recognizing

that their differences arose from a misunderstanding; that their aim, their principles, their methods, their dogmas, being absolutely identical, Government should be shared by them; or rather, that they should consider themselves the complements of each other, and should form their union a one and indivisible Authority.

Such at least would have been the conclusion which Church and State would have perhaps reached, if the laws of the progress of Humanity rendered such reconciliation possible; if the Revolution had not already marked their last hour.

However that may be, it is desirable, in order to convince the mind, to set alongside each other the fundamental ideas of, on the one hand, the politico-religious system (Philosophy, which has for so long drawn a line between the spiritual and the temporal, should no longer recognize any distinction between them); on the other hand, the economic system.

Government then, that is to say, Church and State indivisibly united, has for its dogmas:

1. The original perversity of human nature;
2. The inevitable inequality of fortunes;
3. The permanency of quarrels and wars;
4. The irremediability of poverty.

Whence is deduced:

5. The necessity of government, of obedience, of resignation and of faith.

These principles admitted, as they still are, almost universally, the forms of authority are already settled. They are:

a. The division of the people into classes or castes, subordinate to one another; graduated to form a pyramid, at the top of which appears, like the Divinity, upon his altar, like the king upon his throne, AUTHORITY;

b. Administrative centralization;

c. Judicial hierarchy;

d. Police;

e. Worship.

Add to the above, in countries in which the democratic principle has become preponderant:

f. The separation of powers;

g. The intervention of the People in the Government, by vote for representatives;

h. The innumerable varieties of electoral systems, from the Convocation by Estates, which prevailed in the Middle Ages, down to universal and direct suffrage;

i. The duality of legislative chambers;

j. Voting upon laws, and consent to taxes by the representatives of the nation;

k. The rule of majorities.

Such is broadly the plan of construction of Power independently of the modifications which each of its component parts may receive; as, for example, the central Power, which may be in turn monarchical, aristocratic or democratic . . .

It will be observed that the governmental system tends to become more and more complicated, without becoming on that account more efficient and more moral, and without offering any more guarantees to person or property. This complication springs first from legislation, which is always incomplete and insufficient; in the second place, from the multiplicity of functionaries; but most of all, from the compromise between the two antagonistic elements, the executive initiative and popular consent. It has been left for our epoch to establish unmistakably that this bargaining, which the progress of centuries renders inevitable, is the surest index of corruption, of decadence and of the approaching dissolution of Authority.

What is the aim of this organization?

To maintain *order* in society, by consecrating and sanctifying obedience of the citizen to the State, subordination of the poor to the rich, of the common people to the upper class, of the worker to the idler, of the layman to the priest, of the business man to the soldier.

As far back as the memory of humanity extends, it is found to have been organized on the above system, which constitutes the political, ecclesiastical or governmental order. Every effort to give Power a more liberal appearance, more tolerant, more social, has invariably failed: such efforts have been even more fruitless when they tried to give the People a larger share in Government; as if the words, Sovereignty and People, which they endeavoured to yoke together, were as naturally antagonistic as these other two words, Liberty and Despotism.

Humanity has had to live, and civilization to develop, for six thousand years, under this inexorable system, of which the first term is *Despair*, and the last *Death*. What secret power has sustained it? What force has enabled it to survive? What principles, what ideas, renewed the blood that flowed forth under the dagger of authority, ecclesiastical and secular?

This mystery is now explained.

Beneath the governmental machinery, in the shadow of political institutions, out of the sight of statesmen and priests, society is producing its own organism, slowly and silently; and constructing a new order, the expression of its vitality and autonomy, and the denial of the old politics, as well as of the old religion.

This organization, which is as essential to society as it is incompatible with the present system, has the following principles:

1. The indefinite perfectibility of the individual and of the race;

2. The honourableness of work;

3. The equality of fortunes;

4. The identity of interests;

5. The end of antagonisms;

6. The universality of comfort;

7. The sovereignty of reason;

8. The absolute liberty of the man and the citizen.

I mention below the principal forms of activity:

a. Division of labour, through which classification of the People by INDUSTRIES replaces classification by *caste*;

b. Collective power, the principle of WORKMEN'S ASSOCIATIONS, in place of *armies*;

c. Commerce, the concrete form of CONTRACT, which takes the place of *Law*;

d. Equality in exchange;

e. Competition;

f. Credit, which turns upon INTERESTS, as the governmental hierarchy turns upon *Obedience*;

g. The equilibrium of values and properties.

The old system, standing on Authority and Faith, was essentially based upon *Divine Right*. The principle of the sovereignty of the People, introduced later, did not change its nature; and it is a mistake today, in the face of the conclusions of science, to maintain a distinction which does not touch underlying principles, between absolute monarchy and constitutional monarchy, or between the latter and the democratic republic. The sovereignty of the People has been, if I may say so, for a century past, but a skirmishing line for Liberty. It was either an error, or a clever scheme of our fathers to make the sovereign people in the image of the king-man: as the Revolution becomes better understood, this mythology vanishes, all traces of government disappear and follow the principle of government itself to dissolution.

The new system, based upon the spontaneous practice of industry, in accordance with individual and social reason, is the system of *Human Right*. Opposed to arbitrary command, essentially objective, it permits neither parties nor sects; it is complete in itself, and allows neither restriction nor separation.

There is no fusion possible between the political and economic systems, between the system of laws and the system of contracts; one or the other must be chosen. The ox, while it remains an ox, cannot be an eagle, nor can the bat be at the same time a snail. In the same way, while Society maintains in the slightest degree its political form, it cannot become organized according to economic law. How harmonize local initiative with the preponderance of a central authority, or universal suffrage with the hierarchy of officials; the principle that no one owes obedience to a law to which he has not himself consented, with the right of majorities?

If a writer who understood these contradictions should undertake to reconcile them, it would prove him, not a bold thinker, but a wretched charlatan. This absolute incompatibility of the two systems, so often proved, still does not convince writers who, while admitting the dangers of authority, nevertheless hold to it, as the sole means of maintaining order, and see nothing beside it but empty desolation. Like the sick man in the comedy, who is told that the first thing he must do is to discharge his doctors, if he wants to get well, they persist in asking how can a man get along without a doctor, or a society without a government. They will make the government as republican, as benevolent, as equal as possible; they will set up all possible guarantees against it; they will belittle it, almost attack it, in support of the majesty of the citizens. They tell us: You are the government! You shall govern yourselves, without president, without representatives, without delegates. What have you then to complain about? But to live without government, to abolish all authority, absolutely and unreservedly, to set up pure *anarchy*, seems to them ridiculous and inconceivable, a plot against the Republic and against the nation. What will these people who talk of abolishing government put in place of it? they ask.

We have no trouble in answering.

It is industrial organization that we will put in the place of government, as we have just shown.

In place of laws, we will put contracts. – No more laws voted by a majority, nor even unanimously; each citizen, each town, each industrial union, makes its own laws.

In place of political powers, we will put economic forces.

In place of the ancient classes of nobles, burghers, and peasants, or of business men and working men, we will put the general titles and special departments of industry; Agriculture, Manufacture, Commerce, etc.

In place of public force, we will put collective force.

In place of standing armies, we will put industrial associations.

In place of police, we will put identity of interests.

In place of political centralization, we will put economic centralization.

Do you see now how there can be order without functionaries, a profound and wholly intellectual unity?

You, who cannot conceive of unity without a whole apparatus of legislators, prosecutors, attorneys-general, custom house officers, policemen, you have never known what real unity is! What you call unity and centralization is nothing but perpetual chaos, serving as a basis for endless tyranny; it is the advancing chaotic condition of social forces as an argument for despotism – a despotism which is really the cause of the chaos.

Well, in our turn, let us ask, what need have we of government when we have made an agreement? Does not the National Bank, with its various branches, achieve centralization and unity? Does not the agreement among farm labourers for compensation, marketing, and reimbursement for farm properties create unity? From another point of view, do not the industrial associations for carrying on the large-scale industries bring about unity? And the constitution of value, that contract of contracts, as we have called it, is not that the most perfect and indissoluble unity?

And if we must show you an example in our own history in order to convince you, does not that fairest monument of the Convention, the system of weights and measures, form, for fifty years past, the cornerstone of that economic unity which is destined to replace political unity?

Never ask again then what we will put in place of government, nor what will become of society without government, for I assure you that in the future it will be easier to conceive of society without government, than of society with government.

Society, just now, is like the butterfly just out of the cocoon, which shakes its gilded wings in the sunlight before taking flight. Tell it to crawl back into the silken covering, to shun the flowers and to hide itself from the light!

But a revolution is not made with formulas. Prejudice must be attacked at the foundations, overthrown, hurled into dust, its injurious effects explained, its ridiculous and odious nature shown forth. Mankind believes only in its own tests, happy if these tests do not addle its brains and drain its blood. Let us try then by clear criticism to make the test of government so conclusive, that the absurdity of the institution will strike all minds, and Anarchy, dreaded as a scourge, will be accepted as a benefit . . .

THE DISSOLUTION OF GOVERNMENT

William Godwin
(From *Enquiry Concerning Political Justice*, 1793)

Government can have no more than two legitimate purposes, the suppression of injustice against individuals within the community, and the common defence against external invasion. The first of these purposes, which alone can have an uninterrupted claim upon us, is sufficiently answered, by an association, of such an extent, as to afford room for the institution of a jury, to decide upon the offences of individuals within the community, and upon the questions and controversies, respecting property, which may chance to arise. It might be easy indeed for an offender, to escape from the limits of so petty a jurisdiction; and it might seem necessary, at first, that the neighbouring parishes,* or jurisdictions, should be governed in a similar manner, or at least should be willing, whatever their form of government, to co-operate with us, in the removal or reformation of an offender, whose present habits were alike injurious to us and to them. But there will be no need of any express compact, and still less of any common centre of authority, for this purpose. General justice, and mutual interest, are found more capable of binding men, than signatures and seals. In the meantime, all necessity for causing the punishment of the crime to pursue the criminal would soon, at least, cease, if it ever existed. The motives to offence would become rare: its aggravations few: and rigour superfluous. The principle object of punishment, is restraint upon a dangerous member of the community; and the end of this restraint would be answered, by the general inspection, that is exercised by the members of a

---

* The word parish, is here used, without regard to its origin, and merely in consideration of its being a word, descriptive of a certain small portion of territory, whether in population or extent, which custom has rendered familiar to us.

limited circle, over the conduct of each other, and by the gravity and good sense that would characterize the censures of men, from whom all mystery and empiricism were banished. No individual would be hardy enough in the cause of vice, to defy the general consent of sober judgment that would surround him. It would carry despair to his mind, or, which is better, it would carry conviction. He would be obliged, by a force not less irresistible than whips and chains, to reform his conduct.

In this sketch is contained the rude outline of political government. Controversies between parish and parish, would be, in an eminent degree, unreasonable, since, if any question arose, about limits, for example, the obvious principles of convenience could scarcely fail to teach us, to what district any portion of land should belong. No association of men, so long as they adhered to the principles of reason, could possibly have an interest in extending their territory. If we would produce attachment in our associates, we can adopt no surer method, than that of practising the dictates of equity and moderation; and, if this failed in any instance, it could only fail with him who, to whatever society he belonged, would prove an unworthy member. The duty of any society to punish offenders, is not dependent upon the hypothetical consent of the offender to be punished, but upon the duty of necessary defence.

But however irrational might be the controversy of parish with parish in such a state of society, it would not be less possible. For such extraordinary emergencies therefore, provision ought to be made. These emergencies are similar in their nature to those of foreign invasion. They can only be provided against by the concert of several districts, declaring and, if needful, enforcing the dictates of justice.

One of the most obvious remarks that suggests itself, upon these two cases, of hostility between district and district, and of foreign invasion which the interest of all calls upon them jointly to repel, is, that it is their nature to be only of occasional recurrence, and that, therefore, the provisions to be made respecting them, need not be, in the strictest sense, of perpetual operation. In other words, the permanence of national assembly, as it has hitherto been practiced in France, cannot be necessary in a period of tranquillity, and may perhaps be pernicious. That we may form a more accurate judgment of this, let us recollect some of the principal features that enter into the constitution of a national assembly.

*   *   *   *   *

In the first place, the existence of a national assembly, introduces the evils of a fictitious unanimity. The public, guided by such an assembly, must act with concert, or the assembly is a nugatory excrescence. But it is impossible that this unanimity can really exist. The individuals who constitute a nation, cannot take into consideration a variety of important questions without forming different sentiments respecting them. In reality, all questions that are brought before such an assembly, are decided by a majority of votes, and the minority, after having exposed, with all the power of eloquence, and force of reasoning, of which they are capable, the injustice and folly of the measures adopted, are obliged, in a certain sense, to assist in carrying them into execution. Nothing can more directly contribute to the depravation of the human understanding and character. It inevitably renders mankind timid, dissembling and corrupt. He that is not accustomed, exclusively to act upon the dictates of his own understanding, must fall inexpressibly short of that energy and simplicity of which our nature is capable. He that contributes his personal exertions, or his property, to the support of a cause which he believes to be unjust, will quickly lose that accurate discrimination, and nice sensibility of moral rectitude, which are the principal ornaments of reason.

Secondly, the existence of national councils, produces a certain species of real unanimity, unnatural in its character, and pernicious in its effects. The genuine and wholesome state of mind is, to be unloosed from shackles, and to expand every fibre of its frame, according to the independent and individual impressions of truth upon that mind. How great would be the progress of intellectual improvement, if men were unfettered by the prejudices of education, unseduced by the influence of a corrupt state of society, and accustomed to yield without fear, to the guidance of truth,

however unexplored might be the regions and unexpected
the conclusions, to which she conducted us? We cannot
advance in the voyage of happiness, unless we be wholly a;
large upon the stream that would carry us thither; the anchor,
that we at first looked upon as the instrument of our safety,
will, at last, be found to be the means of detaining our progress. Unanimity of a certain sort, is the result to which
perfect freedom of enquiry is calculated to conduct us; and
this unanimity would, in a state of perfect freedom, become
hourly more conspicuous. But the unanimity that results from
men's having a visible standard by which to adjust their
sentiments, is deceitful and pernicious.

In numerous assemblies, a thousand motives influence our
judgements, independently of reason and evidence. Every
man looks forward, to the effects which the opinions he
avows, will produce on his success. Every man connects himself with some sect or party. The activity of his thought is
shackled, at every turn, by the fear, that his associates may
disclaim him. The effect is strikingly visible in the present
state of the British parliament, where men, whose faculties
are comprehensive almost beyond all former example, may
probably be influenced by three motives, sincerely to espouse
the grossest and most contemptible errors.

Thirdly, the debates of a national assembly are distorted
from their reasonable tenor, by the necessity of their being
uniformly terminated by a vote. Debate and discussion are,
in their own nature, highly conducive to intellectual improvement; but they lose this salutary character, the moment
they are subjected to this unfortunate condition. What can
be more unreasonable, than to demand, that argument, the
usual quality of which is gradually and imperceptibly to enlighten the mind, should declare its effect in the close of a
single conversation? No sooner does this circumstance occur,
than the whole scene changes its character. The orator no
longer enquires after permanent conviction, but transitory
effect. He seeks rather to take advantage of our prejudices,
than to enlighten our judgement. That which might otherwise
have been a scene of patient and beneficient enquiry, is changed
into wrangling, tumult and precipitation.

Another circumstance that arises out of the decision by

vote, is the necessity of constructing a form of words, that shall best meet the sentiments, and be adapted to the preconceived ideas, of a multitude of men. What can be conceived, at once more ludicrous and disgraceful, than the spectacle of a set of rational beings, employed for hours together, in weighing particles and adjusting commas? Such is the scene that is incessantly witnessed in clubs and private societies. In parliament, this sort of business is usually adjusted, before the measure becomes a subject of public inspection. But it does not the less exist; and sometimes it occurs in the other mode, so that, when numerous amendments have been made to suit the corrupt interest of imperious pretenders, the Herculean task remains at last, to reduce the chaos into a grammatical and intelligible form.

The whole is then wound up, with the flagrant insult upon all reason and justice, the deciding upon truth by the casting up of numbers. Thus every thing, that we have been accustomed to esteem most sacred, is determined, at best, by the weakest heads in the assembly, but, as it not less frequently happens, through the influence of most corrupt and dishonourable intentions.

In the last place, national assemblies will by no means be thought to deserve our direct approbation, if we recollect, for a moment, the absurdity of that fiction, by which society is considered, as it has been termed, as a moral individual. It is in vain that we endeavour to counteract the laws of nature and necessity. A multitude of men, after all our ingenuity, will still remain a multitude of men. Nothing can intellectually unite them, short of equal capacity and identical perception. So long as the varieties of mind shall remain, the force of society can no otherwise be concentrated, than by one man, for a shorter or a longer term, taking the lead of the rest, and employing their forces, whether material, or dependent on the weight of their character, in a mechanical manner, just as he would employ the force of a tool or a machine. All government corresponds, in a certain degree, to what the Greeks denominated a tyranny. The difference is that, in despotic countries, mind is depressed by a uniform usurpation; while, in republics, it preserves a greater portion of its activity, and the usurpation more easily conforms itself to the fluctuations of opinion.

The pretence of collective wisdom is among the most palpable of all impostures. The acts of the society, can never rise above the suggestions of this or that individual, who is a member of it. Let us enquire whether society, considered as an agent, can really become the equal of certain individuals, of whom it is composed. And here, without staying to examine what ground we have to expect, that the wisest member of the society will actually take the lead in it, we find two obvious reasons to persuade us, that, whatever be the degree of wisdom inherent in him that really superintends, the acts which he performs in the name of the society will be both less virtuous and less able, than the acts he might be expected to perform in a simpler and more unencumbered situation. In the first place, there are few men who, with the consciousness of being able to cover their responsibility under the name of a society, will not venture upon measures, less direct in their motives, or less justifiable in the experiment, than they would have chosen to adopt in their own persons. Secondly, men who act under the name of a society, are deprived of that activity and energy, which may belong to them in their individual character. They have a multitude of followers to draw after them, whose humours they must consult, and to whose slowness of apprehension they must accommodate themselves. It is for this reason that we frequently see men of the most elevated genius dwindle into vulgar leaders, when they become involved in the busy scenes of public life.

From these reasonings we seem sufficiently authorized to conclude, that national assemblies, or, in other words, assemblies instituted for the joint purposes of adjusting the differences between district and district, and of consulting respecting the best mode of repelling foreign invasion, however necessary to be had recourse to upon certain occasions, ought to be employed as sparingly as the nature of the case will admit. They should either never be elected but upon extraordinary emergencies, like the dictator of the ancient Romans, or else sit periodically, one day for example in a year, with a power of continuing their sessions within a certain limit, to hear the complaints and representations of their constituents. The former of these modes is greatly to be preferred. Several of the reasons already adduced, are calculated to show, that election itself is of a nature not to be employed, but when the occasion demands it. There would probably be little difficulty in suggesting expedients, relative to the regular originating of national assemblies. It would be most suitable to past habits and experience, that a general election should take place, whenever a certain number of districts demanded it. It would be most agreeable to rigid simplicity and equity, that an assembly of two or two hundred districts should take place, in exact proportion to the number of districts by whom that measure was desired.

It will scarcely be denied, that the objections which have been most loudly reiterated against democracy, become null in an application to the form of government which has now been delineated. Here we shall with difficulty find an opening for tumult, for the tyranny of a multitude drunk with unlimited power, for political ambition on the part of the few, of restless jealousy and precaution on the part of the many. Here the demagogue would discover no suitable occasion, for rendering the multitude the blind instrument of his purposes. Men, in such a state of society, might be expected to understand their happiness, and to cherish it. The true reason why the mass of mankind has so often been made the dupe of knaves, has been the mysterious and complicated nature of the social system. Once annihilate the quackery of government, and the most homebred understanding might be strong enough to detect the artifices, of the state juggler that would mislead him.

*   *   *   *   *

It remains for us to consider, what is the degree of authority necessary to be vested, in such a modified species of national assembly as we have admitted to our system. Are they to issue their commands to the different members of the confederacy? Or is it sufficient, that they should invite them to co-operate for the common advantage, and, by arguments and addresses, convince them of the reasonableness of the measures they propose? The former of these might at first

be necessary. The latter would afterward become sufficient.*
The Amphictyonic council of Greece possessed no authority,
but that which flowed from its personal character. In proportion as the spirit of party was extirpated, as the restless-
ness of public commotion subsided, and as the political
machine became simple, the voice of reason would be secure
to be heard. An appeal, by the assembly, to the several
districts, would not fail to unite the approbation of reasonable men, unless it contained in it something so evidently
questionable, as to make it perhaps desirable that it should
prove abortive.

This remark leads us one step further. Why should not the
same distinction between commands and invitations, which
we have just made in the case of national assemblies, be
applied to the particular assemblies or juries of the several
districts? At first, we will suppose, that some degree of
authority and violence would be necessary. But this necessity
does not appear to arise out of the nature of man, but out of
the institutions by which he has been corrupted. Man is not
originally vicious. He would not refuse to listen to, or to be
convinced by, the expostulations that are addressed to him,
had he not been accustomed to regard them as hypocritical,
and to conceive that, while his neighbour, his parent, and his
political governor, pretended to be actuated by a pure
regard to his interest or pleasure, they were, in reality, at
the expense of his, promoting their own. Such are the fatal
effects of mysteriousness and complexity. Simplify the social
system, in the manner which every motive, but those of
usurpation and ambition, powerfully recommends; render
the plain dictates of justice level to every capacity; remove
the necessity of implicit faith; and we may expect the whole
species to become reasonable and virtuous. It might then be
sufficient for juries to recommend a certain mode of adjust-

* Such is the idea of the author of *Gulliver's Travels*, a man who
appears to have had a more profound insight into the true principles
of political justice, than any preceding or contemporary author. It
was unfortunate, that a work of such inestimable wisdom failed, at
the period of its publication, from the mere playfulness of its form,
in communicating adequate instruction to mankind. Posterity only will
be able to estimate it as it deserves.

ing controversies, without assuming the prerogative of dictating that adjustment. It might then be sufficient for them to invite offenders to forsake their errors. If their expostulations proved, in a few instances, ineffectual, the evils arising out of this circumstance, would be of less importance, than those which proceed from the perpetual violation of the exercise of private judgement. But, in reality, no evils would arise: for, where the empire of reason was so universally acknowledged, the offender would either readily yield to the expostulations of authority; or, if he resisted, though suffering no personal molestation, he would feel so uneasy, under the unequivocal disapprobation, and observant eye, of public judgement, as willingly to remove to a society more congenial to his errors.

The reader has probably anticipated the ultimate conclusion from these remarks. If juries might at length cease to decide, and be contented to invite, if force might gradually be withdrawn, and reason trusted alone, shall we not one day find, that juries themselves, and every other species of public institution, may be laid aside as unnecessary? Will not the reasonings of one wise man, be as effectual as those of twelve? Will not the competence of one individual to instruct his neighbours, be a matter of sufficient notoriety, without the formality of an election? Will there be many vices to correct, and much obstinacy to conquer? This is one of the most memorable stages of human improvement. With what delight must every well informed friend of mankind look forward, to the auspicious period, the dissolution of political government, of that brute engine, which has been the only perennial cause of the vices of mankind, and which . . . has mischiefs of various sorts incorporated with its substance, and no otherwise removable than by its utter annihilation!

ARRANGING OUR OWN LIVES

Leo Tolstoy
(From *The Slavery of Our Times*, 1900, translated by
Aylmer Maude)

It is said that without Governments we should not have those
institutions, enlightening, educational, and public, that are
needful for all.

But why should we suppose this? Why think that non-
official people could not arrange their life for themselves,
as well as Government people can arrange it not for themselves but for others?

We see, on the contrary, that in the most diverse matters
people in our times arrange their lives incomparably better
than those who govern them arrange things for them. Without
the least help from Government, and often in spite of the
interference of Government, people organize all sorts of
social undertakings – workmen's unions, co-operative societies,
railway companies, cartels, and syndicates. If collections for
public works are needed, why should we suppose that free
people could not, without violence, voluntarily collect the
necessary means and carry out anything that is now carried
out by means of taxes, if only the undertakings in question are
really useful for everybody? Why suppose that there cannot
be tribunals without violence? Trial, by people trusted by
the disputants, has always existed and will exist, and needs
no violence. We are so depraved by long-continued slavery,
that we can hardly imagine administration without violence.
And yet, again, that is not true: Russian communes migrat-
ing to distant regions, where our Government leaves them
alone, arrange their own taxation, administration, tribunals,
and police, and always prosper until governmental violence
interferes with their administration. And in the same way
there is no reason to suppose that people could not, by
common agreement, decide how the land is to be apportioned
for use.

I have known people – Cossacks of the Oural – who have

lived without acknowledging private property in land. And there was such well-being and order in their commune as does not exist in society where landed property is defended by violence. And I know communes that live without acknowledging the right of individuals to private property. Within my recollection the whole Russian peasantry did not accept the idea of landed property. The defence of landed property by governmental violence not merely does not abolish the struggle for landed property, but, on the contrary, intensifies the struggle, and in many cases causes it.

Were it not for the defence of landed property, and its consequent rise in price, people would not be crowded into such narrow spaces, but would scatter over the free land of which there is still so much in the world. But, as it is, a continual struggle goes on for landed property; a struggle with the weapons Government furnished by means of its laws of landed property. And in this struggle it is not those who work on the land, but always those who take part in governmental violence, who have the advantage.

It is the same with reference to things produced by labour. Things really produced by man's own labour, and that he needs, are always protected by custom, by public opinion, by feelings of justice and reciprocity, and they do not need to be protected by violence.

Tens of thousands of acres of forest lands belonging to one proprietor – while thousands of people close by have no fuel – need protection by violence. So, too, do factories and works where several generations of workmen have been defrauded and are still being defrauded. Yet more do hundreds of thousands of bushels of grain, belonging to one owner, who has held them back to sell them at triple price in time of famine. But no man, however depraved – except a rich man or a Government official – would take from a countryman living by his own labour the harvest he has raised, or the cow he has bred, and from which he gets milk for his children, or the ploughs, the scythes, and the spades he has made and uses. If even a man were found who did take from another articles the latter has made and required, such a man would rouse against himself such indignation, from everyone living in similar circumstances, that he would hardly find his action profitable for himself. A man so immoral as to do it under such circumstances, would be sure to do it under the strictest system of property defence by violence. It is generally said, 'Only attempt to abolish the rights of property in land, and in the produce of labour, and no one will take the trouble to work, lacking assurance that he will be able to retain what he has produced.' We should say just the opposite: the defence by violence of the rights of property immorally obtained, which is now customary, if it has not quite destroyed, has considerably weakened people's natural consciousness of justice in the matter of using articles, i.e. has weakened the natural and innate right of property, without which humanity could not exist, and which has always existed and still exists among all men.

And, therefore, there is no reason to anticipate that people will not be able to arrange their lives without violence.

Of course, it can be said that horses and bulls must be guided by the violence of rational beings – men; but why must men be guided, not by some higher beings, but by people such as themselves? Why ought people to be subject to the violence of just those men who are in power at a given time? What proves that these people are wiser than those on whom they inflict violence?

The fact that they allow themselves to use violence toward human beings, indicates that they are not only not more wise, but less wise than those who submit to them. The examinations in China for the office of Mandarin, do not, we know, ensure that the wisest and best people should be placed in power. And just as little is this ensured by inheritance, or the whole machinery of promotions in rank, or the elections in constitutional countries. On the contrary, power is always seized by those who are less conscientious and less moral.

It is said, 'How can people live without Governments, i.e. without violence?' But it should, on the contrary, be asked, 'How can rational people live, acknowledging the vital bond of their social life to be violence, and not reasonable agreement?'

One of two things: either people are rational beings or they are irrational beings. If they are irrational beings, then they are all irrational, and then everything among them is decided by violence, and there is no reason why certain people should, and others should not, have a *right* to use violence. And in that case, governmental violence has no justification. But if men are rational beings, then their relations should be based on reason, and not on the violence of those who happen to have seized power. And in that case, again, governmental violence has no justification.

WHAT IS AUTHORITY?

MICHAEL BAKUNIN
(From *Dieu et l'état*, 1882, translated by Benjamin Tucker as *God and the State*, 1883)

What is authority? Is it the inevitable power of the natural laws which manifest themselves in the necessary concatenation and succession of phenomena in the physical and social worlds? Indeed, against these laws revolt is not only forbidden – it is even impossible. We may misunderstand them or not know them at all, but we cannot disobey them; because they constitute the basis and fundamental conditions of our existence; they envelop us, penetrate us, regulate all our movements, thoughts, and acts; even when we believe that we disobey them, we only show their omnipotence.

Yes, we are absolutely the slaves of these laws. But in such slavery there is no humiliation, or, rather, it is not slavery at all. For slavery supposes an external master, a legislator outside of him whom he commands, while these laws are not outside of us; they are inherent in us; they constitute our being, our whole being, physically, intellectually, and morally: we live, we breathe, we act, we think, we wish only through these laws. Without them we are nothing, *we are not*. Whence, then, could we derive the power and the wish to rebel against them?

In his relation to natural laws but one liberty is possible to man – that of recognizing and applying them on an ever-extending scale of conformity with the object of collective and individual emancipation or humanization which he pursues. These laws, once recognized, exercise an authority which is never disputed by the mass of men. One must, for instance, be at bottom either a fool or a theologian or at least a metaphysician, jurist, or bourgeois economist to rebel against the law by which twice two make four. One must have faith to imagine that fire will not burn nor water drown, except, indeed, recourse be had to some subterfuge founded in its turn on some other natural law. But these revolts, or, rather, these attempts at or foolish fancies of an impossible revolt, are decidedly the exception; for, in general, it may be said that the mass of men, in their daily lives, acknowledge the government of common sense – that is, of the sum of the natural laws generally recognized – in an almost absolute fashion.

The great misfortune is that a large number of natural laws, already established as such by science, remain unknown to the masses, thanks to the watchfulness of these tutelary governments that exist, as we know, only for the good of the people. There is another difficulty – namely, that the major portion of the natural laws connected with the development of human society, which are quite as necessary, invariable, fatal, as the laws that govern the physical world, have not been duly established and recognized by science itself.

Once they shall have been recognized by science, and then from science, by means of an extensive system of popular education and instruction, shall have passed into the consciousness of all, the question of liberty will be entirely solved. The most stubborn authorities must admit that then there will be no need either of political organization or direction or legislation, three things which, whether they emanate from the will of the sovereign or from the vote of a parliament elected by universal suffrage, and even should they conform to the system of natural laws – which has never been the case and never will be the case – are always equally fatal and hostile to the liberty of the masses from the very fact that they impose upon them a system of external and therefore despotic laws.

The liberty of man consists solely in this: that he obeys natural laws because he has *himself* recognized them as such, and not because they have been externally imposed upon him by any extrinsic will whatever, divine or human, collective or individual.

Suppose a learned academy, composed of the most illustrious representatives of science; suppose this academy charged with legislation for and the organization of society, and that, inspired only by the purest love of truth, it frames none but the laws in absolute harmony with the latest discoveries of science. Well, I maintain, for my part, that such legislation and such organization would be a monstrosity, and that for two reasons: first, that human science is always and necessarily imperfect, and that, comparing what it has discovered with what remains to be discovered, we may say that it is still in its cradle. So that were we to try to force the practical life of men, collective as well as individual, into strict and exclusive conformity with the latest data of science, we should condemn society as well as individuals to suffer martyrdom on a bed of Procrustes, which would soon end by dislocating and stifling them, life ever remaining an infinitely greater thing than science.

The second reason is this: a society which should obey legislation emanating from a scientific academy, not because it understood itself the rational character of this legislation (in which case the existence of the academy would become useless), but because this legislation, emanating from the academy, was imposed in the name of a science which it venerated without comprehending – such a society would be a society, not of men, but of brutes. It would be a second edition of those missions in Paraguay which submitted so long to the government of the Jesuits. It would surely and rapidly descend to the lowest stage of idiocy.

But there is still a third reason which would render such a government impossible – namely that a scientific academy invested with a sovereignty, so to speak, absolute, even if it were composed of the most illustrious men, would infallibly and soon end in its own moral and intellectual corruption. Even today, with the few privileges allowed them, such is the history of all academies. The greatest scientific genius, from the moment that he becomes an academician, an officially licensed *savant*, inevitably lapses into sluggishness. He loses his spontaneity, his revolutionary hardihood, and that troublesome and savage energy characteristic of the grandest geniuses, ever called to destroy old tottering worlds and lay the foundations of new. He undoubtedly gains in politeness, in utilitarian and practical wisdom, what he loses in power of thought. In a word, he becomes corrupted.

It is the characteristic of privilege and of every privileged position to kill the mind and heart of men. The privileged man, whether practically or economically, is a man depraved in mind and heart. That is a social law which admits of no exception, and is as applicable to entire nations as to classes, corporations, and individuals. It is the law of equality, the supreme condition of liberty and humanity. The principal object of this treatise is precisely to demonstrate this truth in all the manifestations of human life.

A scientific body to which had been confided the government of society would soon end by devoting itself no longer to science at all, but to quite another affair; and that affair, as in the case of all established powers, would be its own eternal perpetuation by rendering the society confided to its care ever more stupid and consequently more in need of its government and direction.

But that which is true of scientific academies is also true of all constituent and legislative assemblies, even those chosen by universal suffrage. In the latter case they may renew their composition, it is true, but this does not prevent the formation in a few years' time of a body of politicians, privileged in fact though not in law, who, devoting themselves exclusively to the direction of the public affairs of a country, finally form a sort of political aristocracy or oligarchy. Witness the United States of America and Switzerland.

Consequently, no external legislation and no authority – one, for that matter, being inseparable from the other, and both tending to the servitude of society and the degradation of the legislators themselves.

Does it follow that I reject all authority? Far from me such a thought. In the matter of boots, I refer to the authority of the bootmaker; concerning houses, canals, or railroads, I consult that of the architect or the engineer. For such or such special knowledge I apply to such or such a *savant*. But I allow neither the bootmaker nor the architect nor the *savant* to impose his authority upon me. I listen to them freely and with all the respect merited by their intelligence, their character, their knowledge, reserving always my incontestable right of criticism and censure. I do not content myself with consulting a single authority in any special branch; I consult several; I compare their opinions, and choose that which seems to me the soundest. But I recognize no infallible authority, even in special questions; consequently, whatever respect I may have for the honesty and the sincerity of such or such an individual, I have no absolute faith in any person. Such a faith would be fatal to my reason, to my liberty, and even to the success of my undertakings; it would immediately transform me into a stupid slave, an instrument of the will and interests of others.

If I bow before the authority of the specialists and avow my readiness to follow, to a certain extent and as long as may seem to me necessary, their indications and even their directions, it is because their authority is imposed upon me by no one, neither by men nor by God. Otherwise I would repel them with horror, and bid the devil take their counsels, their directions, and their services, certain that they would make me pay, by the loss of my liberty and self-respect, for such scraps of truth, wrapped in a multitude of lies, as they might give me.

I bow before the authority of special men because it is imposed upon me by my own reason. I am conscious of my own inability to grasp, in all its detail, and positive developments, any very large portion of human knowledge. The greatest intelligence would not be equal to a comprehension of the whole. Thence results, for science as well as for industry, the necessity of the division and association of labour. I receive and I give – such is human life. Each directs and is directed in his turn. Therefore there is no fixed and constant authority, but a continual exchange of mutual, temporary, and, above all, voluntary authority and subordination.

This same reason forbids me, then, to recognize a fixed, constant and universal authority, because there is no universal man, no man capable of grasping in that wealth of detail, without which the application of science to life is impossible, all the sciences, all the branches of social life. And if such universality could ever be realized in a single man, and if he wished to take advantage thereof to impose his authority upon us, it would be necessary to drive this man out of society, because his authority would inevitably reduce all the others to slavery and imbecility. I do not think that society ought to maltreat men of genius as it has done hitherto; but neither do I think it should indulge them too far, still less accord them any privileges or exclusive rights whatsoever; and that for three reasons: first, because it would often mistake a charlatan for a man of genius; second, because, through such a system of privileges, it might transform into a charlatan even a real man of genius, demoralize him, and degrade him; and, finally, because it would establish a master over itself.

THE REVOLUTION AND THE NATION

PIERRE-JOSEPH PROUDHON
(From *Idée générale de la révolution au XIXé siècle*, 1851, translated by John Beverley Robinson, 1923)

Nationality, aroused by the State, opposes an invincible resistance to economic unity: this explains why monarchy was never able to become universal. Universal monarchy is, in politics, what squaring the circle or perpetual motion are in mathematics, a contradiction. A nation can put up with a government as long as its economic forces are unorganized, and as long as the government is its own, the nationalism of the power causing an illusion as to the validity of the principle; the government maintains itself through an interminable succession of monarchies, aristocracies and democracies. But if the Power is external, the nation feels it as an insult: revolt is in every heart, it cannot last.

What no monarchy, not even that of the Roman emperors, has been able to accomplish; what Christianity, that epitome of the ancient faiths, has been unable to produce, the universal Republic, the economic Revolution, will accomplish, cannot fail to accomplish.

It is indeed with political economy as with other sciences: it is inevitably the same throughout the world: it does not depend upon the fancies of men or nations; it yields to the caprice of none. There is not a Russian, English, Austrian, Tartar, or Hindu political economy, any more than there is a Hungarian, German or American physics or geometry. Truth alone is equal everywhere: science is the unity of mankind.

If then science, and no longer religion or authority, is taken in every land as the rule of society, the sovereign arbiter of interests, government being void, all the legislation of the universe will be in harmony. There will no longer be nationality, no longer fatherland, in the political sense of the words: they will mean only places of birth. Man, of whatever race or colour he may be, is an inhabitant of the universe; citizenship is everywhere an acquired right. As in a limited territory the municipality represents the Republic, and wields its authority, each nation in the globe represents humanity, and acts for it within the boundaries assigned by Nature. Harmony reigns, without diplomacy and without council, among the nations: nothing henceforward can disturb it.

What purpose could there be for entering into diplomatic relations among nations who had adopted the revolutionary programme:

No more governments,

No more conquests,

No more custom houses,

No more international police,

No more commercial privileges,

No more colonial exclusions,

No more control of one people by another, one State by another,

No more strategic lines,

No more fortresses?

Russia wants to establish herself at Constantinople, as she is established at Warsaw; that is to say, she wants to include the Bosphorus and the Caucasus in her sphere. In the first place, the Revolution will not permit it; and to make sure, it will begin by revolutionizing Poland, Turkey, and all it can of Russian provinces, until it reaches St Petersburg. That done, what becomes of the Russian relations at Constantinople and Warsaw? They will be the same as at Berlin and Paris, relations of free and equal exchange. What becomes of Russia itself? It becomes an agglomeration of free and independent nationalities, united only by identity of language, resemblance of occupations, and territorial conditions. Under such conditions conquest is meaningless. If Constantinople belonged to Russia, once Russia was revolutionized Constantinople would belong to it neither more nor less than if it had never lost its sovereignty. The Eastern question from the North ceases to exist.

England wants to hold Egypt as she holds Malta, Corfu, Gibraltar, etc. The same answer from the Revolution. It notifies England to refrain from any attempt upon Egypt, to place a limit upon her encroachments and monopoly, and, to make sure, it invites her to evacuate the islands and fortresses whence she threatens the liberty of nations and of the seas. It would be truly a strange misconception of the nature and scope of the Revolution to imagine that it would leave Australia and India as the exclusive property of England, as well as bastions with which she hems in the commerce of the continent. The mere presence of the English in Jersey and Guernsey is an insult to France; as their exploitation of Ireland and Portugal is an insult to Europe; as their possession of India and their commerce with China is an outrage upon humanity. Albion, like the rest of the world, must be revolutionized. If necessary to force her, there are people here who would not find it so hard a task. The Revolution completed in London, British privilege extirpated, burnt, thrown to the winds, what would the possession of Egypt mean to England? No more than that of Algiers is to us. All the world could enter, depart, trade at will, arrange for the working of the agricultural, mineral and industrial resources; the advantages would be the same for all nations. The local power would extend only to the cost of its police, which the colonists and natives would defray.

There are still among us *chauvinists* who maintain absolutely that France must recapture her *natural* frontiers. They ask too much or too little. France is everywhere that her language is spoken, her Revolution followed, her manners, her arts, her literature adopted, as well as her measures and her money. Counting thus, almost the whole of Belgium, and the cantons of Neufchâtel, Vaud, Geneva, Savoy, and a part of Piedmont belong to her; but she must lose Alsace, perhaps even a part of Provence, Gascony and Brittany whose inhabitants do not speak French, and some of them have always been of the kings' and priests' party against the Revolution. But of what are these repetitions? It was the mania for annexations which, under the Convention and the Directory, aroused the distrust of other nations against the Republic, and which, giving us a taste for Bonaparte, brought us to our finish at Waterloo. Revolutionarize, I tell you. Your frontiers will always be long enough and French enough if they are revolutionary.

Will Germany be an Empire, a unitary Republic, or a Confederation? This famous problem of Germanic unity, which made so much noise some years ago, has no meaning in the face of the Revolution; which proves indeed that there has never been a Revolution. What are the States, in Germany as elsewhere? Tyrannies of different degrees of importance, based on the invariable pretexts, first, of protecting the nobility and upper classes against the lower classes; second, of maintaining the independence of local sovereignty. Against these States the German democracy has always been powerless, and why? Because it moved in the sphere of political rights. Organize the economic forces of Germany, and immediately political circles, electorates, principalities, kingdoms, empires, all are effaced, even the Tariff League: German unity springs out of the abolition of its States. What the ancient Germany needs is not a confederation but a liquidation.

Understand once for all: the most characteristic, the most decisive result of the Revolution is, after having organized labour and property, to do away with political centralization, in a word, with the State, and as a consequence to put an end to diplomatic relations among nations, as soon as they subscribe to the revolutionary compact. Any return to the traditions of politics, any anxiety as to the balance of power in Europe, based on the pretext of nationality and of the independence of States, any proposition to form alliances, to recognize sovereignties, to restore provinces, to change frontiers, would betray, in the organs of the movement, the most complete failure to understand the needs of the age, scorn of social reform, and a predilection for counter-revolution.

The kings may sharpen their swords for their last campaign. The Revolution in the nineteenth century has for its supreme task, not so much the overthrow of their dynasties, as the destruction of the last root of their institution. Born as they are to war, educated to war, supported by war, domestic and foreign, of what use can they be in a society of labour and peace? Henceforth there can be no more purpose in war than in refusal to disarm. Universal brotherhood being established upon a sure foundation, there is nothing for the representatives of despotism to do but to take their leave. How is it that they do not see that this always increasing difficulty of existence, which they have experienced since Waterloo, arises, not as they have been made to think, from the Jacobin ideas, which since the fall of Napoleon have again begun to beset the middle classes, but from a subterranean working which has gone on throughout Europe, unknown to statesmen, and which, while developing beyond measure the latent forces of civilization, has made the organization of those forces a social necessity, an inevitable need of revolution?

As for those who, after the departure of kings, still dream of consulates, of presidencies, of dictatorships, of marshalships, of admiralties and of ambassadorships, they also will do well to retire. The Revolution, having no need for their services, can dispense with their talents. The people no longer want this coin of monarchy: they understand that, whatever phraseology is used, feudal system, governmental system, military system, parliamentary system, system of police, laws and tribunals, and system of exploitation, corruption, lying and poverty, all are synonymous. Finally they know that in doing away with rent and interest, the last remnants of the old slavery, the Revolution, at one blow, does away with the sword of the executioner, the blade of justice, the club of the policeman, the gauge of the customs officer, the erasing knife of the bureaucrat, all those insignia of government which young Liberty grinds beneath her heel.

TOPLESS FEDERATIONS

COLIN WARD
(From *Anarchy in Action*, 1973)

> *The fascinating secret of a well-functioning social organism
> seems thus to lie not in its overall unity but its structure,
> maintained in health by the life-preserving mechanism of
> division operating through myriads of cell-splittings and
> rejuvenations taking place under the smooth skin of an
> apparently unchanging body. Wherever, because of age or
> bad design, this rejuvenating process of subdivision gives
> way to the calcifying process of cell unification, the cells,
> now growing behind the protection of their hardened
> frames beyond their divinely allotted limits, begin, as in
> cancer, to develop those hostile, arrogant great-power
> complexes which cannot be brought to an end until the
> infested organism is either devoured, or a forceful opera-
> tion succeeds in restoring the small-cell pattern.*
>
> Leopold Kohr, *The Breakdown of Nations*

People used to smile at Kropotkin when he instanced the
lifeboat institution as an example of the kind of organization
envisaged by anarchists, but he did so simply to illustrate that
voluntary and completely non-coercive organizations could
provide a complex network of services without the principle
of authority intervening. Two other examples which we often
use to help people to conceive the federal principle which
anarchists see as the way in which local groups and associations could combine for complex functions without any
central authority are the postal service and railways. You
can post a letter from here to China or Chile, confident that
it will arrive, as a result of freely arrived-at agreements
between different national post offices, without there being
any central world postal authority at all. Or you can travel
across Europe over the lines of a dozen railway systems –
capitalist and communist – co-ordinated by agreement between

different railway undertakings, without *any kind* of central railway authority. The same is true of broadcasting organizations and several other kinds of internationally co-ordinated activities. Nor is there any reason to suppose that the constituent parts of complex federations could not run efficiently on the basis of voluntary association. (When we have in Britain more than one railway line running scheduled services on time, co-ordinating with British Rail, and operated by a bunch of amateurs, who dare say that the railwaymen could not operate their services without the aid of the bureaucratic hierarchy?) Even within the structure of capitalist industry there are interesting experiments in organizing work on the basis of small autonomous groups. Industrial militants regard such ventures with suspicion, as well they might, for they are undertaken not with the idea of stimulating workers' autonomy but with that of increasing productivity. But they are valuable in illustrating our contention that the whole pyramid of hierarchical authority, which has been built up in industry as in every other sphere of life, is a giant confidence trick by which generations of workers have been coerced in the first instance, hoodwinked in the second, and finally brainwashed into accepting.

In territorial terms, the great anarchist advocate of federalism was Proudhon who was thinking not of custom unions like the European Common Market nor of a confederation of states or a world federal government but of a basic principle of human organization:

In his view the federal principle should operate from the simplest level of society. The organization of administration should begin locally and as near the direct control of the people as possible; individuals should start the process by federating into communes and associations. Above that primary level the confederal organization would become less an organ of administration than of co-ordination between local units. Thus the nation would be replaced by a geographical confederation of regions, and Europe would become a confederation of confederations, in which the interest of the smallest province would have as much expression as that of the largest, and in which all affairs would be settled by mutual agreement, contract, and arbitration. In terms of the evolution of anarchist ideas, *Du Principe Fédératif* (1863) is one of the most important of Proudhon's books, since it presents the first intensive libertarian development of the idea of federal organization as a practical alternative to political nationalism.[1]

Now, without wishing to sing a song of praise for the Swiss political system we can see that, in territorial terms, the twenty-two sovereign cantons of Switzerland are an outstanding example of a successful federation. It is a federation of like units, of small cells, and the cantonal boundaries cut across the linguistic and ethnic boundaries, so that unlike the many examples of unsuccessful political federation, the confederation is not dominated by a single powerful unit, so different in size and scale from the rest that it unbalances the union. The problem of federalism, as Leopold Kohr puts it in his book *The Breakdown of Nations*, is one of division, not of union. Proudhon foresaw this:

Europe would be too large to form a single confederation; it would have to be a confederation of confederations. This is why I pointed out in my most recent publication (*Federation and Unity in Italy*) that the first measure of reform to be made in public law is the re-establishment of the Italian, Greek, Batavian (Netherlands), Scandinavian and Danubian confederations as a prelude to the decentralization of the large States, followed by a general disarmament. In these conditions all nations would recover their freedom, and the notion of the balance of power in Europe would become a reality. This has been envisaged by all political writers and statesmen but has remained impossible so long as the great powers are centralized States. It is not surprising that the notion of federation should have been lost amid the splendours of the great States, since it is by nature peaceful and mild and plays a self-effacing role on the political scene.[2]

Peaceful, mild and self-effacing the Swiss may be and we may consider them a rather stodgy and provincial lot, but

A.R.   L

they have something in their national life which we in the nations which are neither mild nor self-effacing have lost. I was talking to a Swiss citizen (or rather a citizen of Zürich, for strictly speaking that is what he was) about the cutting-back to profitable inter-city routes of the British railway system, and he remarked that it would be inconceivable in a Swiss setting that a chairman in London could decide, as Dr Beeching did in the 1960s, to write off the railway system of the north of Scotland. He cited Herbert Luethy's study of his country's political system in which he explained that:

Every Sunday the inhabitants of scores of communes go to the polling booths to elect their civil servants, ratify such and such an item of expenditure, or decide whether a road or a school should be built; after settling the business of the commune, they deal with cantonal elections and voting on cantonal issues; lastly . . . come the decisions on federal issues. In some cantons the sovereign people still meet in Rousseau-like fashion to discuss questions of common interest. It may be thought that this ancient form of assembly is no more than a pious tradition with a certain value as a tourist attraction. If so, it is worth looking at the results of local democracy.

The simplest example is the Swiss railway system, which is the densest network in the world. At great cost and with great trouble, it has been made to serve the needs of the smallest localities and most remote valleys, not as a paying proposition but because such was the will of the people. It is the outcome of fierce political struggles. In the nineteenth century the 'democratic railway movement' brought the small Swiss communities into conflict with the big towns, which had plans for centralizations . . .

And if we compare the Swiss system with the French which, with admirable geometrical regularity, is entirely centred on Paris so that the prosperity or the decline, the life or death, of whole regions has depended on the quality of the link with the capital, we see the difference between a centralized state and a federal alliance. The railway map is the easiest to read at a glance, but let us now superimpose on it another showing economic activity and the movement of population. The distribution of industrial activity all over Switzerland, even in the outlying areas, accounts for the strength and stability of the social structure of the country and prevented those horrible nineteenth-century concentrations of industry, with their slums and rootless proletariat.[3]

I suspect that times have changed, even in Switzerland, and I quote Dr Luethy, not to praise Swiss democracy, but to indicate that the federal principle which is at the centre of anarchist theory is worth very much more attention than it is given in the textbooks of political science. Even in the context of ordinary political and economic institutions, its adoption has a far-reaching effect. If you doubt this, consult an up-to-date map of British Rail.

The federal principle applies to every kind of human organization. You can readily see its application to communications of all kinds: a network of local papers sharing stories, a network of local radio and television stations supported by local listeners (as already happens with a handful of stations in the United States) sharing programmes,[4] a network of local telephone services (it already happens in Hull, which through some historical anomaly runs its own telephone system and gives its citizens a rather better service than the Post Office gives the rest of us).

It already applies in the world of voluntary associations, unions, and pressure groups, and you will not disagree that the lively and active ones are those where activity and decision-making is initiated at local level, while those that are centrally controlled are ossified and out of touch with their apathetic membership. Those readers who remember the days of CND and the Committee of 100 may recall the episode of the Spies for Peace. A group of people unearthed details of the RSGs or Regional Seats of Government, underground hideouts to ensure the survival of the ruling elite in the case of nuclear war. It was of course illegal to publish this information, yet all over the country it appeared in little anonymous duplicated pamphlets within a few days, providing an enormously interesting example of *ad hoc* federal activity through loose networks of active individuals. We later published in *Anarchy* some reflections on the implications of this:

> One lesson to be drawn from 'Spies for Peace' is the advantage of an *ad hoc* organization, coming rapidly into being and if necessary disappearing with the same speed, but leaving behind innumerable centres of activity, like ripples and eddies on a pond, after a stone has been thrown into it.
>
> Traditional politics (both 'revolutionary' and 'reformist') are based on a central dynamo, with a transmission belt leading outwards. Capture of the dynamo, or its conversion to other purposes, may break the transmission entirely. 'Spies for Peace' seems to have operated on an entirely different basis. Messages were passed from mouth to mouth along the route, documents from hand to hand. One group passed a secret to a second, which then set about reprinting it. A caravan became the source of a leaflet, a shopping basket a distribution centre. A hundred copies of a pamphlet are distributed in the streets: some are sure to reach the people who will distribute them.
>
> Contacts are built on a face to face basis. One knows the personal limitations of one's comrades. X is an expert at steering a meeting through procedural shoals, but cannot work a duplicator. Y can use a small printing press, but is unable to write a leaflet. Z can express himself in public, but cannot sell pamphlets. Every task elects its own workers, and there is no need for an elaborate show of hands. Seekers of personal power and glory get little thrill from the anonymously and skilfully illegal. The prospect of prison breeds out the leader complex. Every member of a group may be called upon to undertake key tasks. And all-round talent is developed in all. The development of small groups for mutual aid could form a basis for an effective resistance movement.
>
> There are important conclusions. Revolution does not need conveyor-belt organization. It needs hundreds, thousands, and finally millions of people meeting in groups with informal contacts with each other. It needs mass con-

sciousness. If one group takes an initiative that is valuable, others will take it up. The methods must be tailored to the society we live in. The FLN could use armed warfare, for it had hills and thickets to retreat into. We are faced by the overwhelming physical force of a State better organized and better armed than at any time in its history. We must react accordingly. The many internal contradictions of the State must be skilfully exploited. The Dusseldorf authorities were caught in their own regulations when the disarmers refused to fasten their safety belts. MI5 cannot conceive of subversion that is not masterminded by a sinister Communist agent. It is incapable of dealing with a movement where nobody takes orders from anyone else. Through action, autonomy and revolutionary initiative will be developed still further. To cope with our activities the apparatus of repression will become even more centralized and even more bureaucratic. This will enhance our opportunities rather than lessen them.[5]

This was a federation whose members did not even know each other, but whose constituent cells had an intimate personal understanding. The passport to membership was simply a common involvement in a common task. Innumerable voluntary organizations from the Scouts to the Automobile Association started in the same impromptu way. Their ossification began from the centre. Their mistake was a faith in centralism. The anarchist conclusion is that every kind of human activity should begin from what is local and immediate, should link in a network with no centre and no directing agency, hiving off new cells as the original ones grow. If there is any human activity that does not appear to fit this pattern our first question should be 'Why not?' and our second should be 'How can we re-arrange it so as to provide for local autonomy, local responsibility, and the fulfilment of local needs?'

1. George Woodcock, *Anarchism: A History of Libertarian Ideas and Movements* (Cleveland, 1962; London, 1963).

2. P.-J. Proudhon, *Du Principe Fédératif* quoted in Stewart Edwards (ed.) *Selected Writings of Pierre-Joseph Proudhon* (London, 1970), p. 325.

3. Herbert Luethy, 'Has Switzerland a Future?' *Encounter*, December 1962.

4. See Theodore Roszak, '*The Case for Listener-supported Radio*', *Anarchy* 93, November 1968.

5. 'The Spies for Peace Story', *Anarchy* 29, July 1963.

REFLECTIONS ON DECENTRALISM

GEORGE WOODCOCK
(From *The Rejection of Politics*, 1972)

I was asked to write on decentralism in history, and I find myself looking into shadows where small lights shine as fireflies do, endure a little, vanish, and then reappear like Auden's messages of the just. The history of decentralism has to be written largely in negative, in winters and twilights as well as springs and dawns, for it is a history which, like that of libertarian beliefs in general, is not observed in progressive terms. It is not the history of a movement, an evolution. It is the history of something that, like grass, has been with us from the human beginning, something that may go to earth, like bulbs in winter, and yet be there always, in the dark soil of human society, to break forth in unexpected places and at undisciplined times.

Palaeolithic man, food-gatherer and hunter, was a decentralist by necessity, because the earth did not provide enough wild food to allow crowding, and in modern remotenesses that were too wild or unproductive for civilized men to penetrate, men still lived until very recently in primitive decentralism; Australian aborigines, Papuan inland villagers, Eskimos in far northern Canada. Such men developed, before history touched them, their own complex techniques and cultures to defend a primitive and precarious way of life; they often developed remarkable artistic traditions as well, such as those of the Indians of the Pacific rain forests and some groups of Eskimos. But, since their world was one where concentration meant scarcity and death, they did not develop a political life that allowed the formation of authoritarian structures nor did they make an institution out of war. They practised mutual aid for survival, but this did not make them angels; they practised infanticide and the abandonment of elders for the same reason.

I think with feeling of those recently living decentralist societies because I have just returned from the Canadian Arctic where the last phase of traditional Eskimo life began as recently as a decade ago. Now, the old nomadic society, in which people moved about in extended families rather than tribes, is at an end, with all its skills abandoned, its traditions, songs and dances fading in the memory. Last year the cariboo-hunting Eskimos probably built their last igloo; now they are herded together into communities ruled by white men, where they live in groups of four to six hundred people, in imitation white men's houses and with guaranteed welfare handouts when they cannot earn money by summer construction work. Their children are being taught by people who know no Eskimo, their young men are losing the skills of the hunt; power élites are beginning to appear in their crowded little northern slums, among a people who never knew what power meant, and the diminishing dog teams (now less than one family in four owns dogs and only about one family in twenty goes on extended hunting or trapping journeys) are symbolic of the loss of freedom among a people who have become physically and mentally dependent on the centralized, bureaucrat-ridden world which the Canadian Government has built since it set out a few years ago to rescue the peoples of the North from 'barbarism' and insecurity.

The fate of the Eskimo, and that of so many other primitive cultures during the past quarter of a century, shows that the old, primal decentralism of Stone Age man is doomed even when it has survived into the modern world. From now on, man will be decentralist by intent and experience, because he has known the evils of centralization and rejected them.

Centralization began when men settled on the land and cultivated it. Farmers joined together to protect their herds and fields from the other men who still remained nomadic wanderers; to conserve and share out the precious waters; to placate the deities who held the gifts of fertility, the priests who served the deities, and the kings who later usurped the roles of priest and god alike. The little realms of local priest-kings grew into the great valley empires of Egypt and Mesopotamia, and overtowering these emerged the first attempt at a world empire, that of the Achaemenian Kings of Persia, who established an administrative colossus which was the prototype of the centralized state, imitated by the despots of Northern India, the Hellenistic god-kings, and the divine Caesars of Rome.

We have little knowledge how men clung to their local loyalties and personal lives, how simple people tried to keep control of the affairs and things that concerned them most, in that age when writing recorded the deeds of kings and priests and had little to say about common men. But if we can judge from the highly traditional and at least partly autonomous village societies which still existed in India when the Moghuls arrived, and which had probably survived the centuries of political chaos and strife that lay between Moghuls and Guptas, it seems likely that the farther men in those ages lived away from the centres of power, the more they established and defended rights to use the land and govern their own local affairs, so long as the lord's tribute was paid. It was, after all, on the village communities that had survived through native and Moghul and British empires that Gandhi based his hopes of *panchayat raj*, a society based on autonomous peasant communes.

In Europe the Dark Ages after the Roman Empire were regarded by Victorian historians as a historical waste land ravaged by barbarian hordes and baronial bandits. But these ages were also in fact an interlude during which, in the absence of powerful centralized authorities, the decentralist urge appeared again, and village communes established forms of autonomy which in remoter areas, like the Pyrenees, the Alps and the Appenines, have survived into the present. To the same 'Dark' Ages belong the earliest free city republics of medieval Europe, which arose at first for mutual protection in the ages of disorder, and which in Italy and Germany remained for centuries the homes of European learning and art and of such freedom as existed in the world of their time.

Out of such village communes and such cities arose, in Switzerland, the world's first political federation, based on the shared protection of local freedoms against feudal monarchs and renaissance despots.

Some of these ancient communes exist to this day; the Swiss Canton of Appenzell still acts as a direct democracy in which every citizen takes part in the annual voting on laws; the Italian city state of San Marino still retains its mountaintop independence in a world of great states. But these are rare survivals, due mainly to geographic inaccessibility in the days before modern transport. As national states began to form at the end of the Middle Ages, the attack on decentralism was led not merely by the monarchs and dictators who established highly organized states like Bourbon France and Cromwellian England, but also by the Church and particularly by the larger monastic orders who in their houses established rules of uniform behaviour and rigid timekeeping that anticipated the next great assault on local and independent freedoms and on the practice of mutual aid; this happened when the villages of Britain and later of other European countries were depopulated in the Agricultural Revolution of the eighteenth century, and their homeless people drifted into the disciplined factories and suffered the alienation produced by the new industrial towns, where all traditional bonds were broken, and all the participation in common works that belonged to the medieval villages became irrelevant.

It was these developments, the establishment of the centralized state in the seventeenth century and of industrial centralization in the eighteenth and nineteenth centuries, that made men for the first time consciously aware of the necessity of decentralism to save them from the soulless world that was developing around them.

Against Cromwell's military state, Gerrard Winstanley and the original Diggers opposed their idea and practice of establishing new communes of landworkers on the waste lands of England, communes which would renounce overlords and extended participation and equality to men, women and even children.

When the French Revolution took the way of centralism, establishing a more rigidly bureaucratic state than the

Bourbons and introducing universal conscription for the first time, men like Jacques Roux and his fellow *enragés* protested in the name of the local communes of Paris, which they regarded as the bases of democratic administration, and at the same time in England William Godwin, the first of the philosophic anarchists, recognized the perils of forms of government which left decision making in the hands of men gathered at the top and centre of society. In his *Political Justice* Godwin envisaged countries in which assemblies of delegates would meet – seldom – to discuss matters of urgent common concern, in which no permanent organs of central government would be allowed to continue, and in which each local parish would decide its own affairs by free agreement (and not by majority vote) and matters of dispute would be settled by *ad hoc* juries of arbitration.

The British and French Utopian socialists of the early nineteenth century, as distinct from the Marxists and the revolutionary socialists led by Auguste Blanqui, were inspired by their revulsion against monolithic industrial and political organization to base the realization of their theories on small communal units which they believed could be established even before the existing society had been destroyed. At that period the American frontier lay still in the valley of the Mississippi, and there was a tendency – which existed until the end of the pioneering days – for the small pioneer societies of trappers and traders, miners and farmers, to organize themselves in largely autonomous communities that managed their own affairs and in many senses of the word took the law into their own hands. In this society, where men responded to frontier conditions by *ad hoc* participatory and decentralist organization, the European and American Utopian socialists, as well as various groups of Christian communities, tried to set up self-governing communes which would be the cells of the new fraternal world. The followers of Cabet and Fourier, of Robert Owen and Josiah Warren, all played their part in a movement which produced hundreds of communities and lasted almost a century; its last wave ebbed on the Pacific coast in the Edwardian era, when a large Finnish socialist community was established on the remote island of Sointula off the coast of British Columbia. Only the religious communities of this era, which had a purpose outside mere social theory, survived; even today some of the Mennonite communities of Canada keep so closely to their ideals of communitarian autonomy that they are leaving the country to find in South America a region where they can be free to educate their children as they wish. The secular communities all vanished; the main lesson their failure taught was that decentralist organization must reach down to the roots of the present, to the needs of the actual human beings who participate, and not upward into the collapsing dream structures of a Utopian future.

Other great crises in the human situation have followed the industrial revolution, and every one has produced its decentralist movements in which men and women have turned away from the nightmares of megapolitics to the radical realities of human relationships. The crisis of the Indian struggle for independence caused Gandhi to preach the need to build society upon the foundation of the village. The bitter repressions of Tsarist Russia led Peter Kropotkin to develop his theories of a decentralized society integrating industry and agriculture, manual and mental skills. World War II led to considerable community movements among both British and American pacifists, seeking to create cells of sane living in the interstices of a belligerent world, and an even larger movement of decentralization and communitarianism has risen in North America in contradiction to the society that can wage a war like that in Vietnam. Today it is likely that more people than ever before are consciously engaged in some kind of decentralist venture which expresses not merely rebellion against monolithic authoritarianism, but also faith in the possibility of a new, cellular kind of society in which at every level the participation in decision making envisaged by nineteenth-century anarchists like Proudhon and Kropotkin will be developed.

As the monstrous and fatal flaws of modern economic and political centralism become more evident, as the State is revealed ever more convincingly as the enemy of all human love, the advocacy and practice of decentralism will spread more widely, if only because the necessity for it will become constantly more urgent. The less decentralist action is tied to rigid social and political theories, and especially to ante-diluvian ones like those of the Marxists, the more penetrating and durable its effects will be. The soils most favourable to the spread of decentralism are probably countries like India, where rural living still predominates, countries like Japan where the decentralization of factories and the integration of agricultural and industrial economies has already been recognized as a necessity for survival, and the places in our western world where the social rot has run deepest and the decentralists can penetrate like white ants. The moribund centres of the cities; the decaying marginal farmlands; these are the places which centralist governments using bankers' criteria of efficiency cannot possibly revivify, because the profit would not be financial but human. In such areas the small and flexible cell of workers, serving the needs of local people, can survive and continue simultaneously the tasks of quiet destruction and cellular building. But not all the work can be done in the shadows. There will still be the need for theoreticians to carry on the work which Kropotkin and Geddes and Mumford began in the past, of demonstrating the ultimately self-destructive character of political and industrial centralism, and showing how society as a whole, and not merely the lost corners of it, can be brought back to health and peace by breaking down the pyramids of authority, so that men can be given to eat the bread of brotherly love, and not the stones of power – of any power.

THE ORGANIZATION OF PRODUCTION

JAMES GUILLAUME
(From *Idées sur l'organisation sociale*, 1876, translated by George Woodcock)

Among the industrial workers, as among the peasants, we have to distinguish between various categories. First of all, there are the trades in which the necessary equipment is relatively slight, in which division of labour hardly exists, and in which the artisan can produce as much working on his own as if he worked in association with others. Typical examples are those of tailors and shoemakers.

Next come the trades in which small numbers of workers pool their collective labour in a small workshop or enterprise: e.g. printers, cabinet-makers, building workers.

Finally, there is a third category of industries in which the division of labour is much further developed and in which production is on a massive scale that calls for the use of heavy machinery and the availability of a great deal of capital. Typical examples are weaving mills, steel mills and mines.

For workers in the first category of industries, there is no need for collective work, and in most cases – no doubt – the tailor or the cobbler will decide to continue working by himself in his little stall. That would be quite natural, especially as in small communes there may well be no more than one worker belonging to each of these trades. Even so – and with no wish to deprecate the value of individual independence – we believe that, wherever it is practicable, it is better to work in common. Among his equals, the worker is stimulated to emulation; he produces more and works more joyfully. Besides, work in common can lead to useful mutual criticism.

As for the workers in the other two categories, it is obvious that the very nature of their work impels them towards association, and that since their instruments of production are not simple tools for individual use, but machines demanding the co-operation of a number of workers, their plant can only be owned collectively.

Each workshop and each factory will therefore form itself into a workers' association, which will be free to organize itself as it wishes, so long as the rights of each worker are protected and the principles of justice and equality are observed in practice . . . Wherever an industry requires complicated machinery and collective work, the means of production should be held in common. But here there remains one point to be considered. Should this communally held property belong only to the workshop in which it is used, or should it be the property of the corporation of workers in the whole of the relevant industry?

Our view is that the second of these solutions is the best.

To take a hypothetical example, if on the day of the revolution the printers of the city of Rome take possession of all the presses, they should immediately meet in a general assembly to declare that the printing houses of Rome as a whole are the common property of all the Roman printing workers. Then, as soon as possible, they should go further, and unite with the typographers of other Italian cities; the result of such an alliance would be the concentration of all the printing establishments of Italy as the collective property of the federation of Italian printers. Through the establishment of such a community, printers from all over Italy would be able to work in any town of their country and find available all the tools of their trade.

Yet if we argue that the means of production should be corporatively owned, we do not suggest that over and above the groups of workers organized in collectives there should be any kind of industrial government that might have the power to dispose capriciously of the instruments of production. It is obvious that the members of the various workshops will have no intention of handing over what they have won to any superior power, under the name of a corporation or any other title. What they will do is to guarantee the reciprocal use, under specific conditions, of the plants which they have taken over, and in return they will acquire similar privileges from their colleagues in other workshops with whom they have concluded their pact of solidarity.

LAZY MEN AND DIRTY WORK

ALEXANDER BERKMAN
(From *What is Anarchist Communism?*, 1929)

'But what will you do with the lazy man, the man who does not want to work?' inquires your friend.

That is an interesting question, and you will probably be very much surprised when I say that there is really no such thing as laziness. What we call a lazy man is generally a square peg in a round hole. That is, the right man in the wrong place. And you will always find that when a fellow is in the wrong place, he will be inefficient or shiftless. For so-called laziness and a good deal of inefficiency are merely unfitness, misplacement. If you are compelled to do the thing you are unfitted for by your inclinations or temperament, you will be inefficient at it; if you are forced to do work you are not interested in, you will be lazy at it.

Every one who has managed affairs in which large numbers of men were employed can substantiate this. Life in prison is a particularly convincing proof of the truth of it – and, after all, present-day existence for most people is but that of a larger jail. Every prison warder will tell you that inmates put to tasks for which they have no ability or interest are always lazy and subject to continuous punishment. But as soon as these 'refractory convicts' are assigned to work that appeals to their leanings, they become 'model men', as the jailers term them.

Russia has also signally demonstrated the verity of it. It has shown how little we know of human potentialities and of the effect of environment upon them – how we mistake wrong conditions for bad conduct. Russian refugees leading a miserable and insignificant life in foreign lands, on returning home and finding in the Revolution a proper field for their activities, have accomplished most wonderful work in their right sphere, have developed into brilliant organizers, builders of railroads and creators of industry. Among the Russian names best known abroad today are those of men considered shiftless and inefficient under conditions where their ability and energies could not find proper application.

That is human nature: efficiency in a certain direction means inclination and capability for it; industry and application signify interest. That is why there is so much inefficiency and laziness in the world today. For who indeed is nowadays in his right place? Who works at what he really likes and is interested in?

Under present conditions there is little choice given the average man to devote himself to the tasks that appeal to his leanings and preferences. The accident of your birth and social station generally predetermines your trade or profession. The son of a financier does not, as a rule, become a woodchopper, though he may be more fit to handle logs than bank accounts. The middle classes send their children to colleges which turn them into doctors, lawyers, or engineers. But if your parents were workers who could not afford to let you study, the chances are that you will take any job which is offered you, or enter some trade that happens to afford you an apprenticeship. Your particular situation will decide your work or profession, not your natural preferences, inclinations, or abilities. Is it any wonder, then, that most people, the over-whelming majority, in fact, are misplaced? Ask the first hundred men you meet whether they would have selected the work they are doing, or whether they would continue in it, if they were free to choose, and ninety-nine of them will admit that they would prefer some other occupation. Necessity and material advantages, or the hope of them, keep most people in the wrong place.

It stands to reason that a person can give the best of himself only when his interest is in his work, when he feels a natural attraction to it, when he likes it. Then he will be industrious and efficient. The things the craftsman produced in the days before modern capitalism were objects of joy and beauty, because the artisan loved his work. Can you expect the modern drudge in the modern factory to make beautiful things? He is part of the machine, a cog in the soulless industry, his labour mechanical, forced. Add to this his feeling that he is not working for himself but for the benefit of someone else, and that he hates his job or at best has no interest in it except that it secures his weekly wage. The result is shirking, inefficiency, laziness.

The need of activity is one of the most fundamental urges of man. Watch the child and see how strong is his instinct for action, for movement, for doing something. Strong and continuous. It is the same with the healthy man. His energy and vitality demand expression. Permit him to do the work of his choice, the thing he loves, and his application will know neither weariness nor shirking. You can observe this in the factory worker when he is lucky enough to own a garden or patch of ground to raise some flowers or vegetables on. Tired from his toil as he is, he enjoys the hardest labour for his own benefit, done from free choice.

Under anarchism each will have the opportunity for following whatever occupation will appeal to his natural inclinations and aptitude. Work will become a pleasure instead of the deadening drudgery it is today. Laziness will be unknown, and the things created by interest and love will be objects of beauty and joy.

'But can labour ever become a pleasure?' you demand.

Labour is toil today, unpleasant, exhausting, and wearisome. But usually it is not the work that is so hard: it is the conditions under which you are compelled to labour that make it so. Particularly the long hours, insanitary workshops, bad treatment, insufficient pay, and so on. Yet the most unpleasant work could be made lighter by improving the environment. Take gutter cleaning, for instance. It is dirty work and poorly paid for. But suppose, for example, that you should get 20 dollars a day instead of 5 dollars for such work. You will immediately find your job much lighter and more pleasant. The number of applicants for the work would increase at once. Which means that men are not lazy, not afraid of hard and unpleasant labour if it is properly rewarded. But such work is considered menial and is looked down upon. Why is it considered menial? Is it not most useful and absolutely necessary? Would not epidemics sweep our city but for the street and gutter cleaners? Surely, the men who keep our town clean and sanitary are real benefactors, more vital to our health and welfare than the family physician. From the viewpoint of social usefulness the street cleaner is the professional colleague of the doctor: the latter treats us when we are ill, but the former helps us to keep well. Yet the physician is looked up to and respected, while the street cleaner is slighted. Why? Is it because the street cleaner's work is dirty? But the surgeon often has much 'dirtier' jobs to perform. Then why is the street cleaner scorned? Because he *earns little*.

In our perverse civilization things are valued according to money standards. Persons doing the most useful work are lowest in the social scale when their employment is ill paid. Should something happen, however, that would cause the street cleaner to get 100 dollars a day, while the physician earns 50, the 'dirty' street cleaner would immediately rise in estimation and social station, and from the 'filthy labourer' he would become the much-sought man of good income.

You see that it is pay, remuneration, *the wage scale*, not worth or merit, that today – under our system of profit – determines the value of work as well as the 'worth' of a man.

A sensible society – under anarchist conditions – would have entirely different standards of judging such matters. People will then be appreciated according to their *willingness to be socially useful.*

Can you perceive what great changes such a new attitude would produce? Everyone yearns for the respect and admiration of his fellow men; it is a tonic we cannot live without. Even in prison I have seen how the clever pickpocket or safe blower longs for the appreciation of his friends and how hard he tries to earn their good estimate of him. The opinions of our circle rule our behaviour. The social atmosphere to a profound degree determines our values and our attitude. Your personal experience will tell you how true this is, and therefore you will not be surprised when I say that, in an anarchist society it will be the most useful and difficult toil that men will seek rather than the lighter job. If you consider this, you will have no more fear of laziness or shirking.

WORK AND THE MACHINE

WILLIAM MORRIS

(From *A Factory as it Might Be*, 1884)

Now as to the work, first of all it will be useful, and, therefore, honourable and honoured; because there will be no temptation to make mere useless toys, since there will be no rich men cudgelling their brains for means of spending superfluous money, and consequently no 'organizers of labour' pandering to degrading follies for the sake of profit, wasting their intelligence and energy in contriving snares for cash in the shape of trumpery which they themselves heartily despise. Nor will the work turn out trash; there will be no millions of poor to make a market for wares which no one would choose to use if they were not driven to do so; everyone will be able to afford things good of their kind, and will have knowledge enough to reject what is not excellent; coarse and rough wares may be made for temporary purposes, but they will openly proclaim themselves for what they are; adulteration will be unknown.

Furthermore, machines of the most ingenious and best-approved kinds will be used when necessary, but will be used simply to save human labour; nor, indeed, could they be used for anything else in such well-ordered work as we are thinking about . . .

Well, the manufacture of useless goods, whether harmful luxuries for the rich or disgraceful makeshifts for the poor, having come to an end, and we still being in possession of the machines once used for mere profit-grinding, but now used only for saving human labour, it follows that much less labour will be necessary for each workman; all the more as we are going to get rid of all non-workers, and busy-idle people; so that the working time of each member of our factory will be very short, say, to be within the mark, four hours a day.

Now, next it may be allowable for an artist – that is, one whose work is pleasant and not slavish – to hope that in no factory will all the work, even that necessary four hours' work, be mere machine-tending; and it follows from what was said above about machines being used to save labour, that there would be no work which would turn men into mere machines; therefore, at least some promotion of the work, the necessary and in fact compulsory work I mean, would be pleasant to do; the machine-tending ought not to require a very long apprenticeship, therefore in no case should any one person be set to run up and down a machine through all his working hours every day, even so shortened as we have seen; now the attractive work of our factory, that which was pleasant in itself to do, would be of the nature of art; therefore all slavery of work ceases under such a system, for whatever is burdensome about the factory would be taken turn and turn about, and so distributed, would cease to be a burden – would be, in fact, a kind of rest from the more exciting or artistic work.

THE TIME STORE

JOSIAH WARREN
(From *Practical Details in Equitable Commerce*, 1852)

The inventions which have, from time to time, been adopted by society and by men in power, for the preservation of order and the establishment of justice, have had a long, full, and fair trial; and all of them have proved fallacious and abortive; and, upon close examination, they are found to be too full of error to compensate society for the evils they produce. The total failure of all plans of government and schemes of legislators, and the general confusion into which society is thrown, call forth and excuse the proposal of

A NEW STATE OF SOCIETY,

different from any heretofore attempted.

There are a few individuals who will at once recognize more or less of their own feelings and conclusions in what has already been said, and who are already too familiar with the vices, the follies, and miseries which surround them, and with the repeated failures of proposed remedies. With these, therefore, I need not dwell upon the disease, nor have I ventured to bespeak their attention to remedies merely theoretical, but shall proceed at once to the *practical part* of my subject, and shall speak of *results already obtained*, rather than of the uncertain future.

The foundation of these experiments is laid in the broadly-admitted principles of human nature, and in the experience of the Communistic experiments in New Harmony during the two years 1825 and 1826, which may, with truth, be called the experience of a world.

I will not now delay to detail the reasonings which led to the conclusion that SOCIETY MUST BE SO RECONSTRUCTED AS

TO PRESERVE THE *sovereignty of every individual* INVIOLATE. *That it must avoid all combinations and connections of persons and interests, and all other arrangements, which will not leave every individual at all times at* LIBERTY *to dispose of his or her person, and time, and property, in any manner in which his or her feelings or judgement may dictate,* WITHOUT INVOLVING THE PERSONS OF OTHERS.

That there must be

Individuality of Interests,

Individuality of Responsibilities,

Individuality in the deciding power; and, in one sense,

Individuality of action.

The idea of the sovereignty of each over his own property made it necessary to determine what *is* truly and legitimately one's property. The answer would seem to be, *the whole produce or results of his own labour.* This would result, of course, if each lived on a separate island, and supplied all his own wants, and he would use the sunshine, air, water, stone, and other minerals, land, spontaneous fruits, and all other NATURAL WEALTH, without paying any other persons for the privilege; but how could all these considerations be adjusted through the complicated ramifications of exchange and division of labour, and yet the individual retain at all times an amount equal to the product of his own labour? This could only be effected by an exchange for *equivalents* – *Labour for Labour* – and by not giving any labour for the use of NATURAL WEALTH. Now came in the proposition of Robert Owen to exchange *hour for hour.* This was seen not to be perfect, because some labours were harder than others; but, then, as the sovereignty of every one was to be preserved through all the operations, each could make such exceptions to the rule as he or she might choose to make, and all would be comparatively harmless.

With these views an individual went to Cincinnati, Ohio, after the experiments in New Harmony; without waiting for the concurrence of others, opened, on the 18th of May, 1827, a store on a very small scale, on the north-west corner of Fifth and Elm Streets, for the purpose of testing the views in their practical bearings in the mercantile line – that being a branch of business (particularly the retail branch) in which every citizen is immediately interested. The predetermination was – if the operation was successful and promising – that this store would be wound up, and land was to be taken outside the city to build up a model village, all without saying much to the public till it should be in successful operation, so as to demonstrate every particular *practically* beyond all possible doubt or cavil, so that there would be nothing left to do but to *explain how it was done*, and to multiply these villages or cities. On the other hand, if, upon bringing the views to this severe test, it should appear that there was some unforeseen radical defect, or unconquerable obstacle, then the keeper had determined to convert the store into one of the ordinary kind, and let all systematic reforms entirely alone, and abandon them as hopeless; and, in view of this possible result, he did not give out any public pledges nor scarcely any public announcements.

In this store the principal peculiar feature was, that the compensation of the merchant was to be measured by the labour performed and exchanged, hour for hour, with other labours. Of course it became necessary to '*disconnect*' the compensation of the merchant from the price of the goods, because he might purchase and sell a hundred barrels of flour in the same time he could purchase and sell one barrel; and, if his compensation was charged on one barrel, he would be a hundred times paid in selling a hundred barrels; but by *separating* – '*Individualizing*' – the two elements, he would be just paid, and no more nor less than paid, whether he sold one pound or a thousand barrels.

A clock stood ready to measure the time employed in every transaction, which completely demolished all the chances of disputes about the compensation, *and made it for the interest* of the purchaser not to take up the time of the keeper in higgling about price or anything else; for the more of this was done the farther the clock moved on, and the more time there was to pay for!

Then, as money does not represent any definite quantity of labour, and cannot be made to do so (a dollar sometimes commanding twenty pounds of flour, and sometimes double that quantity), and all other supplies of our wants being subject to similar fluctuations while bought and sold for money, therefore money could not be made to work as the medium for the exchange of equivalents; and, as purchasers could not possibly foresee how much labour they would owe the storekeeper till after the purchase was completed, it was impossible to come provided with any article of labour that would exactly compensate him. At this point came in the *labour-note* proposed by Robert Owen, as a medium of exchange between different organized communities, but which had never been reduced to practice, and the form of which had not been practically digested. When the purchaser had received the goods, and paid the keeper for their cost, then he was to pay him for his labour, for which he gave him a labour-note; or he deposited some article of labour with the keeper, for which the keeper gave his own labour-note, for labour in merchandizing, and the purchaser afterwards paid the keeper in his own notes till they were exhausted – these being divisible, like money, into any amounts, from one minute up to ten or a hundred hours.

A *report of the demand*, corrected every morning, or as often as the supply came in, showed at all times what articles would be received by the keeper for his labour, he being governed by his own wants or the known wants of others. A notice was put up in the store, of which the following is a copy:

'NOTICE'
'Whatever arrangements may be made from time to time in this place, they will always be subject to alteration, or to be abolished, whenever circumstances or increasing knowledge may exhibit the necessity for change.'

These were all the peculiar preparations that were made; the greatest peculiarity of all being that which was left *un*made or what was left UNDONE. For instance, the avoiding very scrupulously all 'constitutions', all artificial machinery of 'organization', avoiding everything that produced either direct or indirect *'combined interests', or united Responsibilities; refraining from laying down laws, rules, and regulations, assum-*

*ing control over any interest but that of the storekeeper;
avoiding all necessity for appointing governors, heads, etc.;
or establishing rules or creeds, assuming control over individual
judgement and* FREEDOM *of action. Shunning all pledges,
promises and contracts that would not leave the individual at*
LIBERTY *to change with changing circumstances.* All this
was done in simple regard to the great, ever-present, and un-
controllable instinct of SELF-PRESERVATION, which
taught the keeper that *the very first* step toward doing any
good to others was to prove to them that he possessed no
power to do them harm, and to *run away* from power, with
as much alacrity as it had hitherto been pursued. Yet, notwithstanding the utmost pains had been taken to show that
there was no possible chance for the keeper to take any
advantage of the customer in any manner whatever, neither
by the delegated power of office, nor by any of the operations
in trade, such were the effects of all past attempts of this
kind, especially on the very heels of our recent failure in
New Harmony, that no one would listen, except through
personal courtesy, to any proposition to co-operate in the
design. Strangers denounced it as some new visionary Utopian
scheme, or a new-fangled trick for speculation or swindling,
and real friends begged the keeper not to pursue any longer
the *ignis fatuus* of reform, but to turn round now, and look
to his own interests to repair the damages of the Harmony
defeats, and let others, if they chose, bear the burden of
new experiments; and they offered to aid him in commencing
a profitable business. But the experimenter saw that his
advisers had not the least idea of what he intended, and,
therefore, their opinions could have no weight; but he went
to a friend and endeavoured to induce him to come to the
store and purchase an article or two, as the means of learning what the operation was to be; through courtesy he consented to come at a certain hour. The keeper was there in
waiting, but he never came! He then went to a second
friend, who also promised to come at a certain hour, but he
came not! He went to a third, who promised to come and
try the experiment at a certain hour; the keeper was on the
spot at that hour, but no friend came! Desperate with dis-

appointment and chagrin, he went to a relation and said, 'G., *you*, perhaps, will allow that I have no design to swindle *you*, at least. If you will come and purchase a few articles for your family, and if you do not like the results, I will take the goods back, and give you your money. You know, of course, that you do not join any society, nor in any way compromise your freedom of person or property. You do not in any way become responsible for my acts, nor, consequently, for my success or that of the experiment; you are as much an individual in all things after the transaction as you are now, and I can get nobody to try the first experiment.' G. promised to come and make a purchase. He did come, and purchased to the amount of about one dollar and fifty cents, or the proceeds of about three hours of his labour by the equal exchange of about fifteen minutes! and this in the purchase of coffee, sugar, writing-paper, and other articles of common necessity. He was not desirous of giving back the articles, but let the transaction stand, and the keeper held G.'s labour-note for fifteen minutes' labour on demand.

G. spoke of the transaction to P., who came immediately to the store and exclaimed, 'My God! what fools we were at Harmony! Why did we not see such a simple thing as this? Here, give me (such and such) articles.' He purchased about five dollars' worth of common necessaries, and saved about a dollar and fifty cents in about twenty minutes! He went away immediately, and reported to a female acquaintance, who was supporting a sick husband with her needle. She came and purchased two articles of medicine, the common price of which would have been $62\frac{1}{2}$ cents, but, upon this principle, the price was 17 cents, and she saved the proceeds of about nineteen hours of her labour, and paid the keeper for his labour with ten minutes of her needle-work! Had the keeper received the common price for these two articles, amounting to only $62\frac{1}{2}$ cents, his profit of ten minutes would have enabled him to command a hundred and fourteen times as much of the labour of the woman as he gave her in return!

The information spread from the last purchaser to another, and from him to others, so that on about the fifth day, a

Mr F., a very much respected member of the Methodist Episcopal Church, came in and said, 'Sir, I am a stranger to you, but my neighbour, Mr. N., was trying last night to initiate me into your new mode of dealing, and I, without giving much thought to it, called it some new humbug; but when I went to bed, I could not sleep; there were some striking points about it, that the more I thought about them, the more impossible it was for me to sleep, and I have not slept all night; and I came to ask you (if you can spare the time) if you will give me an understanding of the enterprise?'

'Yes, sir, certainly, with pleasure; my great difficulty has been to get inquirers or listeners.' A kind of outline of the subject was then given, and the prices of various articles stated –

Mr F. – 'There! You need go no further; I see it – I see it all. I will send some corn-meal here. You must give me small labour-notes for it, and I will explain it to my friends. Goodbye, till I see you again.' The corn-meal came, and the keeper paid for it all in five and ten minute notes, and from that time the customers increased rapidly, and it was not more than three months before there was a throng in the store that amounted to confusion. The storekeeper on the next corner came to the keeper and said, 'I can sell nothing. I must either open a store like this or shut up. I wish you would tell me how to do it.'

'Certainly, sir'; and the next storekeeper opened a second 'Time Store' (as the public called it), because of the clock measuring the time of the merchant. There was a constantly increasing rush of customers to both stores, and the retail trade all over the city began to be affected by it; and this is not surprising when the prices upon this principle are contrasted with the common prices in the ordinary way. Not that retailers of groceries, etc., always get extravagant profits in the long run, but the new arrangement gave rise to economies that are entirely unknown to and impossible in the ordinary way. A retailer may make twenty-five cents in one minute twice a day, and sell twenty other articles so nearly their cost, that his income for the whole day, over and above rent, may not exceed a dollar, but he is employed, perhaps, not a quarter of his time; but being employed all his time at the same rate (the rent being no more), his income might amount to six dollars. The keeper of this place was employed *all* the time. Then again, there was no higgling about price, none of that petty warfare and roundabout manoeuvring between the seller and the buyer, that consumes so much time in the common way. It was all entirely stopped by the simple principle of equivalents, which admits of no variation of price, when once set, and the keeper has no time to throw away in inveigling customers, nor setting traps, spreading nets, or anything of the kind, therefore the time generally consumed in that way was saved and employed in selling. There was an account kept, always open to the inspection of the customers, in which they could see all the items of expenditure and income of the establishment; where items of rent, firewood, cartage, breakage, leakage, etc., were recorded, and a regular percentage was added to the prime cost of articles to pay all these contingencies. If this percentage proved more than sufficient for these purposes, it was to be reduced, and if insufficient it was to be increased, but never without previous notice to that effect. The goods were exposed to view with the prices all marked, so that customers had only to examine and decide for themselves, without ever taking up any of the time of the keeper, as, according to the common practice, by which he is obliged to repeat the whole catalogue of answers, perhaps a hundred times a day. With these and other economies, growing out of the fact, that as much time as the customer took up of the keeper, *so much he had to pay for*, enabled the keeper of that establishment to retail as many goods in an hour as are commonly retailed in a day or two, and all with the best possible feelings between both buyer and seller, growing out of the well-established fact that the whole was perfectly equitable toward both parties. The bills of all the purchases were carefully and promptly posted before the eyes of all the customers, who, by this means, perceived that there was no departure from, no violations of, the professions and principles announced. A few notes, taken during the bustle of business, will show some of the practical bearings upon the minds and interests of the dealers better, perhaps, than any abstract description could:

June, 1827 – Mr M. purchased –

	Cost price	Common price
1 quart brandy	37½	62½
1 pair men's shoes	90	$1.50
4 pounds mackerel	16	25
4 oz. ess. lemon	5	25
	$1.48½	$2.62½
		$1.48½
	Gain	$1.14

In this case the purchaser was a blacksmith. I have given the articles to show that they were of the most ordinary kind; yet in this simple operation of spending $1.48, he saved $1.14 in twenty minutes, which last he paid to the keeper in blacksmith's work. The blacksmith in this simple operation saved nearly the whole proceeds of a day's work. Had the articles been sold in the common way, the keeper would have obtained nine or ten hours of the work of the blacksmith for twenty minutes of his own, although the labour of the blacksmith is much more repugnant than that of store-keeping.

A widow with a family of children dependent on the proceeds of her needle, and who obtains about twenty-five cents a day, purchased a few of the common necessities of life, paid the keeper in an hour of her labour, and saved $1.52, or the proceeds of six days of her labour! Had these articles been sold in the common way the keeper could have obtained sixty or seventy times an equivalent for his labour from the widow! ...

The store was gradually wound up, and the keeper came out of it with just about the same amount of property with which he commenced it, having tested the principle, and cleared all he consumed while engaged in it, but nothing more; a large portion of the time having been occupied in answering questions, and giving explanations, which the just development of the principles rendered necessary; but in villages where the subject had once become familiar, this expenditure of time would not be necessary. Let it be particularly observed here, that throughout all the ramifications of this business, it was regulated by entirely new *principles*, and that there principles *did regulate*, instead of the customary machinery of organization, constitutions, laws, rules and rulers. No organized or artificial power of any description was erected *above the individual*. No votes of majorities were taken for any other purpose than as an economical mode of learning the wishes of others, but not to compel anyone to conform to them any further than he or she chose to yield to the wishes of others. The vote of an unanimous meeting was not intended nor expected to rise above or assume control over the inclination of the individual – *all necessity for such compulsion had been provided against* and avoided in the strict individuality of interests which enabled each to move in his own particular sphere, time, and mode, without involving the persons or interests of others. We have, therefore, thus far demonstrated that *the erection of any power over the individual is unnecessary.*

EXCHANGE AND DISTRIBUTION

JAMES GUILLAUME
(From *Idées sur l'organisation sociale*, 1876, translated by George Woodcock)

In the new society, there will no longer be *commerce, in the sense that we understand today.*

Each commune will establish a *Bank of Exchange*, whose mechanism we shall now explain.

The associations of workers, and the individual producers in those trades where individual production continues, will deposit their products at the Bank of Exchange. The value of these various products will already have been fixed by agreement between the regional syndical federations and the different communes on the basis of statistical information.

The Bank of Exchange will hand the producers *vouchers* representing the value of their products; these vouchers will have an area of circulation equal to the territory of the federation of communes.

Among the products deposited in this way at the Bank of Exchange, some will be for consumption in the commune itself, and others will be exported to other communes and in the process exchanged for other products.

The first class of products will be distributed among the various communal markets, which for the time being will be located in the most convenient of the former shops and stores. Some of these markets will be devoted to food, others to clothes, others to household utensils, etc.

The products for export will be kept in general warehouses until such time as they can be sent on to communes which are in need of them.

Here we can anticipate an objection. It will be said: 'The Bank of Exchange gives the producers vouchers representing the value of their products before being assured that these products will be disposed of. But if they are not disposed of, what will be the Bank's position? Does it not risk losses, and is not this kind of operation somewhat hazardous?'

To that, we reply that each Bank of Exchange plans in advance the disposal of the products it will receive, and thus encounters no difficulty because of the vouchers it has issued.

There will of course be certain categories of workers who will be unable to take their products to the Bank of Exchange, the obvious example being that of the building workers. In this case the Bank of Exchange will still have its function as an intermediary; it will register the works performed according to the values arranged beforehand, and will remit that value in vouchers. The same will happen with workers employed in communal administrative services; their work consists not in manufactured products but in services rendered, which will be estimated in advance and their value duly paid. The function of the Bank of Exchange will not be merely that of receiving the products brought to it by the workers in the commune; it will maintain contact with other communes and be responsible for obtaining the goods which the commune must import from outside, whether in terms of food, or raw materials, or fuel, or manufactured products. Such products drawn from outside will appear in the communal markets alongside local products.

The consumers will go to the various markets with their vouchers which can be divided into coupons of varying worth, and they will obtain at uniform prices the goods they need.

Up to now what we have said of the operations of the Bank of Exchange differs in no essential manner from the operations of present-day commerce, the operations of buying and selling. The bank buys their products from the producers and sells them to the consumers. But we believe that in time the practice of the Banks of Exchange may be modified without any inconvenience, and a new system be gradually substituted for the old one: exchange in the strict sense of the word will vanish and give place to simple *distribution*.

We envisage it in this way. So long as a product is scarce and finds its way into the markets in quantities less than the population might consume, a certain restraint has to be observed in its distribution, and the easiest manner of rationing it to the consumers is to sell it to them, that is to say, to release it only to those who are willing to place a value on it. But when there is a vast development of production, which can not fail to take place once it is organized on rational lines, then we can abandon the practice of selling, which has merely been a brake on immoderate consumption; the communal markets will no longer sell the products to the consumers; they will distribute them in response to the expression of need.

This substitution of distribution for exchange may take place very soon in the case of objects of prime necessity, for the efforts of the associations of producers will first of all be directed towards an abundant availability of such objects. Afterwards other objects, which today are scarce and expensive and consequently are regarded as luxuries, will in their turn be produced on a large scale and enter into the domain of distribution, the field of universal consumption. On the other hand there are some objects, which exist in small quantities and have little real importance (such as pearls, diamonds and precious metals), that will never become abundant because their quantity is naturally limited; however, they will cease to command the price which opinion now gives them and they will mainly be sought by scientific associations which seek to place them in museums of natural history or to use them in the construction of certain instruments.

ON THE WAGE SYSTEM

PETER KROPOTKIN
(From *The Wage System*, 1889)

UNEQUAL REMUNERATION

We have said that most Collectivist writers demand that in a Socialist society remuneration should be based upon a distinction between qualified or professional labour and simple labour. They assert that an hour of the engineer's, the architect's, or the doctor's work should be counted as two or three hours' work from the blacksmith, the mason, or the nurse. And the same distinction, say they, ought to be established between workers whose trades require a longer or shorter apprenticeship and those who are mere day labourers.

This is the case in the present middle-class society; it must be the case in the future society of Collectivism.

Yes, but to establish this distinction is to maintain all the inequalities of our existing society. It is to trace out beforehand a demarcation between the worker and those who claim to rule him. It is still to divide society into two clearly defined classes; an aristocracy of knowledge above, a horny-handed democracy below; one class devoted to the service of the other; one class toiling with its hands to nourish and clothe the other, whilst that other profits by its leisure to learn how to dominate those who toil for it.

This is to take the distinctive features of middle-class society and sanction them by a social revolution. It is to erect into a principle an abuse which today is condemned in the society that is breaking up.

We know very well what will be said in answer. We shall be told about 'Scientific Socialism.' The middle-class economists, and Marx too, will be cited to prove that there is a good reason for a scale of wages, for the 'labour force' of the engineer costs society more than the 'labour force' of the navvy. And indeed, have not the economists striven to prove that, if the engineer is paid twenty times more than the navvy, it is because the cost necessary to produce an engineer is more considerable than that necessary to produce a navvy? And has not Marx maintained that the like distinction between various sorts of manual labour is of equal logical necessity? He could come to no other conclusion, since he took up Ricardo's theory of value and insisted that products exchange in proportion to the quantity of the work socially necessary to produce them.

But we know also how much of all this to believe. We know that if the engineer, the scientist, and the doctor are paid today ten or a hundred times more than the labourer, and the weaver earns three times as much as the toiler in the fields and ten times as much as a match-girl, it is not because what they receive is in proportion to the various costs of production. Rather it is in proportion to the extent of monopoly in education and in industry. The engineer, the scientist, and the doctor simply draw their profits from their own sort of capital – their degree, their certificates – just as the manufacturer draws a profit from a mill, or as a nobleman used to do from his birth and title.

When the employer pays the engineer twenty times more than the workman, he makes this very simple calculation: if an engineer can save him £4000 a year in cost of production, he will pay him £800 a year to do it.. And if he sees a foreman is a clever sweater and can save him £400 in handicraft, he at once offers him £80 or £90 a year. He spends £100 where he counts upon gaining £1000; that is the essence of the capitalist system. And the like holds good of the differences in various trades.

Where then is the sense of talking about the cost of production of labour force, and saying that a student who passes a merry youth at the University, has a *right* to ten times higher wages than the son of a miner who has pined in a pit since he was eleven? Or that a weaver has a *right* to wages three or four times higher than those of an agricultural labourer? The expenditure needed to produce a weaver is not four times as great as the necessary cost of producing a field worker. The weaver simply benefits by the advantageous position which industry enjoys in Europe as compared with parts of the world where at present there is no industrial development.

No one has ever estimated the real cost of production of labour force. And if an idler costs society much more than an honest workman, it still remains to be known if, when all is told (infant mortality among the workers, the savages of anemia, the premature deaths) a sturdy day labourer does not cost society more than an artisan.

Are we to be told that, for example, the 1s a day of a London workwoman and the 3d a day of the Auvergne peasant who blinds herself over lace-making, represent the cost of production of these women? We are perfectly aware that they often work for even less, but we know also that they do it entirely because, thanks to our splendid social organization, they would die of hunger without these ridiculous wages.

The existing scale of wages seems to us a highly complex product of taxation, government interference, monopoly and capitalistic greed – in a word, of the State and the capitalist system. In our opinion all the theories made by economists about the scale of wages have been invented after the event to justify existing injustices. It is needless to regard them.

We are, however, certain to be informed that the Collectivist wage scale will, at all events, be an improvement. 'You must admit,' we shall be told, 'that it will, at least, be better to have a class of workers paid at twice or three times the ordinary rate than to have Rothschilds, who put into their pockets in one day more than a workman can in a year. It will be a step towards equality.'

To us it seems a step away from it. To introduce into a Socialist society the distinction between ordinary and professional labour would be to sanction by the Revolution and erect into a principle a brutal fact to which we merely submit today, considering it all the while as unjust. It would be acting after the manner of those gentlemen of the Fourth of August, 1789, who proclaimed, in high-sounding phraseology, the abolition of feudal rights, and on the Eighth of August sanctioned those very rights by imposing upon the peasants the dues by which they were to be redeemed from the nobles. Or, again, like the Russian government at the time of the emancipation of the serfs, when it proclaimed that land henceforth belonged to the nobility, whereas previously it was considered an abuse that the land which belonged to the peasants should be bought and sold by private persons.

Or, to take a better known example, when the Commune of 1871 decided to pay the members of the Communal Council 12s 6d a day, whilst the National Guards on the ramparts had only 1s 3d, certain persons applauded this decision as an act of grand democratic equality. But, in reality, the Commune did nothing thereby but sanction the ancient inequality between officials and soldiers, governors and governed. For an Opportunist parliament such a decision might have seemed splendid, but for the Commune it was a negation of its own principles. The Commune was false to its own revolutionary principle, and by that very fact condemned it.

In the present state of society, when we see Cabinet Ministers paying themselves thousands a year, whilst the workman has to content himself with less than a hundred; when we see the foreman paid twice or three times as much as the ordinary hand, and when amongst workers themselves there are all sorts of graduations, from 7s to 8s a day down to the 3d of the seamstress, we disapprove of the large salary of the minister, and also the difference between the artisan's eight-shillings and the seamstress's three-pence. And we say, 'Let us have done with privileges of education as well as of birth.' We are Anarchists just because such privileges disgust us.

How can we then raise these privileges into a principle? How can we proclaim that privileges of education are to be the basis of an equal Society, without striking a blow at that very Society? What is submitted to today, will be submitted to no longer in a society based on equality. The general above the soldier, the rich engineer above the workman, the doctor above the nurse, already disgust us. Can we suffer them in

356 *The Anarchist Reader*

a society which starts by proclaiming equality?

Evidently not. The popular conscience, inspired by the idea of equality, will revolt against such an injustice, it will not tolerate it. It is not worth while to make the attempt.

That is why certain Collectivists, understanding the impossibility of maintaining a scale of wages in a society inspired by the influence of fhe Revolution, zealously advocate equality in wages. But they only stumble upon fresh difficulties, and their equality of wages becomes a Utopia, as incapable of realization as the wage scale of the others.

A society that has seized upon all social wealth, and has plainly announced that all have a right to this wealth, whatever may be the part they have taken in creating it in the past, will be obliged to give up all idea of wages, either in money or in labour notes.

EQUAL WAGES VERSUS FREE COMMUNISM

'To each according to his deeds,' say the Collectivists, or rather according to his share of service rendered to society. And this is the principle they recommend as the basis of economic organization, after the Revolution shall have made all the instruments of labour and all that is necessary for production common property!

Well, if the Social Revolution should be so unfortunate as to proclaim the principle, it would be stemming the tide of human progress; it would be leaving unsolved the huge social problem cast by past centuries upon our shoulders.

It is true that in such a society as ours, where the more a man works the less he is paid, this principle may seem, at first sight, an aspiration towards injustice. It is with this principle that the wage-system started, to end where it is today, in crying inequalities and all the abominations of the present state of things. And it has ended thus because, from the day on which society began to value services in money or from any other sort of wages, from the day on which it was said that each should have only what he could succeed in getting paid for his work, the whole history of Capitalism (the State aiding therein) was written beforehand; its germ was enclosed in this principle.

Must we then return to our point of departure and pass once more through the same process of capitalist evolution? These theorists seem to desire it; but happily it is impossible; the Revolution will be Communistic; or it will be drowned in blood, and must be begun all over again.

Service rendered to society, be it labour in factory or field, or moral service, cannot be rendered in monetary units. There cannot be an exact measure of its value, either of what has been improperly called its 'value in exchange' or of its value in use. If we see two individuals, both working for years, for five hours daily, for the community, at two different occupations equally pleasing to them, we can say that, taken all in all, their labours are roughly equivalent. But their work could not be broken up into fractions, so that the product of each day, each hour or minute of the labour of one should be worth the produce of each minute and each hour of that of the other.

Broadly speaking, we can say that a man who during his whole life deprived himself of leisure for ten hours daily has given much more to society than he who has deprived himself of but five hours a day, or has not deprived himself of any leisure at all. But we cannot take what one man has done during any two hours and say that this produce is worth exactly twice as much as the produce of one hour's work from another individual and reward each proportionately. To do this would be to ignore all that is complex in the industry, the agriculture, the entire life of society as it is; it would be to ignore the extent to which all individual work is the outcome of the former and present labours of society as a whole. It would be to fancy oneself in the Stone Age, when we are living in the Age of Steel.

Go into a coal mine and see that man stationed at the huge machine that hoists and lowers the cage. In his hands he holds a lever whereby to check or reverse the action of the machinery. He lowers the handle, and in a second the cage changes the direction of its giddy rush up or down the shaft. His eyes are attentively fixed upon an indicator in front of him which shows exactly the point the cage has reached; no sooner does it touch the given level than at his gentlest pressure it stops dead short, not a foot above or below the required place. And scarcely are the full trucks discharged or the empties loaded before, at a touch to the handle, the cage is again swinging up or down the shaft.

For eight or ten hours at a time he thus concentrates his attention. Let his brain relax but for an instant, and the cage would fly up and shatter the wheels, break the rope, crush the men, bring all the work of the mine to a stand-still. Let him lose three seconds upon each reverse of the lever, and, in a mine with all the modern improvements, the output will be reduced by from twenty to fifty tons a day.

Well, is it he who renders the greatest service in the mine? Or is it, perhaps, that boy who rings from below the signal for the mounting of the cage? Or is it the miner who risks his life every moment in the depths of a mine and will end one day by being killed by fire-damp? Or, again, the engineer who would lose the coal seam and set men hewing bare rock, if he merely made a mistake in the addition of his calculations? Or, finally, is it the owner, who has put all his patrimony into the concern, and who perhaps has said, in opposition to all previous anticipations, 'Dig there, you will find excellent coal'?

All the workers engaged in the mine contribute to the raising of coal in proportion to their strength, their energy, their knowledge, their intelligence, and their skill. And we can say that all have the right to *live*, to satisfy their needs, and even gratify their whims, after the more imperious needs of everyone are satisfied. But how can we exactly value what they have each done?

Further, is the coal that they have extracted entirely the result of *their* work? Is it not also the outcome of the work of the men who constructed the railway leading to the mine, and the roads branching off on all sides from the stations? And what of the work of those who have tilled and sown the fields which supply the miners with food, smelted the iron, cut the wood in the forest, made the machines which will consume the coal, and so on?

No hard and fast line can be drawn between the work of one and the work of another. To measure them by results leads to absurdity. To divide them into fractions and measure them by hours of labour leads to absurdity also. (One course remains: not to measure them at all, but to recognize the right of all who take part in productive labour first of all to live, and then to enjoy the comforts of life.)

Take any other branch of human activity, take our existence as a whole, and say which of us can claim the highest reward for his deeds? The doctor who has divined the disease or the nurse who has assured its cure by her sanitary cares? The inventor of the first steam engine or the boy who one day, tired of pulling the cord which formerly served to open the valve admitting the steam beneath the piston, tied his cord to the lever of the machine, and went to play with his companions, without imagining that he had invented the mechanism essential to all modern machinery – the automatic valve? The inventor of the locomotive or that Newcastle workman who suggested that wooden sleepers should take the place of the stones which were formerly put under the rails and threw trains off the line by their want of elasticity? The driver of the locomotive or the signalman who stops the train or opens the way for it?

To whom do we owe the trans-Atlantic cable? To the engineer who persisted in declaring that the cable would transmit telegrams, whilst the learned electricians declared that it was impossible? To Maury, the scientist, who advised the disuse of thick cables and the substitution of one no bigger than a walking stick? Or, after all, is it to those volunteers, from no one knows where, who spent day and night on the deck of the *Great Eastern*, minutely examining every yard of cable and taking out the nails that the shareholders of the maritime companies had stupidly caused to be driven through the isolating coat of the cable to render it useless?

And, in a still wider field, the vast tract of human life, with its joys, its sorrows, and its varied incidents, cannot each of us mention someone who during his life has rendered him some service so great, so important, that if it were proposed to value it in money he would be filled with indignation? This service may have been a word, nothing but a word in season, or it may have been months or years of devotion. Are you going to estimate these, the most important of all services, in labour notes?

'The deeds of each'! But human societies could not live

for two successive generations, they would disappear in fifty years, if each one did not give infinitely more than will be returned to him in money, in 'notes' or in civic rewards. It would be the extinction of the race if the mother did not expend her life to preserve her children, if every man did not give some things without counting the cost, if human beings did not give most where they look for no reward.

If the middle-class society is going to ruin; if we are today in a blind alley from which there is no escape without applying axe and torch to the institutions of the past, that is just because we have calculated too much. It is just because we have allowed ourselves to be drawn into giving that we may receive; because we have desired to make society into a commercial company based upon debit and credit.

Moreover, the Collectivists know it. They vaguely comprehend that a society cannot exist if it logically carries out the principle 'To each according to his deeds.' They suspect that the *needs* (we are not speaking of the whims) of the individual do not always correspond to his deeds. Accordingly, De Paepe tells us:

> This eminently individualistic principle will be *tempered* by social intervention for the purpose of the education of children and young people (including their maintenance and nurture) and by social organizations for the assistance of the sick and infirm, asylums for aged workers, etc.

Even Collectivists suspect that a man of forty, the father of three children, has greater needs than a youth of twenty. They suspect that a woman who is suckling her child and spends sleepless nights by its cot, cannot get through so much work as a man who has enjoyed tranquil slumber.

They seem to understand that a man or woman worn out by having perhaps worked over hard for society in general may find themselves incapable of performing as many 'deeds' as those who take their hours of labour quietly and pocket their 'notes' in the privileged offices of State statisticians.

And they hasten to *temper* their principle. Oh, certainly, they say, society will feed and bring up its children. Oh, certainly it will assist the old and infirm. Oh, certainly *needs* not *deeds* will be the measure of the cost which society will impose on itself to temper the principle of deeds.

What, Charity? Yes, our old friend, 'Christian Charity', organized by the State.

Improve the foundling hospital, organize insurance against age and sickness, and the principle of deeds will be 'tempered'. 'Wound that they may heal,' they can go no further.

Thus, then, after having forsworn Communism, after having sneered at their ease at the formula, 'To each according to his needs,' is it not obvious that they, the great economists, also perceive that they have forgotten something, i.e. the needs of the producers? And thereupon they hasten to recognize these needs. Only it is to be the State by which they are to be estimated; it is to be the State which will undertake to find out if needs are disproportionate to deeds.

It is to be the State that will give alms to him who is willing to recognize his inferiority. From thence to the Poor Law and the Workhouse is but a stone's throw.

There is but a stone's throw, for even this stepmother of a society, against which we are in revolt, has found it necessary to temper its individualistic principle. It too has had to make concessions in a Communistic sense, and in this same form of charity.

It also distributes halfpenny dinners to prevent the pillage of its shops. It also builds hospitals, often bad enough, but sometimes splendid, to prevent the ravages of contagious disease. It also, after having paid for nothing but the hours of labour, receives the children of those whom it has itself reduced to the extremity of distress. It also takes account of needs – as a charity.

Poverty, the existence of the poor, was the first cause of riches. This it was which created the earliest capitalist. For, before the surplus value, about which people are so fond of talking, could begin to be accumulated it was necessary that there should be poverty-stricken wretches who would consent to sell their labour force rather than die of hunger. It is poverty that has made the rich. And if poverty had advanced by such rapid strides by the end of the Middle Ages, it was chiefly because the invasions and wars, the creation of States and the development of their authority, the wealth gained by exploitation in the East, and many other causes of a like nature, broke the bonds which once united agrarian and urban communities, and led them, in place of the solidarity which they once practised, to adopt the principle of the wage-system.

Is this principle to be the outcome of the Revolution? Dare we dignify by the name of a Social Revolution – that name so dear to the hungry, the suffering and the oppressed – the triumph of such a principle as this?

It cannot be. For, on the day when ancient institutions splinter into fragments before the axe of the proletariat, voices will be heard shouting: Bread for all! Lodging for all! Right for all to the comforts of life!

And these voices will be heeded. The people will say to themselves: 'Let us begin by satisfying our thirst for the life, the joy, the liberty we have never known. And when all have tasted happiness, we will set to work; the work of demolishing the last vestiges of middle-class rule, with its account-book morality, its philosophy of debit and credit, its institutions of mine and thine.' 'While we throw down we shall be building,' as Proudhon said; we shall build in the name of Communism and Anarchy.

CRIME IN A FREE WORLD

PETER KROPOTKIN
(From *In Russian and French Prisons*, 1887)

Let us organize our society so as to assure to everybody the possibility of regular work for the benefit of the common-wealth – and that means of course a thorough transformation of the present relations between work and capital; let us assure to every child a sound education and instruction, both in manual labour and science, so as to permit him to acquire, during the first twenty years of his life, the knowledge and habits of earnest work – and we shall be in no more need of dungeons and jails, of judges and hangmen. Man is a result of those conditions in which he has grown up. Let him grow in habits of useful work; let him be brought by his earlier life to consider humanity as one great family, no member of which can be injured without the injury being felt by a wide circle of his fellows, and ultimately by the whole of society; let him acquire a taste for the highest enjoyments of science and art – much more lofty and durable than those given by the satisfaction of lower passions, – and we may be sure that we shall not have many breaches of those laws of morality which are an unconscious affirmation of the best conditions for life in society.

Two-thirds of all breaches of law being so-called 'crimes against property', these cases will disappear, or be limited to a quite trifling amount, when property which is now the privilege of the few, shall return to its real source – the community. As to 'crimes against persons', already their numbers are rapidly decreasing, owing to the growth of moral and social habits which necessarily develop in each society, and can only grow when common interests contribute more and more to tighten the bonds which induce men to live a common life.

Of course, whatever be the economical bases of organization of society, there will always be in its midst a certain number of beings with passions more strongly developed and less easily controlled than the rest; and there always will be men whose passions may occasionally lead them to commit acts of anti-social character. But these passions can receive another direction, and most of them can be rendered almost or quite harmless by the combined efforts of those who surround us. We live now in too much isolation. Everybody cares only for himself, or his nearest relatives. Egotistic – that is, un-intelligent – individualism in material life has necessarily brought about an individualism as egotistic and as harmful in the mutual relations of human beings. But we have known in history, and we see still, communities where men are more closely connected together than in our Western European cities. China is an instance in point. The great 'compound family' is there still the basis of the social organization: the members of the compound family know one another perfectly; they support one another, they help one another, not merely in material life, but also in moral troubles; and the number of 'crimes' both against property and persons, stands at an astonishingly low level (in the central provinces, of course, not on the seashore). The Slavonian and Swiss agrarian communes are another instance. Men know one another in these smaller aggregations: they mutually support one another; while in our cities all bonds between the inhabitants have disappeared. The old family, based on a common origin, is disintegrating. But men cannot live in this isolation, and the elements of new social groups – those ties arising between the inhabitants of the same spot having many interests in common, and those of people united by the prosecution of common aims – is growing. Their growth can only be accelerated by such changes as would bring about a closer mutual dependency and a greater equality between the members of our communities.

And yet, notwithstanding all this, there surely will remain a limited number of persons whose anti-social passions – the result of bodily diseases – may still be a danger for the community. Shall humanity send these to the gallows, or lock them up in prisons? Surely it will not resort to this wicked solution of the difficulty.

There was a time when lunatics, considered as possessed by the devil, were treated in the most abominable manner. Chained in stalls like animals, they were dreaded even by their keepers. To break their chains, to set them free, would have been considered then as a folly. But a man came – Pinel – who dared to take off their chains, and to offer them brotherly words, brotherly treatment. And those who were looked upon as ready to devour the human being who dared to approach them, gathered round their liberator, and proved that he was right in his belief in the best features of human nature, even in those whose intelligence was darkened by disease. From that time the cause of humanity was won. The lunatic was no longer treated like a wild beast. Man recognized in him a brother.

The chains disappeared, but asylums – another name for prisons – remained, and within their walls a system as bad as that of the chains grew up by-and-by. But then the peasants of a Belgian village, moved by their simple good sense and kindness of heart, showed the way towards a new departure which learned students of mental disease did not perceive. They set the lunatics quite free. They took them into their families, offered them a bed in their poor houses, a chair at their plain tables, a place in their ranks to cultivate the soil, a place in their dancing-parties. And the fame spread wide of 'miraculous cures' effected by the saint to whose name the church of Gheel was consecrated. The remedy applied by the peasants was so plain, so old – it was liberty – that the learned people preferred to trace the result to Divine influences instead of taking things as they were. But there was no lack of honest and good-hearted men who understood the force of the treatment invented by the Gheel peasants, advocated it, and gave all their energies to overcome the inertia of mind, the cowardice, and the indifference of their surroundings.

Liberty and fraternal care have proved the best cure on our side of the above-mentioned wide borderland 'between insanity and crime'. They will prove also the best cure on the other boundary of the same borderland. Progress is in that direction. All that tends that way will bring us nearer to the solution of the great question which has not ceased to preoccupy human societies since the remotest antiquity, and which cannot be solved by prisons.

ANARCHISM AND ECOLOGY

MURRAY BOOKCHIN
(From *Post-Scarcity Anarchism*, 1974)

There is more to anarchism than decentralized communities. If I have examined this possibility in some detail, it has been to demonstrate that an anarchist society, far from being a remote ideal, has become a precondition for the practice of ecological principles. To sum up the critical message of ecology: if we diminish variety in the natural world, we debase its unity and wholeness; we destroy the forces making for natural harmony and for a lasting equilibrium; and, what is even more significant, we introduce an absolute regression in the development of the natural world which may eventually render the environment unfit for advanced forms of life. To sum up the reconstructive message of ecology: if we wish to advance the unity and stability of the natural world, if we wish to harmonize it, we must conserve and promote variety. To be sure, mere variety for its own sake is a vacuous goal. In nature, variety emerges spontaneously. The capacities of a new species are tested by the rigours of climate, by its ability to deal with predators and by its capacity to establish and enlarge its niche. *Yet the species that succeeds in enlarging its niche in the environment also enlarges the ecological situation as a whole.* To borrow E. A. Gutkind's phrase, it 'expands the environment', both for itself and for the species with which it enters into a balanced relationship.

How do these concepts apply to social theory? To many readers, I suppose, it should suffice to say that, inasmuch as man is part of nature, an expanding natural environment enlarges the basis for social development. But the answer to the question goes much deeper than many ecologists and libertarians suspect. Again, allow me to return to the ecological principle of wholeness and balance as a product of diversity. Keeping this principle in mind, the first step towards an answer is provided by a passage in Herbert Read's 'The Philosophy of Anarchism'. In presenting his 'measure of progress', Read observes: 'Progress is measured by the degree of differentiation within a society. If the individual is a unit in a corporate mass, his life will be limited, dull and mechanical. If the individual is a unit on his own, with space and potentiality for separate action, then he may be more subject to accident or chance, but at least he can expand and express himself. He can develop – develop in the only real meaning of the word – develop in consciousness of strength, vitality and joy.'

Read's thought, unfortunately, is not developed, but it provides an interesting point of departure. What first strikes us is that both the ecologist and the anarchist place a strong emphasis on spontaneity. The ecologist, in so far as he is more than a technician, tends to reject the notion of 'power over nature'. He speaks, instead, of 'steering' his way through an ecological situation, of *managing* rather than *recreating* an ecosystem. The anarchist, in turn, speaks in terms of social spontaneity, of releasing the potentialities of society and humanity, of giving free and unfettered rein to the creativity of people. Both, in their own way, regard authority as inhibitory, as a weight limiting the creative potential of a natural and social situation. Their object is not to *rule* a domain, but to *release* it. They regard insight, reason and knowledge as means for fulfilling the potentialities of a situation, not as replacing its potentialities with preconceived notions or distorting their development with dogma.

Turning to Read's words, what strikes us is that both the ecologist and the anarchist view differentiation as a measure of progress. The ecologist uses the term 'biotic pyramid' in speaking of biological advances; the anarchist, the word 'individuation' to denote social advances. If we go beyond Read we will observe that, to both the ecologist and the anarchist, an ever-increasing unity is achieved by growing differentiation. *An expanding whole is created by the diversifications and enrichment of its parts.*

Just as the ecologist seeks to expand the range of an ecosystem and promote a free interplay between species, so the anarchist seeks to expand the range of social experience and remove all fetters from its development. Anarchism is not only a stateless society but also a harmonized society which exposes man to the stimuli provided by both agrarian and urban life, to physical activity and mental activity, to unrepressed sensuality and self-directed spirituality, to communal solidarity and individual development, to regional uniqueness and worldwide brotherhood, to spontaneity and self-discipline, to the elimination of toil and the promotion of craftsmanship. In our schizoid society, these goals are regarded as mutually exclusive, indeed as sharply opposed. They appear as dualities because of the very logistics of present-day society – the separation of town and country, the specialization of labour, the atomization of man – and it would be preposterous to believe that these dualities could be resolved without a general idea of the *physical* structure of an anarchist society. We can gain some idea of what such a society would be like by reading William Morris's *News from Nowhere* and the writings of Peter Kropotkin. But these works provide us with mere glimpses. They do not take into account the post-World-War-II developments of technology and the contributions made by the development of ecology. This is not the place to embark on 'utopian writing', but certain guidelines can be presented even in a general discussion. And in presenting these guidelines, I am eager to emphasize not only the more obvious ecological premises that support them, but also the humanistic ones.

An anarchist society should be a decentralized society, not only to establish a lasting basis for the harmonization of man and nature, *but also to add new dimensions to the harmonization of man and man*. The Greeks, we are often reminded, would have been horrified by a city whose size and population precluded a face-to-face, often familiar, relationship between citizens. There is plainly a need to reduce the dimensions of the human community – partly to solve our pollution and transportation problems, partly also to create *real* communities. In a sense, we must *humanize* humanity. Electronic devices such as telephones, telegraphs, radios and television receivers should be used as little as possible to mediate the relations between people. In making collective decisions – the ancient Athenian ecclesia was, in some ways, a model for making social decisions – all members of the community should have an opportunity to acquire in full the measure of anyone who addresses the assembly. They should be in a position to absorb his attitudes, study his expressions, and weigh his motives as well as his ideas in a direct personal encounter and through face-to-face discussion.

Our small communities should be economically balanced and well rounded, partly so that they can make full use of local raw materials and energy sources, partly also to enlarge the agricultural and industrial stimuli to which individuals are exposed. The member of a community who has a predilection for engineering, for instance, should be encouraged to steep his hand in humus, the man of ideas should be encouraged to employ his musculature; the 'inborn' farmer should gain a familiarity with the workings of a rolling mill. To separate the engineer from the soil, the thinker from the spade, and the farmer from the industrial plant promotes a degree of vocational overspecialization that leads to a dangerous measure of social control by specialists. What is equally important, professional and vocational specialization prevents society from achieving a vital goal: the humanization of nature by the technician and the naturalization of society by the biologist.

I submit that an anarchist community would approximate a clearly definable ecosystem; it would be diversified, balanced and harmonious. It is arguable whether such an ecosystem would acquire the configuration of an urban entity with a distinct centre, such as we find in the Greek *polis* or the medieval commune, or whether, as Gutkind proposes, society would consist of widely dispersed communities without a distinct centre. In any case, the ecological scale for any of these communities would be determined by the smallest ecosystem capable of supporting a population of moderate size.

A relatively self-sufficient community, visibly dependent on its environment for the means of life, would gain a new respect for the organic interrelationships that sustain it. In the long run, the attempt to approximate self-sufficiency would, I think, prove more efficient than the exaggerated national division of labour that prevails today. Although there would doubtless be many duplications of small industrial facilities from community to community, the familiarity of each group with its local environment and its ecological roots would make for a more intelligent and more loving use of its environment. I submit that, far from producing provincialism, relative self-sufficiency would create a new matrix for individual and communal development – a oneness with the surroundings that would vitalize the community.

The rotation of civil, vocational and professional responsibilities would stimulate the senses in the being of the individual, creating and rounding out new dimensions in self-development. In a complete society we could hope to create complete men; in a rounded society, rounded men. In the Western world, the Athenians, for all their shortcomings and limitations, were the first to give us a notion of this completeness. 'The *polis* was made for the amateur,' H. D. F. Kitto tells us. 'Its ideal was that every citizen (more or less, according as the *polis* was democratic or oligarchic) should play his part in all of its many activities – an ideal that is recognizably descended from the generous Homeric conception of *arete* as an all-round excellence and an all-round activity. It implies a respect for the wholeness or the oneness of life, and a consequent dislike of specialization. It implies a contempt for efficiency – or rather a much higher ideal of efficiency; an efficiency which exists not in one department of life, but in life itself.' An anarchist society, although it would surely aspire to more, could hardly hope to achieve less than this state of mind.

If the ecological community is ever achieved in practice, social life will yield a sensitive development of human and natural diversity, falling together into a well-balanced, harmonious whole. Ranging from community through region to entire continents, we will see a colourful differentiation of human grounds and ecosystems, each developing its unique potentialities and exposing members of the community to a wide spectrum of economic, cultural and behavioural stimuli. Falling within our purview will be an exciting, often dramatic, variety of communal forms – here marked by architectural and industrial adaptations to semi-arid ecosystems, there to grasslands, elsewhere by adaptation to forested areas. We will witness a creative interplay between individual and group, community and environment, humanity and nature. The cast of mind that today organizes differences among humans and other life-forms along hierarchical lines, defining the external in terms of its 'superiority' or 'inferiority', will give way to an outlook that deals with diversity in an ecological manner. Differences among people will be respected, indeed fostered, as elements that enrich the unity of experience and phenomena. The traditional relationship which pits subject against object will be altered qualitatively; the 'external', the 'different', the 'other' will be conceived as individual parts of a whole all the richer because of its complexity. This sense of unity will reflect the harmonization of interests between individuals and between society and nature. Freed from an oppressive routine, from paralyzing repressions and insecurities, from the burdens of toil and false needs, from the trammels of authority and irrational compulsion, individuals will finally, for the first time in history, be in a position to realize their potentialities as members of the human community and the natural world.

The Anarchists: A Biographical Supplement

ARSHINOV, PETER (1887—?). Peter Arshinov was a metal worker from the Ukraine who in 1904 joined the Bolshevik Party, turning to anarchism after the 1905-6 revolution. He was involved in terrorist acts, was imprisoned, and escaped to France, returning to Russia in 1909; having been caught transporting arms from Austria, he was imprisoned in Moscow, where he met Nestor Makhno. Both men were released early in the 1917 revolution, and in 1919 Arshinov joined Makhno in the Ukraine and became involved in cultural and educational work in the area controlled by the Makhnovite insurrectionary army. In 1921 Arshinov left the Ukraine, and, hiding in Moscow, wrote his *History of the Makhnovist Movement*.

BAKUNIN, MICHAEL ALEXANDROVICH (1814—1876). Michael Bakunin the most spectacular of all the anarchists, was born into a rich Russian landowning family. Relatives on his mother's side were implicated in the Decembrist uprising of 1825, but Bakunin's early rebellion was philosophic, when he discovered Hegel and Fichte. Alexander Herzen began his conversion to political radicalism, and later, in 1843, when he had gone to Europe for philosophic studies, he became a social revolutionary under the influence of Wilhelm Weitling and Proudhon. During 1848-9 he took an active part in uprisings in Paris, Prague and Dresden; captured after the failure of the Dresden rebellion, he was imprisoned in Saxon and Austrian jails, then handed over to the Tsarist police, and kept for years in the Peter-and-Paul fortress until, toothless from scurvy, he was sent to exile in Siberia, whence he escaped via Japan and the United States to Europe. He took part in an abortive Polish uprising and then, abandoning his pan-Slavist visions, developed his anarchist theories and founded a secret Alliance of Social Democracy. In 1868 he joined the First International and led the opposition to Marx; he was formally expelled from the International in 1872, but the Italian, Spanish, Belgian and many French and Swiss members followed him in establishing a separate organization, the so-called St Imier International. In the 1870s he took part in anarchist risings in Lyon and Bologna, and died in Berne, where he is buried. His writings were powerful but ill-organized; he had, as he admitted to Herzen, no sense of literary architecture, and he rarely finished any work longer than an article. It was as an activist that he lived, and he is perhaps most notable as the real founder of the historic anarchist movement, which came to a virtual end with the destruction of the Spanish anarcho-syndicalist organizations in 1939.

BERKMAN, ALEXANDER (1870—1936). Alexander Berkman was a member of a prosperous Jewish family in Vilna. Some of his relatives were Socialist Revolutionaries, and Berkman himself was expelled from the gymnasium for writing an atheistic essay. He fled from Russia in 1887 at the age of 17, and five years later made an attempt on the life of Henry Frick, for which he served twenty years of imprisonment. Later, with Emma Goldman, he became involved in anti-militarist agitation during the Great War, and in 1919 he was deported to Russia. At first he attempted to work with the Bolsheviks, but his disillusionment was completed by Trotsky's ruthless suppression of the Kronstadt Revolt, and he returned to western Europe to write *The Bolshevik Myth. Prison Memoirs of an Anarchist* and *The ABC of Anarchist Communism* are his other main works. A penniless refugee in France, he committed suicide in 1936.

BOOKCHIN, MURRAY. Murray Bookchin, author of many articles on urban problems and ecological matters, as well as anarchism, teaches at the Alternative University in New York, and is one of the editors of *Anarchos. Post-Scarcity Anarchism* is his most important book.

BORKENAU, FRANZ (?—1957). Franz Borkenau, the son of an Austrian judge, became converted to Communism in the 1920s, and worked for the Comintern until, in the 1930s, he abandoned the Communist movement. He was never an anarchist, but in the two trips he made to Spain late in 1936 and again in 1937 he was an acute observer of anarchist attitudes and achievements, as his book, *The Spanish Cockpit*, reveals.

BOURNE, RANDOLPH (1886—1918). Bourne was an American intellectual, who wrote on literary subjects for *The Dial, The Seven Arts* and the *New Republic*, and established a name for himself as a sharp critic of social pretences before his untimely death of influenza at the age of 32. He published no book in his life, but his essay, 'The State', left uncompleted at his death, created a posthumous reputation for him. The best collection of his essays is *War and the Intellectuals: Collected Essays, 1915-1919*, which Carl Resek edited.

COMFORT, ALEX. The English writer Alex Comfort has made many reputations for himself, as a poet and novelist, as a gerontologist and an advocate of sexual liberation, fields that all border on his anarchist interests, which have been expressed directly in a considerable number of essays, together with pamphlets and books, of which the most important is *Authority and Delinquency in the Modern State*, essentially a study in the criminology of power.

COURBET, GUSTAVE (1819—1877). Courbet, the leader of the Realist school in French painting, was a fellow-countryman and friend of Proudhon, whose ideas he accepted, and a member of the International. He collaborated with Proudhon in the latter's *Du principe de l'art*, one of the first libertarian discussions of the social implications of art, and completed it after his friend's death. Courbet was active in the Paris Commune of 1871, and briefly imprisoned as a result. Later he was unjustly accused of responsibility for the Commune's destruction of the Vendôme Column, and fined so heavily that he had to flee into exile in Switzerland, where he died.

DURUTTI, BUENAVENTURA (1896—1936). Durutti was the most famous of the militant activists who were so numerous in the Spanish anarchist movement. He wrote nothing, he made no contribution to the theory of anarchism, yet he was an arresting personality whom even Malraux admired, and a man willing to risk everything for the cause in which he believed. In boyhood he became a railway mechanic and, after taking an active part in a strike in 1917, he fled to France, whence he returned to Spain to join the CNT and become an anarchist. He became one of a group of terrorists who robbed banks for the cause and were involved in assassinations, the most notorious that of the Cardinal Archbishop of Salamanca at his high altar. In and out of prison and exile under both the monarchy and the republic after 1932, Durutti took a leading part in the fighting in Barcelona against the Francoist generals, and later led an anarchist column into Aragon, where he recovered much territory before he led his men to the defence of Madrid. There he died in November, 1936, from a shot in the back. His killer was never identified.

EICHENBAUM, VSEVOLOD MIKHAILOVICH (1882—1945). Eichenbaum, who is known usually by his revolutionary pseudonym of Voline, was a Russian poet, son of a prosperous doctor of Voronezh. He joined the Social Revolutionary Party during the revolution of 1905 and was sent into exile, but managed to escape to France, where, in 1911, he became an anarchist. Later he went to the United States and served on the staff of *Golos Truda*, organ of the Union of Russian Workers. In 1917 he returned to Russia, and continued editing *Golos Truda* in Petrograd. Later he went to Kharkov to help organize the Nabat Federation, and when the Bolsheviks began to persecute the anarchists he joined Makhno's insurrectionary army. Early in 1920 he was arrested by the Cheka, and finally released and allowed to leave Russia after protests by delegates to the Red Trade Union International Congress in 1921. After a period in Berlin, he left for France, where he lived in hiding throughout the Nazi occupation, to die shortly after the liberation of France. *The Unknown Revolution*, describing aspects of the Russian revolution suppressed by the Bolsheviks, was the masterpiece that occupied his years of exile.

GODWIN, WILLIAM (1756—1836). Godwin was born into a family of dissenting ministers, and began his career as a country pastor, but lost faith, unsuccessfully attempted to found a school, and then became a professional writer for the rest of a life marred by poverty and by political ostracism. The problems of government, illuminated by the French revolution and the conservative reaction to it in England, led him to write his masterpiece, *Enquiry Concerning Political Justice*, a thorough-going criticism of authoritarian patterns which is in effect the first full exposition of anarchist doctrine. Later, in *The Enquirer*, he put forward a plea for free education, and his *Caleb Williams* is a novel of pursuit which critics still regard highly. In 1797 he married Mary Wollstonecraft, who died shortly afterwards, giving birth to the girl who became Mary Shelley; besides being Godwin's son-in-law, the poet Shelley was his disciple and on occasion his financial benefactor. Coleridge and Lamb were among Godwin's friends, as, in a later generation, was Bulwer Lytton; he is a figure in English literary history as well as in the history of anarchist thought.

GOLDMAN, EMMA (1869—1940). Emma Goldman went from Russia to the United States in 1886, when she was seventeen; she married young and unhappily, and joined the many Jewish immigrants who worked in the garment-makers' sweatshops. Settling in New York, she came under the influence of Johann Most, and was converted to anarchism. She broke with Most in 1892 because he criticized the attempted assassination of Henry Frick by her companion Alexander Berkman, and in her own right became a noted anarchist orator, and a defender of women's rights, birth control and free speech. In 1919 she was deported to Russia, where she became bitterly disillusioned with the Bolshevik regime, leaving Russia in 1921 with the personal mission of exposing the dictatorship to the world. The rest of her life was spent wandering between England, Canada (where she established a residence in Toronto) and Spain during the Civil War. Her autobiography, *Living my Life,* reveals an intensely ego-oriented personality.

GOODMAN, PAUL (1911—1972). Paul Goodman was born in New York and though teaching assignments took him to many other parts of the United States, his links with the city remained close, even while he preached decentralism and ennobling poverty, which gained him a wide hearing in the youth culture of the 1960s. His experience in experimental education and psychotherapy was extensive, and out of it emerged some of the classic works of contemporary anarchism, such as *Growing Up Absurd* and *Communitas*, a book on urban organization which he wrote in collaboration with his brother Percival.

GUILLAUME, JAMES (1844—1916). James Guillaume became interested in anarchism when he was a student in Zurich, and later as a printer in Neuchâtel, he became one of the leading members of the Jura Federation of the First International. Having accepted anarchist beliefs, he associated himself with Bakunin, with whom he was expelled from the International at the Hague Congress in 1872. Later he was active in founding the rival St Imier International. He played a decisive role in Kropotkin's conversion to anarchism, and worked with him at anarchist agitation in Switzerland during the later 1870s. Early in the 1880s, Guillaume withdrew from anarchist involvements, to become active again twenty years later in the anarcho-syndicalist movement. The four-volume work he wrote during this later period, *L'International: Documents et Souvenirs*, is the most important source of information from the anarchist point of view relating to the First International.

HENRY, EMILE (1872—1894). Emile Henry was born in Spain, the son of a Communard who was then in exile. Returning with his family to Paris, he became a brilliant student and was admitted to the prestigious Ecole Polytechnique. But, having been convinced by anarchist teachings, he abandoned his studies and decided to devote himself to propaganda by deed. He placed a bomb in the offices of a mining company notorious for its strike-breaking methods; taken from the building, the device exploded and killed several policemen. Henry was not detected, and in February 1894 he placed a bomb in the Café Terminus which killed one person and injured many others. This attack on innocent people shocked even many of the anarchists, but Henry justified it with chill logic at his trial and went to the guillotine unrepentant.

HERZEN, ALEXANDER (1812—1870). Though he never explicitly called himself an anarchist, and spent his life struggling for constitutional democracy in Russia, Herzen was personally close to the anarchists and shared many of their views. He was Bakunin's personal friend from the early 1840s and financed his departure to western Europe. He befriended Proudhon and financed his journals in 1848-9. From exile he was for years the most powerful individual opponent of Tsarism, principally through the oppositionist journal, *The Bell*, which he edited from London and which percolated into the highest levels of Russian society. He distrusted governments, was sceptical of western democratic forms, and had great faith in the power of peasants and other ordinary people to organize themselves.

KROPOTKIN, PETER ALEXEYEVICH (1842—1912). Peter Kropotkin was born in Moscow into a noble family, traditionally Princes of Smolensk and descended from Rurik, medieval Grand Prince of Kiev. Attracting as a boy the attention of Tsar Nicholas I, he was trained in the select Corps of Pages, and became an officer in Siberia, where his scientific interests led him to explorations of great geographical significance. His experiences in Siberia sharpened an existing inclination towards rebellion; he resigned from the army to become a geographer, and in turn gave up science to become an anarchist, joining the International in Switzerland in 1872 and returning to Russia to carry on clandestine propaganda. He was imprisoned and dramatically escaped to western Europe, where he founded and edited *Le Révolté* until he was imprisoned in France in 1882. In 1885, after wide protests by writers, scientists and academics, he was released, and went to England, where he spent the next three decades and wrote his most important books, *The Conquest of Bread*, *Mutual Aid*, *Memoirs of a Revolutionist* and *Fields, Factories and Workshops*. When the Russian revolution took place in 1917 he returned to his country, but was disillusioned by the Bolshevik dictatorship, found himself without influence, and spent most of his final years working on his unfinished *Ethics*. He wrote many pamphlets, and though he abandoned active scientific research, the scientific spirit imbued his works to the end.

LEVAL, GASTON. Born in the 1890s, Gaston Leval became a war-resister before the Great War, and in 1915 sought refuge from military service in Spain, where he entered the syndicalist movement and became so accepted that he was named a member of the Spanish delegation to the Red Trade Union International Congress in Moscow in 1921. Under the dictatorship of Primo de Rivera he left Spain for Argentina, where he remained from 1923 to 1936, when he returned to Spain and decided that his contribution to its revolution should be to observe the experiments in social transformation going on in towns and cities alike and to make a record for posterity. Out of this emerged a number of early pamphlets, followed by his major work, *Collectives in the Spanish Civil War*. For the past twenty years Leval, who returned to France when an amnesty for war-resisters was granted after World War II, has been editing his monthly journal, *Cahiers de l'Humanisme Libertaire*.

MAKHNO, NESTOR (1889—1935). Nestor Makhno was born in the Ukrainian village of Gulyai-Polye which in later years was to become the centre of his guerilla exploits. He worked as a farmboy on the large estates of the locality, and during the revolution of 1905 he was converted to anarchism and began a life of revolutionary activity. In 1908 he was imprisoned for participation in terrorist acts and was not released until the revolution of 1917, when he returned to Gulyai-Polye to organize the local Soviet. When the Austrians and Germans occupied the Ukraine in 1918, he organized guerilla action against them, and gradually developed the insurrectionary army which he used so effectively in 1919 and 1920 against the White armies of Denikin and Wrangell. The Bolsheviks were anxious to benefit from Makhno's military prowess without allowing him to detach the Ukraine as an anarchist region, and once the Whites were defeated, the Red Army was turned against him. For many months he resisted, but eventually in 1921 he fled to Rumania. There he was interned and fled again to Poland, where he was arrested for alleged crimes against Poland; in 1923 he was acquitted and allowed to go to Paris, where he died poor and almost friendless. It was under Makhno that anarchism achieved its greatest influence in Russia, but essentially as a local, Ukrainian movement.

MALATESTA, ERRICO (1853—1932). Malatesta was the son of well-to-do South Italian parents. As a medical student he joined the First International and came under the personal influence of Bakunin. He abandoned his profession and devoted the remaining sixty years of his life to anarchist agitation, in his native Italy and in countries of exile as far apart as Turkey and Argentina. He took part in insurrections and strikes in Belgium and Spain as well as in Italy. Occupied in this way as an activist, and supporting himself by work as an electrician, he did not write any major book, but his pamphlets—of which *Anarchy* is best known to the English-speaking world—and his articles are among the most clear-sighted writings in anarchist literature. His last years were spent in Italy, where, under the fascist regime, he was kept under house arrest, so feared by the authorities that on his death his body was thrown into a common grave, lest his monument should become a symbolic rallying point for dissenters.

MORRIS, WILLIAM (1834—1896). William Morris, the English poet and craftsman, is usually regarded as a socialist, and indeed always described himself as such. But he belonged to the extreme libertarian wing of socialism, worked with anarchists in the Socialist League and in the editing of *Commonwealth,* was a close friend of Kropotkin, and in *News from Nowhere* wrote an account of a society without government that is the nearest thing to an anarchist utopia.

ORWELL, GEORGE (1903—1950). Except for a brief period during the early 1930s, George Orwell did not regard himself as an anarchist, though he was a libertarian socialist. In Spain he fought in the militia of the dissident Marxist POUM movement, but during the May days of 1937 in Barcelona this brought him into the fighting on the side of the anarchists against the Communists, and partly for this reason his writing on the anarchist aspects of Spain during the Civil War is both informed and sympathetic.

PELLOUTIER, FERNAND (1867—1901). During his short but brilliant life Fernand Pelloutier became one of the most influential figures in French working-class history. He began life as a journalist, and joined the Marxist Parti Ouvrier Français, but became disgusted with the dogmatism of the leaders and turned to anarchism. In 1895 he became the secretary of the Fédération des Bourses de Travail, the equivalent of local trades councils in English-speaking countries, and there he developed his anarcho-syndicalist idea that the trades union or syndicate could become at the same time a means of carrying on the struggle for social change and a model for the free communist world of the future.

PROUDHON, PIERRE-JOSEPH (1809—1865). Proudhon was born of peasant stock in the Franche-Comté, his father a cooper and tavern-keeper. He himself became a printer, and later representative of a transport firm based in Lyon where he first became associated with socialists and began to develop his own characteristic theories of a non-governmental system based on co-operative economic organization and the liberation of credit from usury. In 1840 he published *Qu'est-ce-que la propriété?* in which he made the first specific declaration for anarchism, and which was admired by Karl Marx, later Proudhon's bitter critic. During the 1848-9 revolution Proudhon became an independent deputy in the National Assembly, founded a People's Bank to demonstrate his theories of free credit, and edited a series of highly critical journals, beginning with *Le Representant du Peuple*; which earned him a long term of imprisonment under Napoleon III. A later book, *De la Justice*, led to a prosecution which forced him into exile in Belgium; returning to Paris, his fearless criticism made him a respected leader among the workers, and a group of his disciples, the Mutualists, was active in founding the First International. His posthumous work, *De la capacité politique des classes ouvrières,* provided the theoretical basis for anarcho-syndicalism. Bakunin called him 'The Master of us all!'

READ, HERBERT (1893—1968). Herbert Read was born on a remote

Yorkshire farm, and never ceased to be at heart a dalesman peasant. His experiences as a miraculously surviving officer in the First World War left him with a profound hatred of war and an equally profound distrust of the state. He became a poet and art critic, a publisher and lecturer; he wrote one extraordinary novel, *The Green Child*, and an equally pellucid autobiography, *Annals of Innocence and Experience*. His anarchism lasted from youth to death, and though he always moved on the edge of the organized movement, he wrote some of the libertarian classics, including *Poetry and Anarchism*, *The Philosophy of Anarchism* and *Education through Art*, which devises a mode of education that is in fact a method of creating anarchists by stealth.

SPOONER, LYSANDER (1808—1887). Spooner was a Massachusetts lawyer and libertarian who turned his knowledge and vigour to combating the encroachment of the state on the liberty of the individual. Before the Civil War he wrote on the unconstitutionality of slavery; afterwards he wrote on the unconstitutionality of the constitution. His opposition to the state often took very practical forms; for example, when he was opposing the postal monopoly, he set up a private postal system which succeeded so well that, even if he did not succeed in ending the postal monopoly, he at least forced a considerable reduction in postal rates. His conceptions of democracy were so direct and participatory as to be virtually undistinguishable from anarchism.

STIRNER, MAX (1806—1856). Kaspar Schmidt was a German school teacher, employed in a Berlin academy for young ladies, when he wrote his single important book, *The Ego and His Own*. This extremely individualist anarchist was closely associated with the radical Young Hegelians who clustered around Arnold Ruge and Bruno Bauer, and took the nom-de-plume of Max Stirner because of the loftiness of his brow (*stirn*). The victim of an unhappy marriage, he became in his later years a hack translator, and *The Ego and His Own*, which influenced Nietzsche, remains his only work of real significance.

THOREAU, HENRY DAVID (1817—1862). Born in Concord, Massachusetts, Thoreau returned there after he received his degree at Harvard in 1837, and apart from occasional excursions into other parts of New England, this small, quiet town of the Transcendentalists remained the microcosmic centre of his life, thought and writing. His most famous book, *Walden*, was an essay in withdrawal from the over-complications of modern life as Thoreau saw them in the 1840s. Apart from the period at Walden Pool which inspired his book, the principal event in Thoreau's life was probably the imprisonment for a single night incurred for refusing to pay his taxes as a protest against the American war against Mexico, with its territorial motivations. It was a small martyrdom, but out of it emerged the essay on Civil Disobedience which inspired not only later generations of American rebels but also the great Indian liberationist, M. K. Gandhi. For his elevation of the individual reason against reasons of state and of the individual conscience against national loyalties, Thoreau ranks among the true anarchists.

TOLSTOY, LEO (1828—1910). Tolstoy was already a great novelist, author of *Anna Karenina* and *War and Peace*, and a wealthy titled landowner (with a record as a military officer), when in his fifties he abandoned his past to become a Christian pacifist and sought to live like a Russian peasant. He never called himself an anarchist, wishing to avoid the connotations of violence which he saw in the appellation, but he came to views of government and authority that were essentially anarchistic, and he was deeply influenced by Proudhon. In 1910, at the age of 81, he finally decided to abandon all links with his privileged past, and left his home, only to die at Astapova railway station.

TUCKER, BENJAMIN (1854—1939). Benjamin Tucker was perhaps the most eloquent of the American individualist anarchists. From 1881 to 1908 he published from Boston the lively periodical, *Liberty*, to which Bernard Shaw and many other distinguished writers of the time contributed; Tucker sustained the periodical through his earnings as an engineer. His principal work was *Instead of a Book*, but he also wrote a number of essays not included therein; 'State Socialism and Anarchism', from which the extract we reproduce is taken, is the most important. Like Kropotkin, Tucker supported the Allies in the Great War, which alienated him from his fellow anarchists, and from that time he remained virtually silent until his death at Monte Carlo in 1939.

WALTER, NICOLAS. Nicolas Walter is a contemporary British anarchist theoretician who has contributed many historical and polemical articles to *Anarchy*, *Freedom* and other libertarian journals. For some years he worked on the staff of the *Times Literary Supplement* and is now editing a rationalist review.

WARD, COLIN. Colin Ward was converted to anarchism while serving in the armed forces during World War II, and immediately on demobilization began an active participation in anarchist activities which continued for at least two decades. He was one of the editors of *Freedom*, and later founded *Anarchy*, which during the 1960s became the best libertarian journal ever published in English, and perhaps the best in any language. Colin Ward has been a teacher and an architect, and he has written widely on town planning and related subjects. *Anarchy in Action* is probably his most important book.

WILDE, OSCAR (1854—1900). Wilde's acceptance of anarchism was in part an expression of the inclination of literary and artistic rebels of the 1890s to regard anarchism as a political expression of their attitudes, but it sprang also from a personal interest that made Wilde an admirer not only of William Morris but also of Kropotkin, who he felt had led a nearly perfect life. *The Soul of Man under Socialism* was Wilde's most clearly anarchist work, but his interest in social revolutionary activity was also shown in his early play, *Vera, or the Nihilists,* and in later years personal experience led him to write, in *The Ballad of Reading Gaol,* a remarkable poetic indictment of prison and punishment.

WOODCOCK, GEORGE. Born in Canada, George Woodcock went to England in early childhood and lived there until his return to Canada in 1949. He wrote first as a poet, and began publishing in the little magazines of the Thirties. Pacifism led him logically to anarchism (to deny violence implies to deny coercion); his friendship with Marie Louise Berneri was the most important influence in leading him to anarchist activism between 1940 and 1949, when he was one of the editors of *War Commentary* and *Freedom* and also founding editor of the libertarian literary review, *Now.* Among his forty books are biographies of anarchists like Kropotkin, Proudhon and Wilde, and near-anarchists like Aldous Huxley and George Orwell; his *Anarchism* is one of the leading histories in English of libertarian ideas and movements.

Bibliographical Note

This is not intended as a complete bibliography of anarchism, the literature of which has grown vastly in recent years. The important works of the anarchists—and some of the less important ones—are listed in the Introduction to this volume and in the notes appended to the various extracts. A substantial bibliography of the literature of anarchism up to the beginning of the 1960s is included in my own *Anarchism*, of which the most recent Penguin edition appeared in 1975; the list is carried a decade further in Nicolas Walter's 'Anarchism in Print: Yesterday and After: A Bibliographical Note', which formed one of the essays in a useful little symposium on contemporary libertarian movements entitled *Anarchism Today* (1971) and edited by David E. Apter and James Joll.

However, there is a point in indicating recent and easily available books that will expand the informational horizons of anyone who has used this *Reader* and wishes to inform himself more thoroughly on anarchist history and the writing of the anarchists.

First, there are the general histories that have appeared in recent years: my own *Anarchism* (1962), James Joll's *The Anarchists* (1964), Daniel Guérin's narrowly anarcho-syndicalist *Anarchism* (1970), and *The Anarchists* by Roderick Kedward (1971), a well-illustrated popular account.

Among the accounts of anarchism in various nations are Paul Avrich's *The Russian Anarchists* (1967) and two other works on the Russian movement, Voline's *The Unknown Revolution* (most complete edition being that of 1975) and Franco Venturi's *Roots of Revolution* (1960), which is very illuminating on the links between anarchism and Russian populism; Jean Maitron's *Histoire du movement anarchiste en France 1880-1914* (1955) and, for the link between anarchism and the arts in France during the later nineteenth century, *The Artist and Social Reform* by Eugenia W. Herbert (1961); *The Chinese Anarchist Movement* by Robert A. Scalopino and George T. Yu (1961); *The Gentle Anarchists: A Study of the Sarvodaya Movement for Non-Violent Revolution in India* by Geoffrey Ostergaard and Melville Currell (1971); *The London Years* by Rudolf Rocker (1956) and *East End Jewish Radicals 1875-1914* by William J. Fishman (1975); Richard Hostetter's *The Italian Socialist Movement*, which includes much information on early Italian anarchism (1958). So far as Spain is concerned, a definitive history of the great anarchist movement there still remains to be written in English; in the meantime, the best account is still that given in Gerald Brenan's *The Spanish Labyrinth* (1943), which should be read in connection with the chapter entitled 'The Andalusian Anarchists' in E. J. Hobsbawm's *Primitive Rebels* (1959); on the role of anarchists in the Spanish Civil War the best accounts are *Lessons of the Spanish Revolution* by Vernon Richards (1972) and Gaston Leval's *Collectives in the Spanish Revolution* (1975).

Biographies and semi-biographies of the anarchists include E. H. Carr's *Michael Bakunin* (1937) and *Bakunin: The Father of Anarchism* by Anthony Masters (1974); *The Anarchist Prince: A Study of Peter Kropotkin* by George Woodcock and Ivan Avakumovic (1950); *Pierre-Joseph Proudhon* by George Woodcock (1956); Richard Drinnon's biography of Emma Goldman, *Rebel in Paradise* (1961); and George Woodcock's *Herbert Read: The Stream and the Source* (1974).

A number of the anarchist classics have recently been reprinted, including Kropotkin's *Mutual Aid, Fields, Factories and Workshops, Memoirs of a Revolutionist* and *The Conquest of Bread*, Emma Goldman's *Living My Life* and *Anarchist Essays*, Bakunin's *God and the State*, Proudhon's *What is Poverty?* and Alexander Berkman's *ABC of Anarchism*. As relatively little of Proudhon and Bakunin has been translated, three recent volumes of representative selections of their work should be noted: *Michael Bakunin: Selected Writings*, edited by Arthur Lehning (1973), *Bakunin on Anarchy*, edited by Sam Dolgoff (1971), and *Selected writings of P.-J. Proudhon*, edited by Stewart Edwards (1969). Since so little by or on Malatesta has been available in English, notice should also be taken of *Errico Malatesta: His Life and Ideas*, compiled and edited by Vernon Richards (1965).

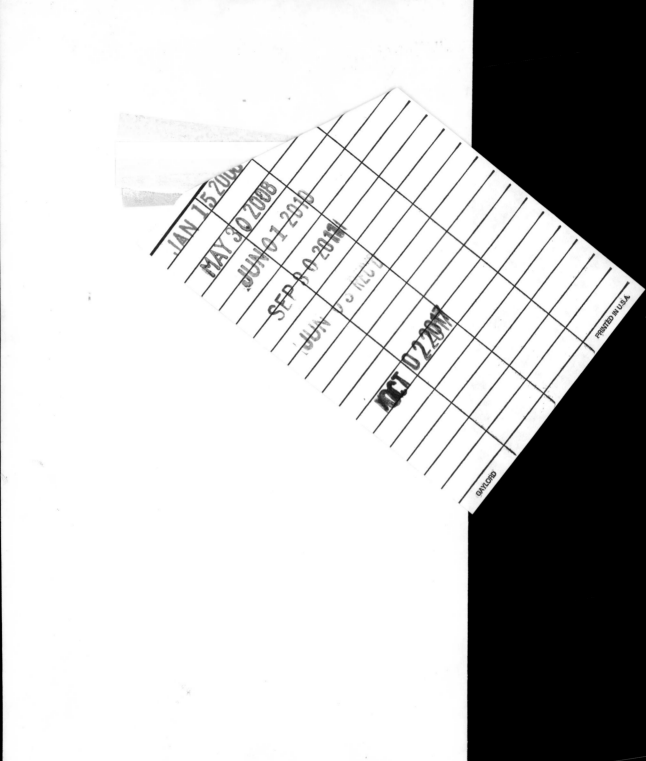

JAN 15 2008

MAY 3 0 2008

JUN 0 1 2010

SEP 3 0 2011

JUN 0 5 2012

OCT 0 2 2014

GAYLORD

PRINTED IN U.S.A.